Lecture Notes in Computer Science 10476

Commenced Publication in 1973
Founding and Former Series Editors:
Gerhard Goos, Juris Hartmanis, and Jan van Leeuwen

More information about this series at http://www.springer.com/series/7410

Frank Stajano · Jonathan Anderson
Bruce Christianson · Vashek Matyáš (Eds.)

Security
Protocols XXV

25th International Workshop
Cambridge, UK, March 20–22, 2017
Revised Selected Papers

 Springer

Editors
Frank Stajano
University of Cambridge
Cambridge
UK

Jonathan Anderson
Memorial University of Newfoundland
St. John's, NL
Canada

Bruce Christianson
University of Hertfordshire
Hatfield
UK

Vashek Matyáš
Masaryk University
Brno
Czech Republic

ISSN 0302-9743 ISSN 1611-3349 (electronic)
Lecture Notes in Computer Science
ISBN 978-3-319-71074-7 ISBN 978-3-319-71075-4 (eBook)
https://doi.org/10.1007/978-3-319-71075-4

Library of Congress Control Number: 2017960873

LNCS Sublibrary: SL4 – Security and Cryptology

Printed on acid-free paper

This Springer imprint is published by Springer Nature
The registered company is Springer International Publishing AG
The registered company address is: Gewerbestrasse 11, 6330 Cham, Switzerland

Preface

In 2017, for its 25th edition, the International Security Protocols Workshop returned to Cambridge, UK, but moved from charming Sidney Sussex to the majestic grounds of Trinity College, where it will remain for the foreseeable future as one of us is now a Fellow there.

Our theme this year was "multi-objective security". Security protocols often have more than one objective. For example, entity authentication holds only during the protocol run, but data implicitly authenticated by the session persists long afterwards. When are such temporal disparities essential and when are they inadvertent? Protocols may also have multiple objectives because they have multiple stakeholders with potentially-competing interests. Alice's access may be Bob's risk: how do we design protocols to satisfy both? How do we detect protocols serving one master better than the other? Do we even know where the protocol came from and what its authors' objectives are? How do they interact with the policies of resource owners? What about data provenance?

As usual, the workshop theme at SPW is not prescriptive. It is not intended to restrict the topic of the paper, but to help provide a particular perspective and focus to the discussions. Our intention is to stimulate discussion likely to lead to conceptual advances, or to promising new lines of investigation, rather than to consider finished work. If you are considering participating in a future SPW, and we hope you do, please consider the year's theme as a springboard rather than a fence.

An initial draft of each position paper was circulated informally at the workshop. The post-proceedings volume you hold in your hands contains revised versions that were edited and updated by the authors to reflect the discussions and contributions triggered by the lively discussions accompanying the workshop presentations. Following SPW tradition, for each paper we also present a curated transcript of the ensuing discussion. Wherever possible we have excised the initial monologue in which the presenter said the same things that can be found in more polished form in the post-proceedings paper.

The SPW admits participants by invitation only. To be considered for invitation, please send us a short, indicative submission by the announced deadline. The call for papers for the next available workshop, while not yet out at the time of writing, is widely distributed: with a modest amount of luck you will be able to find it on the web using your favourite search engine.

August 2017

Frank Stajano
Jonathan Anderson
Bruce Christianson
Vashek Matyáš

Previous Proceedings in This Series

The proceedings of previous International Security Protocols Workshops are also published by Springer as *Lecture Notes in Computer Science* and are occasionally referred to in the text:

24th Workshop (2016)	LNCS 10368	ISBN 978-3-319-62033-6
23rd Workshop (2015)	LNCS 9379	ISBN 978-3-319-26096-9
22nd Workshop (2014)	LNCS 8809	ISBN 978-3-319-12399-8
21st Workshop (2013)	LNCS 8263	ISBN 978-3-642-41716-0
20th Workshop (2012)	LNCS 7622	ISBN 978-3-642-35693-3
19th Workshop (2011)	LNCS 7114	ISBN 978-3-642-25866-4
18th Workshop (2010)	LNCS 7061	ISBN 978-3-662-45920-1
17th Workshop (2009)	LNCS 7028	ISBN 978-3-642-36212-5
16th Workshop (2008)	LNCS 6615	ISBN 978-3-642-22136-1
15th Workshop (2007)	LNCS 5964	ISBN 978-3-642-17772-9
14th Workshop (2006)	LNCS 5087	ISBN 978-3-642-04903-3
13th Workshop (2005)	LNCS 4631	ISBN 3-540-77155-7
12th Workshop (2004)	LNCS 3957	ISBN 3-540-40925-4
11th Workshop (2003)	LNCS 3364	ISBN 3-540-28389-7
10th Workshop (2002)	LNCS 2845	ISBN 3-540-20830-5
9th Workshop (2001)	LNCS 2467	ISBN 3-540-44263-4
8th Workshop (2000)	LNCS 2133	ISBN 3-540-42566-7
7th Workshop (1999)	LNCS 1796	ISBN 3-540-67381-4
6th Workshop (1998)	LNCS 1550	ISBN 3-540-65663-4
5th Workshop (1997)	LNCS 1361	ISBN 3-540-64040-1
4th Workshop (1996)	LNCS 1189	ISBN 3-540-63494-5

No published proceedings exist for the first three workshops.

Contents

Multiple Objectives of Lawful-Surveillance Protocols

Joan Feigenbaum[1]([✉]) and Bryan Ford[2]

[1] Computer Science Department, Yale University, New Haven, CT 06520, USA
Joan.Feigenbaum@yale.edu
[2] Swiss Federal Institute of Technology (EPFL), Lausanne, Switzerland
Bryan.Ford@epfl.ch

Abstract. In recent work on *open, privacy-preserving, accountable surveillance*, we have proposed the use of cryptographic protocols that enable law-enforcement and intelligence agencies to obtain actionable information about targeted users of mass-communication systems without intruding on the privacy of untargeted users. Our suggestion that appropriate technology, combined with sound policy and the rule of law, can afford typical users significantly more privacy than they have now without hindering lawful and effective actions by law-enforcement and intelligence agencies has met with considerable skepticism. In this paper, we summarize the principal objections to our approach and address them.

1 Introduction

As networked devices become more available, more capable, and more ubiquitous in everyday life, tension mounts between users' desire to safeguard their personal information and government agencies' desire to use that personal information in their pursuit of criminals and terrorists. Since the Snowden revelations began in June of 2013, many people have asserted that society faces an unpleasant, stark choice: Citizens can either have control over their personal information, or they can have law-enforcement and intelligence agencies with the tools needed to keep the country safe. Others regard this stark choice as a false dichotomy and assert that, by deploying appropriate cryptographic protocols in the context of sound policy and the rule of law, citizens can have both user privacy and effective law enforcement and intelligence.

In this paper, we begin by briefly recapping our recent work on lawful, privacy-preserving surveillance, in which we adopt the second point of view and demonstrate its technical feasibility. We then present and address the principal objections to this viewpoint that we have heard from members of the cryptography, security, and privacy research communities.

2 Overview of Previous Work

In our work on *open, privacy-preserving, accountable surveillance*, we distinguish between *targeted users* (*i.e.*, those who are under suspicion and the subjects of

© Springer International Publishing AG 2017
F. Stajano et al. (Eds.): Security Protocols 2017, LNCS 10476, pp. 1–8, 2017.
https://doi.org/10.1007/978-3-319-71075-4_1

properly authorized warrants) and *untargeted users* (everyone else, *i.e.*, the vast majority of the users of any general-purpose, mass-communication system). We also distinguish between *known users* (*i.e.*, those for whom the relevant agency has a name, phone number, or other piece of personally identifying information (PII)) and *unknown users* (*i.e.*, those for whom no PII is available but who might nonetheless be legitimate targets of investigation). At first glance, it may seem nonsensical to describe a user as both "unknown" and lawfully "targeted," but it is not. For example, a "John Doe warrant" [1] might be issued for persons of interest for whom no PII is known but for whom relevant times and locations are known and for which the warrant can adequately demonstrate to a judge that reasonable suspicion is attached to that particular combination of times and locations.

We have explored the design and implementation of open processes and procedures for bulk surveillance that protect the privacy of all untargeted users but reveal information about lawfully targeted users, both known and unknown. Here, an "open" process or procedure is one that is unclassified and laid out in public laws that all citizens have the right to read, to understand, and to challenge through the political process. Our solutions make essential use of computation on encrypted data; roughly speaking, they enable agencies to obtain a large set of encrypted data about both targeted and untargeted users, feed it into a cryptographic protocol that winnows it down to the records of users targeted by a John Doe warrant, and decrypt only those records. Protocol-design principles include division of trust, limitations on scopes of individual warrants, sealing times and eventual target notifications for all warrants, and publicly reported statistics about the use of warranted-access mechanisms.

We have provided experimental evidence that actionable, useful information can indeed be obtained in a manner that preserves the privacy of innocent parties and that holds government agencies accountable. In particular, we have presented practical, privacy-preserving protocols for two operations that law-enforcement and intelligence agencies have used effectively: *set intersection* and *contact chaining*. Experiments with our protocols suggest that privacy-preserving contact chaining can perform a 3-hop privacy-preserving graph traversal producing 27,000 ciphertexts in under two minutes. These ciphertexts are usable in turn via privacy-preserving set intersection to pinpoint potential unknown targets in a set of 150,000 ciphertexts within 10 min, without exposing personal information about non-targets. Details of these experiments can be found in [7,8], along with a comprehensive overview of our approach to openness and accountability in lawful surveillance.

Other researchers have addressed privacy and accountability in government surveillance; a full review of the literature is beyond the scope of this paper. Most closely related to ours is the work of Kamara [3] and Kroll *et al.* [5], who propose cryptographic protocols that achieve privacy and accountability in the surveillance of *known* targets, and that of Kearns *et al.* [4], who propose differential-privacy-based, graph-search algorithms that distinguish targeted users from untargeted users.

3   Principal Objections and Responses

Our proposal for open, privacy-preserving, accountable surveillance is tantamount to an endorsement of a *social contract* that binds the cryptography, security, and privacy research communities together with the law-enforcement and intelligence communities. The contract requires us to provide technology that enables government agents to identify and pursue criminals and terrorists with minimal (if any) intrusion upon innocent users of information and communication systems. It requires democratic governments to conduct their pursuit of criminals and terrorists in a truly democratic fashion (employing *open processes*, as explained in Sect. 2) and a technologically sound fashion. We now summarize and respond to the wide range of objections to such a social contract that we have encountered since we first presented these ideas in [9].

3.1   The "Don't Be Evil" Objection

Unsurprisingly, we have encountered members of the cryptography, security, and privacy research communities who believe that our communities should not work with law-enforcement and intelligence agencies at all. They believe that the communities' goal should be "no surveillance" – of anyone by anyone ever for any reason.

This view is "unsurprising," because it exemplifies the cyber-libertarian tendency that has always been present in our communities. We anticipated this objection and pre-emptively responded to it in [9]:

> Before proceeding, we wish to address the question of why "privacy-preserving, accountable surveillance" is an appropriate topic for a workshop on "free and open communications on the Internet." While it may be interesting and appealing to contemplate an Internet in which there is little or no surveillance, it would not be an effective way to increase the degree to which "Internet freedom" is a lived experience for ordinary people. Law-enforcement and intelligence agencies have been and currently are active in every national- or global-scale mass-communication system, and the Internet will be no exception. The Snowden revelations may have provided an opportunity to design protocols that allow government agencies to collect and use data that are demonstrably relevant to their missions while respecting the privacy of ordinary citizens and being democratically accountable. The FOCI community should seize that opportunity.

3.2   The "Political and Social Infeasibility" Objection

Many have objected to our proposals simply on the grounds that they are politically unrealistic and will never be adopted. The law-enforcement and intelligence communities will not enter into a social contract of the type we support. Division of trust, scope limitations, mandatory statistical reporting, *etc.*, are incompatible with "the way surveillance works," and thus even democratic governments will never commit to them. A very closely related objection is that such principles are vacuous: A scope limit, for example, could be set so high as to allow the decryption of all records obtained in a cell-tower dump or other act of bulk collection (and would be by a FISA court or equivalent "rubber-stamp" judicial system).

We acknowledge that this is a reasonable point of view. However, it is a description of "the way surveillance *currently* works" rather than an essential feature of the way it must work. To date, citizens of democratic countries have not demanded that their governments respect their privacy, autonomy, and other individual rights online as well as offline. On the contrary, citizens have been quite vocal in their demands that their governments stop criminals and terrorists from using the Internet in pursuit of violent aims, and many seem unconcerned ("I have nothing to hide") about whether their own civil rights would be trampled if governments heeded their demands.

This state of affairs could change. Political and social reality has changed drastically just in the last few years; for better and for worse, the range of feasible government policy has expanded. Citizens who once seemed complacent about (or even oblivious to) important societal problems have started to demand that their governments take action. Courts have ruled inadmissible some fruits of warrantless electronic searches, and presidential commissions have rejected blanket collection of call records. In time, law-enforcement and intelligence agencies may demand that we provide them with technology that has been thoroughly vetted by independent experts, that produces evidence that will not be ruled inadmissible, and that need not be keep secret and hence unavailable to prosecutors.

In summary, we believe that it would be foolish to abandon the study of open, privacy-preserving, accountable surveillance protocols simply because their adoption will take time.

3.3   The "Technical Infeasibility" Objection

We have heard several times that, although secure, multiparty computation is very interesting theoretically, it is not usable in practice. It is described as too hard for software developers to understand and implement, too slow even when implemented well, or to hard to explain to our target users (law-enforcement and intelligence agencies). Sadly, this dismissive attitude is on display even in the cryptographic-research community, members of which have told us that they think "fancy crypto" or "exotic protocols" are ill-suited for this problem domain.

It is simply not true that secure, multiparty protocols for specific problems of interest in this context are too hard to implement or too slow to use on realistic-sized data sets; for example, the experimental results that we reported in [7] refute such criticisms. In general, there has been great progress in recent years on implementation and application of privacy-preserving computational techniques, including secure, multiparty computation, homomorphic encryption, and private information retrieval. An overview of DARPA and IARPA[1] efforts in this area can be found in [2,6]. Whether the fruits of this research can be adequately explained to our target users is an empirical question, and we remain optimistic.

3.4   The "Lack of Generality" Objection

Use of a privacy-preserving protocol for set intersection, contact chaining, or any particular computation requires an upfront commitment to the design and implementation of not only the protocol itself but also the necessary data infrastructure. The data that may be input to such a protocol, *e.g.*, phone-call records or IP-packet headers, must be formatted appropriately, encrypted under multiple public keys using the cryptosystem that is used in the protocol, and stored by an approved data custodian that may or may not be the communications-service provider whose system originally produced the data. Some people have rejected our proposals on the grounds that it does not make sense to create a data infrastructure to support only one operation (or even a small number of operations). Their claim is that government agencies would be willing to fund the creation and maintenance of such an infrastructure only if it were fully general-purpose, *i.e.*, if the encrypted data that it contained could be fed into *all* surveillance and data-mining protocols that the agencies use now or may use in the future.

Although a general-purpose data infrastructure may be a good long-term goal, we disagree that it is an appropriate goal at this time. In order to promote the use of privacy-preserving protocols in law enforcement and intelligence, we believe that the best starting point is a specific operation (or small number of them) that government agencies use routinely (and admit to using routinely) and that we know, based on rigorous experimental research, can be done efficiently, in a privacy-preserving manner, with current technology. Given that set intersection is a standard tool of law enforcement and intelligence (used, *e.g.*, in the NSA CO-TRAVELER program [10]) and that it is a well studied problem for which there are mature and practical privacy-preserving protocols that require only modest infrastructural investment, why would government agencies *not* be willing to compute set intersections in a privacy-preserving manner? We would be entirely justified, both as technologists and as citizens, in demanding that they do.

3.5   The "Don't Give Aid and Comfort to the Enemy" Objection

Finally, some people readily agree that particular cryptography-based solutions that we have proposed are clearly technically feasible and that they would enable government agencies to conduct in a privacy-preserving manner surveillance

---

[1] The Defense Advanced Research Projects Agency and the Intelligence Advanced Research Project Activity are technology-research organizations within the US Department of Defense and the US Office of the Director of National Intelligence, respectively.

operations that they currently conduct in a privacy-invasive manner. Nonetheless, they believe that these solutions should not be adopted and that, merely by proposing them, we may be causing harm.

Essential to this objection is the belief that our proposals will be overinterpreted and/or misinterpreted by pro-surveillance zealots. Although we have clearly stated that we are proposing solutions to very specific problems, *e.g.*, how to find the records in the intersection of multiple cell-tower dumps without exposing the records that are not in the intersection, some critics claim that law-enforcement and intelligence agencies will, because they either don't understand or deliberately misrepresent our proposals, claim that we've provided fully general solutions. These agencies could assert that "academic cryptographers have shown that data-mining and surveillance operations can be done without compromising the privacy or security of innocent parties" and then interpret this assertion to mean that there would be no harm in their conducting whatever warrantless mass-surveillance operations they wish to conduct. Technically informed people who are paying attention will see immediately that the implied universal quantifier is not in fact present in what "academic cryptographers have shown," but the government officials who could grant a broad mandate for mass surveillance will not, in general, be technically informed and may not realize that they need expert advice (or may be convinced by the wrong "expert").

Another way in which we could do harm by proposing technically workable solutions that would provide privacy protection for untargeted users is by creating *function drag*. This term was coined by Paul Syverson to describe a situation in which it is preferable (for security, performance, or other reasons) to migrate to a new technology, but a particular function of the status quo technology appeals very strongly to a powerful constituency and thus exerts a drag on migration. Our existing communication infrastructure creates and stores a great deal of metadata, including phone-call records and IP-flow statistics, that is useful to law-enforcement and intelligence agents but potentially destructive of users' privacy. Infrastructure evolves, however, and we may someday be faced with the opportunity to route phone calls and IP packets without creating massive amounts of privacy-destructive metadata. Government agencies may resist the adoption of such a surveillance-resistant communication infrastructure, because they are increasingly dependent on communications metadata for their investigations. If we provide them with techniques for accessing those metadata in a privacy-preserving manner, we may make it easier for them to block desirable evolution of communications systems, because we will erode one of the reasons (*i.e.*, lack of privacy) that current systems are undesirable.

No doubt, these are reasonable concerns. Taken to their logical conclusions, they vitiate the very notion of a social contract that binds the cryptography, security, and privacy research communities together with the law-enforcement and intelligence communities. While acknowledging the risks of misinterpretation and function drag, we believe that research into privacy-preserving surveillance is still worth pursuing and that researchers should advocate for deployment of whatever workable solutions we obtain. As explained in Sect. 3.1, we simply don't see a better alternative. Democratic governments will continue to seek access to private information that they believe will enable them to catch criminals and terrorists, because their citizens will continue to demand that they do so. Currently, it is fairly easy for law-enforcement and intelligence agencies to collect large amounts of information in plaintext form, most of which will prove to be irrelevant to their investigations. The cryptography, security, and privacy research communities have been saying for decades that our techniques can be used to compute a particular fact about a large, distributed data set without revealing anything about the data except what is implied by that fact and prior knowledge. It now behooves us to deploy these techniques in order to ensure that large-scale surveillance operations *of the sort that are routinely done now and that will continue to be done for the foreseeable future* are conducted in as privacy-respectful a manner as possible.

4 Conclusion

Stepping back from the specific points discussed in Sect. 3, we sense that much of the resistance to our notion of a social contract boils down to skepticism about whether government agencies should be trusted with technically sophisticated surveillance tools. More accurately, there is deep skepticism about whether they should be trusted with a larger arsenal of such tools than they already have. Obviously, the cryptography, security, and privacy research communities cannot stop government agencies from developing their own tools or from contracting with technology companies to develop them, but we could decide not to participate in such development efforts. If it were clear that our efforts would do more harm than good, then refusal to participate would be the only honorable choice.

The social contract that we envision would eliminate the need for trust without verification. Laws and processes governing surveillance would have to be open, as explained in Sect. 2, and would apply to everyone, including government officials. Users of surveillance technology in law enforcement and intelligence would have to abide by that part of the contract *and to show that they are abiding by it.* They would have to come out of the shadows, submit their needs to public scrutiny, and accept that one of the worthwhile prices of democracy is that rule of law will occasionally enable a criminal to evade surveillance who otherwise might not have. Crucially, their surveillance tools would have to be publicly proposed, publicly debated in a technically informed fashion, embodied in open-source designs and implementations, analyzed in public by technology and privacy experts, and verifiably deployed in configurations that technically enforce proper division of trust and rule of law.

We would sign that contract if they would.

Acknowledgements. This work was supported by US National Science Foundation grants CNS-1407454 and CNS-1409599, William and Flora Hewlett Foundation grant 2016-3834, and the AXA Research Fund.

We are grateful to our collaborator and former student Aaron Segal for all of his good work in this area and for helpful discussions.

References

1. Bieber, M.A.: Meeting the statute or beating it: Using John Doe indictments based on DNA to meet the statute of limitations. Univ. PA Law Rev. **150**(3), 1079–1098 (2002)
2. Greenberg, A.: DARPA will spend $20 million to search for crypto's holy grail. Forbes, 6 April 2011
3. Kamara, S.: Restructuring the NSA metadata program. In: Böhme, R., Brenner, M., Moore, T., Smith, M. (eds.) FC 2014. LNCS, vol. 8438, pp. 235–247. Springer, Heidelberg (2014). https://doi.org/10.1007/978-3-662-44774-1_19
4. Kearns, M., Roth, A., Wu, Z.S., Yaroslavtsev, G.: Private algorithms for the protected in social network search. Proc. Nat. Acad. Sci. **113**(4), 913–918 (2016)
5. Kroll, J.A., Felten, E.W., Boneh, D.: Secure protocols for accountable warrant execution (2014). http://www.cs.princeton.edu/~felten/warrant-paper.pdf
6. Lohr, S.: With 'Brandeis' project, DARPA seeks to advance privacy technology. The New York Times, 14 September 2015
7. Segal, A., Feigenbaum, J., Ford, B.: Open, privacy-preserving protocols for lawful surveillance (2016). https://arxiv.org/abs/1607.03659
8. Segal, A., Feigenbaum, J., Ford, B.: Privacy-preserving contact chaining [preliminary report]. In: Proceedings of the 15th Workshop on Privacy in the Electronic Society. pp. 185–188. ACM, New York NY, USA, October 2016
9. Segal, A., Ford, B., Feigenbaum, J.: Catching bandits and only bandits: privacy-preserving intersection warrants for lawful surveillance. In: Proceedings of the 4th Workshop on Free and Open Communications on the Internet. USENIX, Berkeley CA, USA, August 2014
10. Soltani, A., Gellman, B.: New documents show how the NSA infers relationships based on mobile location data. The Washington Post, 10 December 2013

Multiple Objectives of Lawful-Surveillance Protocols
(Transcript of Discussion)

Joan Feigenbaum[✉]

Computer Science Department, Yale University, New Haven, CT, USA
joan.feigenbaum@yale.edu

It's great to be back in Cambridge.

I want to talk about the supposedly competing objectives of personal privacy and national security. More generally, I'm interested in the alleged tension between proper handling of sensitive data and pursuit of criminals and terrorists. Many people claim that these are irreconcilable objectives, but I don't believe that they necessarily are.

The topic fits into this year's SPW theme of multiple-objective security.

Let me take you back to three years ago, when we had the first Cambridge Security-Protocols Workshop after the summer of Snowden. At that 2014 SPW, I gave a talk that was essentially an angry lament about the mass surveillance that had been revealed by Snowden in tremendously dramatic fashion. One of the bullets that I had on my slides read "all around catastrophic failure of institutions and individuals."

That was my description of the surveillance morass. One of the "institutions" that I singled out as having failed was us: the crypto- and security-research community. The failure that I was lamenting in that talk – our failure – was that we as a group had not really stepped up and made forceful, principled statements opposing the kind of mass surveillance that Snowden had revealed. That was true at the time; it's a little bit less true now. My co-author Jérémie Koenig and I said in that paper that the antidotes to mass surveillance and passive acceptance were mass encryption and active protest. When I finished my lament, Jérémie took over, explained that the "feudal Internet" (a term that I believe was coined by Bruce Schneier) had enabled the surveillance morass, and advocated grass-roots, decentralized cloud services.

That was I at the 2014 Security-Protocols Workshop. Later the same year, another I (actually not literally I but Bryan's and my graduate student and co-author Aaron Segal) presented a paper[1] on "privacy-preserving surveillance" at the 2014 USENIX FOCI Workshop. The view expressed in that paper was *not* "All surveillance is terrible. There shouldn't be any." Rather, it was "There are bad guys out there, and there is a role in society for law-enforcement and

---

[1] A. Segal, B. Ford, and J. Feigenbaum, "Catching Bandits and *Only* Bandits: Privacy-Preserving Intersection Warrants for Lawful Surveillance," in *Proceedings of the Fourth USENIX Workshop on Free and Open Communications on the Internet*, 2014.

© Springer International Publishing AG 2017
F. Stajano et al. (Eds.): Security Protocols 2017, LNCS 10476, pp. 9–17, 2017.
https://doi.org/10.1007/978-3-319-71075-4_2

intelligence agencies; they have to surveil some of the people some of the time." Of course, that does not mean that they are supposed to surveil everybody all the time, which is what I had been lamenting at SPW 2014. Is there a privacy-respecting way for them to identify targets? Not just to surveil known targets but to *identify* targets and to obtain actionable information without intruding on all of the rest of us.

Back in 2014, I assumed that the knee-jerk reaction of anybody in the crypto and security community would be "Sure there's a way." In the framing that I used in my 2014 SPW talk, this is certainly one front on which our community has not failed at all. For decades, we've been doing work on secure multi-party protocols, private information retrieval, and related cryptographic techniques for mining a single pertinent fact from a distributed data set without learning anything else about that data set. Enabling law enforcement and intelligence to obtain one particular piece of information that they need but not have everybody's private data revealed to them: That's exactly what we know how to do, right? We've certainly been claiming we know how to do that for many years.

In our 2014 FOCI paper, we considered lawful, accountable, privacy-preserving surveillance. The idea is to combine cryptographic protocols (SMC, PIR, *etc.*) with black-letter law. (I've always thought that was an interesting phrase, because it sort of sounds like the opposite of what it is; but, apparently "black-letter law" means known, open, public processes that the voters can read, can understand, and then can challenge through the political process. That's what we want.) More generally, we advocated combining technical protocols with legal and social protocols, and we sought to build into these protocols the kind of things that are always recommended in crypto papers: Limit the scope of the warrant; distribute the power to authorize a surveillance operation so that no one party has too much power over who gets surveilled and who doesn't; build in oversight, *e.g.*, public reporting of statistics on how much surveillance has been authorized. What could a FOCI audience possibly think was wrong with that?

Our motivating example in the 2014 FOCI paper was the so-called "high-country bandits" case. In 2010, there were three old-fashioned F2F bank robberies in Arizona and Colorado. In three banks in three different towns, a gang of bank robbers with guns stormed in and said "Stick'em up. Give me the cash." They took the cash and left – I don't think there were any fatalities. Because it was an inter-state crime, the FBI pursued it, and they got a tip at some point that one of the bank robbers was talking on a cell phone during the heist. So the FBI got three cell-tower dumps: all of the cell-phone numbers that sent or received calls at the times of the robberies via the cell towers nearest to the banks that were robbed. That's metadata on a total of about 150,000 users. The FBI intersected the three sets, and it turned out that the intersection contained a single phone number. They went to the carrier that served that number, got the name and address of the customer, and arrested him. Sure enough, he was one of the robbers; he ratted out his friends, and that was the end of high-country bandits.

Success, right? When I get to that point, most people say, "Wow that's great." But I say, "Well, they succeeded in catching the bandits, but there's a problem. What about the 149,999 innocent bystanders whose cell-phone metadata were sucked in by the FBI?" Perhaps the FBI claims that it has destroyed those data; I don't know whether they made that claim, but we should not just take their word for it even if they did. Moreover, the possibility that data about innocent people – people never even charged with crimes, much less convicted of them – can be retained and misused by law enforcement is not a hypothetical problem. Remember the controversy about stop and frisk in New York. The NYPD had a policy of stopping people on the street who they thought "looked suspicious" and frisking them for weapons, drugs, or something else illegal; the police department claimed that stop and frisk was a success and pointed out that many of the people on whom they found something illegal turned out to have outstanding warrants against them. Ultimately the policy was declared by a judge to be unconstitutional; the main objection to it was its disparate racial impact. But there was at least one other major problem that the judge and civil-rights advocates called attention to: The police department was keeping records of the descriptions, names, and addresses of completely innocent people who were stopped, frisked, discovered not to be doing anything wrong, and let go without being charged. A lot of these people were later questioned when a crime occurred and their descriptions matched the suspect's. Once the information was in a government database, there was a significant chance that it would be used. So we want to keep irrelevant personal data out of government databases.

It's important to note that our motivating example in this work is a scenario in which law enforcement *already has lawful access to a lot of personal data.* We're not saying, "Let's enable pursuit of criminals and terrorists by using fancy protocols to justify law-enforcement access to data they're not getting now." Rather, we're asking, "How can law enforcement perform the same task that it is performing now in a less privacy-destructive manner?" In particular, how can privacy of innocent bystanders be maintained?

It's also important to note that the goal in this scenario is to identify a target (or a small set of targets). The government seeks access to sensitive data about a large set of people; most of the people are "untargeted" data subjects or, as I've been calling them, innocent bystanders. A small number (perhaps just one, as in the high-country bandits case) are targeted data subjects – there is evidence that they have committed crimes or, more generally, are directly relevant to an investigation. Why can't the government agency just get a warrant for data on the targets? Because these are "unknown targets." That sounds like an oxymoron (how can someone be both "unknown" and "targeted"?), but it is not. The government can describe the data subjects very precisely by saying that they are the only people who were at these k places at these k times; if the targets happened to be using cell phones or otherwise leaving electronic bread crumbs that mark their presence, then intersecting k sets of data should identify them. But the government does not have any PII on these people when it goes to get a warrant; it can't get a warrant to track "Mr. Smith's phone" or to track "phone number 917-359-4081." It needs what's referred to in the US as a John Doe warrant: permission to track or search a person or people who fit a precise description that has been presented to a judge but whom the agency seeking the warrant cannot (yet) identify. Technically speaking, we want to identify the unknown, targeted subjects of a "John Doe" warrant *without* identifying all of the unknown, untargeted people whose data may be indistinguishable from those of the targets before the warrant is executed.

In our FOCI 2014 paper, we pointed out that the high-country bandits could have been captured without the FBI's obtaining cell-phone numbers of any untargeted users. Privacy-preserving set-intersection is a well studied problem. In this particular application, we used a variant of the Vaidya-Clifton protocol; it works on sets of *encrypted* data, outputs the cleartext of data items in the intersection of all of the input sets, and leaves the items not in the intersection encrypted. Our proposal was to have repositories store call records in encrypted form – specifically to encrypt them using the public keys of multiple authorities all of whom would have to participate in the execution of the set-intersection protocol in order for it to run to completion and decrypt the records in the intersection; that is equivalent to "distributing the power to authorize a surveillance operation," which is one of our design principles. Aaron Segal implemented the protocol and found that it could handle a set of 150,000 encrypted call records very efficiently.

Beyond privacy-preserving set intersection, we advocated surveillance regimes that obtain a large set of encrypted data about both targeted and untargeted users, feed it into a cryptographic protocol that winnows it down to the records of users targeted by the John Doe warrant, and decrypt only those records. As I said earlier, how could a FOCI audience object to any of that?

In fact, many in the FOCI audience objected to everything we proposed. We've heard similar objections from many people in the crypto- and security-research community in the intervening three years. Now that I know that the our ideas are so controversial, I figure that a Cambridge SPW is the perfect place to present them.

Frank Stajano: Those operators: Do they have access to plain text?

Reply: I'm not sure exactly what you mean by "operators." In the bandits example, the plain texts are phone-call records; they're produced by the phone networks as a byproduct of network operation. So, of course, the phone companies have access to them. But no one else need have access to them. The encrypted records that may be subpoenaed can be stored by the phone companies themselves or by neutral repositories. Our framework is very general: Large sets of sensitive data about both targeted and untargeted data subjects should be encrypted by multiple authorities and used in cryptographic protocols only if all of the authorities agree that a legitimate warrant has been obtained. Who stores the encrypted records will depend on the use case.

Frank Stajano: Why can't the FBI just say to a phone operator "give me the records of the people who were there at the time"?

Reply: That's exactly what the FBI did, and it wound up getting the records of all of the untargeted phone users as well as those of the single target. We're trying to prevent that.

Paul Wernick: If you get the information from the phone companies, won't they know that the person you're looking for is the target of an investigation by the security services?

Reply: They'll know that the target may be identified by *one* element of the large set of data that they supply, but they won't know which one.

Fabio Massacci: I think there's a big error. You need to tell the phone operator what it's going to be used for. They have to encrypt the raw data in a way that makes it usable in the protocol.

Reply: Good, you're making an important technical point. Data that might be collected in bulk in encrypted form and fed into a cryptographic protocol by government agencies in order to identify targets (or, more generally, to discover something about *a priori* unknown targets) need to be encrypted in a particular way. They need to be prepared to serve as input to a specific privacy-preserving protocol. Notice that I mentioned ElGamal encryption on a previous slide; that's because our set-intersection protocol uses ElGamal and Pohlig-Hellman. This requirement that repositories store encrypted data in precisely the form that will be needed by the protocol that the authorities later execute implies that the government must know in advance what operations it plans to perform on the sensitive data in question. That may ultimately limit the applicability of our whole approach. Still, we do know that set intersection is used regularly by law enforcement and by the NSA. They could be using it in a privacy-preserving manner instead of the privacy-invasive manner in which they're now using it. The same applies to some other common operations.
  Go ahead Ross.

Ross Anderson: The problem is that, under the UK Investigative Powers Act, for example, we get something called Internet connection records, which phone companies must support with cleared staff and appropriate enclaves, and these give not just intersections but joins. What the UK government now entitles itself to do is to say, "Tell me all of the websites that have been visited both by wicked Dr. Sierra and wicked Professor Anderson and then show us everybody else in Britain who visited those websites in the last month."

Reply: So that's *this* objection to the entire approach (speaker points to a bullet on her slide), which is that it's a non-starter politically.

Ross Anderson: You should have sold this in the 1990s. (Laughter)

Reply: (Turns to another member of the audience.) Yes, go ahead.

Partha Das Chowdhury: In a place like Kashmir, when you do operations, you have loads of people coming from the street, throwing stones, and preventing the police or the army from targeting the militants. So whatever they (the police) do in such a situation, they do to everyone. They can't target anyone. The same applies in other places; we have loads of Maoists in the eastern and central parts of India. In those places, how would you define your target? Because the young soldier you are sending down, he has a family to take care of; he's not going to listen to "privacy, etc."

Also, government agencies don't want large quantities of data. Forensics is very slow ... getting data, analyzing them. The agents are not willing to deal with large amounts of data.

Reply: It sounds like you're actually saying two different things, the first one of which isn't directly relevant to our framework. We're addressing precisely the scenario in which there *is* a specific target, but it's an unknown target, and the only apparent way to get the data on that target is to sort through a much larger superset. You're saying that there are situations in which you cannot properly target. Fine. There may be situations in which you actually need to surveil a crowd, because there's a threat from an entire crowd. Those are not the situations that are addressed by our framework.

Now to your point that government agencies don't want a lot of data. Perhaps *some* government agencies don't want a lot of data. The US intelligence agencies seem to want every bit of data in the whole damned world.

Partha Das Chowdhury: Forensic tools are very slow; you don't want to use them on a large data set when you're trying to investigate.

Reply: Well, that's one of the arguments that computer scientists make to intelligence agencies: No, you shouldn't be sucking in every single bit that's sent anywhere on the Internet, because you don't have computational techniques that can actually use all those data. But that has been a tough sell. Anyway, in our high-country bandits case, we're not talking about big data: We're talking about 150,000 records; so what?

We skipped over one slide, but I don't think it's all that important. We are actually having the discussion that I wanted to have. Since FOCI'14, I have been very surprised by the knee-jerk negative reaction to the idea of "privacy-preserving surveillance" and by the immense technical pessimism about the possibility of using cryptographic protocols to simultaneously enable legitimate pursuit of targets and privacy of non-targets. I even heard Ron Rivest pooh-pooh the idea; he said "I don't know whether exotic protocols should be used for law enforcement and intelligence." These aren't "exotic protocols"! I saw a DIMACS Workshop talk about efficient privacy-preserving set intersection more than 20 years ago! I've had this experience before, often in discussions of Internet voting. Members of my own research community sort of nay say the idea of using our own tools for some social objective by saying, "oh it's never going to work." It drives me crazy.

Ross Anderson: I think that's an unfair criticism of Ron, because he, like I, was an author of the "Risks" report in 1998. When a bunch of people in the crypto-research community were quite happily proving mathematical theorems, we were prepared to roll up our sleeves and get engaged in the struggle. Those of us who have been on the front lines know what this is like. We know what's even remotely likely to fly, and we know what simply doesn't have a chance. So I support Ron 100% on this.

Reply: So ... back to this bullet? (Points to a bullet on her slide) Because technical ...

Ross Anderson: Because Ron, like me, has been in dozens of contretemps with policemen – in the first crypto war, in the second crypto war. We've been in private meetings in Washington, we've been private meetings in Brussels, we've been sitting down with industry people. You know, we've got the form. We know this fight, we know what it's about. It's not about technical control mechanisms. It's about policy.

Reply: Okay, so then you're not saying what Ron said to me in that particular discussion, which was that SMC protocols *per se* are just not usable for this purpose. That nobody could ever implement them and deploy them at this kind of scale or in this kind of situation. You're saying that, politically, they won't fly.

Ross Anderson: Well, it's not where the fight is. You see, no sensible person has got an objection to ... Remember the case here in Britain about ten years ago, in which a man conducted a number of rapes in the east end of London? Nobody was bothered about the police going in and taking cell-tower dumps from the relevant places until they found the guy. In those days, however, if you took a cell-tower dump, it involved serious manual labour by phone-company employees, and it cost the police tens of thousands of pounds. What's changed is that, now, this has all been automated. Government has spent hundreds of millions of pounds in up-front cost to ensure that the marginal cost of getting cell-tower dumps is basically zero.

Reply: All right. That was not Ron's objection in the conversation I had with him, but I understand your objection.
(Turns to another audience member.) Yes. You have to identify yourself.

Tuomas Aura: You are treating surveillance like a logical proposition. I think you have to understand that the ability to find someone depends on data mining and technical forensics. If you are the police desperately looking for clue, you look for the link in forensics. It's based on statistical likeness.

Reply: What you just said is actually related to what you said. (Points to Fabio Massacci.)

Tuomas Aura: It's brittle.

Reply: Yes, there is brittleness here and potential limitation of applicability. That's not what most of the controversy is about. It actually is not true that privacy-preserving data mining, even privacy-preserving data mining that uses cryptography, can only be applied to deterministic, well defined functions. There is a lot of ongoing work right now on privacy-preserving statistical data mining.

Tuomas Aura: It's ongoing but there are no complete solutions.

Reply: I'm not at all saying this framework is universally applicable. Its Achilles heel might be that, ultimately, there are not robust enough methods for pre-processing data to both hide them – make the whole end-to-end operation privacy preserving – and actually use them for enough data mining operations that anybody would bother.

Tuomas Aura: If you say that this is the limit on the low end, then, unfortunately, these agencies have only one function that they can use.

Reply: No, I'm absolutely *not* saying that.

Tuomas Aura: You will be blocking more creative methods of mining the data.

Reply: First of all, I'm not saying if this framework doesn't apply, then law enforcement cannot do anything. Nor is it true that there's only a small number of deterministic operations that this will work for. But nonetheless, you're absolutely right that, for this whole thing to be interesting, we have to demonstrate its applicability to more than set intersection, contact chaining, and graph searching.

By the way, the differentially private graph-searching algorithms to which these techniques apply *are* probabilistic algorithms.

Okay! I think we're now having the discussion I wanted to have, in which the question is "why this combination of hostility and pessimism?" George Danezis – I was hoping he was going to be here ... too bad he isn't – burst out of his chair during a workshop talk that I gave and said, "This is really interesting cryptographically, but we shouldn't be working on this stuff! We should be fighting for a world in which there is no surveillance. By anybody, of anything, anytime." I was very surprised that anybody would say that; of course, that was a PETS workshop, and PETS people say things like that all the time. But what has subsequently been revealed to me is that these last two bullets (points to a slide) are a less emotional way of saying the same thing.

On another front, Paul Syverson coined the term "function drag," which is supposed to be the evil twin of "function creep." He cautioned that, someday, phone companies may be able to provide service and bill customers without retaining any records of individual calls. Paul is worried that, if we put in place a system that enables data mining of encrypted phone-call records, the FBI will get used to mining all of those records and won't let a memoryless phone system be built.

Frank Stajano: We can take one more I think.

Reply: Right.

Jonathan Weekes: So, if I understand the process correctly, the phone company collects the data and encrypts it; if the FBI needs it, they get the encrypted data.

Reply: The general framework includes a number of different parties that have different roles to play in accountable, privacy-preserving surveillance.

There are entities that create (or otherwise acquire) sensitive data in the normal course of doing business. In the bandits use case, those are cell-phone companies whose networks create call records in their normal course of operation.

There are repositories that store encrypted data. They could be the same entities that create the data, but they need not be in every use case.

There are multiple authorities that must agree on the legitimacy of a request for data and participate in a cryptographic protocol that ultimately decrypts only a subset of the data. This is how power is distributed so that no one person or government body has too much say over which sensitive data are revealed and when. In the bandits use case, which occurred under the American legal system, it is natural to think of these authorities as employees of different (even competing) government bodies or officials of the three different branches of government. But that's not essential in our framework; the requirement is simply that power be distributed in the sense that it is vested in multiple independent parties. The parties don't even have to be parts of the government.

The data that are stored in repositories are encrypted under the public keys of all of the authorities; that is why all of the authorities must participate in the protocol if the targeted data records are to be decrypted. Encryption of the original cleartext data records might be done by the entities that created them or by some other party – it depends on the use case.

So at the beginning of the process, someone in law enforcement or intelligence requests access to data. In the bandits case, the requester would be an FBI agent, and he would request the intersection of three cell-tower dumps. The requester must go to a judge and get a warrant. If the judge grants the request, he may put restrictions on the warrant; for example, in the bandits case, he might say that the number of records ultimately decrypted and sent to the FBI must be small – at most the number of robbers that held up the banks. The requester submits the warrant to all of the authorities, who must authenticate it. If they all agree that it is a legitimate warrant, they execute the protocol, verify that the output satisfies whatever restrictions the judge imposed, and send the decrypted records to the requester.

I think we don't have any more time for questions now, but we have the whole rest of the workshop for discussion.

Thank you!

Getting Security Objectives Wrong: A Cautionary Tale of an Industrial Control System

Simon N. Foley[✉]

IMT Atlantique, LabSTICC, Université Bretagne Loire, Rennes, France
simon.foley@imt-atlantique.fr

Abstract. We relate a story about an Industrial Control System in order to illustrate that simple security objectives can be deceptive: there are many things that can and do go wrong when deploying the system. Rather than trying to define security explicitly, this paper takes the position that one should consider the security of a system by comparing it against others whose security we consider to be acceptable: Alice is satisfied if her system is no less secure than Bob's system.

1 Introduction

Contemporary systems are convoluted arrangements of frameworks, software stacks, services and third party components. It is in this complexity, that mistakes are made and that security threats emerge. Despite our best efforts, we continue to have difficulty accurately capturing security objectives, identifying threats and implementing and configuring the security mechanisms that mitigate the threats. The history of the definition of information flow security style properties is a case in point: in the course of forty years of research [5,12,18,21,22], there has been much debate over its meaning and how it might be used in practice. If there can be such variations over what appears to be a conceptually simple security objective—preventing high information from flowing down to low—then what hope have we of providing a meaning for security in a convoluted enterprise system, scalability notwithstanding?

Security practitioners have tended to take a more operational approach to dealing with security in convoluted systems. Rather than attempting to provide a declarative meaning for security, security objectives are defined operationally. Threats are identified and operational controls are used to mitigate those threats, usually according to some notion of best practice. Thus, for instance, the network administrator does not define the meaning of security of an N-tier enterprise network in a declarative sense, rather, the security of the system is defined in terms of its operation: by organising the enterprise network in tiers, the innermost subnet hosts critical data, following best practices, and so forth.

Security Risk/Threat Management [9,17,25] is an example of this operational approach to security, and, while it may scale to convoluted systems, it is in itself convoluted and error-prone. Standards and best practices may help an administrator to identify security risks and to deploy defences, however their

F. Stajano et al. (Eds.): Security Protocols 2017, LNCS 10476, pp. 18–29, 2017.
https://doi.org/10.1007/978-3-319-71075-4_3

extensive catalogues encourage a focus on checkbox-style security compliance, rather than security outcomes. At the extreme, approaches such as the Security Content Automation Protocol (SCAP) family of standards [26] champion catalogues with a tremendous amount of detail, leading to challenges in comprehension. For example, the scope for inconsistencies within and between OVAL, CPE, CVE and CCE repositories in SCAP are considered in [6].

Rather than attempting to define security objectives declaratively or operationally, this paper takes the position that one should consider the security of a system by comparing it against others whose security we consider to be acceptable. This is characterised as a refinement relation between systems: Alice is satisfied if her system is no less secure than Bob's system, or, if Alice makes a change to her system configuration then it should be no less secure than her previous configuration. For consistency, one would expect this ordering relation to form a partial order, with the properties of reflexivity, anti-symmetry and transitivity. If it can be shown than the refinement relation also forms a lattice then its greatest lower, and lowest upper bound, operators provide useful forms of composition. If Alice is happy when her system is no less secure than Bob's system and no less secure than Clare's system then the lattice join operator ensures Alice has the best possible secure replacement.

In this paper we do not attempt to put forward a general refinement relation (other than it should form a lattice), nor suggest what is meant by a system or security objectives. Rather, we suggest that one should use the notion of refinement as a strategy when considering convoluted systems, or protocols, that have multiple security objectives. This strategy of defining security in terms of comparison has been previously considered for mandatory access control policies [7,10] and formal security properties [8,16]. It is revisited in this paper, where we consider how it might be used in a broader and less-formal setting as a potential approach to dealing with convoluted systems.

This challenges of capturing the full meaning of security in a convoluted system is illustrated in the paper using a ethnographic style study of the connection of an Industrial Control System to the Internet. Shodan.io was used to locate what appeared to be a vulnerable ICS connected to the Internet; the apparent operators of the system were contacted, the vulnerability highlighted and remediation suggested. No further contact was made and Shodan.io was used to track subsequent changes between March 2016 and March 2017. At face value, securing this ICS infrastructure connection should be trivial in terms of network security objectives. However, in our use case we see that there are many objectives to be understood and met, some of which can be contradictory, others are out of the operator's control, and mistakes are made. Focussing on just the firewall aspects of the system, we illustrate how thinking about the security in terms of refinement may provide a means to deal with this convolution.

2   A Convoluted System Use Case

Despite the widespread availability of information on how to defend against infrastructure threats, security can be overlooked or misunderstood when

Industrial Control Systems are connected to the Internet. For instance, the UK Centre for the Protection of National Infrastructure (CPNI) recommends that the control network should not be accessible from the public network. Siemen's S7comm protocol runs over Port 102 and is used for supervisory communications in SCADA systems. When we began this work a Shodan search found a large number of systems with Port 102 open to the Internet, that is, they appeared not to follow best security practice. In this section we explore one such case: a Siemens SIMATIC S7-300 universal controller that was believed to be used by a public organisation, as depicted in Fig. 1.

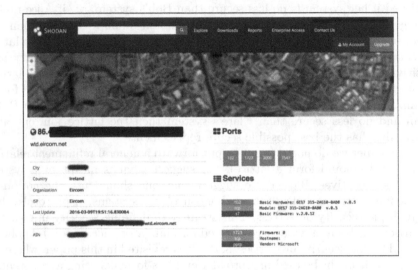

Fig. 1. Shodan report on an Internet connected S7 Service.

Based on CPNI best practice [2,3] the controller and PLCs should be deployed on an internal control network and a VPN tunnel used when accessing the controller over the Internet/public network. The service should not be directly accessible over a public network. In the following discussion we *speculate* on the threats to which this system might be exposed, based on the information provided by Shodan, vulnerability repositories, and other information in the public domain. Our purpose here is to illustrate the convoluted nature of the system and the security objectives. No attempt was made to access the system nor test our speculation.

CPE. An Internet connection is provided via a commercial ISP. Based on the headers (Fig. 1), the Customer Premise Equipment (CPE)/gateway router appears to be a Huawei Home Gateway.

It is not immediately evident which particular model is used, however various vulnerabilities have been reported against numerous Huawei Home Gateway models. For example, CVE-2015-7254 (CVSS 5.0) reports *"Directory traversal vulnerability on Huawei HG532e, HG532n, and HG532s devices allows remote attackers to read arbitrary files via a.. (dot dot) in an icon/ URI".* Huawei routers use the Allegrosoft embedded webserver, which, for example, has had reported buffer overflow vulnerabilities CVE-2014-9223 (CVSS 10.0) and cross-site scripting vulnerabilities CVE-2013-6786 (CVSS 4.3). Huawei [13] reason that backdoor password vulnerabilities on older Home Gateway models can be mitigated by replacement/identifying them as being at *"End of Service"*.

CWMP. The gateway router is deployed with the CPE WAN Management Protocol (CWMP) running on TCP/HTTP at Port 7547 of the router. CWMP provides communication between the router and the ISP and supports auto-configuration and management of the router by the ISP.

Running on HTTP, means that the router may be vulnerable to a misfortune cookie attack (CVE-2014-9222,CVE-2014-9223) [4], among others. This vulnerability is a consequence of an HTTP cookie mechanism that allows an attacker to forge session cookies so that its session has administrator privileges. A number of Huawei Home Gateway routers are vulnerable [29] which can be mitigated via a firmware update. However, we note that the installation relies on HTTP digest authentication, which is not generally advised: a remarkable number of routers run CWMP over an unencrypted connection and that an authenticated HTTPS connection would be more appropriate [4], although this is something over which the user has little control.

VPN connection. VPN access to the local Control Network appears to be provided via PPTP on Port 1723.

A variety of security vulnerabilities related to using the PPTP protocol have been published over the years [19,23]. Rather than using PPTP, it is suggested, for example, to use OpenVPN or IPSec in certificate mode [19].

Control Network. Access to a SCADA/PLC controller uses the S7comm protocol over TCP/TSAP on Port 102, possibly intended via the VPN service.

While this may be the intended configuration, Port 102 remains open to the Internet, meaning that the controller is directly accessible via the S7Comm protocol from the Internet. This does not follow best practice recommendations [2,3], although the (subsequently removed) Siemens FAQ [24] at the time of the study could be misinterpreted when it noted that

> *"[...] if the data is transferred over routers or if firewalls are used, the port must be enabled in the router or firewall according to the service implemented"* and recommends that *"Port 102 is blocked by default in routers and firewalls and must be enabled for the complete transfer route". [...]*

CVE-2015-2177 notes that versions of the SIMATIC S7-300 is vulnerable to a denial of service attack via this protocol as described by Beresford [1], who also discovered a hardcoded user-id/password ('Basisk') used to access internal diagnostic functions [14]. Based on the header information provided by Shodan, we conclude that the SIMATIC S7-300 is a 315-2DP CPU, running firmware

V2.6, which has this vulnerability [14]. Our speculation here is that in setting up VPN access, closing direct access to the S7 service via Port 102 was overlooked in the firewall/CPE settings.

Web servers. Its not evident from the network footprint, nor the documentation, that the SCADA system in the use case incorporates an embedded web-server. Embedded web-servers are supported by some SCADA devices and are used to serve up SCADA administration panels.

An example of an embedded web server is GoAhead. Various vulnerabilities have been published for the GoAhead server, including an application-level (Slow Loris) denial of service attack (CVE-2009-511) and a directory path traversal (CVE-2014-9707). While a software update is recommended to mitigate the directory path traversal vulnerability, it is also suggested that a larger `ulimit` helps defend against the Slow Loris attack. However, this latter recommendation is an example of the need for a trade off, as a larger `ulimit` may make the hosting system vulnerable to a fork-bomb attack.

Changing configurations. Based on the geographic location of the system as reported by Shodan (Fig. 1), the (likely) Director of IT responsible for the system was informally contacted by email in March 2016. The mis-configuration of the S7/VPN and its vulnerabilities were hi-lighted and remediation by blocking Internet access to Port 102 suggested, with reference to the CPNI Best Practices [2,3]. Receipt of the email was acknowledged, with a response that it would be investigated. No further contact was made and Shodan was used to track subsequent changes between March 2016 and March 2017.

- March 2016. Shortly after sending the email, the configuration changed with the addition of Microsoft Remote Desktop Protocol on Port 3389, however Port 102 remained open.
- May 2016. The system and all services disappeared from Shodan. This might indicate that the system was successfully configured and VPN access concealed. However, we speculate that all services, including Port 102, were blocked from the Internet, since it re-appeared the following month.
- June 2016. The system re-appeared, this time with Port 102 (S7), Port 3389 (RDP) and Port 7547 (CWMP) open.
- October 2016. Port 102 was closed, however Port 3389 (RDP) was discoverable, displaying a Windows login with a specific user-id and prompting for a password.
- December 2016. The system and all services disappeared from Shodan. At the time, the hope was that Port 3389 (RDP) was successfully concealed, however in.
- March 2017, the system re-appeared, this time with Port 2000 discoverable with a "RemotelyAnywhere" login prompt that was available over HTTPS.

3   What is the Likely Setup Behind the Scenes?

The use case is intended to illustrate the convoluted nature of a contemporary system and how easily mistakes are made in achieving security objectives.

Informed by this, we give a simplified interpretation of how deploying the VPN went wrong. The configuration is depicted in Fig. 2 where a PLC/controller (Port 102) and Front End Processor FEP (Port 3389) are on an internal network, behind a firewall. Access is required by the external enterprise/administrator (ADMIN), but the attacker (EVIL) should not have access.

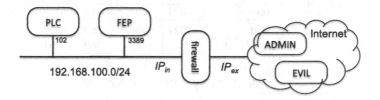

Fig. 2. A network connected ICS

Policy UPol. In the initial configuration, following Siemens FAQ8970169 *"Port 102 is blocked by default in routers and firewalls and must be enabled for the complete transfer route"*, and naively setting up a VPN, gives rise to the following firewall policy.

Index	[...]	Src IP	Src Port	Dst IP	Dst Port	Action
1	...	*.*.*.*	≥1024	PLC	102	ALLOW
2	...	*.*.*.*	≥1024	FEP	3389	ALLOW

For ease of presentation we assume that RDP provides the VPN from the outset.

Policy CPNI. CPNI recommendation *"SCADA communications should be encrypted and routed through a VPN tunnel through corporate IT or other non-critical networks"* is implemented as the policy:

Index	[...]	Src IP	Src Port	Dst IP	Dst Port	Action
1	...	*.*.*.*	≥1024	PLC	102	ALLOW
2	...	*.*.*.*	≥1024	FEP	3389	ALLOW

Policy RPol. Access to the VPN should be limited to authorised IPs:

Index	[...]	Src IP	Src Port	Dst IP	Dst Port	Action
1	...	ADMIN	≥1024	FEP	3389	ALLOW
2	...	*.*.*.*	*	FEP	3389	DROP

Composition I. A common strategy for managing firewall policies is to compose policies in sequence. On understanding that policy *CPNI* must be enforced, we speculate that the policy was revised as (*UPol* ; *CPNI*) and then further extended to (*UPol* ; *CPNI* ; *RPol*) in order to limit RDP access (Table 1). The resulting anomalies whereby *CPNI* and *Rpol* are shadowed/redundant by *UPol* mean that we do not achieve the *CPNI* nor *RPol* objectives.

Table 1. Composition *UPol*; *CPNI*; *RPol*

Index	[...]	Src IP	Src Port	Dst IP	Dst Port	Action
1	...	*.*.*.*	≥ 1024	PLC	102	ALLOW
2	...	*.*.*.*	≥ 1024	FEP	3389	ALLOW
3	...	192.168.100.0/24	≥ 1024	PLC	102	ALLOW
4	...	*.*.*.*	*	PLC	102	DROP
5	...	external	≥ 1024	FEP	3389	ALLOW
6	...	ADMIN	≥ 1024	FEP	3389	ALLOW
7	...	*.*.*.*	*	FEP	3389	DROP

Table 2. *CPNI*; *RPol*; *UPol*

Index	[...]	Src IP	Src Port	Dst IP	Dst Port	Action
1	...	192.168.100.0/24	≥ 1024	PLC	102	ALLOW
2	...	*.*.*.*	*	PLC	102	DROP
3	...	external	≥ 1024	FEP	3389	ALLOW
4	...	ADMIN	≥ 1024	FEP	3389	ALLOW
5	...	*.*.*.*	*	FEP	3389	DROP
6	...	*.*.*.*	≥ 1024	PLC	102	ALLOW
7	...	*.*.*.*	≥ 1024	FEP	3389	ALLOW

Composition II. Having realised the mistake, the administrator revises the policy to enforce the *CPNI* policy objectives first, followed by the remaining policy, that is, *CPNI*; *RPol*; *UPol* (Table 2). However, while blocking Port 102, there is an anomaly between Rules 2 and 4, which means that the RDP objective that only ADMIN should have access to the FEP is not enforced.

Composition III. The administrator tries another re-arrangement of the policy as *RPol*; *CPNI*; *UPol* (Table 3) which happens to be anomaly-free and meets our objectives. However, re-arranging policies in this ad-hoc manner so that they

Table 3. Composition *RPol*; *CPNI*; *UPol*

Index	[...]	Src IP	Src Port	Dst IP	Dst Port	Action
1	...	ADMIN	≥1024	FEP	3389	ALLOW
2	...	*.*.*.*	*	FEP	3389	DROP
3	...	192.168.100.0/24	≥1024	PLC	102	ALLOW
4	...	*.*.*.*	*	PLC	102	DROP
5	...	external	≥1024	FEP	3389	ALLOW
6	...	*.*.*.*	≥1024	PLC	102	ALLOW
7	...	*.*.*.*	≥1024	FEP	3389	ALLOW

are anomaly-free does not necessarily always achieve our objectives, especially when policies may run to a large number of rules.

4   Comparing Configurations

4.1   Refining Firewall Policies

In the following we use a refinement relation for firewall policies that is a simplification of the more general iptables firewall algebra described in [11,20]. In particular, packets are modelled in terms of source and destination IP addresses and Ports:

$$Packet == IP \times PORT \times IP \times PORT$$

where (ip_s, p_s, ip_d, p_d) denotes a packet from source IP ip_s, source port p_s, with destination IP ip_d and destination port p_d. A firewall policy $P : Policy$ defines a set of packets $accepts(P)$ that are accepted and a set of packets $denies(P)$ that are denied/dropped. We have

$$Policy == \{Accepts, Denies : \mathbb{P}\, Packet \mid Accepts \cap Denies = \emptyset\}$$

and we assume a default deny for packets not referenced by P. This is a very simple representation of an anomaly-free policy that is adequate for our purposes; our discussion here can be extended to the more general firewall algebra [20] that supports iptables policies with IP and port ranges, and numerous other attributes. Two types of constructor provide a simple policy notation.

Weak allow/deny. Packets not in $X : \mathbb{P}\, Packet$ are default deny:

   Allow $X = (X, \emptyset)$;   Deny $X = (\emptyset, X)$

For example, permit S7 traffic from the internal network (IP_{in}) to the PLC:

   Allow($IP_{in} \times PORT \times \{\text{PLC}\} \times \{102\}$)

Strong allow/deny. Packets not mentioned in X are explicitly denied/accepted:

   Allow$^+ X = (X, Packet \setminus X)$;   Deny$^+ X = (Packet \setminus X, X)$

For example, block external S7 traffic to PLC, everything else permitted:

   Deny$^+(IP_{ex} \times PORT \times \{\text{PLC}\} \times \{102\})$

Policy Replacement. Policy Q can be replaced by policy P, if $P \sqsubseteq Q$, that is, P is no less restrictive than Q. For all $P, Q : Policy$:

$$P \sqsubseteq Q \Leftrightarrow (accepts(P) \subseteq accepts(Q)) \wedge (denies(P) \supseteq denies(Q))$$

The most restrictive policy is $\bot == (\emptyset, Packet)$ and the least restrictive policy is $\top == (Packet, \emptyset)$ and we have $\bot \sqsubseteq P \sqsubseteq \top$ for any policy P.

Policy intersection and union. The least restrictive safe replacement for P and Q is $P \sqcap Q$, where

$$P \sqcap Q == (accepts(P) \cap accepts(Q), denies(P) \cup denies(Q))$$

The most restrictive policy that can be safely replaced by P or Q is $P \sqcup Q$:

$$P \sqcup Q == (accepts(P) \cup accepts(Q), denies(P) \cap denies(Q))$$

The set *Policy* is a lattice under partial order $\sqsubseteq$, greatest lower bound operator $\sqcap$, and lowest upper bound operator $\sqcup$ [11, 20]. Figure 3 gives an example of some policy orderings.

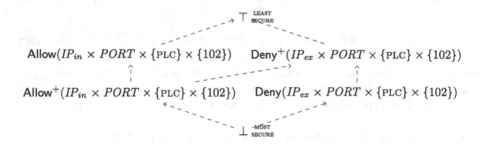

Fig. 3. Some policy orderings

4.2 Comparing the ICS Firewalls

CPNI recommendation. The CPNI objective specifies that internal S7 traffic to the PLC is permitted while external traffic should be blocked but no constraints on other external traffic.

$$CPNI == \mathsf{Allow}(IP_{in} \times PORT \times \{\text{PLC}\} \times \{102\})$$
$$\sqcap \mathsf{Deny}^+(IP_{ex} \times PORT \times \{\text{PLC}\} \times \{102\})$$

Remote Desktop recommendation. The RDP objective permits administrator VPN access to the Front end processor, and to deny all other traffic.

$$RDP == \mathsf{Allow}(\{\text{ADMIN}\} \times PORT \times \{\text{FEP}\} \times \{3389\})$$
$$\sqcap \mathsf{Deny}^+(IP_{ex} \times PORT \times \{\text{FEP}\} \times \{3389\})$$

For any packet the *CPNI* or *RDP* policy should apply. Therefore, if the initial policy was *Pol*, then changing it to incorporate CPNI on a RDP based VPN gives:

$$Pol' == Pol \sqcap (CPNI \sqcup RDP)$$

and since $(Policy, \sqsubseteq)$ forms a lattice the administrator can be sure that the new policy *Pol'* a safe replacement of the original policy, and the new security objectives. Furthermore, it is the best secure replacement under $\sqsubseteq$.

5 Conclusion

In the spirit of Jackson [15] we have related a story about an Industrial Control System in order to illustrate that simple security objectives can be deceptive: there are many things that can and do go wrong when deploying the system. We suggest that rather than tying to reason about the security objectives explicitly, we capture them indirectly by comparison in the form of a refinement relation. In developing this idea, we limit ourselves in this paper to just firewall policies which is a homogenous collection of objectives.

We believe that this strategy of defining security by comparison can be extended to heterogenous objectives and we are currently exploring how other, non-firewall, aspects of the ICS use case can be incorporated into the refinement relation. In doing this, one must be mindful to ensure that the composition of the underlying security mechanisms is consistent/preserves the composition of the respective objectives that they uphold [27]. Additionally, while the use-case helps to illustrate the difficulty in securing convoluted systems, and, we believe, provides a convincing technical argument, research is required to establish whether the proposed strategy of security through comparison is conducive to a more user-centered approach [28] to security.

Acknowledgement. This research was supported in part by the CHIST-ERA project *DYPOSIT: Dynamic Policies for Shared Cyber-Physical* Infrastructures under Attack and by the Cyber CNI Chair of Institute Mines-Télécom which is held by IMT Atlantique and supported by Airbus Defence and Space, Amossys, EDF, Orange, La Poste, Nokia, Société Gén érale and the Regional Council of Brittany; the Chair is recognized by the French Centre of Excellence in Cybersecurity.

References

1. Beresford, D.: Exploiting Siemens SIMATIC S7 PLCs. In: Black Hat (2011)
2. Center for the Protection of National Infrastructure: Firewall deployment for SCADA and process control networks. Guide (2005)
3. Center for the Protection of National Infrastructure: Securing the move to IP-based SCADA/PLC networks. Guide, November 2011
4. Checkpoint Software Technologies: Protecting against misfortune cookie and TR-069 vulnerabilities (2014). http://mis.fortunecook.ie/
5. Cohen, E.: Information transmission in sequential programs. In: DeMillo, R., et al. (eds.) Foundations of Secure Computation. Academic Press, Cambridge (1978)
6. Fitzgerald, W.M., Foley, S.N.: Avoiding inconsistencies in the security content automation protocol. In: Proceedings of the 6th Symposium on Security Analytics and Automation. IEEE (2013)
7. Foley, S.N.: A model for secure information flow. In: IEEE Symposium on Security and Privacy, Oakland, CA, May 1989
8. Foley, S.N.: A non-functional approach to system integrity. IEEE J. Sel. Areas Commun. **21**(1), 36–43 (2003)
9. Foley, S.N.: Security risk management using internal controls. In: ACM CCS Workshop on Information Security Governance (2009)
10. Foley, S.N.: The specification and implementation of commercial security requirements including dynamic segregation of duties. In: Proceedings of the 4th ACM Conference on Computer and Communications Security, CCS 1997, Zurich, Switzerland, 1–4 April 1997, pp. 125–134 (1997)
11. Foley, S.N., Neville, U.: A firewall algebra for openstack. In: 2015 IEEE Conference on Communications and Network Security, CNS 2015, Florence, Italy, 28–30 September 2015, pp. 541–549 (2015)
12. Goguen, J.A., Meseguer, J.: Security policies and security models. In: Proceedings 1982 IEEE Symposium on Security and Privacy, pp. 11–20. IEEE Computer Society (1982)
13. Huawei: Security notice - statement on password disclosure/change vulnerability in huawei home gateway products (2015). http://www.huawei.com/en/psirt/security-notices/hw-443302
14. ICS-ALERT-11-204-01-A: SIEMENS S7-300 hardcoded credential (2011)
15. Jackson, M.: Getting it wrong: a cautionary tale. In: Cameron, J. (ed.) JSP & JSD: The Jackson Approach to Software Development. IEEE CS Press (1989)
16. Jacob, J.: Security specifications. In: Proceedings 1988 IEEE Symposium on Security and Privacy, pp. 14–23. IEEE Computer Society Press, New York, April 1988
17. Johnson, M., Goetz, E., Pfleeger, S.: Security through information risk management. Secur. Priv. IEEE **7**(3), 45–52 (2009)
18. Mantel, H.: Information flow and noninterference. In: van Tilborg, H.C.A., Jajodia, S. (eds.) Encyclopedia of Cryptography and Security, 2nd edn, pp. 605–607. Springer, New York (2011). https://doi.org/10.1007/978-1-4419-5906-5_874
19. Marlinspike, M.: Divide and conquer: cracking MS-CHAPv2 with a 100% success rate. In: DefCON 20 (2012)
20. Neville, U., Foley, S.N.: Reasoning about firewall policies through refinement and composition. In: Ranise, S., Swarup, V. (eds.) DBSec 2016. LNCS, vol. 9766, pp. 268–284. Springer, Cham (2016). https://doi.org/10.1007/978-3-319-41483-6_19
21. Ryan, P.Y.A.: Mathematical models of computer security. In: Focardi, R., Gorrieri, R. (eds.) FOSAD 2000. LNCS, vol. 2171, pp. 1–62. Springer, Heidelberg (2001). https://doi.org/10.1007/3-540-45608-2_1

22. Schneider, F.B.: Enforceable security policies. ACM Trans. Inf. Syst. Secur. **3**(1), 30–50 (2000). https://doi.org/10.1145/353323.353382
23. Schneier, B., Mudge, Wagner, D.: Cryptanalysis of microsoft's PPTP authentication extensions (MS-CHAPv2). In: Baumgart, R. (ed.) Secure Networking - CQRE [Secure] 1999. LNCS, vol. 1740. Springer, Heidelberg (1999). https://doi.org/10.1007/3-540-46701-7_17
24. Siemens: FAQ: which ports are used by the various services for data transfer by means of TCP and UDP and what should you watch out for when using routers and firewalls? Frequently Asked Question 8970169 (2012). https://support.industry.siemens.com/cs/document/8970169/which-ports-are-used-by-the-various-services-for-data-transfer-by-means-of-tcp-and-udp-and-what-should-you-watch-out-for-when-using-routers-and-firewalls?dti=0&lc=en-WW. Accessed 3 Jan 2017 (subsequently removed)
25. Stoneburner, G., Goguen, A.Y., Feringa, A.: SP 800–30: risk management guide for information technology systems. Technical report, National Institute of Standards & Technology, Gaithersburg, MD, United States (2002)
26. Waltermire, D., Quinn, S., Scarfone, K., Halbardier, A.: The technical specification for the security content automation protocol: SCAP version 1.2. Recommendations of the National Institute of Standards and Technology, NIST-800-126, September 2011
27. Zhou, Z., Yu, M., Gligor, V.D.: Dancing with giants: wimpy kernels for on-demand isolated I/O. In: 2014 IEEE Symposium on Security and Privacy, SP 2014, Berkeley, CA, USA, 18–21 May 2014, pp. 308–323 (2014)
28. Zurko, M.E., Simon, R.T.: User-centered security. In: Proceedings of the 1996 Workshop on New Security Paradigms, pp. 27–33. ACM Press (1996). http://doi.acm.org/10.1145/304851.304859
29. Zyxel: Guard against "misfortune cookie" vulnerability. http://www.zyxel.com/support/announcement_misfortune_cookie_vulnerability.shtml

Getting Security Objectives Wrong: A Cautionary Tale of an Industrial Control System (Transcript of Discussion)

Simon N. Foley[✉]

IMT Atlantique, LabSTICC, Université Bretagne Loire, Rennes, France
simon.foley@imt-atlantique.fr

Simon Foley: This is work that evolved by accident. Last year I started a project on industrial control system security, and by way of educating myself about the kinds of things that can go wrong, I used Shodan to search for an existing Industrial Control System connected to the Internet. I gave my first version of this talk in March 2016, and have given it a couple of times in the interim. Each time I prepared for the talk, I revisited the ICS, and each time its configuration had changed. This talk is what I learned from that experience.

Firstly, a short overview of the motivation for this talk. My focus is on Industrial Control Systems that are connected to public networks, with one very simple security objective, provided by the UK Centre for the Protection of National Infrastructure, which is that any SCADA communication with the ICS over a public network should be encrypted and routed through a VPN tunnel. At face value this seems like a straightforward security objective. To investigate, I used Shodan to search for ICS systems connected to the Internet with Port 102 open. Siemens use this port to host their S7 protocol for SCADA control packets, enabling a system to interact with the control system over a network. The search found many such systems, connected to the Internet and willing to speak S7 on Port 102. I chose one such connected ICS system. For my tale, its not important where it was: it looked like it was owned by a public organisation.

Studying the Shodan report for this system, we discover that the S7 service may be vulnerable to a denial of service attack and may have a default backdoor userid/password. In being connected to the Internet with Port 102 open, in principle anyone could exploit these vulnerabilities and compromise this system. Of course, I didn't try to access the system; I viewed it through the eye of Shodan. The deployment of the system appeared not to meet the CPNI security objective, which should be to send all this SCADA traffic encrypted over a VPN and block the service from direct access over the public network[1]

Perhaps the engineer deploying the system followed the CPNI objective and installed the VPN, however he or she didn't realise that securing the system was much more complex and would require multiple objectives to be met.

---

[1] Shodan reported other services available, including PPTP and CWMP, and the reader of this transcript is directed to Sect. 2 of the associated paper for further details. In short, it illustrates that security is not as simple as ensuring that just one objective is met.

© Springer International Publishing AG 2017
F. Stajano et al. (Eds.): Security Protocols 2017, LNCS 10476, pp. 30–37, 2017.
https://doi.org/10.1007/978-3-319-71075-4_4

The question then is this: what exactly are the security objectives for a simple system like this? From even our cursory look at the system using Shodan, it is apparent that there are multiple security objectives. The further we drill into the details of the system the more security objectives we are likely to have to consider. Its not likely that the typical engineer deploying an ICS will have this understanding.

How might a security expert approach the problem of identifying the necessary security objectives in this case? Many of us have looked at how to define and reason about security objectives in terms of formal security properties; our view of the system will be necessarily simple and we hide much of the complexity to make the modelling tractable. Whatever about agreeing on how these properties should be specified, we will very likely overlook security objectives for the actual system deployed. For example, if our ICS was a potato processing plant then the reality is closer to this Heath Robinson contraption[2] for peeling potatoes than to a Jonas potato peeler. Faced with this particular PLC, the commercial router box and all the legacy services and software that go with it, then how do we define what is meant by security in this case? We know that this is difficult and it is more likely that the efficacy of the deployment will be based on the expertise of the individual setting it up, best practises, and so forth. Thus, rather than attempting to directly define what we mean by security in terms of exact objectives, we should instead, consider it indirectly in terms of comparison.

If Alice believes that Bob's system is secure then she would like configure her system to be like his. Alice does not need to know what it is about Bob's security objectives that make his system secure, other than to know that her resulting system is no less secure than Bobs. We capture this in terms of a security comparison relation, whereby $P \sqsubseteq Q$ means that security objective P is no less secure that security objective Q. This gives us a basis for secure replacement. If Alice currently requires security objective Q then she can safely replace it by a P, where $P \sqsubseteq Q$, and then have P as her new objective; perhaps the result is more secure, but regardless it is no worse in security terms than her original requirement. The idea then is that instead of defining security explicitly, for example, in terms of the exact objectives of Alice, we define it implicitly, by comparison, that Alice's objectives should be no less secure than Bobs.

Joan Feigenbaum: I don't understand how you can prove that one is more secure than the others who don't define their security.

Reply: Its a question of semantics. We still have define security, implicitly, using the comparison relation. However, we do not then have to explicitly define the security objectives for Alice, other than they are no worse than those of Bob. Alice's new objectives P will block more packets than her previous objectives Q.

Vashek Matyas: Maybe the question is not about security, but compliance?

Reply: I agree, compliance fits within this view. Alice would like to replace her objectives by something stronger which ensures the CPNI requirement that

---

[2] A cartoon entitled *The Professor's invention for peeling potatoes* by Heath Robinson.

traffic is encrypted over a VPN; if $CPNI \sqsubseteq P$ holds then Alice is happy since her new objective $CPNI$ is no less secure than her previous objective P. She's not checking that she's just compliant with some CPNI objective, but also that her new objective does not break whatever other objectives she might have.

It is reasonable to expect that secure replacement should form a partial order over the set of objectives. If we can show that the ordering relationship also forms a lattice, then we get intersection and union operations which gives us a way not only to compare our objectives, but to also compose them. So for example, if I have two objectives P and Q, and I want my system to uphold these two objectives or at least I want an objective that's suitable replacement for P and Q, then I'll take their intersection. Intersection, as a greatest lower bound operator, gives us the most flexible/least restrictive objective that is a secure replacement for P and Q. This is a much more useful objective than, for example, the most restrictive objective that permits nothing and is also a secure replacement for P and Q; however, at the bottom of the lattice it is overly restrictive.

Bryan Ford: The example you used to motivate this I think really nicely illustrates my question. One of the problems with this approach, it seems to me, is that if you have an ideal model, for example that requires that the only traffic emerging from this SCADA system has to come out of the VPN. But the only possible way to implement the VPN is that at a lower of level of abstraction, at the implementation level, packets do have to emerge out of the physical device and that point where they emerged out of the physical device was exactly one of the places you point out where the implementation failed to be more secure.

Reply: I have some examples later which hopefully answer that.

Bryan Ford: Okay, I'll let you get to that then.

Paulo Esteves Verissimo: If we're considering that we can substitute secure parts of the system with other more secure parts then how do you deal with emergence? In this case it may turn out that while a replacement part may be more secure than the part it replaces, some new behaviour may emerge, that breaks security, as a result of the interoperation between this new part and the rest of the system.

Reply: That's an important point. Security is not a functional property and we know that the composition of two secure systems is not necessarily secure. For my purposes, I assume that this is dealt with by the context in which you define and use the comparison ordering relation. Thus far I have only considered objectives; it becomes a much harder problem if we are to also consider the security controls that are intended to meet those objectives. If security controls A meet objective P and security controls B meet objective Q then we would need to be very careful defining how to compose the systems/controls A and B if we wanted their composition to meet the intersection of the objectives. I show a simple example of this working for a firewall control later, but for arbitrary collections of controls it will be a challenging problem.

I don't want to prescribe a specific secure replacement operation. If you're dealing with multiple objectives then perhaps what you should do is think about them in terms of "what does it mean to compare the objectives?" and see is there a partial order in it, and whether it form a lattice. Because if it does form a lattice, then it gives me an algebra that I can use to compare and compose my objectives. And this is hard. We've done it for a secure replacement ordering for iptables and it was a lot of work just for something as simple as a firewall policy.

Virgil Gligor: When you talk about security objectives you implicitly have in mind some sort of a definition of an adversary. Unless you have some sort of adversary, the security objectives are useless, right?

Reply: Yes.

Virgil Gligor: Now if you have a correct and complete definition of an adversary, it turns out that you might get your lattices. And, in fact, I have a bunch of examples in a paper presented at 2014 IEEE Security and Privacy Symposium about how to define an adversary completely and correctly such that you can measure such you can have a lattice. So having said that, I understand that your problem here is much harder than that. Because you have to combine not only the adversary definition in some way to your security replacement but you also functionally have to combine it with protocols that are really fine in some sense. So it's integration that causes the composition problem.

Reply: That's a good point because what happens then is that, for all the attraction to be able to say, "It's a lattice," and you'll end up with this problem again.

Virgil Gligor: Exactly.

Reply: The question is then one of "What's the right level of abstraction?". I don't want to build a formal model of the entire system's behavior with a Dolev-Yao style attacker built into it because, good and all as it is, unless we abstract away detail we'll end up with the professor's potato peeler, the Heath Robinson contraption that's so complex that we've likely overlooked something. And the same applies to compliance, even though the aspiration of compliance is good. Again, the problem is one of complexity. If you have an organisation that has tens or even hundreds of thousands of security controls for which you've got to check compliance, then you're back to this problem of complexity again and trying to figure out what your security objectives are. So we've got to choose some level of abstraction to work with. And further, instead of trying to explicitly define what is meant by security I suggest we should implicitly define it using comparison.

With this in mind, we return to the cautionary tale about the Industrial Control System, an apparently simple system connected over the Internet. Based on the Shodan reports I conjecture what happened behind the scenes; it is speculation, but regardless, it does make for a nice way to illustrate the challenge of dealing with multiple security objectives.

We likely have a local network with a PLC/SCADA system with Port 102 open for the control system traffic and a front end processor FEP. These are behind a firewall/router with a VPN tunnelling service on Port 3389, using the remote desktop protocol. On the external network/Internet we have an Administrator and the attacker Evil. We imagine that the engineer deploying the system, set up the VPN to tunnel traffic to Port 102. That's all good, however, its complicated because the engineer may also have consulted the Manufacturer FAQ[3] where they advise that "Port 102 is blocked by default in routers and firewalls and must be enabled for the complete transfer route". If the engineer follows this advice then they may reconfigure the firewall to permit traffic to Port 102, despite the presence of the VPN and the CPNI recommendation. We have an apparent conflict between objectives.

When I first looked at the Shodan report for this system, I emailed the people who I believed operated this system. I pointed out to them that they hadn't set up their VPN correctly, gave them the documentation on the vulnerabilities, noted that they should to setup their network/VPN correctly and pointed them to the CPNI information on best practices. They responded that they would investigate. That was in March of last year (2016) and later that month, when I consulted Shodan they had changed the configuration of their system. Their change was to add a further VPN service running on a new port, but they didn't disable the previous VPN service nor block off Port 102. A new security objective was added, but they didn't address the previous objectives/setup which were flawed. Over the intervening months Shodan reported various changes on how the system was connected to the Internet and the services that were exposed[4].

Fabio Massacci: Could not this be the case that they were installing other things, then at the central point of the click through process it just kept accepting these things though the firewall?

Simon Foley: Yes, it could be, although SCADA systems have a reputation for having poor update management. Nevertheless and however we interpret things, it does illustrate how easy it is for us to get the objectives wrong. Even though the rules appear quite straightforward, if were not paying attention, how do we compose them correctly?

Fabio Massacci: Yes but my challenge is whether they actually know what the objectives are.

Reply: Indeed, what are the objectives!

Fabio Massacci: The system didn't work previously for them, they click through a notice from windows that says we want launch through the firewall, they tried it didn't work, they redid it again, now it works, now they have the login and password screen. This is actually a feature; it not a bug, it's taking you directly to login.

---

[3] On being alerted to this issue, the advice was removed from the Manufacturer's website.

[4] The reader of this transcript can find the account of these changes and their security implications in Sect. 4 of the accompanying paper; they provide the tale on how difficult it can be to get multiple security objectives right.

Reply: Yes. What they likely want in this case is "I'd like to replace my current configuration with the system is no less secure than the previous configuration," regardless of how the installation might work.

The cautionary tale is about misunderstanding of firewall objectives. In another piece of work we have developed an algebra for constructing firewall policies. This algebra, provides a lattice ordering which gives us a definition for secure replacement. A firewall Policy Q can be replaced by another firewall policy P, if P is no less restrictive than Q, that is if all the packets accepted by P are accepted by Q and all the packets denied by Q are denied by P. This is a simple definition; the original paper provides a full comparison operation for IPtables firewall policies and we managed to prove that it forms a lattice with a greatest lower bound and lowest upper bound operators. This means that we can compose firewall policies while providing secure replacements.

Ross Anderson: That presumably assumes that the firewall policies are all stateless.

Reply: We can manage some information about stateless policies also.

Ross Anderson: I had a research student who looked at what access control meant in Software Defined Networks. And it turns out that access control and VPN is pretty much the same as Cheswick-Bellovin firewall rule. So you could port across what we know about access control from the past 60 years and compare it to the last 25 year's worth of firewall rules. The interesting thing is that what happens to state, which we deal with differently.

Simon Foley: We had thought about how the idea of a lattice of firewall rules might be adapted to Software Defined Network routing rules. Building a similar algebra for SDN would be tricker than the algebra for single firewalls, but it should be possible. In another paper we had looked at modelling multiple firewalls in terms of compositions of upstream/downstream policies.

That's more or less what I wanted to talk about today. We have convoluted systems where there's many pieces to the many components, many people involved, many objectives, lots to go wrong. And as a way of trying to deal with this complexity is, rather than trying to define directly what we mean by security, defining it by comparison instead. Alice is happy if her system is no less secure than Bob. There's a simple example of the firewall algebra in the paper, but we reference another paper, which gives all of the details.

Lastly, I have a question for the audience about the ethical considerations for this kind of work. As I mentioned at the start, it was quite accidental that I ended up studying this particular SCADA system over a period of a year. It was only after that I'd written the paper that I started to think about the ethical considerations. The British Psychological Society gives some recommendations on ethics and conduct. Which is, "unless informed consent has been obtained, one should restrict research based on observations of public behaviour to those situations in which persons being studied would reasonably expect to be observed by strangers, with reference to cultural values" and so forth. The users in this case connected their system to the public network, albeit incorrectly. Presumably, they had an expectation that they were doing all of this in private and that they wouldn't be observed. Is it ethical for me to have carried out this ethnographic style study of the behaviour (albeit through the eye of Shodan) of these users without their knowledge, and do research and write some commentary on it?

Frank Stajano: Yes. I would say that the fact that you are doing research puts you in a safe place, both legally and ethically, because they have connected their system to the network, any bad guy can see that, why should they think that the good guy can't see what the bad guys can see.

Ross Anderson: I think I would take a different view of it. I'm on our University Research and Ethics Committee and this comes up again and again. The reason that Cambridge has a school-level ethics committee as well as a unified one, for example as CMU does, is that if you try and apply the psychologist rules and the clinical medics rules to ours, we can't get any work done at all.

There's a second issue that there is a legal expectation of privacy as the Mirror vs. Campbell case showed, that even celebrities behaving on the public street can sometimes have an expectation of privacy. So I would say that users in your study could say that, yes, you violated something by Shodaning them, but whether that was the privacy of any identifiable individual is another question.

Reply: Yes, apart from the user-identifier revealed in the screenshot of the RDP login prompt. The target of this study is a public organisation, so there is a duty of care on them, that if they're going to connect to the network, then they do it properly. Does the public expectation that they should be competent competency outweigh privacy?

Fabio Massacci: Was there any accident in the meanwhile?

Reply: No that I know of.

Fabio Massacci: So this means they were competent enough? Forget about the part about the vulnerability and so on, from our perspective, they were competent enough.

Frank Stajano: There was no *known* incident.

Fabio Massacci: Sure, but that's the point, right? If there was some incident of serious consequences, it would have ended up in the news, we'd find something on the newspaper. But everything was fine.

Paulo Esteves Verissimo: I would opt for something in the middle. You don't want to protect yourself legally completely, you don't want to be very stringent. I think I have the right to publish it. And if you have something to say about it and if you want to fix it.

Bryan Ford: I'd like to go back to the actual content of your topic of your, as opposed to the ethical issues surrounding, which are also interesting, I agree. Your example is interesting and a nice example of what goes wrong, for example, if you try to reason about security policies in the form of linear allow, deny lists. But it's not that surprising that linear allow/deny lists are a bad way of reasoning about security policies. On the other hand, it seems, completely implausible that the average person setting this kind of thing up is going to be able to reason in formal reasoning system. At the same time, do you know anything in the middle that's better than allow/deny lists which are incomprehensible to the average Joe, at least?

Reply: We have our IPtables algebra, and while we do define policies in terms of allows and denies, we don't have to worry about how we sequence them. We use the join and intersection operators to build policies that are suitable secure replacements for previous policies. We could build a tool where the user thinks not in terms of rules, but in terms of compositions of policy objectives. In the case of our study, the engineer would take the original policy and extend it by composition to include the CPNI objective; the result will be a secure replacement for the previous policy so there'll be no security surprises, at least. Or, perhaps I'll take a part of Bob's policy and compose that with my own.

Bryan Ford: It seems likely that what's going to happen in that case is the only secure way that two policies that can compose is for each component to shut down the other's component and then nothing works.

Reply: Yes, and that's a fair point. But, if the composition of two objectives gives you 'bottom', the most restrictive policy, then that should indicate that the objectives need to be checked. At least I now have an algebra where I can compare policies and discover that there might be a problem, which is better than what we had before.

Bryan Ford: Yes. I guess this is the question. As attractive as an ordering is from a formal sense, is that practical as an answer for an average Joe to reason about security?

Reply: I'll answer using the theme of the presentation, which is about comparison. I believe that its better than what was there.

Paul Wernick: How do you address the situation where a change makes one part of the apparatus more secure, and one part a bit less secure?

Reply: That's a good question, and it is related to the earlier question about emergence. To deal with it you need to consider how the security objectives are upheld by the system components and security controls, and how these components behave and interoperate. For now, I've focussed on comparing just the objectives. It will be interesting to see how we might extend it to include the behaviour of the security controls.

Assuring the Safety of Asymmetric Social Protocols

Virgil Gligor[1] and Frank Stajano[2(✉)]

[1] Carnegie Mellon University, Pittsburgh, PA, USA
[2] University of Cambridge, Cambridge, UK
frank.stajano@cst.cam.ac.uk

Abstract. Most studies of security protocols in the literature refer to interactions between computers. Nowadays, however, more and more fraud (such as phishing, Nigerian scams and the like) is carried out by abusing social protocols—that is to say, computer-mediated interactions between human subjects. We call a social protocol "asymmetric" when the initial sender benefits from execution of the protocol but the recipient is not guaranteed against dishonesty of the sender. Can a recipient ever safely engage in an asymmetric social protocol?

Over the past decade or two, computer-mediated communications and purchasing transactions have become pervasive among the general public. As a consequence, attacks on social protocols have grown in prominence and value. We need a principled and systemic response to this problem, rather than ad-hoc patches.

Our contribution is to introduce a framework, the "marketplace of social protocol insurers", in which specialised providers compete to offer safety guarantees, for a fee, to subjects who wish to engage in social protocols. Providers need to develop accurate classifiers for rating protocol inputs as safe or dangerous, and the providers with the most accurate classifiers can price their insurance premiums more competitively, thereby winning a greater share of the customers.

Our solution offers, through competition amongst providers, aligned incentives for the development and deployment of accurate classifiers to distinguish fraudulent and legitimate inputs and it offers a safe way for ordinary users to engage in asymmetric social protocols without having to become experts at detecting fraudulent proposals.

1 Introduction

People participate in a variety of socio-economic activities over computer networks such as social networking, commerce, crowdsourcing and so forth. We call "social protocols" these interactions of human subjects with networks that involve computers and other humans. People therefore engage in a variety of social protocols with subtle security and privacy consequences. Increasingly, these protocols lead to online manipulation, deception, and scams on an unprecedented scale. Particularly vulnerable to scams and deception is a growing aging population who engages in social protocols over the Internet daily for a variety of

© Springer International Publishing AG 2017
F. Stajano et al. (Eds.): Security Protocols 2017, LNCS 10476, pp. 38–48, 2017.
https://doi.org/10.1007/978-3-319-71075-4_5

life-enriching activities. Protocols between computer-based principals have been extensively studied. We focus instead on interactive social protocols in networks of computers and humans, and on the susceptibility of unsuspecting participants to psycho-social manipulation and deception by skilled adversaries.

The overarching questions that we ask are:

- How can computer systems and network services help people make critical decisions that affect the individuals' own security and privacy, that of organizations, and of entire social networks?
- How can network services protect themselves from manipulation, deception, and scams?

We offer the following contributions in this paper.

- We introduce the "marketplace of social protocol insurers" to assure the safety of asymmetric social protocols for end users.
- We show how competition in this marketplace provides a virtuous circle of incentives that results in safer online interactions for end users. (More specifically, competition among insurers rewards the development of more accurate classifiers to distinguish fraudulent inputs from innocuous ones—a task that is much better performed by dedicated expert operators than by naïve end users. Additionally, competition among insurers ultimately deters insurers from taking easy shortcuts to the detriment of the users.)
- We show how the classifiers employed by insurers don't need to be perfect in order to provide a tangible benefit.
- We show how non-technical end users can safely engage in asymmetric social protocols by paying an insurer to assess which interactions can be pursued and which ones should be avoided.
- We analyse ways of abusing the system and offer preventive countermeasures.

2   Social Protocols

Past research identified the following three key characteristics of social protocols that lead to scams, deception, and manipulation [2,3,5].

Value perception: Honest participants perceive that engaging in the social protocol will ultimately be beneficial to them, despite an implicit risk. For example, a person may willingly disclose private information to a service provider, accept a certificate of uncertain origin, or click on an unknown link based on the expectation that they will receive a better service. Or open an attachment to an email message from an otherwise trustworthy sender for timely response to a question of common interest.

Irreducible asymmetry: Dishonest participants are better off after executing the protocol, while honest participants cannot a priori protect themselves from negative consequences of interacting with participants who may turn out to be dishonest. For example, an unscrupulous service provider may profitably misuse personal data disclosed by a user, who will have no recourse after the fact against the unauthorized disclosure of their private information. Or a fraudster may direct a participant's machine to connect to a server that offers malicious software for download, which surreptitiously accesses the unwitting participant's data.

Safety states: Despite the asymmetry, honest participants must have ways of establishing well-founded beliefs in the honesty of other participants and the (positive or negative) value accruing from protocol interaction. For example, by relying on a network of trustworthy parties or commercially available services, a participant can gain visibility into the protocol originator's identity, network presence, reputation, and validity of their value offer.

Several open research questions arise about the safety of interactive social protocols. Under what conditions do safe protocols exist? And if they do, how can we identify them? If we can identify them, are they usable in practice? In other words, can they be understood and used by ordinary members of the public without undergoing extensive training? Can users engage in these protocols without relying on networks of trusted entities? For example, can users exploit "social collateral models" (e.g., all protocol participants putting some financial, reputational or other value at stake as a guarantee against their own misbehaviour) to derive safety conditions without relying on globally trusted authorities? Can we use decision science to help users behave securely in cyberspace? Can we improve interactive social protocols to guard not only against external adversaries but against misuse of legitimate privileges by insiders—an increasingly significant concern? Can we devise effective retribution mechanisms and formally prove that they would deter misuse by adversaries exhibiting rational behaviour[1]?

In this paper we address the subset of these questions that help frame (1) the dilemma faced by a receiver of an offer to engage in a social protocol from an unknown and possibly dishonest participant, and (2) the network services that assure a receiver that the protocol will reach a safe state.

3   Receiver's Dilemma and Past Attempts to Solve it

When engaging in an interactive social protocol, a receiver must first *assess the value proposition*. In particular, the receiver must determine whether the face value of an offer received represents a scam or an attempt to deceive/manipulate, or a mutually beneficial transaction.

Second, the receiver must *assess the trustworthiness* of the offer sender for the current protocol run. The assessment may be residual: it may account for the fact that an offer sender proved trustworthy in the past. In general, trustworthiness can be established only in the context of the receiver's beliefs and preferences.

---

[1] Although we must accept the existence of irrational adversaries—the cyber equivalent of suicide bombers—whom such retribution mechanisms will not deter.

For example, the receiver may attempt to determine the offer sender's public reputation, or may rely on recommendations of others.

Third, the receiver may also want to lower his risk of using a social protocol by *finding ways to insure himself* in case of misbehaviour of the offer sender.

Fourth, the receiver may want to determine whether accountability mechanisms exist that can be used in conjunction with graduated punishment such that the offer maker[2] can be *deterred from perpetrating* a scam.

We identify three broad approaches to help with the assessments required to resolve the receiver's dilemma.

3.1 Asymmetric-Protocol Exclusion

One way to deal with the irreducible asymmetry is to detect it in a protocol and avoid using that protocol. This limits social interactions to symmetric protocols. For example, a third party that is trusted by both the offer maker and receiver may in fact act as an escrow agent and ensure that neither participant can cheat without losing their escrow deposit [3]. This approach is hard to adopt because trusted third parties are difficult to find in practice. Even when they can be found, agreement among participants on the appropriate escrow value may be difficult to reach.

3.2 Protocol Compensation for Asymmetry

Another potential solution to the receiver's dilemma is to add an explicit *asymmetry reduction step* to a protocol to compensate for the otherwise irreducible asymmetry. For example, protocols based on social collateral models [3] add a message exchange phase with an outside party who has collateral with the receiver and who is able to establish whether an offer sender is accountable. Although making a sender accountable does not remove protocol asymmetry, it can reduce the receiver's risk and placate his betrayal aversion. This approach has been used in practice in other domains, such as money lending in third-world countries. However, it is not always possible to find an outsider who can hold specific offer makers accountable and has sufficient receiver collateral. Even if such a party is found, whether the aversion reduction is sufficient to guarantee receiver engagement depends on whether a safe state can be established; i.e., whether accountability can lead to sufficient punishment to deter sender misbehavior.

3.3 Conditional Asymmetry Acceptance

Perhaps the most common way to solve the receiver's dilemma is to enable the receiver to *assess the trustworthiness of an offer maker* when the value

---

[2] We maintain a subtle distinction between the *offer maker*, who creates the offer in the first place, and the *offer sender* who sends it to the recipient. These may be the same principal, as when a Nigerian operator sends a "419" to a victim, or not, as when a naïve user passes on the fake alert that the email password must be changed.

proposition is not in question. For example, in e-commerce services, both Ebay and Amazon (1) enable a receiver's belief formation by providing a reputation assessment system that is well-tuned to certain classes of services, (2) lower a receiver's risk aversion by providing reasonably-priced insurance against cheating by high-reputation offer senders, and (3) lower a receiver's betrayal aversion by banning known cheaters from using their services. However, the use of these protocols outside e-commerce settings may be limited by other factors such as service scalability, deployment cost and profitability.

Conversely, other protocols in this class attempt to help recipients *establish the face value of an offer* when the trustworthiness of the offer sender is not in question. These protocols are necessary because beliefs of offer sender's trustworthiness are intransitive, and also because honesty is not correlated with technical competence. For example, a recipient may trust an offer sender (e.g., a relative, a friend, a colleague, an employer) but not the offer sender's social contacts who might have scammed him into accepting deceptive email messages which he unwittingly forwards to the receiver—a common vector of malware propagation. Services offering trustworthiness assessments already appeared on the market and may become viable in the longer term as add-ons to popular services, such as email.

Finally, the last type of protocols in this class *balances cost of assessment of sender trustworthiness against value offered*. For example, if the cost of the trustworthiness assessment is impractically high and the value offered is comparatively low, the recipient's recommended response is to deny acceptance of the offer. This is an effective better-safe-than-sorry approach, which trades off value lost against safety.

4 Our Solution: A Marketplace of Social Protocol Insurers

We argue, based on available evidence, that most people are demonstrably unable to perform trustworthiness assessments of a stranger, and equally unable to assess the face value of his offers accurately. In fact, most people seem to fall for the same type of scam repeatedly, even after appearing to understand the underlying scammers' protocols [4]. More alarmingly, even experts at detecting scams occasionally accept a too-good-to-be-true offer. The use of the Internet exacerbates this problem because possible telltale signs provided by a scammer's body language are unavailable; i.e., as Peter Steiner's 1993 cartoon in *The New Yorker* illustrates, "on the Internet, no one knows that you are a dog."?

On that basis, we propose the creation of a framework in which Internet services can perform assessments of both sender trustworthiness and offer value. Our framework takes the shape of a *marketplace of social protocol insurers.*

One of the core ideas of our solution is for end users to *offload the burden of assessment to expert third parties*, in exchange for a modest fee. This allows specialisation, economies of scale and, from the third parties, investment in advanced techniques to improve such assessments. Another core idea is to *have several such third parties in competition with each other*, in order to keep fees low and to provide incentives for improving the accuracy of the assessments. The third core idea is for these third parties to *back their assessments by offering insurance*: if an assessor declares to a customer that a certain action is safe, the assessor promises to refund the customer if he incurs a loss as a consequence of taking that action.

Our framework offers the following advantages.

From the viewpoint of the user, social protocols are no longer dangerous. The user shows the available inputs to his preferred insurer, who issues a verdict about the risk of engaging in the protocol. If the verdict of the insurer says it's dangerous, the user does not proceed and stays safe. (In case of true positive[3], the user has avoided an attack. In case of false positive, the insurer has been overcautious and the user has needlessly given up on the value of that interaction. We'll revisit the case of false positives later, in Sect. 5.2.) Otherwise, if the verdict said it was safe, the user proceeds and, assuming it was a true negative, enjoys the value deriving from the interaction. If it was a false negative, that is to say if the insurer said it was safe but it wasn't, and therefore the user incurs a loss, then the insurer steps in and offers a refund[4].

From the viewpoint of the insurer, payment is received for two conceptually different services: (1) offering an expert verdict on whether a potential interaction is dangerous; (2) offering insurance against false negatives for interactions that the insurer declared not to be dangerous. The insurer has an obvious incentive to keep a low rate of false negatives (because he must pay out for each of them). This in turn is an indirect incentive to make the classifier accurate (which reduces both false positives and false negatives). There is still the risk that a dishonest insurer would tackle the issue not by improving the classifier but by moving the threshold so as to have almost no false negatives even if this means many false positives (saying that everything is dangerous, even if it is not), but the fact that in our framework we competitively pit many insurers against each other

---

[3] To avoid misunderstanding, the obvious definitions are as follows. *True positive:* the input was dangerous and was flagged as such. *True negative:* the input was not dangerous and was flagged as such. *False positive:* the input was flagged as dangerous despite not being dangerous. *False negative:* the input was flagged as not dangerous despite being dangerous.

[4] Note that insurance and refund are only able to "undo the evil deed" for certain types of threats, such as those that result in financial loss, where the victim may be fully refunded. For others, such as those that result in confidentiality loss, compensation may still be offered but it is impossible to undo the disclosure and restore the state of the world to that before the occurrence of the attack. This is an inherent limit of any approach involving remedial compensation and is not specific to our framework. It should also be noted that our approach only resorts to compensation in the case of false negatives, but that in the case of true positives it employs prevention (not engaging in the protocol that would result in, say, confidentiality loss), which is much better. Note also that, as detailed in the following paragraph, the financial incentives for insurers in our framework are aligned to favour true positives against false negatives, which is precisely the intended outcome.

acts as a deterrent for such dishonest behaviour, because the user may notice the too many rejections and may decide to switch to an insurer offering fewer false positives.

5   The Details: How the Marketplace Protects End Users

5.1   An Example: Email Protection

Since so many computer-mediated frauds and scams arrive through email, let's consider, by way of example, how our marketplace framework would protect end users from fraudulent emails.

A basic service could offer receivers a number of security features based on measurement of the receiver's untrusted inputs (email messages) according to proprietary metrics. The general idea here is that the end user (customer) buys a service from one of several competing insurers (provider). The customer forwards all his emails to the provider[5] and receives a risk rating for each message. The risk rating indicates the provider's opinion about whether it is safe for the customer to engage in the interaction offered by the sender (opening an attachment, sending money to a stranger, purchasing a blue pill and so forth). The risk rating is backed by an insurance, in that the provider will compensate the customer if engaging in an interaction that had been deemed safe results instead in a loss[6].

The insurance needs to be paid for with a premium. One might at first imagine that the cost itself of the premium could be used as the rating (if a message is safe then it's cheap to insure and vice versa) but this simple-minded strategy backfires and opens the system to abuse. The user would normally be expected to pay the premium for each message in order to feel safe in opening the message. However the user might simply consider that a high premium means "risky" and therefore choose not to open the message (without paying), and similarly consider a low premium as a signal that the message is "safe" and

---

[5] We are glossing over the obvious confidentiality problems, which would have to be addressed by an appropriate service level agreement. On the other hand, we observe that a not insignificant fraction of battle-hardened security researchers nonchalantly forward all their emails to Google or Yahoo without batting an eyelid.

[6] The trust* protocol by Clarke et al. [1] also attempts to protect the recipient against spam by paying an insurance broker, but there it's the sender who pays, rather than the recipient: the sender, who wishes her own mail to get through, pays the broker to offer a guarantee to the recipient that the mail is not spam. It is assumed that a recipient may choose not to open any emails that arrive without such guarantees. Until such a system becomes widespread, however, most emails will arrive without guarantees anyway (because senders won't even know about the existence of the trust* scheme), so the recipient will have to decide for himself whether to open them without protection from the broker. In our system, by contrast, once the recipient establishes an insurance contract with a broker, the recipient is protected against all incoming emails, whether the senders play the game or not. This means the scheme in this paper offers its benefits to its early adopters even before it becomes mainstream.

therefore open it without buying the insurance. The user would not pay in either case, and would free-ride on the signalling provided by the price set by the insurer.

It is difficult for the insurer to extract payment of the premium without revealing its amount: why would the user want to commit to paying an unknown price? If the insurer attempts to aggregate messages and price them as a bundle (such as a batch of 100 messages, or a batch of one day's worth of messages), the user experiences unacceptable delays: who would want to get all their emails one day late? Moreover, if the insurer offered a premium for the bundle, with the semantics that he will compensate the user if the user is damaged by opening one of the messages in the bundle, then the user would be entitled to be careless and open any messages without precaution (moral hazard). Attempting to counter this situation by charging a premium equal to the maximum possible loss would make the insurance unattractive and pointless.

The core mistake of this naïve approach is the attempt to "price" and therefore insure *all* messages—even the ones that are blatantly fraudulent. Both provider and subscriber are better off if the provider refuses to insure the messages it deems too risky. At a conceptual level it is advantageous to separate the service of rating the messages from that of insuring the customer's actions. The provider can then safely sell a rating service[7] whereby each email for the subscriber is given a risk rating. Then, as a complementary service that would normally go together, the provider can also sell insurance, possibly at several levels with different prices. For a given premium[8], the provider would guarantee to compensate the subscriber for engaging with any message that had been rated as not exceeding a defined risk threshold—the threshold being a function of the premium.

From a marketing viewpoint, this conceptual separation could be totally hidden: the subscriber simply pays to have each message rated and guaranteed. The guarantee is that, if he acts upon the rating as recommended (i.e., if he only opens messages that have been deemed to be below the agreed risk threshold for the paid premium), then he will be safe, either because nothing bad will happen or because he will be made whole by the insurer.

5.2 False Positives

One remaining problem for the subscriber is that an unscrupulous insurer could honour the above agreement simply by being overcautious and labelling almost all messages as too risky. This would indeed provide a safe experience for the subscriber (and a lucrative one for the provider, who would pocket the premiums without hardly ever having to pay on insurance claims) but the subscriber would lose out on the value proposition of many false-positive innocuous messages that had been unnecessarily marked as dangerous.

---

[7] Conceptually with a per-message charge, though commercially this might be more easily sold as flat-rate subscription with reasonable-use quotas.

[8] Again, ideally per-message but potentially as a flat-rate subscription with quotas.

In our framework, this is couterbalanced by the competition between the providers. Given a common fee, from the user's viewpoint the best provider is the one that labels more messages as safe. A user, or more likely an association of consumers, could subscribe to several providers simultaneously and rate them on the proportion of messages that they label as safe. Providers cannot simply mark all messages as safe because they would be liable for enormous payouts when users open malware; therefore market forces would oblige insurers to compete on classification accuracy, with the most accurate classifier getting the most business and making the greatest profits.

5.3   Service Offered

In summary, the service offered by the provider gives a risk rating to each message and defines a threshold level above which a user's actions on rated input messages are insured by the service; i.e., a level of compensation a service subscriber receives for his losses incurred when accepting a malformed or deceptive input from a sender incorrectly assessed to be trustworthy by the service. The level of protection is defined according to state-of-the-art detection of malformed and deceptive input and known-to-be-malicious sender domains; e.g., spear phishing, encoded malware in email attachments and possibly text, or links to malicious servers. Zero-day attacks may be ruled out by the service, which limits the scope of the assessment to known attacks and due state-of-the-art diligence. Just as with anti-virus tools, the level of protection offered increases over time, as the service's database of known attacks increases. The security features offered are tailored to a subscriber's expectation of trustworthiness, his risk tolerance, and betrayal aversion. The assessment service learns these levels as it analyses subscriber-selected security features and subscription levels, which may change in time.

The assessment service needs to deliver a state-of-the-art level of due diligence to the point that it becomes a useful, profitable business. However, it need not be perfect. It would only need to ensure that its subscribers are better off than those who do not use the service. The existence of multiple competing services in the Internet assures that a service provider offers good value to its subscribers. In the absence of ground truth for complete solutions to the receiver's dilemma, competition in the marketplace will undoubtedly end up establishing which services are the de facto holders of ground truth.

The availability of multiple assessment services also assures subscriber choice in the marketplace. Independent *Consumer Reports*-like agencies could offer ratings of different services and provide users the opportunity to make informed choices in selecting a service. In addition, for subscribers who use multiple services that offer different assessments for the same input messages, these ratings may provide help in selecting the best assessment, since services' ratings reflect different levels of accuracy for common security metrics.

Services can also offer additional benefits, such as deterrence mechanisms against scam perpetrators, which include social protocol auditing and naming and shaming miscreants. They could also create honeypots for scammers, which would reveal the scammers' strategies, and publish those, along with naming and shaming them.

5.4 Subscriber Protocols

Subscribers pick the level of protection they desire and issue a subscription request to the service. This provides an initial indication of the subscriber's need for accuracy in trustworthiness and value proposition assessment to the service provider. Before acting on an input message, the subscriber sends it to the service, which performs the assessment. The assessment is returned to the subscriber, who then decides how to act on it; e.g., accept the message, read its contents, open an attachment, follow a link, accept a certificate, or discard the message.

The subscriber-service protocol needs to assure that a subscriber gets an assessment only if s/he has a required type of subscription and the subscriber's actions on the security-measured input are in accordance with the level of insurance provided. In effect, the service returns a sealed object to the subscriber with a certain set of actions that can be performed on the input message and logged by the service.

5.5 Thwarting Further Attacks on Providers

The framework must ensure that neither the subscriber nor the service can deny the assessment request and response. Neither can cheat the other directly.

The subscriber (who may be the service's competitor) could send different versions of malformed inputs to a service to discover the service's "secret assessment sauce" and level of protection. Similarly, a subscriber's adversary may try to learn the assessment metric, adapt/bypass it, and attack the service's subscribers. For example, a subscriber may operate botnets that could issue multiple requests at a very high rate. The quota mechanisms and the cost of a subscription should be set such that an adversary's learning of the "secret sauce" by issuing multiple requests at a high rate becomes too high to be practical. The desired effect is that the adversary would not adapt and would instead target "non-insured" users, if any.

6   Conclusion

Past analyses of scam, deception or manipulation attacks via interactive social protocols have common characteristics; i.e., value perception by receivers of various types of offers, irreducible asymmetry in terms of the gains achieved by honest and dishonest participants, and the existence of safe states despite asymmetry. Past research in human psychology indicates that most people are generally unable to perceive the value of offers made via social protocols nor assess the trustworthiness of the offer senders correctly. Motivated by these observations, we propose a framework, the marketplace of social protocol insurers, in which users are able to delegate these assessments to specialists. This framework fosters the development of accurate services that measure a receiver's untrusted input (e.g., email message), and offer assessments of sender's trustworthiness and value offered. The service insures user actions on rated inputs according to a subscription scheme that compensates the user for losses incurred by acting on incorrectly rated inputs. Preliminary evidence of service viability appeared recently: new companies that discover the identity of email senders already exist[9]. We anticipate that rapid development of machine learning techniques will soon provide the ability to discern and understand the value proposition offered both in email text and encoded (e.g., *pdf*) attachments.

Subscriber-service protocols can be designed to protect services from miscreant subscribers and a service provider's adversaries. Market competition assures that security measurements of receivers' untrusted inputs by services can increase subscriber security at reasonable cost despite the absence of established ground truth.

Acknowledgements. We are grateful to Trinity College and the Computer Laboratory for hosting Virgil Gligor for part of his sabbatical in summer 2016 while much of this research was carried out.

References

1. Clarke, S., Christianson, B., Xiao, H.: Trust*: using local guarantees to extend the reach of trust. In: Christianson, B., Malcolm, J.A., Matyáš, V., Roe, M. (eds.) Security Protocols 2009. LNCS, vol. 7028, pp. 171–178. Springer, Heidelberg (2013). https://doi.org/10.1007/978-3-642-36213-2_21
2. Gligor, V., Wing, J.M.: Towards a theory of trust in networks of humans and computers. In: Christianson, B., Crispo, B., Malcolm, J., Stajano, F. (eds.) Security Protocols 2011. LNCS, vol. 7114, pp. 223–242. Springer, Heidelberg (2011). https://doi.org/10.1007/978-3-642-25867-1_22
3. Kim, T.H.-J., Gligor, V., Perrig, A.: Street-level trust semantics for attribute authentication. In: Christianson, B., Malcolm, J., Stajano, F., Anderson, J. (eds.) Security Protocols 2012. LNCS, vol. 7622, pp. 96–115. Springer, Heidelberg (2012). https://doi.org/10.1007/978-3-642-35694-0_12
4. Konnikova, M.: The Confidence Game. Viking, New York City (2016)
5. Stajano, F., Wilson, P.: Understanding scam victims: seven principles for systems security. Commun. ACM **54**(3), 70–75 (2011). https://doi.org/10.1145/1897852.1897872

---

[9] www.agari.com.

Assuring the Safety of Asymmetric
Social Protocols
(Transcript of Discussion)

Frank Stajano[✉]

University of Cambridge, Cambridge, UK
frank.stajano@cst.cam.ac.uk

This is joint work with Virgil Gligor, over there, who will intervene when appropriate.

Most security protocols studied in the literature are between machines. We are interested in protocols, which we call "social", that happen between people, even though they are mediated by machines. This is a fertile area for fraud. Someone, for example, receives an email that promises wealth from a Nigerian prince, or some magic blue pill that makes some part of your anatomy longer, and has to decide whether it's a good idea or not to respond to that email.

We call social protocols "asymmetric" when the entity that sends the offer knows that, if the offer is accepted, they're going to get a good deal out of it; while instead the recipient cannot really have a guarantee that they will be in a good situation after responding. With this premise, should anyone ever want to engage in an asymmetric protocol if they are the receiving party? And are there ways to make an asymmetric social protocol become secure for the receiver?

Consider the case where a sender sends an offer to a receiver. The offer could be a useful app, free coupons, a program to remove adware or spyware from your computer, timely news, important or sensitive email attachments. The receiver has to decide whether to take action on this offer or not.

The *receiver's dilemma* is as follows: first of all, how can I assess the value of the offer? It looks good on paper, but what's the true value? How can I assess the trustworthiness of the offer sender? That's rather orthogonal to the value of the offer. We also need to make a subtle distinction between the offer *sender* and the offer *maker*: the offer maker is the one who invents the offer, whereas the offer sender is the one who sends it to me. Sometimes I may have an honest but somewhat clueless sender, passing on an offer that is actually fraudulent. "Oh! Apparently there is a big virus doing the rounds unless you install this software in order to be protected." They send it to me as well. The sender is actually genuine and trustworthy, as far as their honesty is concerned, but clueless and therefore untrustworthy if we consider their technical competence.

Can I insure myself against misbehaviour of the offer maker? Is there a party that would be willing to make me whole in case things go wrong, and how much is owed to them? Are there accountability mechanisms and punishments that could be a threat to deter the sender, or the offer maker, from this behaviour?

© Springer International Publishing AG 2017
F. Stajano et al. (Eds.): Security Protocols 2017, LNCS 10476, pp. 49–59, 2017.
https://doi.org/10.1007/978-3-319-71075-4_6

There have been a few attempts at solving the receiver's dilemma and we summarize them in the paper. Among others, there is *conditional asymmetry acceptance*. For example, services like Amazon and Ebay offer this kind of promise: "I will build a reputation system for the offer makers such that you have some indication of how well they behaved in the past". For the offer makers that have a long track record of having behaved well, Amazon or Ebay is willing to give you an extra guarantee that, if something goes bad with one of their reputable sellers, then Amazon or Ebay themselves will compensate you.

Ross Anderson: There's an even older scheme: if you go back to the days before the internet, when stuff was sold by mail order, there was a thing called the "Mail Order Protection Scheme" whereby, if you bought something through a newspaper ad and it turned out to be dodgy or didn't arrive, then the newspaper would make good. Given that Google makes all the advertising revenue in the world nowadays, perhaps now Google should be the insurer of last resort, and of first resort too.

Virgil Gligor: Yes. This falls into this broad category, but basically the idea is that Google (or Ebay) has already made sure that the advertising party has a good reputation.

Reply: Yes, we are also in a situation where there is basically a wrapping entity around the offer makers. In our case Ebay or Amazon. In Ross's case, the newspaper or Google. Or it could be the legal framework that imposes extra constraints on what may happen.

Tuomas Aura: My experience is that this kind of one-shot purchases from an unknown and untrusted party have decreased. But with some parties we have a continuous relationship, with repeated purchases or interactions. That's the only thing that will force the other party to behave well. They will because they want to keep the customer happy and willing to do further business with them in the future.

Reply: Yes, and the interesting thing is that, due to the presence of this intermediary, even if it is a one-off interaction with this particular seller, for the buyer it is a many-times interaction with the intermediary, be it Ebay or Amazon.

Virgil Gligor: This works extremely well, except when one of them decides to defect. In other words, at some point one of them might in fact defect and cut the relationship. If so, there is a loss at the last step. Now, will they defect? This is the question. You can figure out if they defect if you know the discount rate. In our 2012 paper[1] we described this case. The problem is that you can almost never find the discount rate.

Partha Das Chowdhury: Coming back to this mail order thing, there was a huge Ponzi scheme in India. Billions of dollars. Public figures were arrested, put in prison and deported. This is similar to those newspaper ads.

---

[1] LNCS 7622, p 96.

Bruce Christianson: The point that Ross has made is that, in the case of Google or the newspaper, the *sender* is paying the insurance premium, not the receiver. The newspaper is making an assessment of the risk they run and is charging the sender up front.

Reply: There are two ways in which the sender/seller is paying. One is an actual fee to be a sender in that particular market (e.g. on Amazon). And another one is the danger of being kicked out if they misbehave. For the sellers, if they have an actual business there, the second penalty may even be greater than the first.

Bruce Christianson: Yes, but this is slightly different from the model that you're putting on this slide.

Virgil Gligor: Well, it's not clear that it's different from our point A.

Reply: It's what we're doing here [points at slide], where we say that someone who has high reputation gets covered by a guarantee from Ebay or Amazon. For them, the disincentive against cheating is that then they will be kicked out. So this mechanism lowers the betrayal aversion of the receiver of the offer by banning the high reputation senders from using the service once they cheat. So, if you have earned high reputation and you become a cheater, then you can no longer use the service and all the work you did in the past to build that reputation is lost.

We think it is too difficult a task for every ordinary user to make an accurate assessment of the value of an offer and of the trustworthiness of a random offer maker. Therefore the core of our solution is that we would like to encourage the development of very accurate classifiers, created by experts whose sole job is to make the best classifiers possible. How do we encourage this? We have devised a framework where the best performance of classifiers is rewarded with more business. This is in the context of a marketplace between competing insurers.

An insurer is someone who can both evaluate an offer and then, when they are confident about their assessment, make me a deal that, if I pay a certain premium, they will refund me if their assessment was wrong. So the secret sauce of the insurer is an accurate classifier to distinguish good offers from bad ones. The classifier is at the core of this mechanism. The insurers with the best classifiers are in a position to make the most profit.

A "positive" verdict from the classifier means that the offer under evaluation is dangerous, whereas "negative" means it's not dangerous. So this gives us the usual four quadrants: true positive, true negative, false positive, false negative. If they say it's dangerous and it really *was* dangerous (a "true positive"), then I should not engage in this offer, I should reject it. The user avoids an unsafe state and is happy because he is not defrauded. Fraud is averted. Great.

If the classifier says it's not dangerous and it really was not dangerous, we have a true negative, which is a safe state. I can just enjoy the interaction. The offer really was not dangerous and, here too, everything is great.

Now, in the case of misjudgment from the classifier, we have the "false" cases. If the classifier said the offer was not dangerous, but it was, this is a false negative: I am told that it was safe to engage in this transaction and instead

I get defrauded. This is bad for me but this is covered by the insurance. The insurer promises: "if I get it wrong and you get into a problem, I shall refund you of your losses". This is an incentive for the insurer to be accurate and never come up with a false negative, because every time they have one they have to pay out.

(Now I should point out that refunding someone only works for some types of damage. I can be refunded if I have lost some money, but I cannot be refunded if there has been a breach of confidentiality, because that cannot be reversed and undone. I may be offered compensation in lieu, but I cannot be restored to the previous situation.)

Bruce Christianson: You talk about the purpose of the premium of the insurance payout as being to restore the receiver to the state they were in before, and that's one model. But a second model is to force just enough of a payoff to act as a disincentive to the insurer for getting it wrong; because, if you adopt a collegial view, it's enough that everybody calls out the insurer every time there's a false negative. And okay, victims don't get back to where they were, but collectively they can either drive the bad insurer out of business or force them to improve their algorithm.

Reply: Yes, that is certainly a valid viewpoint. From the viewpoint of the receiver, though, obviously I prefer to engage in this insurance-backed business only if I have some confidence that the insurance will cover me, otherwise I'm putting myself at risk in order to make the world a better place, and I'm not sure if everyone is so altruistic.

Of course, when you have a classifier, you have an overlap between the positives and the negatives. What is always easy to do is to move the threshold one way or another to decide what I'm going to call positive and what I'm going to call negative; and what is difficult to do is to separate the two Gaussians so that you have less of an overlap. The latter requires improving the classifier, whereas the former is just changing a number, a trade-off, fewer false positives but more false negaties or vice versa. If you are a lazy insurer and you want to make a quick buck you can say that basically everything is unsafe and you tell the user never to engage in any transaction. You have eliminated all your false negatives at the price of introducing a lot more false positives. Of course you'll never have to pay out but that's not very helpful for me as the insured party because I will have to refuse many offers that would have been beneficial and actually quite safe. This is bad. As receiver I don't like the false positive, where "positive" means the insurer said it was dangerous, "false" means it was *not* dangerous and I have to reject it and I lose an otherwise good interaction whereas the unscrupulous insurer pockets my premium.

The way we counteract this is precisely by arranging the insurers into a market. I can see that this insurer is saying "dangerous" too often, compared to others, and therefore I will give my business to the insurer that says "dangerous" least frequently, provided he covers me for the cases where he gets it wrong.

Ross Anderson: Hang on a second. It took a lot of time and effort for the Consumers' Association to become established in the UK as an organisation that would give people advice on bargains, offers and coupons in a pre-incident role. In the end, the only way they could make their business fly was as a mass-membership organisation. It's very well to say "let's have a marketplace", but how do you actually incentivise insurers to enter the business? What will my business plan look like if I want to set up in competition with the Consumers' Association?

Virgil Gligor: The question is: how does such a market appear?

Ross Anderson: Well, we've got one supplier, the Consumers' Association. If I want to compete with them...

Reply: Wait a minute: the Consumers' Association gives out *ratings* but has never promised to *insure* you!

Virgil Gligor: Precisely. The Consumers' Association simply rates these insurance agencies (like the ones we are talking about) *once they exist*, but the question is: how do they come up? Is there a need that arises that is satisfied by these guys?

It turns out that you are now beginning to see some of these insurers here. For example there is a start-up company that provides assessments of the validity of the email address using machine learning. They can tell you if this is a phoney address or not a phoney address, among other things. In other words, they are now beginning to look at the emails that you receive and give you some warnings based on the analytics in the network. The company is called Agari and was set up by cryptographer Markus Jakobsson. Apparently they are doing very well: a lot of large companies, including Google, use their services. But what we suggest here goes a step further. This insurance service that we are talking about not only tells you whether or not the email comes from a reasonable source but it is able to assess, in some sense, the *content* of the email, which is much harder than simply figuring out if the email comes from a legitimate source.

Ross Anderson: But if I want my money back, the thing that exists at the moment in the UK (and the US under different laws but with roughly the same effect) is my credit card company. If I get sold scammy goods by some trader in Mongolia, I go through my credit card company and they make me good. This is the critical magic that makes internet commerce scalable internationally.

Virgil Gligor: That's absolutely true and might work here as well.

Ross Anderson: It exists.

Virgil Gligor: It exists, but not in this domain. Right now, the insurance associations are beginning to look at this model.

Ross Anderson: So what you should be doing is selling this idea to Visa and MasterCard, whose members are currently experiencing the pain.

Reply: At the moment, insurers have no say on which emails you should be clicking on; whereas, with this model, if they had an accurate classifier, they could make a lot of money if they only paid out the premiums for the offers that they were happy to insure.

Bryan Ford: It seems like credit card companies are already providing this service on credit card transactions, but they're getting in the way all the time! Who hasn't had their credit card denied when they're travelling because of a false positive in the credit card system? I think this highlights an important potential issue, here: it seems there's this tremendous pressure for the insurance providers to be extremely conservative and not to produce false negatives, but there is only very little weak collective incentives to not produce false positives. That's because, most probably, the user is only being mediated by this one insurer and won't even know that they are missing other offers that their insurer blocked.

Reply: Well, this is precisely the point that's addressed by the marketplace. If it were easier to move between insurers in the marketplace...

Bryan Ford: It sounds like a lemons market to me!

Reply: In the lemons market you don't really know whether something is any good or not, so you have to assume that everything is bad. But in this case you can tell: this is a credit card company that always gives me a "don't do it" verdict, so you know they are playing it too safe and ripping you off.

Bryan Ford: The insurers are only going to pass Disney to you. You will only ever get to hear from Disney or other similarly very safe senders, and nobody else will get through.

Virgil Gligor: There are two problems with the restrictions that they put. This protocol is not intended exclusively, or not even at all, for sales. This might work in a "drive-by" model. I am browsing the web and I see this attractive website: do I click or not? Or in an authentication case: do I click on this certificate? This has nothing to do with any sales of any goods.

Bryan Ford: I wasn't saying it did. Even if we only consider who would be classed as acceptable mail senders, the insurers are going to say: "okay, you get emails from Disney but everybody else is too unsafe from our conservative viewpoint".

Virgil Gligor: This is precisely the point that we are addressing.

Ross Anderson: Virgil, I still say this is Google's job because Google has got a copy of the internet sitting on 10,000 servers in Oregon and they can automatically monitor the whole world and see which senders are bad.

Marios Omar Choudary: Earlier on, you mentioned a book that said that actually it's possible to fool anyone. Does this mean that, suddenly, there is no point in doing anything?

Virgil Gligor: Essentially what the *confidence game* (Konnikova) book argues is that even very sophisticated people occasionally fall for scams.

Marios Omar Choudary: Ah, *occasionally!*

Virgil Gligor: Occasionally. And, in addition to that, even sophisticated people fall for *the same scams* repeatedly. The first book (Akerlof and Shiller, *Phishing for Phools*) actually says that this is a constant situation: it's part of the economic equilibrium. This is what they call "the phishing equilibrium", and they claim it's part of economic life. In other words, the invisible hand of Adam Smith now has a component which is... an invisible hand that gets into your pocket. And that should not be ignored. In other words, this is a staple of life.

Bruce Christianson: It's quite shocking.

Paul Wernick: How does your insurer protect you and the receiver against a long-term fraud? I mean, one where a bad sender builds up a good reputation over time, but then suddenly floods lots of receivers with a virus?

Reply: That is a problem that the insurers have to address in their business model, depending on how much they are willing to cover for, based on how confident they are in their classifier. And so they have to set a premium, and a willingness-to-compensate, that is compatible with the confidence that they have in the accuracy of their detection service.

Paul Wernick: So, if the, bad sender who's planning to go bad knows what the insurance classifying mechanism is, then they can game it.

Reply: Sure. It is certainly possible to defraud the insurer, right? It's not that you become invulnerable just because you become an insurer. You can still go out of business by being scammed.

Paul Wernick: But as a receiver relying on an insurer, I might then find my insurer's model being broken.

Reply: If your insurer goes bankrupt, and that's what you relied on, yes, we have the next slide on this. But I hadn't finished with this one yet...

Partha Das Chowdhury: If I understand this correctly, there are implicit reputation systems where you get your money back. But this is an explicit reputation system I'm relying on, isn't it?

Reply: Well, it's not quite a reputation system. The eBay one is definitely a reputation system, but in here the reputation is not really made explicit. It's something that is part of the secret sauce of each insurer, to decide which sender I'm rating as one I can insure and which one I won't.

Partha Das Chowdhury: You might distribute that reputation mechanism among various parties, say Google and the people who promote the product.

Reply: Well, in this model, the insurers are not cooperating. They are actually competing.

Virgil Gligor: There is one more thing. That distribution that you're talking about is, in some sense, implied: I, as the receiver, can actually compare the services against each other. If I'm reasonably well off, I can even actually subscribe to three different insurance companies, for example. And that would take care of that distribution that you're talking about.

Fabio Massacci: How real-time do you need to be? Because, in theory, for most of the phishing attacks, the big danger is in the first 30 min. So I might offer a physical business in which I just tell customers: "Just wait for 45 min, then [if we haven't blocked it] you can click on it if you still want to". This would probably require no studies, no effort, nothing. Just a random delay of 45 min.

Virgil Gligor: A telltale sign of a bad offer that you get is that you have to act *now*, otherwise you lose this offer. This is a telltale sign, equivalent to a warning in capitals that says DON'T CLICK!.

Bruce Christianson: The insurer might offer a time-dependent deal: the insurance premium is very high if you click now, but it goes down.

Reply: Indeed. You can price it differently. Also, if you are the party that is providing the classification service, you can have many observation points. For example you may have several different unrelated email addresses; if you get the same email message in several of them, then you're pretty sure that it's a fraud.

Fabio Massacci: I meant that you could run the business in the following way: I just keep a little clock waiting. It tells you to keep on waiting for 45 min. After this, do whatever you want. In 99% of cases, this would work.

Reply: Bruce has given a good answer to this, which is you can charge more for someone who wants an answer within 2 seconds, compared to someone who wants an answer within a minute, because I can be more confident in my classifier after seeing what happened after one minute. So, if you want a super snappy answer, then pay more, fine. And I, as an insurer, incur more risk, but then I can extract more value.

Back to our contribution. We were looking at how this insurance premium could be sold, and we had a few iterations of me suggesting stupid things and Virgil fixing them (or sometimes vice-versa). One thing that didn't work was to say that the insurer will offer a different premium for every message depending on how risky it looks. Then, if you're willing to pay the premium, you will be covered, but if the message looks risky then you'll have to pay a lot more before you're going to be covered for opening it. This naive strategy doesn't work. First of all, there may be things that are clearly scams and then the premium would have to be absurdly high in order to cover the potential damage. Secondly, the receiver could free-ride on this pricing signal and see, based on the amount of the premium, whether the insurer considers the message risky or not. If they consider that this is dangerous (which I, the receiver, can tell because I notice that the insurer put a high premium on it), I don't open it; if they consider it cheap, then I open it; in both cases without ever paying any of the premiums, whether high or low. And so this is not a service that the insurer can profitably sell.

Another flawed solution is for the insurer to try to aggregate messages and say: "I will give you a price for the next hundred messages". But again, there's uncertainty, until I've seen the hundred messages, as to what the price should be. If I (insurer) wait until you (receiver) have received the hundred messages, and then I price them, the resulting delay is unacceptable for the customer. So this doesn't work either.

What we decided would work better instead is to make receiver pay for the *service* of having the messages classified. And, with that, will come a promise of an insurance, which is conceptually separate even though it may be sold together. So the recipient forwards the message to the insurer and the insurer says: "If you want me to tell you whether this is safe or not, you have to pay this amount, which is independent of the message—it's just the price of the assessment. And if I tell you that it is safe, and you have also paid me the insurance, if it turns out that it was not safe, I'm going to make you whole in that case." But, if the insurer says it was unsafe and you nonetheless still click on it, then you're on your own. You're not going to be refunded just because you've bought the insurance (just like your car insurer won't buy you a new car if you intentionally crash your old one).

This, on a conceptual level, is done on a per-message basis—although, on a commercial level, it is probably going to be done with a subscription, maybe with a quota on the number of messages. This is because people who buy insurance want to have certainties. They want to just say, "I'm devoting so much per month to being safe with respect to this threat". They don't want to have to keep track of every message. For this service not to be abused, and maybe even resold, then the insurer will have to put quotas on how many interrogations there can be.

Next, attacks to discover the "secret sauce". We look at the situation where the insurer has enemies, who are other insurers, who wish to figure out what the special criterion of this insurer's classifier is, and they try to interrogate it repeatedly. We want to set the fees such that doing this is not advantageous for the competitor. We want to ensure that they may not resell the service to someone else. We don't want any free-rider to be able to get away with not doing the assessment themselves, but reselling the service just by copying a competitor's response.

Khaled Baqer: So the sender has an incentive to collude with the insurer. So you get more money out of lying to the receiver than if you colluded with the sender. So who insures you against that insurer?

Partha Das Chowdhury: That's why it's distributed.

Khaled Baqer: So you're saying you have to subscribe to many of them?

Partha Das Chowdhury: You can.

Paul Wernick: Doesn't that mean that, with every insurer you subscribe to, you're adding them to a list of people who are reading your emails?

Reply: Yes, there is that. One might object: "Wait a minute! But in order for these offers to be assessed, I have to send them my emails in plain text? That sounds like crazy!" Then you look at people in this room, who are all privacy-minded, and yet half of them are crazy enough to use Gmail...

Virgil Gligor: And there are also some fancy academic solutions to that. We'll send them the email encrypted in such a way that they can actually query some fields that are of interest.

Joan Feigenbaum: Sounds familiar!

Virgil Gligor: What's needed here is probably weaker than what you described in your earlier talk. If the sender is more like cryptdb, you run queries on data that's encrypted in a way that lets you run the queries.

Joan Feigenbaum: Some people have been known to do that.

Simon Foley: Unrelated question. Are people paying a fixed price for the service, regardless of what the costs would be and what's being insured?

Reply: No. Depending on what premium they are willing to pay, they may get a different service; for example they may be insured against higher risks or, as Bruce suggested earlier, they may receive more timely responses.

Simon Foley: In terms of the high risks, does the consumer then have a way of being able to detect what is high risk and what is not high risk, or is it hidden behind the insurer?

Reply: If the answer of the classifier is not a Boolean but a real number between 0 and 1, then you can say, "If you pay me this premium, I only insure you for risks up to this level; but if you pay me this higher premium, I will insure for these other risks as well". And so on.

To summarize this presentation: we discuss the class of *asymmetric social protocols*, which are the ones where people talk to other people but the interaction is mediated by machines. *Asymmetric*, because the value proposition is clear to the potential fraudster but not to the potential victim. These protocols form the basis of many scams. We want to address this asymmetry not with an ad hoc solution for the particular scam but with a systematic framework to try to reduce the risk for everything. The asymmetric social protocols are in fact being used in the real world. Guccifer, here on the slide, is the Romanian unemployed taxi driver and social engineer who was responsible for the attacks into Hillary Clinton's email server. And Guccifer 2.0 is allegedly the group that hacked into the US Democratic Party's network and leaked its documents to Wikileaks. Whatever. This type of scam is not going to go away. Social engineering is now a major source of fraud on the internet.

So, for most users, it is not possible to establish what is a safe protocol state. Users are not able to assess the value and, frankly, we just think it's unfair: you have to live in the computer society because, in this century, you can't get out of it anymore; but, because of that, you are being asked to take complex decisions that no regular human being could. And so we encourage a situation where these decisions are taken by technical entities who make it their job to be accurate about them, and we pit them against each other so they have a strong incentive to be accurate, in the interest of their own business model.

For everyone's good, we are interested in obtaining accurate classifiers. We have said nothing about how you build the machine learning that is necessary for building the actual classifiers: instead, we have just provided a framework (shaped like a marketplace) in which the people who are smart enough to make classifiers can become rich, if they are more accurate than others, and if they are not so greedy that they would always say "Dangerous, dangerous, dangerous", because that's an easy way for the insurer never to issue false negatives but is not helpful for the insured.

Simulating Perceptions of Security

Paul Wernick[✉], Bruce Christianson, and Joseph Spring

University of Hertfordshire, Hatfield, UK
p.d.wernick@herts.ac.uk

Abstract. Systems complicated enough to have ongoing security issues are difficult to understand, and hard to model. The models are hard to understand, even when they are right (another reason they are usually wrong), and too complicated to use to make decisions.

Instead attackers, developers, and users make security decisions based on their *perceptions* of the system, and not on properties that the system actually has. These perceptions differ between communities, causing decisions made by one community to appear irrational to another.

Attempting to predict such irrational behaviour by basing a model of perception on a model of the system is even more complicated than the original modelling problem we can't solve. Ockham's razor says to model the perceptions directly, since these will be simpler than the system itself.

1 Introduction and Rationale

The theme of SPW 2017 is "Multi-objective security". In this position paper we consider security mechanisms in the light of the different perceptions, by different communities, of the degree of vulnerability of a computer system[1] to various attacks. We portray these differences by means of a graphical model, which is intended to capture quantitative changes in these perceptions over time.

We identify three distinct communities involved in the development and use of a system. These communities are likely to have very different opinions on the vulnerabilities of the system. The communities are, first, people planning to attack systems or computer-based devices, or who have already done so (intruders); second, those developing or augmenting the defence mechanisms of those systems (developers); and third, people who lack deep technical knowledge, and simply use the systems (users). A person can belong to one community with respect to one system, and to others for other systems; for example, a person can be an attacker for one system whilst relying for their own security on a tool they are using such as an operating system or language compiler.

Incomplete knowledge means that no community has platonic access to an "objective" reality about the security of the system with which it interacts, and so communities perforce make decisions on the basis of *their* perceptions,[2]

---

[1] The term 'system' as employed here includes a computer's operating system, as well as any countermeasures such as antivirus and other programs, and mobile and other inter-connected devices. Our argument applies to all of these.

[2] cf. [1].

© Springer International Publishing AG 2017
F. Stajano et al. (Eds.): Security Protocols 2017, LNCS 10476, pp. 60–68, 2017.
https://doi.org/10.1007/978-3-319-71075-4_7

along with any internal models in which *they* have trust. It is a brute fact that divergences between the beliefs held by the communities cause them to act in ways that other communities perceive as being "irrational". So, rather than trying to ignore these differences as symptoms of a "mistake" on the part of one or another stakeholder, we seek to model them as essentially rational from their community's perspective.

2   Perceptions of Vulnerability

The three communities to which we have referred have very different viewpoints of the security of a system at any particular time:

1. A potential or actual *intruder*, who will attempt to subvert the use or gain control of that device for some reason, and who may be aware of weaknesses unknown to the developers. We include within this community knowledgeable hackers, hacking tool developers, and unsophisticated 'script kiddies'.
2. The *developers* of the software in the device, who may be aware of some weaknesses not yet exploited by intruders but may also be unaware of other vulnerabilities undiscovered by, available to, or already exploited by those intruders.
3. The *users*, whether commercial organisations or individual owners, of these devices, who must rely on the *publicising* of weaknesses to support any decision to update the operating software on their devices.

It is the user community's perception of safety in device or system use which particularly concerns us. Given the lack of reliable information – and the presence of misinformation – available to them, particularly online, they are often unable to make decisions as to how safe their devices or systems are that are as rational as they might make if they were informed better and/or earlier. Consequently, they are vulnerable not only to attacks on their technology but also to a false sense of security in using it [4].

The tensions between the different perceptions of risk implicit in the use of devices with insecure software to access sensitive services such as online banking is heightened when users are unaware of known risks embedded in their equipment. This situation is made even worse when we note that one of the most active areas of growth in mobile banking – Africa – is where it is likely that for cost reasons many people will be using previously-owned devices exported from richer areas of the world.

One impetus for the work described here arises from a paper presented at SPW 23 [8] in which the authors appear to suggest that users of mobile technology are likely to upgrade their devices' operating software at a sufficient speed to ensure that it is sufficiently up-to-date to minimise security risks. We believe this assumption cannot be sustained in an environment in which security holes are not revealed to users; security fixes are not provided to users on an ongoing basis (Android devices are updated at the whim of the manufacturer); and older devices (which may have an increasing number of security issues as support tails off [2] are not destroyed but passed on to subsequent users: see, for example "Once you've been paid, your phone may be refurbished and sold to insurance channels or sent abroad to be sold on there."[3]

Thomas et al. also note that there are security holes in Android devices still in current use but running older versions of the operating system. A growing number of these vulnerabilities will never be fixed due to the failure of the manufacturers responsible for providing users with updated versions of Android. These permanent weaknesses will inevitably include some of which those users remain unaware, resulting in a false feeling of confidence in the security and confidentiality of their activities. We feel that it is not desirable to *assume* that security is adequately maintained simply by older, insecure devices falling out of use. Nor does it suffice to leave users' security to the whim of commercial organisations with an interest in selling new equipment to people who already have working systems, as suppliers currently seem able to avoid responsibility for loss or damage to users who do not upgrade. A system provider such as an internet bank might seek to pass the risk on to their customer base. In the past card issuers have denied liability for card fraud by stating as fact that the victim must have told somebody their PIN, and tried to fight off their liability.

3   Deciding When to Update

The decisions of users when (or whether) to update are likely to be influenced by their *perceptions* of the *risks* to continued operation incurred by performing these updates, as well as of the benefits of doing so. The behaviour of these users can be influenced by statements by interested parties, such as antivirus authors whose concerns are often quoted in the media, and news media who rely on a stream of potentially-overstated stories of data loss or damage to attract people to their websites and increase advertising revenue.

An example of an issue which we are exploring is whether users should install updates published by software suppliers as they are issued, a common concern for users of technology. Users may be impelled to update their systems if they have been attacked themselves.[4] Under these circumstances they might adopt all future upgrades. They might buy new versions of software as they believe they need to – or as they are told they need to. Alternatively, if they are not currently aware that they have been attacked or are at risk, they might not update their systems, on the basis that they don't think they need to, or have been scared away from doing so, perhaps by potential attackers telling them not to upgrade because the upgrade will damage their systems.

If a user does decide to update their system this may not be a painless process for the non-technical user, and may also incur a subsequent risk to the continued operation of the device, even with modern updating procedures (e.g. [5]; [7]). So if the updating procedure is under the user's control then it must be expected that

---

[3] http://www.comparemymobile.com/, accessed 11 October 2016.

[4] Many commercial organisations test updates received from suppliers before distributing them to their user base, a protection unavailable to the private user.

a proportion of users will choose to defer updating, preferring to let others find the landmines, until it is imperative or even beyond. This may be one reason for Microsoft updating Windows 10 without user permission or control; there may also be commercial reasons for this policy relating to their move to a subscription model of revenue generation.

In future work we intend to modify the model to reflect the real-world circumstances of one or more specific systems and the media stories surrounding their security history, and calibrate the model to explore the dynamics of the three communities' perceptions of how secure those systems have been over time.

4 The Simulation Environment

Our model has been developed using the Vensim [9] system dynamics [6] (SD) environment. In this approach to simulation, which is based on an analogy with a hydraulic system, movements of tangible elements, and intangible aspects such as belief, are seen as equivalent to liquids moving from one state (represented by a rectangular box and referred to in SD as a 'level') to another via pipes (double lines) whose flow is constrained by valves ('flows'). Levels and flows are named variables in the quantified simulation; the equations which calculate their values are based in part on their type, the value of a level for example being the integration over time of its inputs minus its outputs, typically commencing with a given initial value at the start of the simulation run. The value of a variable is computed based on the values of other model variables, and the constant numbers and look-up tables which link the model variables to real-world values.

The benefit of this simulation approach is not limited to what can be found from running a quantified model; as Professor Lehman told the first author of this paper, "90% of the value of a simulation comes from building the model".[5] This is because the modeller is forced to eliminate ambiguities and resolve misunderstandings in their appreciation of the situation under consideration, and the resulting model structure diagram becomes a vehicle for discussion between the model builder and the different groups of stakeholders ehicvh can improve understanding of the situation being analysed.

5 The Model Described

Our intention in developing this model is to enable a comparison to be made between the relative degrees of confidence (whether well-justified or otherwise) of three groups of people who are stakeholders in the security of a software-based system. These are: people who are attacking the security of that system, or wish to be in a position to do so in the future; the people responsible for developing, maintaining and upgrading that system; and the end users of that system. Our current model reflects a generic situation; discussions at SPW have convinced

---

[5] Manny Lehman, conversation with Paul Wernick, 1997.

us that it needs to be refined to reflect the events and influences in the history of a specific system before it can be usefully calibrated.

We have included in our model different causes of perceptions of vulnerability for the communities which we have identified. This requires us to simulate the ability of an attacker to exploit a vulnerability of the software running on a system, the ability of the developers of its software to fix that vulnerability, and the ability and motivation of a user of that system to access the necessary security fixes. Our approach to modelling has been to ignore detailed differences between specific vulnerabilities or exploits, and attempt to improve our understanding of the situation from a high, more general, level; this approach is typical when using a continuous simulation environment such as system dynamics. Our current uncalibrated model shows how the differences in perception can arise; the final, quantified, model will also be able to quantify the degree to which these perceptions diverge over time.

Once this configuration and calibration of the model are complete, it will be possible to trace changes in these levels of belief over time. We expect this to show that attackers will be confident in their ability to attack such a system using techniques such as zero day exploits, that the developers will have some confidence that the current version is resilient, and that the confidence of end users – those most vulnerable to loss – in the security of the system may be considerably greater than that of the other two groups.

The current model consists of three main parts:

1. The flow of vulnerabilities from implicit through discovery by potential or actual intruders, the identification and fixing of these issues by software developers, and the releasing of these fixes to the field. This is modelled as an SD *aging chain.*
2. The developers' willingness to devote effort to fixing security holes, whether these holes have been identified in the field and fixed for release or identified within the development organisation and prepared for release but not fielded until the issue is subsequently exploited in the field.
3. The process which cause users of these devices to realise that their systems are vulnerable, identify relevant fixes made available to them, and adopt them. An important concern here is whether developers provide users with fixes to security weaknesses exploited in their model of device.

In some cases security and other updates are provided and installed automatically without user intervention, whilst at the other end of the scale there are many devices still in use which will never receive any further fixes to security weaknesses. These weaknesses, whether exploited on a specific device or not, will remain until the device is taken out of use. The users of these vulnerable devices may be aware of the problem, for instance people still using Windows XP for which discontinuance of support has been well publicised, or they may be unaware of the security holes in their devices, which we believe is the case for owners of mobile phones running older versions of Android. This issue is also likely to be relevant to users of many other software-based systems, including the security failures of the Internet of Things (cf. [3]).

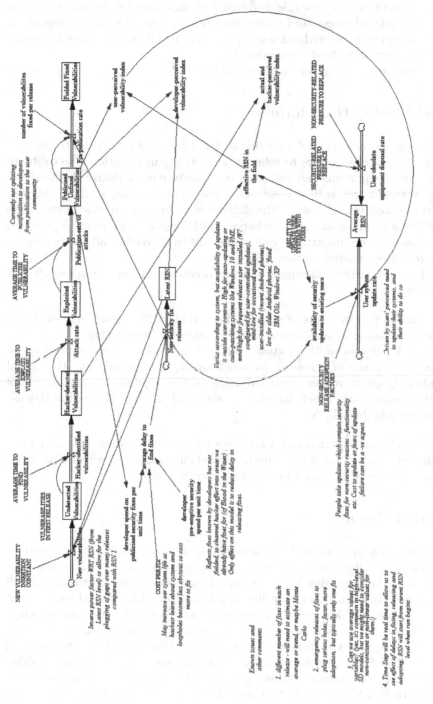

Fig. 1. Model of degree of confidence in system security

At the same time it is likely that users will install updates for reasons other than security (for example additional or improved functionality, fixes to non-security-related bugs), and these updates may contain security fixes which improve user protection without users perceiving it. Of course, those fixes may also include new or revived vulnerabilities.

The structure of the model is shown in Fig. 1.

6   Calibrating the Model

Following the identification of a specific system for consideration and the modification of the model structure to reflect that system, our intention is to calibrate our model with equations and values so as to produce quantitative results showing any divergent trends in perceptions of the security of the system. This will allow us to quantitatively assess the differences in perception of security of the three different communities and, we hope, explain trends in, for example, changes in the rates of successful attacks on examples of that system and the take-up of new more secure versions as they appear.

We have made the following tentative decisions on how to approach this calibration:

- The time step is in terms of elapsed time, to allow the significance of delays in, for instance, releasing fixes to known issues, to be considered
- Successive releases of the software under consideration are assumed to be a single sequence of releases. To avoid having to contend with the actual numbers given to releases and sub-releases, the sequence is indicated by a single integer value which increments with each release; this is the Release Sequence Number (RSN).

We will rely on expert opinion for input values which cannot be easily measured directly, such as numbers of undiscovered vulnerabilities; we have used this approach previously in earlier modelling activities [10].

7   Initial Results

Even before we adapt the model to a specific system and calibrate it to produce quantified results, we can derive some initial insights. Some of these are well-known, but it is reassuring that the model supports them, a situation which gives us more confidence in the utility at a high level, of the model structure as a representation of the current security situation. We expect that as we adapt the model structure it will be possible to draw further conclusions of this type.

An advantage of the Vensim environment is that a built-in analysis tool allows the modeller to see easily where feedback loops exist between variables; these loops will have a strong influence on the behaviour of the overall model and the perceptions which it seeks to represent. Even without a quantified model, we believe representing the situation in a graphical notation helps to clarify the relationships between different stakeholder groups. Examples of this include showing how users of a system can be left behind the current state of security mechanisms without realising until it is too late, and the sources of pressures on software developers to fix security flaws.

As an example of the stories that the uncalibrated model structure can tell, here is one feedback loop in the model; this loop involves 11 variables:

New security fix releases
    Latest RSN
    New vulnerabilities
    Undetected Vulnerabilities
    Hacker-identified vulnerabilities
    Hacker-detected Vulnerabilities
    Attack rate
    Exploited Vulnerabilities
    Publication rate of attacks
    Publicised Unfixed Vulnerabilities
    Developer spend on publicised security fixes per unit time
    Average delay to find fixes
New security fix releases

This loop tells a story of newly-released security fixes themselves generating new vulnerabilities. After deployment of the new release, these vulnerabilities can be identified and exploited by hackers. The exploits are then either privately reported to the developers or publicised in the media, which causes the system's developers to deploy effort to close the security holes, an activity which inevitably takes time. The fixes are then released, causing a new set of vulnerabilities to arise or old vulnerabilities to re-emerge in new forms, in addition to existing problems, which are then identified by hackers, and so on.

It is unlikely that users, system developers and hackers will share the same appreciation of the current level of security in their systems, and of how vulnerable they are to attack. Some users' systems are no longer being evolved to fix security vulnerabilities; some users do not receive updates to security holes in a timely manner; and some will choose, if they have the option, to not update their systems. These groups of users are likely to be more vulnerable than they believe to be the case. Contrary to one possible inference from Thomas et al.'s [8] work, our model demonstrates how the failure of systems developers to maintain the security of their customers' systems can result in users being made more vulnerable to attack *without their realising that this is the case*. This is particularly true for users of systems which are no longer being supported with security fixes, and who are unaware of the seriousness of the threat, or who are otherwise persuaded not to replace their systems, or cannot afford to do so, or are buying old devices with operating software containing security holes. Even if they are aware of the risk, the situation is entirely outside the users' control unless they spend the money (if they have it), and take the time, to replace their systems.

8   Future Work

We intend to develop this work by identifying a specific long-lived software system with many security fixes issued over time. Following any necessary modifications to the model structure to capture this history we will complete its quantitative calibration. This will reflect trends in the rates of attacks and of the development, fielding and adoption of fixes. Further outputs will include estimates of the degree of confidence each group holds in the completeness and/or accuracy of their knowledge. We then hope to involve industrial collaborators such as antivirus software developers in helping to improve our understanding of how and why each of the groups we have identified acts as they do on the basis of their differing perceptions of the security of the software they use.

References

1. Christianson, B.: Living in an impossible world: real-izing the consequences of intransitive trust. Philos. Technol. **26**(4), 411–429 (2013)
2. Clark, S., Blaze, M., Smith, J.: Blood in the water: are there honeymoon effects outside software? In: Christianson, B., Malcolm, J. (eds.) Security Protocols 2010. LNCS, vol. 7061, pp. 12–17. Springer, Heidelberg (2014). https://doi.org/10.1007/978-3-662-45921-8_4
3. Leverett, E., Clayton, R., Anderson, R.: Standardisation and certification of the 'Internet of Things'. In: Proceedings of WEIS 2017 (2017)
4. Murayama, Y., Fujihara, Y., Nishioka, D.: The sense of security and a countermeasure for the false sense. In: Christianson, B., Crispo, B., Malcolm, J., Stajano, F. (eds.) Security Protocols 2011. LNCS, vol. 7114, pp. 205–214. Springer, Heidelberg (2011). https://doi.org/10.1007/978-3-642-25867-1_20
5. Robinson, D.: Windows 10 backlash: which? demands compo for forced upgrades; The Register (2016). www.theregister.co.uk/2016/09/22/windows_10_backlash_begins_which_calls_for_upgrade_compensation/. Accessed 21 Nov 2016
6. System Dynamics Society: What is System Dynamics? (2016). http://www.systemdynamics.org/what-is-s/. Accessed 7 Dec 2016
7. Tepper, F.: Updating to iOS 10 is bricking some iPhones and iPads; TechCrunch (2016). https://techcrunch.com/2016/09/13/updating-to-ios-10-is-bricking-some-iphones-and-ipads/. Accessed 11 Oct 2016
8. Thomas, D.R., Beresford, A.R., Coudray, T., Sutcliffe, T., Taylor, A.: The lifetime of android api vulnerabilities: case study on the javascript-to-java interface. In: Christianson, B., Švenda, P., Matyáš, V., Malcolm, J., Stajano, F., Anderson, J. (eds.) Security Protocols 2015. LNCS, vol. 9379, pp. 126–138. Springer, Cham (2015). https://doi.org/10.1007/978-3-319-26096-9_13
9. Ventana Systems, Inc. (2016). https://vensim.com/. Accessed 7 Dec 2016
10. Wernick, P., Lehman, M.M.: Software process dynamic modelling for FEAST/1. J. Syst. Softw. **46**, 193–201 (1999)

Simulating Perceptions of Security
(Transcript of Discussion)

Paul Wernick[✉]

University of Hertfordshire, Hatfield, UK
p.d.wernick@herts.ac.uk

One of the things that's come through, particularly in Simon's and in Virgil and Frank's work, is that different people might have different perceptions of how secure a system is, and that's the basis of what I'm going to be talking about.

People have different perceptions, on which they base what they believe at any particular time. How we might model these perceptions? At the moment, in the form of a diagram we can do some analysis on, looking for loops and so on, but in future work we intend to quantify these degrees of perception to compare them with each other and, as a result of feedback, improve the structure we already have by calibrating and exercising it.

There are different views of how a system can be, and we should accept the brute fact that people might reasonably adhere to very different beliefs. Earlier today, it was suggested that somebody was completely mad for thinking a particular way: yet from their point of view, it might be entirely rational. We have to be able to understand and maybe even predict changes in behaviour between different communities, different types of people involved in a particular situation, based on those differing perceptions. In the position paper we think about an intruder, a software developer maintainer, and an end-user.

Developers know how much money they make from the system, from selling people upgrades to make things safer, and selling entirely new pieces of software to replace the ones they say are no longer to be kept safe. They will tell you that Windows XP cannot be kept safe anymore, so you should upgrade to Vista or Windows 7 (whilst at the same time, if you've got enough money, continuing to keep XP secure). They also have a view about what reputational damage or actual damage they will incur if those systems are breached, and whether it's worth making a commercial decision just to take the hit.

Given that amount of information, bear in mind they don't have the same information the bad guys have, how might the developers act?

Ross Anderson: This discussion about the business model for fix-it becomes serious when we start talking about cars. Cars upgrade maybe once a decade, cars don't last for just three years like mobile phones. A Land Rover sold today was 30 years old. Riding around in a car like that, who's going to be paying for the security fixes? Who even knows how to fix software that's 30 years old? Where does the money to fix it come from?

© Springer International Publishing AG 2017
F. Stajano et al. (Eds.): Security Protocols 2017, LNCS 10476, pp. 69–75, 2017.
https://doi.org/10.1007/978-3-319-71075-4_8

Reply: I think that's a very good question! When a car model goes out of production, by law you have to be able to produce spare parts for 10 years. But they're saying nothing about software fixes, as you say. At the same time we're moving toward autonomous cars that are already being hacked. If an autonomous car goes out of production, does that mean that everyone's capable of being hacked and everybody will be told to throw their car away?

Ross Anderson: What's a car going to cost if we invent a car that you have to scrap after 10 years? And what does this tell us about how a socially optimal model for patching is going to evolve?

Reply: I'll confess, I'm not considering the social model. I'm considering it from the point of view of the software developer, and what they might rationally do from their own commercial perspective. Now if you say that society's got to kick them until they do something different, that's something else to add to the model later on.

Bruce Christianson: It might be nice to be able to quantify how much kicking it would take. Just how much would their profit and/or reputation have to suffer before they would change?

Reply: Cars are a longer-term thing. But the mobile phone issue is immediate, with new versions coming out every few months. The mobile phone I've got in my wallet here runs an old version of Android that will never be updated.

Bruce Christianson: Ouch. Those phones are going to be used for mobile banking.

Virgil Gligor: In fact, there may be a demand for very old devices that cannot be hacked, such as a 1955 Chevy. Like, my phone certainly cannot be hacked via Bluetooth. A vacuum tube computation system cannot be hacked by the NSA, as we noticed in Somalia. So these vintage pieces of equipment do have some useful properties.

Reply: I've heard stories that the FSB are using typewriters.

Virgil Gligor: Absolutely, yes. Although we do worry about acoustics.

Reply: So, sound-proof rooms.

The user is going to make rational decisions based on what they believe is the case. They might be told by the developers that the system needs updating. They get a message that says, "Your system needs to be updated." I got one recently on this machine, and I didn't recognise it at all. I had to do a bit of work before I realised it was Lenovo, the manufacturer saying it. But it could have been a bad guy saying, "Your system needs updating! It needs updating because I want to put my malware on it."

Bruce Christianson: So what is the user to do?

Reply: Well, what the users believe out of what they're being told is an interesting question. They know what they've been told. It could be marketing hype.

"Your computer needs updating, which means we want to get another subscription to our anti-virus service." Or it could be a bad guy. Users know whether fixes are being made available, or they might realise, "Hang on a minute, my phone has not been updated for three years, maybe it's not being updated anymore, maybe it's vulnerable. I don't know. But how much is it going to cost me? Do I need to go and get a new phone? Do I need to throw my 10 year old car away and buy a new car, because it's vulnerable? Who's telling me this anyway?"

Bruce Christianson: Perhaps you haven't had any upgrades because they've fixed everything and it's perfectly secure now.

Reply: Perhaps I'll believe that.

Sven Uebelacker: A few years ago, for xLinux, there were various versions. The problem was that they had security bugs, but the distributers were not reliably packaging the latest version. So the developers put a small function inside the software in the xScreenSaver saying, "This version is from that date, and after six months there should have been an update." If there is no update, the user got a pop-up saying, "You are running an old version, you need to update."

So here is a different way to get the software upgrades into the car from somewhere: to implement the security mechanism to check this into the software, and not rely upon waiting for the user.

Reply: Firstly, the user has to believe that it is the right software that's promoting the update notice. Second issue is that users might rationally believe there are certain pieces of software that don't have security implications. Like screensavers. They may believe that certain things are intrinsically safe, because they've been told that.

The mechanism we are using to simulate beliefs is system dynamics. How many people are familiar with this simulation environment? The model is based on a hydraulic system. Imagine a bath. You've got taps to pour water in, and a plug, that way you can let water out.

Bruce Christianson: Basically our approach is simply that belief is an incompressible fluid.

Reply: So what's the attacker's perception? How does the attacker believe the world is? Bearing in mind that they can't know everything. Our idea is predicated on each group having a different subset of all possible beliefs. Nobody has perfect knowledge. They have the software that's actually out there in the real world, and the vulnerabilities they know they've found.

For the developer, how vulnerable they think the system is, is the vulnerabilities they know about compared with the current version, even if it hasn't yet been fielded. They know where they are in terms of fixing those problems.

The user: all they know about is what's actually going on in the field from the publicity. How many vulnerabilities have turned up on page one of the Daily Mail that they believe they haven't been given a fix for?

So each of these three groups has a different view of reality, and will make potentially rational decisions based on that view. That's the big thing we're trying to bring out, which is that people do not necessarily make irrational decisions. It's easy to say, "Well, the user's being stupid." But nobody knows what is *actually* true (or actually stupid). Certainly not the developers.

This is the current version of the model where you've seen, briefly, this ageing chain of vulnerabilities. The developers are working here. They're fixing things, whether they actually fix things as they're publicised, or they're actually spending time to pre-fix known vulnerabilities, or not necessarily fielding them until they need to. And the users are updating as appropriate, although they may be limited in their ability to put updates in, or they may say, "I'm not going to do it."

Partha Das Chowdhury: But do developers release fixes to threats that they think might happen? Or only to the things that actually happen?

Reply: I believe both. Developers will say, "We have a fix to this particular problem. We know there's a vulnerability and the thing to do is fix it but not necessarily field that fix because we have a suspicion that will introduce new vulnerabilities." So, stay stable, as long as the bad guys haven't found that hole, let's not field a fix to it.

Ross Anderson: The standard criticism of system dynamics, which a lot of people did 20 or 30 years ago, is that's it all very well to draw boxes and arrows between them but there's no way in which this can be tested. One guy can write one network of boxes and arrows. Another guy can write another network of boxes and arrows. And whether one is better than the other is difficult to relate to evidence. Now, when people do economics of security, they tend to assume very much simpler models so that they can actually test them with data that can be collected from the real world. So, what does this approach actually buy us? We already know about the vulnerability of life-cycle models. There have been lots of these proposed in the security economics literature. What do we get from adding a few extra arrows.

Reply: I hope what we get is an ability to see the big picture. To see how these three parallel views of vulnerable systems fit together.

Simon Foley: I guess my question is, if you're looking at the real system, where is this information going to come from? If you consider the size of the databases that describe all the different assets, are you saying somebody needs to sit down and input all of this information in order to derive the beliefs that the different communities have in the system?

Bruce Christianson: We're not attempting to model the system. We're attempting to model the beliefs of different communities well enough to predict their behaviour.

Simon Foley: But will that be at the granularity of the individual components? Like, look here's a component version of each belief?

Reply: No, no. System Dynamics, I think, works best at the very big, broad level. And that's one of the things, Ross, that we can buy with System Dynamics, an understanding of what goes where. I've produced emulations in the past based on expert opinions of some of the factors I couldn't directly measure and they worked surprisingly well. You get outputs in terms of graphs you can take back to the experts and say them, "Is this what you expected to happen?" Sometimes yes and sometimes no. And the no can be interesting because then you (and they) learn.

Bruce Christianson: The extra modelling step we've taken is that peoples' actions are based on their beliefs, which are based in turn on their perceptions. We know that the real system is a lot more complicated than peoples' perceptions of it, because that's why there are security issues. So Ockham's razor says don't bother to model reality first, and then model how people perceive it, just directly model their perceptions.

Reply: System Dynamics is particularly good at feedback loops. An example here is where what happens if we release a new security fix. In the model that introduces new vulnerabilities because we've fixed something and put some more code in and that introduces new vulnerabilities. They're identified by the hackers. They're then attacked and exploited and publicised, at which point the developers spend some time and money fixing them. It then takes a bit of time to do that. They then go out into the field, at which point you go right back to the start

Virgil Gligor: One important type of vulnerability to look at is design vulnerabilities. Let me give an example. There is a vulnerability in LAN MAN, which was a Microsoft local area network system dating from about 1080[1]. The vulnerability was very simple, it was in the LanMan hash. They had an administrative domain where you logged in once, there is a hash of your password associated with your name, and that stayed online as a valid authenticator no matter how many sessions you had. So if somebody got your authenticator and the name, they could reuse it and become you. Now, that vulnerability, which was a design vulnerability, was apparently patched in Windows NT in 1995. This design bug was actually rediscovered and reimplemented a little later, in 1997. And then, over the years, there are patches against this until 2013 when Chinese hackers, the Shanghai group, used this past hash vulnerability, with a new version of Windows, to penetrate the US Office of Personnel Management (OPM). So finally, Microsoft, after about 20 years of knowing about this, got the message and really fixed the design problem instead of the implementation bug.

So essentially, if you have a design flaw then the cycles of using the new system and patching a little bit but not changing the design will come and bite you. And that might fit in your model.

Reply: I think that fits this loop very nicely. If we say that the old problem has been fixed, but the new problem is actually the same one again ...

Virgil Gligor: ... in the new version of the system.

---

[1] `Wikipedia.org/wiki/LAN_manager`.

Reply: So that keeps going round and round until ...

Virgil Gligor: ...until the design is fixed.

Fabio Massacci: At the end of the day, what's your final goal? How can I use this model, through inference or something, on what the user is to do differently? What's better about this model than the ones we already have?

Reply: This model works at a higher level than what the individual does in any specific circumstance. We hope that once the model is fully featured and calibrated, you could ask: What is the effect of the user stopping taking updates? What is the effect of the developer no longer supplying updates? How do those three different perceptions compare over time?

Bruce Christianson: And we want to use it to predict what changes to their perception would alter the behaviour of users, and the developers, and even maybe the attackers, in more desirable directions.

Joan Feigenbaum: I think you hit on something that is underappreciated when you mentioned hype. Our users, maybe our developers, and maybe even researchers are going to wonder whether all of the scary stories we've heard about insecurity are actually to be taken quite so seriously. Should we really be as scared as some people want us to be?

Reply: Well, I suppose they ought to be scared at the right level of being scared. Their perception of reality has got to be somewhere.

Joan Feigenbaum: Right. And I think that this is one of the loci of maximum uncertainty. Like, how scared should you be? At some point you just have to ask yourself this. I've heard the sky is falling rhetoric so many times, and every time supposedly that was it, that was computer security Armageddon. But no, actually not. We carry on. Networks carry on. What do we make of all this?

Reply: One of the elements of the user's perception is, what does it cost me? A few people have got their data completely scrubbed. A lot more people have had duff payments on their credit cards, but they know the credit card company will pay them out, so why worry? What they believe depends partly on their personal experience and, as you say, partly on what they're told. Is it actually Armageddon, or is it a cry of Wolf promoted by the person who wants to sell us an upgraded computer? There's always somebody[2] down the line who will say, "Well, I can't afford an upgraded computer. I'll just buy an old second-hand one running Windows XP and hope for the best." I think it's precisely a matter of perception.

Partha Das Chowdhury: Your feedback approach resonates with the paper Bruce Christianson and I gave at the 18th workshop in 2010[3]. We argued that it's more important for security to be resilient against the unexpected than for it to be provably correct.

---

[2] Two months after the Workshop, the NHS turned out to be an example.

[3] More Security or Less Insecurity, Security Protocols 18, LNCS 7061, pp 115–126.

Reply: But that also brings out the lovely idea of security being good enough. It doesn't have to be perfect.

Partha Das Chowdhury: But how do you identify the limitations of your model? A model is good to have, but like a map it also has limitations.

Reply: Models are always abstractions. I'm taking a very high level view of what's going on, driven by what I need to know in order to capture those perceptions.

Self Attestation of Things

Partha Das Chowdhury[1]($\boxtimes$) and Bruce Christianson[2]

[1] Aberystwyth University, Aberystwyth, UK
partha.dc@gmail.com
[2] University of Hertfordshire, Hatfield, UK
b.christianson@herts.ac.uk

Abstract. Various devices including our mobile phones are increasingly used as the intermediary (gateway) between IoT peripherals (like the smart lock at our homes) and the larger cloud infrastructure. In this paper we introduce the novel notion of Caveat instances on the cloud together with a novel application of MQTT (the communication protocol designed for peripherals) to stamp our will on how data about us can be used when it travels and resides outside our immediate boundary. Even when we cannot keep our personal data private, we can still prevent it from being misused, for example to commit identity theft, by ensuring that the attacker cannot produce an appropriate attestation for the data.

1 Introduction

The Internet now senses, thinks and acts through devices we term Things. We live in a world where we have Things (e.g. refrigerators, heart monitors, cars) including computers[1]. In the process, the uncertainty and noise of the real world is interacting with the precision of computing. The Internet of Things provides tremendous opportunities but these opportunities are fraught with tremendous risks. The IoT world is the ultimate Panopticon[2]. IoT enables data collection at a granularity like never before, so there is considerable rush in integrating the enormous stream of data from physical devices along with our existing data. The IoT infrastructure is used to collect the data and then, using analytics, the goal is to have a single view of (all the) data pertaining to corresponding data subjects.

In this paper we propose a mechanism using (nearly) already deployed infrastructure to tag personal sensitive information with our policies regarding potential uses of the data. We build on the explicit realization that in the world we live in we need to collaborate with the enemy to achieve a meaningful distributed service; thus we do disclose identifying information where needed, but with

---

[1] http://nymag.com/selectall/2017/01/the-internet-of-things-dangerous-future-bruce-schneier.html.

[2] A institutional building designed by English philosopher Bentham where all the inmates can be observed by an observer without the inmates knowing when they are being observed and when not.

© Springer International Publishing AG 2017
F. Stajano et al. (Eds.): Security Protocols 2017, LNCS 10476, pp. 76–84, 2017.
https://doi.org/10.1007/978-3-319-71075-4_9

the explicit expression of the permitted uses of the information. Thus misuse of the information can be identified. The ability to track misuse of identifying information is novel, relevant in the context of a world with software in everything, and a significant conceptual as well as technical departure from conventional approaches to protecting personal sensitive information and preventing identity theft. This departure is intended to boost research into applications (e.g. differential pricing) impeded so far by the all or nothing approach to personal information disclosure, as well as lack of accountability. The role of an effective information governance mechanism in spawning newer applications has been discussed by economists [1,2] long before this paper was conceived. A tamer Panopticon lies right at the heart of wider user participation in the IoT world.

On the other hand systems, traditionally, are not built keeping in mind the need that they may be used by a third party to gather evidence against their users or against the system itself. However the conventional need of evidence gathering in the electronic world appears in the IoT world as well. For example, on October 21, 2016, a collection of digital video recorders pushed Twitter off the Internet[3]. It is a legitimate need that data can be preserved and subsequently collected from those video recorders in a manner that satisfies the evidence acts of various countries. Legally admissible evidence can not only prove guilt but also exonerate the innocent owners of some of the video recorders.

2 Related Work

We are particularly interested in two approaches designed to allow peripherals (e.g. a smart watch or a smart lock) to communicate with the larger Internet infrastructure, particularly the cloud, for analytics as well as storage. One is known as Beetle [11] and the other is known as MQTT [13]. Both run as an OS service at the gateway (e.g. mobile phones), and subscription remains a key requirement in both these approaches to receive messages from the peripherals. There are thus ways to control passive snooping and who can subscribe to what.

Beetle virtualizes peripherals at the application layer, thus multiple applications can share peripherals: for example two applications can concurrently access the heart monitor or inter peripheral communication; for example the door lock can be activated from the smart watch. Also, one application can access various peripherals; for example an application can read the battery level of various devices. Beetle provides a significant improvement in regard to this interoperability, as conventionally peripherals and their applications operate in silos similar to a walled existence i.e. one peripheral and its application does not talk to another peripheral and their corresponding application. Conventionally Bluetooth Low Energy (BLE) devices use GATT (Generic Attribute Profile) at the application layer. Beetle interprets the GATT byte streams and allows fine grained security policies like *no access, read only access, and read write access* which prevents any application from having complete control over a device it has

---

[3] https://www.theguardian.com/technology/2016/oct/26/
ddos-attack-dyn-mirai-botnet.

access to. Thus Beetle achieves virtualization without allowing any application that can access a peripheral from having complete control over the peripheral.

MQTT on the other hand is a lightweight publish/subscribe protocol that operates through service (functionally a broker) and is known as Mosquitto. The notion of a Topic is at the core of MQTT, where a service of the heart rate monitor, such as the heart rate, can be a topic. Mosquitto allows user applications and servers to publish and/or subscribe to messages from the Topics. The publication and subscription can be managed through a fine grained access management using a configuration file[4], a access control (ACL) file and a password file. Mosquitto allows multiple subscription to a peripheral, or a single instance can subscribe to multiple topics, and peripherals can be reached via callback.

3   Case for Departure

There is considerable previous work [4–8] protecting sensitive personal information on the Internet; there are also fine grained access control mechanisms using gateways proposed in some of the current approaches [11,13] in the IoT world. A reasoned scrutiny [14] of the distributive implications of decisions relating to disclosure/non disclosure of personal sensitive information, reveal that failure to take into account the consequences of enhanced protection, leads to discrimination, anticompetitive behavior and other manifest injustices. For example research [10] into use of data for medical research shows that lack of an *accountable* data sharing mechanism creates an atmosphere of mistrust between patients and doctors; thus preventing patients from sharing health information (consumers of data lose due to lack of privacy). Lack of credible health information adversely affects the shared common interest of society; better health care. The technical abilities proposed in this paper to express purpose, through tags along with the data, while allowing for controlled exceptions for collective interest proposed in this paper, is an apt systems manifestation of the nuanced understanding of the distributive implications. Our approach can be implemented using infrastructure which is (nearly) already deployed for other reasons. Our protocol semantics is structured so that other agents in the cloud (which form part of the larger IoT infrastructure) may benefit by respecting or storing these tags. The users play a key role in the tagging process.

3.1   Assumptions

We make one assumption at the cloud infrastructure and another at the gateway between the peripherals and the cloud.

---

[4] A file that enumerates to allow or disallow arbitrary access, along with the location of the access control file which lists users allowed to read and/or write to a topic, along with the location of the password file containing user names and passwords the broker can verify.

– In a simple scenario where each instance on a hyper-visor represents an individual owner and their peripherals, let us assume one additional instance
known as the Caveat instance along with the tenant instances. The Caveat
instance is a 'monition', a probate[5] (to peripherals as well as the instances
on the cloud), that certain actions may not be taken by one (either tenant instances or peripheral owners) without informing the other. The Caveat
instance acts as a policy repository including owners' policies at the cloud[6].
The peripheral owner chooses what data it wants to protect (the user might
want the external fire responders to continuously monitor the kitchen temperature but not the bedroom temperature) and informs the Caveat instance
during the peripheral set up phase (and subsequently only to notify changes
to the policy). The Caveat instance in turn informs the corresponding tenant
about the users' preferences and lays down forensically[7] compliant access and
audit rules. The user cannot tag the data with a policy that is against established law. Caveat instances do not need to know about all data, only those
that are sensitive to the user. As well as the initial policy, periodic policy
updates can be communicated to the Caveat instance.
The tenant instances hence receive data from devices independently (maybe
or maybe not through the gateway), without any intervention of the Caveat
instance. Non-standard access like audit/modify/delete policy requests goes
through the Caveat instance. The Caveat instance will prevent any illegal
requests by the peripheral owners as well. The peripheral owners can request
an audit trail of their corresponding tenant instance through the Caveat
instance.
– The Caveat instance communicates with the peripheral owners via a child OS
(COS) service at the gateway (e.g. mobile phone). For our purposes we assume
the existence of either a Beetle or a MQTT service in between the peripheral
and the cloud. We do not adhere to a particular technology, although for
exposition we exploit the abilities of Mosquitto at the gateway in our example.
MQTT topics can well serve the ability to redirect packets from peripherals
to application based on their needs[8], however the topic discovery process is
not as friendly as in GATT. Nonetheless MQTT topics can be bridged to
GATT and then one can exploit the message interpreting ability of Beetle.
We are technology-agnostic in spirit. We assume the COS is running in our
mobile phone, which acts as the gateway between the peripherals and the
cloud. Users communicate through the COS.

---

[5] Traditionally a formal notice from a bishop or ecclesiastical court admonishing a
person not to do something specified.

[6] The Caveat instance is not the door through which instances communicate, except
during policy initiation and subsequent updates. So there is no bottleneck due to
the Caveat instance.

[7] ACPO - Association of Chief Police Officers UK.

[8] The battery monitoring application only needs the topic to access the battery but
not the heart rate.

3.2   Self Attestation

Our approach is influenced by a popular fraud counter measure (against identity theft) used in India.

– We often issue self attested photocopies of credential documents. However there used to be widespread misuse of such self attested photocopies. Hence credential owners started writing the name of the intended purpose on the photocopies before signing them[9]. Thus one can limit the options of a potential identity thief as to where he could use it, and also place the onus on a service provider if they accept a document that was not intended for them. In the IoT world we intend to limit the potential use and validity of information by self attesting information from sensors and controllers of devices.
– It can happen that sensors responsible for publishing information at regular intervals crash without any notice. MQTT provides sensors with the ability to define their intentions in the event of an unexpected crash through a attribute known as Last Will and Testament (LWT). This mirrors the real world ability of individuals to define their will on their assets after they cease to breathe. For now we propose to tweak this feature to use it for our system. We keep the name LWT for consistency with the MQTT nomenclature, however the way we use it is not the same as mentioned in the standard.

3.3   Protocol Steps

The system outline is as follows:

– There is a topic Temperature which will receive temperature data from a sensor named tempsen.
– The configuration file (at the remote broker in the cloud) is defined to deny anonymous connections. Only password-based connections for both subscription and publishing to the Topic Self Attestation will be accepted.
– The mosquittopasswd utility is used to create a user tempsen with the password it will use to publish to the Topic Temperature.
– The mosquittopasswd utility is used to create the subscriber TempI in this example to subscribe to messages from the Topic Temperature. The user TempI is an instance in the cloud but separate from the Caveat instance.
– The ACL file is populated with the policy that the user tempsen can only publish, and the user TempI can only subscribe, by presenting a secret only known to them.

---

[9] For example someone who gave a photocopy for a SIM card would write on the photocopy "For Vodafone SIM Application".

- The conopts (the connection option syntax) of tempsen is defined as in Fig. 1, with the user name and password along with the LWT. The owner of the device say tempsen in our example sets the LWT[10] thus expressing his will.
- In our approach the LWT, if set to a Topic, will limit the Topic to be perused only by TempI as indicated in the message until further notice in the LWT.
- The COS (at the gateway e.g. our phone) upon the user setting a LWT (during the sensor configuration phase) communicates it to the Caveat instance. The Caveat instance in turn communicates the owner's policy to TempI. There is no further involvement of the Caveat instance in data exchanges between the sensor and TempI while the policy remains in effect.
- It is an important assumption in our system that the Caveat instances are not biased to the owner of the peripherals or the cloud. They supervise on behalf of the peripheral owner that information flow does not violate their policies but sensitive operations such as deletion and modification are always carried out with mutual consent of the cloud and the peripheral owner and duly accounted.

```
public void dodemo()
{
    String topica       = "Self Attestation";
    String user         = "tempsen";
    String lwttopica    = "Attestation";
    //String topicb      = "Multiple Subscription";
    //String topicc      = "Policy";
    String contenta     = "Message from ATTESTATION for topic A";
    //String contentb    = "Message from MqttPublishSample for topic B";
    int qos             = 2;
    String broker       = "tcp://localhost:1883";
    String clientId     = "JavaSample";
    MemoryPersistence persistence = new MemoryPersistence();

    try {
        MqttClient sampleClient = new MqttClient(broker, clientId, persistence);
        MqttConnectOptions connOpts = new MqttConnectOptions();
        connOpts.setCleanSession(true);
        connOpts.setUserName(user);
        connOpts.setPassword("passwordtemp".toCharArray());
        connOpts.setWill(lwttopica, "For Cloud Only".getBytes(), 2, false);
        System.out.println("Connecting to broker: "+broker);
        sampleClient.connect(connOpts);
        //sampleClient.setCallback(this);
        System.out.println("Connected");
        System.out.println("Publishing message: "+topica);
```

Fig. 1. Tempsen communicating with Mosquitto with password and LWT

---

[10] Once configured the packets will be either LWT marked, or not marked, till further notice. However there is no extra overhead in setting the LWT in every packet, as the Gateway has mechanisms to interpret the attributes and *not* send further packets to the Caveat instance unless a change in policy is detected. The policy information is stored in the Access Control file (a text file) standard to every Mosquitto broker implementation.

3.4 Accountability

If the owner of tempsen wants to check at a later date whether the policy is being adhered to by TempI at the cloud, then it can contact the Caveat instance and seek a audit report of TempI, say for a period of 24 h. The Caveat instance verifies if it can allow the request and acts as per prior policy agreements. There is no involvement of Caveat instance in routine information exchange. In some cases information can be copied to the Caveat instance (say a hash of packets at random intervals) but those are for archive and the Caveat instance is not responsible for forwarding them to the tenant. They can be used to detect any modification (by the cloud) at a later date. None of the communications between the peripheral owner and the Caveat instances happens on a regular basis. The ability to randomly verify digests can be another level of deterrence on top of the ability to do random audits.

Another useful mechanism to achieve accountability in the Caveat instance can be built using localized trust assumptions. In our scheme the user is not against information sharing, but wishes to share only with morally relevant parties with accountability. Our Caveat instance can act as the log and decryption agent, and the user can share a symmetric key with either the Caveat instance or TempI, in such a way that each decryption requires concurrence and explicit entry into the log at the Caveat instance. Thus, with a publicly verifiable log, the remote infrastructure remains accountable to the user and vice versa. Moreover, in contrast with the original use of the scheme proposed in [12], the users do not need to trust a remote decrypting agent and a remote trusted device with the decrypting key. This localizes the assumed trust. Furthermore, since in our model the user is present[11] and willing to disclose information, having the key only with the user enables the user to allow controlled exceptions to information disclosure policy[12] yet eliminate the need to trust TempI or Caveat instance with the key.

4 Future Directions

The Caveat instance can be extended to facilitate matters like legal obligations which the users are responsible for obeying, but not competent to enforce/implement, by ensuring that legal obligations to information access and modification are maintained and do not conflict with the laws. The audit trail maintained by the Caveat instance is independent of the owner as well as of the Cloud. Any fudging of the audit trail by either the peripheral owner or the cloud can be credibly challenged by the other. Collusion between the peripheral owner and cloud can only happen to the peril of at least one of them, and is consequently unlikely. A general oversight of the Caveat instances can thus provide a pathway to standardization of forensics across the cloud.

---

[11] In the original scheme the protocol assumes that information will only be decrypted in cases when the user is not present; for example a parent can decrypt provided the child is late arriving home.

[12] for example for medical research.

We can't keep our personal data invisible, but our objective is rather to ensure that misuse of it can't be concealed either. The ability to locate misuse of our data allows evolutionary pressure to be applied to the systems which process personal information; including eventual regulation of attestation, and public policies concerning the burden of proof.

The pursuit of excellence is pernicious in security. A good system is one where the problems are easy to identify and the system is easy to change [9]. For example our immune system is not perfect but moderates itself against attacks. Our approach can potentially evolve with society as it evolves rather than forcing users to adhere to a fixed threat model increasingly disjointed from the reality. The OS service, as well as the Caveat instance, can also be equipped to learn from attacks and moderate the defense mechanism, thus allowing feedback based incremental improvements [3] throughout the life of the system. An approach which evolves with societal realizations is more inclusive and prevents discrimination against the elderly[13] and less privileged.

References

1. Acquisti, A.: Identity management privacy and price discrimination. In: IEEE Security and Privacy (2007)
2. Acquisti, A., Varian, H.: Conditioning prices on purchase history, Technical report. University of California Berkeley (2001)
3. Anderson, R.: Why cryptosystems fail? In: 1st Conference Computer and Communications Security. ACM (1993)
4. Camenisch, J., Lysyanskaya, A.: An efficient system for non-transferable anonymous credentials with optional anonymity revocation. In: Pfitzmann, B. (ed.) EUROCRYPT 2001. LNCS, pp. 93–118. Springer, Heidelberg (2001). https://doi. org/10.1007/3-540-44987-6_7
5. Camenisch, J., Herreweghen, E.V.: Design and implementation of the idemix anonymous credential system. In: Proceedings of the 9th ACM Conference on Computer and Communications Security, pp. 21–30 (2002)
6. Chaum, D.: Untraceable electronic mail, return addresses and digital pseudonyms. Commun. ACM **24**(2), 84–90 (1981)
7. Chaum, D.: Security without identification: transaction systems to make big brother obsolete. Commun. ACM **28**(10), 1030–1044 (1985)
8. Chaum, D.: Achieving electronic privacy. Sci. Am. **267**, 96–101 (1992)
9. Chowdhury, P.D., Christianson, B.: More security or less insecurity. In: Christianson, B., Malcolm, J. (eds.) Security Protocols 2010. LNCS, vol. 7061, pp. 115–119. Springer, Heidelberg (2014). https://doi.org/10.1007/978-3-662-45921-8_18
10. Nuffield Council on Bio Ethics: The Collection, Linking and Use of Data in Biomedical Research and Health Care: Ethical Issues (2015)
11. Levy, A., Hong, J., Riliskis, L., Levis, P., Winstein, K.: Beetle: flexible communication for bluetooth low energy. In: Mobisys 2016. ACM (2016)

---

[13] The use of biometrics in India to transfer government subsidies to the poor discriminates against the aged farmers without recognizable prints.

12. Ryan, M.D.: Making decryption accountable. In: Stajano, F., Anderson, J., Christianson, B., Matyáš, V. (eds.) Security Protocols 2017. LNCS, vol. 10476, pp. 93–98. Springer, Heidelberg (2017). https://doi.org/10.1007/978-3-319-71075-4_11
13. Stanford-Clark, A., Truong, H.L., Hunkeler, U.: Mqtt-S Űa publish/subscribe protocol for wireless sensor networks. In: 3rd International Conference on Communication Systems Software and Middleware and Workshops (COMSWARE 2008) (2008)
14. Strahilevitz, L.J.: Toward a positive theory of privacy law. Harvard Law Rev. **126** (2013). https://harvardlawreview.org/authors/lior-jacob-strahilevitz/

Self Attestation of Things
(Transcript of Discussion)

Partha Das Chowdhury[✉]

Aberystwyth University, Aberystwyth, UK
partha.dc@gmail.com

This is a picture of the Panopticon. I live in a world now, where everybody can observe me without me knowing when I am being observed and when not. So, that's the threat model I'm primarily aiming at. Last year I was working for a large software company. They had an insurance company as their client. They were trying to get data on people out of the on-board diagnostics. Not only the speed, et cetera, to do pay-as-you-drive insurance, but also the location information from the on-board diagnostics. This is similar to the government U-turn on health privacy that we heard about from Ross. And most of the times, the software that lies in my car (or in my toaster) I do not own or control. It's owned by the company who manufactured it. Like, the Jeeps that John Deere manufactures, they say that the software is owned by them. The user has no access, no control, nothing to do with it. But forensics is a important concern. If my car (or my toaster) happens to kill me, then the investigator should be able to find out exactly what happened when I was murdered.

While installing CCTV systems for smart cities, I experienced a practical manifestation of this quote, "You will never strike oil by drilling through a map." In the IoT world, we do not even have a map. I do not underestimate the power of maps, but they come with limitations as well. So, we are drilling without a map.

What is my goal? My goal is to fairly control what our devices tell about us, and to whom. Say, for example, the first responders monitoring my home temperature should be able to know the kitchen temperature, but I might not be willing to share my bedroom temperature with them.

I take inspiration from popular fraud countermeasures we use in India. Some time back, when we were applying for SIM cards or other services, we used to give a photocopy of our credential document, and we signed below the image. There used to be agencies between me and the service provider. They used to take the photocopy, and go and apply for a loan. So, people started clearly stating on the photocopy for what purpose the copy was being given. So, we mention, say, "for Vodaphone SIM application." below the image and sign with date. So the liability is no longer on me if that is misused, because I have clearly spelled out for what I am submitting this particular document.

We can replicate this in the world of Things, where data about us leaks from sensors owned or used by us, outside our immediate physical boundary. So, the assumptions we make are: There is an additional instance in the cloud, which

© Springer International Publishing AG 2017
F. Stajano et al. (Eds.): Security Protocols 2017, LNCS 10476, pp. 85–92, 2017.
https://doi.org/10.1007/978-3-319-71075-4_10

we term as the caveat instance. The caveat instance is like a policy repository. It's like a monition that, if the tenant at the cloud does something using my data, I cannot be held liable for that without my consent. At the level of the gateways where most of the BLE devices operate through our phones, there is a OS service at the link layer, or we can use MQTT as well.

The caveat instance will communicate with the peripheral owners or the peripherals themselves through the child OS service that I have at the gateway. I'll give an example how it works. Alice buys a temperature sensor. The sensor can be configured via the mobile phone. The sensor will communicate the temperature information to its corresponding instance, AliceI. at the cloud. Now, Alice decides that data from the sensor should not be shared with any entity other than AliceI, so Alice, via her phone, sets that policy. If we are using MQTT, there is a flag called, "Last Will and Testament (LWT)." It is used for a different purpose, but we can propose to use it for this application, where Alice sets the LWT of the first packet exchange between the sensor and the cloud. So, when the LWT is set, the gateway notifies the caveat instance that this data cannot be shared without explicit consent of Alice. The caveat instance in turn communicates the policy to AliceI.

Now, the role of the caveat instance finishes thereafter. The caveat instance is not involved in every exchange between the sensor and AliceI, so it's not a bottleneck. If Alice wants to check at a later date if the policy's being adhered to by AliceI, it can ask for an audit report through the caveat instance from AliceI. So, the caveat instance is only involved in, the first policy communication, if there is a change later on in the policy and if there is some external request[1] for access to data from AliceI. Now, policy changes are not very frequent, so caveat instance is not involved regularly in communications between Alice and AliceI. Now, if Alice wants to change or modify or delete any information, even that goes through caveat instance, because there are regulatory requirements as well, of keeping data in a manner that can be used later on.

So, the caveat instance is similar to formal verifications we find in the signaling systems. Human beings have legal obligations, but we might not be competent to implement those legal obligations. Say, for example, the ACPO[2] guidelines. So, the caveat instance can be used to enforce or implement those legal obligations. The gateway service is similar to active user involvement in the avionics model. We advocate the principle of consent and audit in data collection, and the child OS service can potentially evolve with the changing threat model. Say it is observed while systems are being implemented, that they tend to discriminate against the elderly, the less-educated or the less privileged. So, the child OS service is not a input-only parameter. It can evolve with the life cycle of the system.

Mark Ryan: Just to clarify. This caveat instance resides in the cloud, but is trusted by the user Alice. So, Alice has some reason for believing that this VM or whatever it is in the cloud is obeying her policies?

---

[1] e.g. investigations.

[2] Association of Chief Police Officers, UK Forensic guidelines.

Reply: Well, Alice, on her part, primarily trusts her ability to communicate to the cloud that, "Please don't share this data with anybody else."

Mark Ryan: But how does she trust that the cloud will adhere to that request?

Reply: Even if the cloud does not adhere, Alice's policy is still in force. So, what can the cloud do? How might the cloud use this data? If the cloud reveals it to somebody, Alice has no liability to take ownership of that data. Because I have given my credential for a Vodaphone SIM application, if that is misused to apply for a loan elsewhere, I don't have liability on the loan, so long as I have clearly spelled out that the credential was provided for a SIM application.

Mark Ryan: So, what happens if the person who receives this application cuts off the bit that says, "for Vodaphone SIM application," and writes down, "for purchase of a house".

Reply: Yes, but counterfeiting is not part of our threat model here. I deal with counterfeiting as an orthogonal issue from this.

Bruce Christianson: That's where you wave your hands and say there's some sort of cryptographic protection.

Mark Ryan: Right. Well, I don't see how there can be. You put data into the cloud, and now whoever possesses it, whoever runs that cloud can in principle do what they like with the data. They can separate the purpose that you've attached to it, and put a different purpose there.

Reply: Yes, but Alice retains an audit record of what Alice communicates to the cloud.

Mark Ryan: You see, there's no point to saying, but I attached, "for Vodaphone SIM application," when the bank is pursuing you for the loan that was taken out. They will say, "Well, that's too bad." You're still in the same place. You're still suffering.

Bruce Christianson: The objective isn't really to stop the information from getting out of the cloud. It's to give participating entities a way of defending themselves against the accusation that they're misusing the data. Now, people might not want to pay for that. They might say, "Well, I'm just going to use the data." But once you get into personal information brokerage, it's an open question whether this is politically dead, as Ross said to Joan yesterday[3], or whether it's just a matter of finding appropriate mechanisms to get this approach accepted.

But suppose you are in a position where the courts will say, or the Information Commissioners will say, "Well, if you're holding this personal data and it's got the appropriate use certificate attestations with it, then the onus is on the user to show that you were misusing it. But, if it hasn't, then it's the other way around, and the onus is on you to explain how it is that you happen to be using this data to do what you are doing."

---

[3] Feigenbaum and Ford, these proceedings.

Mark Ryan: Ah. Okay. Right. So I think the answer to my question is, we do have to trust the cloud provider. This is just a language, if you like, for its end user.

Bruce Christianson: You have to trust that there are certain elements running in the cloud. They're effectively a policy repository.

Paulo Esteves Verissimo: I probably still feel after this clarification that the cloud becomes irrelevant. Because, as Mark just pointed out, either you trust the cloud provider or you don't trust. If you trust the cloud provider, you can surely ignore that the cloud sysadmin will allow the cloud provider to get the data out and leave it somewhere, so then it counterfeits it. So, I have a hard time understanding that you don't protect this whatever credential against counterfeiting. Why don't you make it a formal credential? That's, I think, what you should do, because it's not about confidentiality, we have seen, it's about mis-use. And the way you do it, the cloud is irrelevant, right?

If it's irrelevant, then I'm not understanding the protection your scheme offers, because you're actually not protecting this little bit, which you should. But then it could be posted on a website. It was the same thing.

Reply: I am telling the data that's leaving my physical boundary that, please don't share it. So, yes, in a way the cloud becomes irrelevant, because I don't want to trust a feudal cloud, and I don't know what they will do with the data. So, the protection I'm providing is an ability on the part of the user to stamp their policy on the data about them.

Bruce Christianson: It's not so much the cloud as it is the Internet of Things that provides the very low friction threshold for data escaping.

Paulo Esteves Verissimo: But you say you are not thinking about counterfeiting?

Bruce Christianson: Counterfeiting is an orthogonal issue. Plenty mechanisms exist for that. Pick your favourite one and use it for this. We're not claiming to make any contribution to the state of the art in that area.

Reply: I am only focusing on providing the users with the ability, at the gateway level, where they can say, "Okay, this data is leaving my sensor. I don't want to share it. This data is leaving my sensor. This can be shared." So, that's what I'm providing at the level of the gateways.

Paulo Esteves Verissimo: There is something indelible that should accompany it. We agree, right? Because the danger is that it'll stop being protected by an ensemble, the system, in all its travelling. So, it must be self-protected. The same idea about certificates. Because, this thing that says, "You cannot be shared," is something that mustn't be able to be nullified, because otherwise someone else can put "You can be shared," or, "You can be shared with these other guys."

Reply: Yes! So, that stamp I'm doing at the level of the gateways, that this data cannot be shared. And say, for example, if Alice and AliceI., choose to collude to do something evil. Then that harms them. So collusion between Alice and AliceI, there in the cloud, is not in the interest of either of them. Alice has the ability to say, "This, my data, this data about me, pertaining to this, cannot be shared." So, that's the small ability I aim to provide now.

Bryan Ford: Going forward, have you thought about what examples of this might be amenable to watermarking techniques? Where the data that goes out of the gateway gets watermarked invisibly, along with the public stamp. So, if the data later turns up in a random place, you know which version they have. On the other hand, that would be subject to the abuse that, I could try to frame someone. I could perhaps send the data with a public Vodaphone watermark, but say it's really about this other thing, and then blame that person for, like, leaking what they had, and then that brings in, potentially, issues of, can you use fancy crypto or something to prove that their watermark is the same as the public label as it goes out? I think there's some interesting questions here to explore.

Fabio Massacci: So, in reality, there's never a black and white decision, shared or unshared. It's always fragments, like your bank address. Your address needs to be shared by your bank to the post office, so that you can receive your bank statement. So, how does it work in that case? Does the caveat instance need to be contacted every time, to okay people sharing each fragment of the data, like this? Will this scale?

Bruce Christianson: We're not trying to have a policy mechanism that makes all these decisions for you. We're trying to have a policy mechanism (and an audit trail) that allows a human or somebody, perhaps a court, or perhaps the Information Commissioner, to decide whether a particular act of sharing was reasonable or not. So, for example, my insurance says, "We share data with other insurance companies to make sure you're not committing fraud." Eventually a court has to decide whether the sharing of the piece of information was reasonable without my consent, and that's unchanged, but at least now there's a way of working out whether the company really had my explicit consent to share that specific piece of information or not.

Fabio Massacci: But my argument is, you never share the entire things for something. You shared a fraction of it in many cases. And this fraction needs to automated in all sorts of cases. If you start adding humans into the loop, it's just like calling a call centre each time you have to share something.

Bruce Christianson: Oh no no.You can only have humans setting a policy, you can't have them involved in executing every instance.

Reply: And the policy's set right at when I sign for my sign-on for my bank account, or when I buy a sensor, when I log in the cloud. The policy is decided at that point in time. The policy's only revisited if I have a good reason to change it, and I change it adhering to laws and regulatory mechanisms. So the caveat instance actually is not coming into play every time data is shared, because that policy is decided right at the beginning.

Ross Anderson: I don't really understand what incentive any sort of things would have to do this. Because it's a sort of physical object with some attached cloud service in the smart phone app, and the default way of operating for Thing salesmen is to promise us privacy, and then sell our information to the spammers.

So, for such a thing to be viable, you'd presumably need a regulated environment such as the armed forces, or perhaps a hospital, where some third party can say, "You will use our approved, classified, GCHQ-approved mechanism" in the case of government, or something else in the case of health care, and there will be enough Thing salesmen that would relish the prospect of selling a thing for £200 rather than £20. They will do this. What are the likely markets for this, and what are the likely requirements of the regulators of the forced adoption of such a mechanism?

Reply: Well, not having privacy is not always beneficial for the sellers either. Similarly, privacy also creates losers among the consumers. So, yes, we need a regulatory mechanism to have such things in place–

Ross Anderson: Well, in regulated environments it's almost never about privacy. It's about MLS rules. It's about keeping the top secret stuff and the confidential stuff apart, or it's about safety rules. Not putting explosives and detonators in the same truck.

Reply: Yes. So, in the regulated environment, a way of selling it would be that we keep the data in a way that is, say, for example, compliant with the forensic guidelines. We say to the caveat instance to ensure that the data is stored in a manner which can be presented as evidence. So, selling it to the regulator can be done in various ways. Like, yesterday in Joan's talk, what we are discussing is, something selling this to the police would be that this will get you evidence quicker than having loads of data on your table to sniff through.

Bruce Christianson: We're not trying to prevent personal information from getting into the public domain. The issue is, if all your personal information is going to get into the public domain anyway, how do you prevent identity theft?

Reply: How do you prevent misuse of that personal information, and if there is a misuse, then you have a way to tell, "Okay, I did not give this information out to do this, but it has been used to do this."

Bruce Christianson: Ross and I talked last year in Brno[4] about the issue of the Information Commissioner looking at databases and saying, "Is it appropriate for you to have this data, or should I fine you?" The approach we discussed then was to attach some audit trail information to the legitimate data, and if that isn't present, then there's an instant fine from the regulator. This talk can be thought of an attempt to extend that sort of approach to a more open environment.

Ross Anderson: But this kind of mechanism, from the security economics point of view, will never run in a global environment, because the vendor will

---

[4] Wernick and Christianson, 2016, "The Price of Belief : Insuring Credible Trust", Security Protocols xxiv, discussion.

never let it, right? It costs money and decreases profits. A mechanism like this will only ever sell in a closed environment, where GCHQ says, "No, you shall not have the Thing in the Cabinet Office unless it is an Evaluated Thing, which communicates to an appropriately sharpened clone of the properly audited BLP substrate." Then, something like this can run.

Bruce Christianson: Well, the question I'm thinking of asking is the counter-point question, what would persuade somebody to start using the hooks that this system provides them with? Why would anybody say, "No, I don't just want to whiz your data through the cloud platform. I really want the self certificate to come with it." And they'll only do that if there's some protection for them that comes piggybacked off the self-certificate.

Bryan Ford: Okay. One possible answer to that specific suggestion is some analogue to the, "Wall of Shame," policy, right? So, a law that says, "If the vendor voluntarily chooses to get into this program, and use this and promise to be closed to it, then their liability for screw-ups is limited to X." And if they don't do that, then their liability is not limited. This, "Wall of Shame," mechanism works really nicely in the U.S. for this one specific thing regarding HIPAA data.

It's not perfect, but it's way better than nothing, and it's a nice incentive, right?

Reply: And privacy does creates winners and losers. Another way of selling the virtualized service would be that you can open the door with your smart phone. So, there is interoperability between various sensors you have. So, that would be a way of getting the virtualized service to the users, I guess. There would be incentives to use it, because right now, they all operate in silos. The app I have will talk to my smart phone, but it doesn't talk to my smart lock. So, if there is a way that my smart watch can also talk to my smart lock. And on that, we can piggyback a service like this. I think there is a way of taking this to the user.

Bruce Christianson: And the argument is that this particular approach relies on software that's already deployed for other reasons.

Reply: Yes. Exactly. The virtualized services are there, and the apps exist. It's only to make the app inter-operable across various devices, and this is technically possible as of now, because you can read those attributes that the operating system passes between the devices, and through the gateway.

Simon Foley: Another way of looking at this is, it's almost like digital rights management system, where I'm giving away the right to my data in various ways, and the function there is this attestation as the enforcement mechanism. But we know that the digital rights apps are really rare.

Bruce Christianson: No. Because they are designed to prevent things from ever happening. But once their data is in the public domain, then their game is over. That's a different objective to what we are trying to achieve.

Reply: Here we are trying to give some power to the user in this feudal world, so maybe the users can say, "This data can be used to do X and Y. Data cannot be used to do Z."

Bruce Christianson: And again, the tag isn't primarily about who can use it, but the tag specifies what the data can be used for. So, if you give it to the insurance company, the insurance company says, "to give this data to the bank or post office for some reason, in order to carry out a tax action I was asked to carry out on behalf of the user," that's fine. That's a defence.

Ross Anderson: Well, if it's analogous to a DRM system, then there is a possible point here, because we know historically that the music industry pushed the DRM, and then cut their own throats. Because when you meta-link between two industries, all the power and the money flows to the more concentrated one, and so power and money flows to people like Apple and Google and Amazon, and away from EMI.

So, here's a future environment for something like this. Mr. Google decides that he's going to bring privacy to the world, and so in all the Android apps that you get with your Things, this framework is built in, and this, of course, means that Mr. Google then becomes the dominant player in the System of Things. And eventually, when the Directorate General for Competition in Brussels wakes up to the fact, it's too late.

Bruce Christianson: Hopefully, we're on a slightly different mission. [laughter]

Making Decryption Accountable

Mark D. Ryan[✉]

University of Birmingham, Birmingham, UK
m.d.ryan@cs.bham.ac.uk

Abstract. Decryption is accountable if the users that create ciphertexts can gain information about the circumstances of the decryptions that are later obtained. We describe a protocol that forces decryptors to create such information. The information can't be discarded or suppressed without detection. The protocol relies on a trusted hardware device. We describe some applications.

1 Introduction

When I was a teenager, I wanted to be able to go out in the evening and not have to tell my parents where I was going. My parents were understanding about this wish for privacy, but explained that if for some reason I didn't come back at the expected time, they needed to have some clues to give to the police about where I had been. So we came to the following compromise: I would leave a sealed envelope explaining my activities. This would enable them to search for me if they needed to, but if I came back on time I could retrieve the envelope and see that it had not been opened. This idea seems closely connected to the 'multi-objective' theme of SPW'17: the protocol aims to simultaneously serve the partly conflicting requirements of the teenager and his parents.

To have such a protocol in the digital world, we would need some way of knowing whether someone who has all the needed material to perform a decryption has actually performed it. More generally, we need a way to make decryption key holders accountable in some way for their use of the key. This accountability might take many forms. For example, some applications might need fine-grained accounts of exactly what was decrypted, and when, while in other cases we may be interested only in volumes, frequencies, or patterns of decryption.

In this paper, we informally describe the requirements for making decryptions accountable (Sect. 2), and devise a protocol based on trusted hardware that achieves them (Sect. 3). We describe a few applications at a very high level (Sect. 4).

2 The Requirements

We formulate the requirements as follows:

– Users $U_1, \ldots$ create ciphertexts using a public encryption key ek.

© Springer International Publishing AG 2017
F. Stajano et al. (Eds.): Security Protocols 2017, LNCS 10476, pp. 93–98, 2017.
https://doi.org/10.1007/978-3-319-71075-4_11

- Decrypting agent Y is capable of decrypting the ciphertexts without any help from the users.
- When Y decrypts ciphertexts, it unavoidably creates evidence e that is accessible to the users. The evidence cannot be suppressed or discarded without detection.
- By examining e, the users gain some information about the nature of the decryptions being performed.

Here, the granularity of e is left open. We will see some examples in Sect. 3.2.

Note that we focus on ensuring that if Y decrypts, then the user will be able to achieve evidence that that has happened. The teenager envelope story in the introduction had an additional property: the parents Y can give up the possibility of ever decrypting, if they wish (by returning the unopened envelope). We don't include that additional property in our requirements.

3   Protocol Design

Intuitively, if Y has a ciphertext and a decryption key, it is impossible to detect whether she applies the key to ciphertext or not. This implies that the key has to be guarded by some kind of hardware device D that controls its use. In this section, we propose a simple generic design that achieves some of the desired functionality. The hardware device D embodies the secret decryption key dk corresponding to ek. The secret decryption key dk never leaves the device.

In order to make the evidence e persistent, we assume a log L. The log is organised as an append-only Merkle tree as used in, for example, certificate transparency [1]. The log maintainer publishes the root tree hash H of L, and is capable of generating two kinds of proof about the log's behaviour:

- A proof of presence of some data in the log. More precisely, given some data d and a root tree hash H of the log, the log maintainer can produce a compact proof that d is indeed in the log represented by H.
- A proof of extension, that is, a proof that the log is maintained append-only. More precisely, given a previous root tree hash H' and the current one H, the log maintainer can produce a proof that the log represented by H is an append-only extension of the log represented by H'.

(Details of these proofs can be found in e.g. [8].) This means that the maintainer of L is not required to be trusted to maintain the log correctly. It can give proofs about its behaviour.

3.1   Performing Decryptions

The decrypting agent Y uses the device D to perform decryptions. The device will perform decryptions only if it has a proof that the decryption request has been entered into the provably-append-only log.

The device maintains a variable containing its record of the most recent root tree hash H that it has seen of the log L. On receiving a set R of decryption requests, the decrypting agent performs the following actions:

- Obtain from the device its last-seen root tree hash H.
- Enter the set R of decryption requests into the log.
- Obtain the current root tree hash H' of the log.
- Obtain from the log a proof π of presence of R in the log with RTH H'.
- Obtain from the log a proof ρ that the log with RTH H' is an append-only extension of the log with RTH H.

The decrypting agent presents (R, H', π, ρ) to the device. The device verifies the proofs, and if they are valid, it performs the requested decryptions R. It updates its record H of the last-seen root tree hash with H'.

3.2 Evidence

Evidence about decryptions is obtained by inspecting the log, which contains the decryption requests. There are many ways that this could be organised. We look at two examples:

Example 1: the log contains a hash of the ciphertext that is decrypted. This allows a user U to detect if ciphertexts she produced have been decrypted.

Example 2: the log contains a unique value representing the decrypted ciphertext, but the value cannot be tied to a particular ciphertext (for example, the value could be the hash of a re-encryption [7]). This allows users to see the number of ciphertexts decrypted, but not which particular ones.

3.3 Currency

As described so far, the protocol is insecure because the device D could be tracking a version of the log which is different from the version that the users track. Although both the device and users verify proofs that the log is maintained append-only, there is no guarantee that it is the same log. The log maintainer can bifurcate the log, maintaining each branch independently but append-only.

Gossip protocols of the kind proposed for solving this problem for certificate transparency [5] are insufficient here, because the device D is not capable of reliably participating in them.

To ensure that users track the same version of the log that D tracks, we introduce an additional protocol of D. In this second protocol, D accepts as input a *verifiably current* value v. The value v cannot be predicted in advance, but is verifiable by anyone. D outputs its signature $\text{Sign}_{sk}(v, H)$ on the value v and its current stored root tree hash H of the log. Thus, we require that D has an additional secret key sk for signing. The corresponding verification key vk is published. Like dk, the key sk never leaves the device.

There are several ways in which the verifiably current value v can be constructed. For example, v can be the hash of a data structure containing nonces $v_1, \ldots$, each one produced by one of the users $U_1, \ldots$. Alternatively, v could be the concatenation of the date and the day's closing value of an international stock exchange.

Periodically, the current value of H tracked by the device is published. By means of the proofs of extension, users can verify that it is consistent with their view of the log.

There remains the possibility that users can be denied the possibility of inspecting the log, and/or denied the possibility of interacting with the device to obtain the log root-tree hash H. In these cases, decryptions can take place without the user being aware; but of course, the user knows s/he is being denied access. Thus, if users are denied access they should assume that the agreement concerning accountability has broken down.

3.4   The Trusted Hardware Device

The protocol described relies on having a trusted hardware device D that performs a specific set of operations that are recapped here. The aim is to keep the functionality of D as small and as simple as possible, while still allowing it to support the variety of applications mentioned below (Sect. 4). In summary, D stores persistent keys dk (decryption) and sk (signing), and the current root tree hash H of a log. It offers two services:

Decryption. It accepts a tuple (R, H', π, ρ) as described in Sect. 3.1. It verifies the proof π that R is present in the log with root tree hash (RTH) H', and the proof ρ that H' is the RTH of a log that is an extension of the log of which its current RTH is the H stored in D. (These verifications consist of some hash calculations and comparisons.) If the verifications succeed, it performs the decryptions R, and replaces its stored H with H'.

Attestation. It accepts a value v, and returns $\mathrm{Sign}_{sk}(v, H)$ on the value v and its current stored RTH H.

4   Applications

4.1   Application Areas

Most electronic voting protocols begin with voting clients that encrypt votes with a public key, and end with the result being decrypted by a trustworthy party (or, possibly, a set of trustworthy parties each of which holds a share of the decryption key). The decrypting agents are trusted only to decrypt the result, and not the votes of individual voters. A protocol to make decryption accountable could help make this verifiable.

Finance is an area in which privacy and accountability are often required to be balanced. For this reason, the designers of Zerocash have introduced mechanisms which allow selective user tracing and coin tracing in a cryptocurrency [6]. The limitation of their approach is that authorities have to decide in advance of the relevant transactions which coins or which users they want to trace. This is inconvenient in practice: often, suspects only become clear after transactions have taken place. Making decryptions accountable is another technique which could help obtain the desired combination of privacy and accountability, and would allow retrospective decryption.

The UK government has recently passed legislation allowing government agencies to access information about the communications of private citizens [2], in order to solve crimes. In an effort to provide some kind of accountability, there are stipulations in the law to ensure that the provisions of the act are used in ways that are necessary and proportionate to the crimes being addressed. A protocol that makes decryption accountable could make verifiable the quantity and perhaps the nature of decryptions [7].

Making decryptions accountable potentially addresses the problem of having to trust escrow holders, for example in identity-based encryption [4] and elsewhere [3].

4.2 Access Control

The device and the protocols are desiged to guarantee just one thing: that if decryptions take place, this fact can be detected by the user. Of course, in any real application such as those given above, much more than that is needed. For example, consider an email application, in which authorities are allowed to decrypt emails, and users can detect the extent to which this has been done. Our protocols provide this detectability, but they do not provide other features that would be required to make such a system acceptable. For example, in what circumstances can decryptions be requested, and by whom? How are the decrypted mails to be treated? All these questions would have to be answered by access control mechanisms layered on top of the protocols detailed in this paper.

5 Conclusion

There seems to be a variety of circumstances in which making decryption accountable is attractive. This paper proposes the design of trusted hardware which would assist in this process.

The idea of the design is that the decrypting agent has no way to decrypt data without leaving evidence in the log, unless it can break the hardware device D. This raises the question of who manufactures the device, and how the relying parties (both users $U_1 \dots$ and decrypting agents Y) can be assured that it will behave as specified. It depends on the sensitivity of the information being processed. One idea is that it is jointly manufactured by an international coalition of companies with a reputation they wish to maintain.

References

1. Certificate Transparency (2007). www.certificate-transparency.org
2. Investigatory Powers Act (2016). www.legislation.gov.uk/ukpga/2016/25/contents/enacted

3. Abelson, H., Anderson, R., Bellovin, S.M., Benaloh, J., Blaze, M., Diffie, W., Gilmore, J., Green, M., Landau, S., Neumann, P.G., et al.: Keys under doormats: mandating insecurity by requiring government access to all data and communications. J. Cybersecur. **1**(1), 69–79 (2015)
4. Boneh, D., Franklin, M.: Identity-based encryption from the weil pairing. In: Kilian, J. (ed.) CRYPTO 2001. LNCS, vol. 2139, pp. 213–229. Springer, Heidelberg (2001). https://doi.org/10.1007/3-540-44647-8_13
5. Chuat, L., Szalachowski, P., Perrig, A., Laurie, B., Messeri, E.: Efficient gossip protocols for verifying the consistency of certificate logs. In: IEEE Conference on Communications and Network Security (CNS), pp. 415–423 (2015)
6. Garman, C., Green, M., Miers, I.: Accountable privacy for decentralized anonymous payments. IACR Cryptology ePrint Archive 2016, 61 (2016). http://eprint.iacr.org/2016/061
7. Liu, J., Ryan, M.D., Chen, L.: Balancing societal security and individual privacy: accountable escrow system. In: CSF (2014)
8. Ryan, M.D.: Enhanced certificate transparency and end-to-end encrypted mail. In: Network and Distributed System Security (NDSS) (2014)

Making Decryption Accountable
(Transcript of Discussion)

Mark D. Ryan(✉)

University of Birmingham, Birmingham, UK
m.d.ryan@cs.bham.ac.uk

Mark Ryan: I've given the title *Making Decryption Accountable* to this talk. Let me just start with a little story. When I was a teenager, I wanted to be able to go out in the evening and not tell my parents where I was going because I wanted my privacy. But my parents naturally wanted to make sure that they'd have some recourse if I don't come back at the expected time. They wanted security in other words. We hit upon a compromise whereby I would put my plans in an envelope, and leave it on the kitchen table or something, and then if I came back at the appointed time I could retrieve the envelope, and by the properties of an envelope I could see it hadn't been opened, and therefore I knew my privacy hadn't been violated. But if I didn't come back at the right time, they at least had some clues as to where they should look for me.

Peter Y A Ryan: When you say we hit on the idea, you mean you hit on it?

Reply: I very reluctantly accepted it, that's right.

So that seems to me to be relevant to the theme of this workshop, which is *multi-objective security*. Another kind of situation that we're also familiar with is corporate e-mail or university e-mail. We accept the claim that our employers make that the university mail belongs to them, and that's obviously more true in the case of a corporation like HSBC Bank. But we at universities also feel it belongs a bit to us, so some sort of compromise between their rights to decrypt mail. Of course most mail is sent in the clear, but I'm imagining a world in which it would not be sent in the clear. You might want a situation in which you allow your employer to decrypt the mail, but you want some sort of transparency on how much of that they actually do. So they have the right to decrypt whenever they like, that's a right they claim, but you would like to know how often, with what frequency, and what circumstances they exercise that right. That's another example of the situation that I'm addressing. Now the previous talk [by Partha Das Chowdhury and Bruce Christianson] about mobile phone and IoT sensor data seems also to lend itself to this thing. The specific example that I had in mind is "find my iPhone". As you probably know, that's a service that Apple offers whereby they continuously monitor your location and they have to because at any time you might invoke, "Find my iPhone," and you want them to be able to tell you where it is. But what you would like is to upload that in an encrypted form. Then you would like some information about when they decrypt it, which should be never, except when you invoke "Find my iPhone," that's what you would like to see. Of course, they must be able to decrypt it

© Springer International Publishing AG 2017
F. Stajano et al. (Eds.): Security Protocols 2017, LNCS 10476, pp. 99–108, 2017.
https://doi.org/10.1007/978-3-319-71075-4_12

at any time without needing your assistance because at that point you've lost your iPhone. Just like the corporate e-mail example, they didn't want to have to come to you and ask you for keys, that's not going to work. Now another situation where you might find this would work, and this obviously relates to Joan's talk but obviously fraught with the kind of difficulties that were discussed yesterday, is around governments with claimed entitlement to access our data. In the UK, as we know, the investigative powers act the government has wide range of snooping and interference properties. There is written into that act of parliament some oversight, but of course that oversight is unverifiable. That is to say, we as citizens have no direct evidence of any kind that the oversight works. So making decryption accountable is potentially a step towards verifiable oversight. That's my motivation. Let me just spell out the requirements. After that I'm going to give you the solution I have in one slide, and then I'm going to spend the rest of the time if you permit talking about the solution, but maybe you won't permit, in which case, at least I'll have presented the solution. So the requirements are that users create ciphertext using a public key, PK. This is the problem I want to solve, this problem here. There is a decrypting agent that is capable of decrypting the ciphertext without any help from the users. That's of course the vital point. But when why the decrypting agent decrypts the ciphertext it unavoidably creates some evidence that's accessible to users and the evidence can't be suppressed or discarded without detection. They create this evidence and it can't be got rid of without the users seeing that some evidence has been suppressed or discarded. Therefore, by examining the evidence the users can get some information about the quantity and the nature of the decryptions.

Tuomas Aura: So if you don't have the property of the envelope, namely, that you can dispose of the ciphertext and prevent future reading?

Reply: No, you don't, that's right. In this set of requirements you don't have the property of the envelope that you can dispose of it later. That's correct. I'd have to think through whether that can be added or not. Well no, it probably can't be, you're right. Okay, so you need some hardware to support you in this. You can't do it just by pure cryptography, I think that's kind of obvious. Therefore the question that I'm going to address is what is the minimal specification for this piece of hardware? You'd like it to be as generic as possible, I don't want to attach it to any of the particular applications that I had in mind. I just want a piece of hardware that will help you solve that problem in the abstract form. Now I'm going to tell you exactly what that piece of hardware looks like. It's a little bit perhaps hard to understand the slide when I haven't introduced the background to it, but I want to show you that it's very, very simple. The hardware just stores three items. One is a hash value and the other two are secret keys, one is a decryption key and the other is a signature key. It runs two protocols. The first protocol, it accepts some stuff, which is essentially a decryption request, together with some proofs that the decryption request has been entered into a log. This whole thing uses a log a little bit like the log used by certificate transparency, if you know that, and it verifies that the stuff is in the log and that the log has been maintained only, and if all those things come out correctly, it performs the decryption. Now the other protocol that this device runs, is a protocol intended to prevent the holder of the device, this little device, the holder of a device giving you old values of its output. Essentially this thing allows you to provide a value and get a signature on the value and its current state, which gives you information that the current state is at least as recent as the value that you input. That's all that protocol is doing. So let me explain now a little bit more how this works. There's a log held externally to the device. All decryption requests have to be recorded in the log. The device is able to verify that decryption requests have been recorded in the log and it verifies that before it performs the decryption. So somebody maintains this log, but we try to minimise the trust that's on that person who maintains it, in particular, they're not required to be trusted with regard to integrity of the log; because they're maintaining this log in the manner of certificate transparency, which means that they can prove that they're maintaining the log correctly. That is to say they're maintaining it append only, and when they add something to the log they're able to prove that thing is indeed present in the log. I'm going to just detail those proofs in a moment. But one thing that we can't assume is that the maintainer will respect confidentiality of the log, and therefore the way you set up those entries in the log you have to do it in such a way that you don't require confidentiality. Okay, so I'm going just detail a little bit about the log. It's a Merkle tree. I'm sure that everybody in the room knows what a Merkle tree is; it's some data written in the leaves of the tree and then at each non-leaf node it's a hash of the children leaf nodes. Now this Merkle tree, as in the case of certificate transparency, is maintained in a way that you only add to the right. So when I add new data, when I add a fourth item of data I complete the tree there. Now to add a fifth item of data, I have to add a new root so that I have five there. Then I can add six, seven, and eight, and now if I want to add more data, I add another new root and then complete the tree in that way. So that's how I maintain the tree and that particular way of maintaining the tree means that you can provide two kinds of proofs. The first proof is a proof of the statement that some data is in the tree with a certain root tree hash. That proof is simply some other of the hash values, one per layer over the tree in fact. So that proof is of size and verification time proportional to the log of the number of items that you store in the tree. Then also a proof that a certain root tree hash H' is an append only extension of some previous snapshot H. That's also a proof that you can do with that particular data structure and you can do it again in a way that's compact, namely proportional to the log of the number of items stored. Also, insertion is also something that can be done in log time.

Fabio Massacci: But how can it be $\log N$? Isn't it N if the tree is actually a comb?

Reply: A comb? What's a comb? *(Evidently, the fool doesn't understand Fabio's pronunciation of the word "comb".)*

Fabio Massacci: It's something you use. . .

Reply: A comb. A comb! Right. Okay. The tree is a comb. Is it a comb? It's a tree, I've never heard a tree called a comb before.

Fabio Massacci: You have something that goes directly from the root to node 9, and I assume you go from the root to node 10...

Reply: No, no. You don't go from the root to 10. Let me just ...I didn't show the rest of it. Let me go back to where I detailed how you do that. So here, for example, you have something that goes from the root to five. But when you add six, you don't go from the root to six. You add a little sub-tree there. And then when you want to add some more, you add another little sub-tree. And you keep going until your sub-tree is complete, and then you add a new root. So when I add a new root now, I will keep going until I reach 16 items, and then I'll add another new root.

Partha Das Chowdhury: When you have different data, like data from a sensor, are you considering something like that in your talk?

Reply: Yes, I'm assuming that any of the sensors on your phone, if you want to upload those the Cloud you're going to upload them encrypted with a key and the Cloud can decrypt those at any time because it's got this device in the mechanism that I'm showing. But whenever it does decrypt, it's got to insert the decryption request into the log and you can inspect the log. I should point out if you can't inspect the log because somebody is denying you that possibility, at least that fact is detectable by you.

Hugo Jonker: I was leafing through your paper, see...You talk about how to construct a log and you say you want to avoid suppression of the log but you do not talk about how users query the log, or what if there are different views of the log.

Reply: I think you're saying the log provider could show you a different version of the log to the version that it shows this device D. Right. I'm going to go into a little bit more detail on that particular issue but that's essentially why we have this right-hand protocol here, to allow you to detect if that happens. Okay, so let me just explain how the protocol works if it wasn't understood so far. So you have this decrypting agent which is just an untrusted party that wants to perform a decryption. Then you have this hardware device. So of course we assume that the hardware device adheres to its specification. And by the way you might well ask, "Well, who is going to make this hardware device and why should anybody trust it?" Those are very good questions, and I think the answer is application specific. In particular when it comes to the Investigatory Powers Act I think that would be a very hard question to answer for all the reasons that were discussed yesterday. But for some little applications it might be that you can find a suitable manufacturer to make these devices. You might find that the trust model there is adequate for your purpose. So anyway, how does it work? If the decrypting agent wants to decrypt a certain request, or it receives a certain request, it then asks the hardware device, "What is your latest root tree hash (RTH)?" And then it enters the decryption request into the log and obtains the new RTH of the log and obtains the two proofs: first one that the decryption request is now in the log with RTH H and second one, that H' does indeed extend H. And then it sends those proofs along with the decryption request in H prime to the device. The device verifies that those proofs are all correct, in particular that the decryption request is in the log, and then performs the decryption and sends the result of the decryption back to the decrypting agent.

Tuomas Aura: Yes, I wonder what happens if the hashes don't match, because the device doesn't update its log. I'm the external entity who's decrypting your data and then I just don't care. And the hashes don't match. That's similar to saying, "Oh, the device is broken." Nothing can be proven about what went wrong.

Reply: Yes, that's right. The protocol is not very robust, I agree. Nothing can be proven about what went wrong but your data has not been decrypted. So it's up to the decrypting agent to maintain this hardware device properly. If they screw up, if they get the hash values not to match, if they don't manage to make it work, then they're not going to be able to perform their role.

Tuomas Aura: So an immutable log would be nicer or something. Something like a block chain, where you would publish the data and the device would verify that these events have been one by one published. I'm proposing that you store the hash in a blockchain, like bitcoin.

Reply: Hmmm. How can the device verify that block chain is really published and not some private block chain that you're maintaining just to trick it?

Tuomas Aura: I don't know.

Bruce Christianson: I wanted to ask a different question, but I have a trivial answer to the current one. Use our blog chain which collectively signs all of the locks that it produces. Like have 100 or 1,000 of the recent validators produce a signature of each block. The device could just check that signature.

Tuomas Aura: Okay, there's some assumptions there...

Bruce Christianson: But if I can ask the question I wanted to ask: I didn't see any provision for freshness in this. So it looks like once anybody has decrypted something, the log entry can be reused for another decryption. That's bad. I guess that would be easy to fix if it is bad.

Reply: *(He has misunderstood the question. He thinks its about an unauthorised decryption taking place.)* I'm assuming that there's a whole framework around this that not everyone is free to go and decrypt whatever they want. There's some access control. Somebody maintains this device. They look at requests and decide whether they're valid or not. My only concern here is to provide evidence to users about whether decryptions have happened or not. I'm not trying to prevent decryptions happening; of course that's an important thing to do and there must be other mechanisms to do that.

Bruce Christianson: But do you care how many decryptions have happened?

Reply: I don't care how many provided that number is provided to the user. Each decryption request is unique. *(This is the answer to Bruce's question. Decryption requests can't be used except on the decryption to which they apply.)* I'm going to detail what those decryption requests look like in a moment. Each one is unique so you can't reuse an old one in order to decrypt some new information.

Ross Anderson: Surely the logical thing to do here is to elaborate the design a bit, so one can explore attacks on it. If, for example, you have to end up signing the log in order to prevent somebody producing a private fork of the log. Then to what extent does the signing authority have to be trusted? If you're in an environment where people get a tap on the shoulder from the NSA, it's something that becomes of absolutely crucial importance for some applications, particularly those involving contending jurisdictions. But you could have something signed in three separate jurisdictions, so you can't just have one government abusing the system to the detriment of the interests of other governments that happen to exist. You do not want one government out of the world's 100-plus governments to be able to privately coerce whoever signs the tree to produce privately forked versions of the tree.

Reply: I don't think the attack that you're alluding to will work. You're saying that you could coerce the log maintainer to sign a different version of the log. If that happens, that will be detectable.

Bryan Ford: I think Ross's attack will work if you're relying on certificate transparency for the log maintainer, because certificate transparency only protects the auditability of publicly published versions of the log. It does not prevent private versions signed by the log maintainer.

Reply: So let me please explain how I prevent private versions of the log being maintained. It's by this additional protocol in the device, which accepts an input value and signs its current root tree hash together with that input value. Now, the idea is that ...

Bruce Christianson: That's for freshness.

Reply: That's the freshness, exactly. That means that you get evidence of this thing written in green here, namely, that the device had a given root tree hash at the time the input value was produced. Now how would you produce that value? Well, there's several ways you could do it. One: users could individually contribute nonces that get hashed together in order to produce the value. Users reason: I know that the device saw root tree hash H after I produced my particular nonce. Another way you could do it (if you don't like the idea that users are involved) is to use so-called randomness beacons. There's a whole little industry of producing papers about how you can use financial data like the least significant bits of the closing indexes of stock exchanges as a random beacon. So those are the things that you could do in order to get this freshness property, and I think that's why the problems being described here don't apply. Is that correct?

Bruce Christianson: It comes closer, certainly, but even if the device maintains the last version of the log it saw and consistency checks everything in the history, the last decryption could be based on a fake version of the log in which the owner of the log was coerced to disclose their private key, and that private version of the tree is only used in this last decryption.

Reply: Yes, I concede that it can go wrong on the last decryption. Right, you can be tricked at the very last time, but not over a long period. You'd know that for the last n years that you've been running this system you weren't being tricked. But I agree that in the very last moment you can be tricked, if there is such a last moment. So, now they can pretend to be going along with you until the crucial time and then trick you. They will become verifiable to you only if you get access to the device again, which could be denied. If that's your concern, it wouldn't be usable in that particular application.

Hugo Jonker: I'm wondering, in line with this, could you have a decryption request, and then another one. And then the first one again, and can someone else, the log-maintainer, use that to roll back to the first stage?

Reply: This raises the issue of how log entries are tied to encryptions. I didn't look into this in very much detail, but I wanted to figure out, what are these log entries and what kind of granularity of evidence do you want users to have? Here are two examples on the slide. I think there are probably many more, and this is probably quite an interesting area to kind of refine. In the first version here, the log contains a hash of the cyphertext that's being decrypted. In other words, the device will only decrypt a cyphertext if it sees that a hash of this cyphertext is in the log. Now that very fine grained because a user can see exactly which of their cyphertext were decrypted. They just look in the log and if the hash of the cypher text is there, then that one was potentially decrypted. But that might be too much granularity, depending on your application. You may want users only to be able to see, for example, the proportion of items that were decrypted not the individual items. And that's what example two does. In example two we have some unique representation of the decrypted cypher text, but it can't be tied to any particular cypher text. For example, it could be the hash of a re-encryption, if you imagine ElGamal encryption where you can re-encrypt things. And in that way you would get the number of cypher texts decrypted but not particular ones. Now I think this answers your question, Hugo, because I think your question was roughly, could I reuse evidence about an old decryption in order to perform a new decryption? And the answer in both of these cases is - no you couldn't because the device is going to verify for the particular decryption. You going to have to provide the evidence that it's the particular decryption that you've entered into the log.

Hugo Jonker: I think you could roll back the log.

Reply: You can't roll back the log because of this freshness thing that we've spent ten minutes discussing. You the user get to see what snapshot of the log the device has seen. And if somebody tries to roll the log and show you some old log you'll say, "But no, I've seen that the device has seen a later log than the one you're showing me."

Tuomas Aura: So, I guess when the device releases the decryption key, some trusted log server auditor would at least check that it is now in the real public log.

Reply: Sorry, did you say the device releases its decryption key? Is that what you said? Because the device should never release its long-term decryption key.

Tuomas Aura: No. I meant the decryption key for your data. The sesssion key.

Reply: Yes, sure. The device releases some data, which may indeed be a key.

Tuomas Aura: I'm concerned that the log now has access to this data or key.

Reply: No, the log has no access to the decryption. It knows the decryption *request*, which is a hash of the cypher text. It doesn't have access to the decrypted data.

Fabio Massacci: Can you elaborate more on where the device is actually located. How do I know that the device even exists?

Reply: The device is probably located with the adversary, with GCHQ or the employer or whoever it is, the bad guy. How do you know it exists? Well, the manufacturer made this device and gave you a public key certificate of the two keys that are embedded in it, and you're willing to trust that. That's the assumption. So when you encrypt data, you use the PK that is certified by the device manufacturer.

Bryan Ford: I really like where this is going in general, and I like the exemplar applications, but I'm always suspicious of things that require magic devices. Partly because it's so easy to solve a device problem by just saying, "Just use Intel SGX. Trust Intel, because that will solve all security problems." So I'm wondering, how to dispense with the device? It doesn't seem at all impossible. It seems like you could do this without a device but with some other assumptions, like distribute it.

Reply: Of course you can use distributed decryptors each of which has a fragment of the key. Absolutely. And you can combine the two. This device can be one part of your distributed network that each of which has a fragment of the key. But there's loads of problems with that distributed thing as well. How do you choose?

Joan Feigenbaum: Distributed decryption is a standard, a piece of a framework that any cryptographic researcher would put forward, as we saw yesterday. It just is very hard to sell. There aren't multiple authorities out there that are going to cooperate on something like this, and whose incentives align on something. The way to get something like this going is that some manager actually says, "yes, I'm going to sell this stuff!"

Reply: Yes, it reminds me of a use of the Helios voting system, where one has distributed decryption. Someone running the election at the university had to chose who the decryption key holders would be. So he chose the vice chancellor of the university, the president of the city council, and some other dignitary to act as the decrypting authorities. Of course none of them had a clue what they were meant to be doing, so he had to go around to their offices and do it for them. In other words the decryption was totally centralised in the end.

Bruce Christianson: I really like the idea of having tamper-resistant devices rather than relying on complicated mathematics. Because if people invent quantum computers and cryptography goes away, then tamper-proof devices are really all we've got left to trust. But have you thought about how you're going to verify that the device hasn't been tampered with?

Reply: Yes, that's hard. You can have auditors. That might be enough for some applications. That will give you some assurance.

Bryan Ford: There's definitely places where you can align the incentives so that everyone wants the device to be intact.

Vashek Matyas: Here you are providing a system where people trust the log, and go according to the log. And you can twist your protocols in a way that the attacker would have to spend some computing power, do some calculations and subvert the ability of logs. Spending money or completing logs ...

Reply: Yes, I see direction you're going in. I don't really like the suggestion that you could do it with block chain, or Ethereum or Bitcoin, because it just seems to widen the set of objections that one might have, and add complications about proof of work (or proof of stake, or whatever). The method of maintaining the log with certificate transparency, having a party that proves it is maintaining the log correctly, seems to me to be good enough. The log maintainer signs the RTHs and stakes his reputation on keeping them consistent. There are companies like Google and Apple and so on, that if they say "okay we're going to maintain a service and we're going to prove that we're maintaining it correctly, and you'll be able to detect if we're deviating from that protocol," we can assume that they will go on maintaining it because that's their business model, they've decided to do that. Where as if you widen the scope in the way you're suggesting, it seems to complicate it a lot, and therefore make the security a lot less intuitive.

Tuomas Aura: I can imagine two kinds of trusted entities in the cloud that could help this device. The first one is a public blockchain which is published in a censorship-resistant way.

Reply: Why do you need that?

Tuomas Aura: Because then the device knows, that when you come back home, then you can read the log. It can't be made to disappear.

Reply: Yes. You're addressing the situation whereby the authority says: "Guys, you're not going to see this log anymore. I'm just going to go on decrypting, maintaining the log in private with this device and I'm not going to show you the log anymore." You can detect that, but if additionally you publish in a censor-resistant way you can prevent it happening, which is better.

Tuomas Aura: Another thing is, it could have a secure time server. The device synchronises its clock. And it would refuse to decrypt without getting this secret time.

Reply: Right, yes, interesting idea. If you're willing to accept a secure time server... I wanted to avoid that. But yes I agree with both your points.

Bryan Ford: I want to push back a little on your scepticism on relying on distributed entities because I think your design is already very fundamentally relying on distribution. Certificate transparency, if it's a little bit better than a centralised, trusted third party that you just trust to maintain the log, is only better if other independent parties are actually auditing that log. This is a big, common criticism of certificate transparency, who is auditing the log? We don't really know. Are they doing so reliably? Even if they are, then the attack exists where somebody could steal the log server's private key and use it to create a fake log, maybe not just once but for an extended period. That would be a fake log just for this device that only ever gets shown to that device, right? So the only way to secure the distributed part of your design, which is this certificate transparency part, is a distributed design involving not just the CT log holders but other auditors. You have a very essential, fundamental part of your design that must be distributed in order to be secure anyway. So what's the scepticism about having distributed parts in the design?

Khaled Baqer: Can the user communicate with the device? Because, if so, then maybe you can get rid of the log completely. I'm thinking, this also resolves your issue of the final case where the user can be denied visibility of the log.

Reply: I see, yes. I think you may be right, that what you're saying may work. However, I don't like the assumption that the user can communicate directly with the device because the device may be locked in a drawer, may be with the adversary, may be not available.

Khaled Baqer: The device might be a part of one that's inside of another device. I'm saying, you don't need the key transparency. You're proving to the device owner that something happened, not to the whole world.

Reply: Yep, you could do something like that. It's a bit different from my idea. *(The following thoughts about Khaled's proposal were added during the editing.)* I think Khaled is suggesting that the device will decrypt, and later the user can communicate with the device to find out what it has decrypted. It's a nice idea that dispenses with the log, but I see two problems. (1) The user might be denied the possibility of communicating with the device (because it might be kept offline). (2) To remain secure, the device would have to refuse to decrypt after a certain time if the user hasn't communicated with it. But this now puts the user in a position of power: it can refuse to communicate and thereby prevent further decryptions. This violates a design goal.

Extending Full Disk Encryption for the Future

Milan Brož[1,2](✉)

[1] Faculty of Informatics, Masaryk University, Brno, Czech Republic
xbroz@fi.muni.cz
[2] Red Hat Czech, Brno, Czech Republic

1 Introduction

Full Disk Encryption (FDE) provides confidentiality of a data-at-rest stored on persistent devices like disks or a solid state drives (SSD). Typical examples of widely used FDE systems are Bitlocker on Windows [12], dm-crypt [5] on Linux and Android, TrueCrypt [7] followers or any self-encrypted drives (SED) [18].

The basic required property is length-preserving nature of data encryption [13,17], encrypted data are of the same size as the underlying storage. This precondition limits possible security properties of the system significantly, specifically it limits FDE to provide any kind of viable integrity protection.

Our goal is to show that we can extend FDE to use additional metadata conceptually and provide authenticated encryption on this layer without need to modify any layer above the FDE (filesystem or applications). We believe that such an extension can provide far better security guarantees than commercially available FDE solutions today.

The implementation of our concept would be very simple software-defined storage function and targets commercial off-the-shelf (COTS) devices, with specific focus on SSD drives used in most of the recent laptops.
Our proposal is trying to address these problems with FDE:

- there is neither integrity protection of data nor cryptographically strong authentication (no way to detect data tampering),
- the same data are written to the same sector always produces the same ciphertext (FDE is only partially IND-CPA secure),
- possibility to securely couple FDE with other storage techniques like error correcting codes.

The price of our solution is decreased performance and storage space used for additional metadata.

2 Sector-Based Encryption

Disk drives operate with atomic fixed-length units called *sectors*. In most of COTS devices the sector size is 512 bytes, in more recent and enterprise drives it is increased to 4096 bytes. Sectors on a device are addressed by the sector

© Springer International Publishing AG 2017
F. Stajano et al. (Eds.): Security Protocols 2017, LNCS 10476, pp. 109–115, 2017.
https://doi.org/10.1007/978-3-319-71075-4_13

number that is the linear offset from the device start. Access to each sector is handled independently by the operating system read/write logic.

Transparent and length-preserving disk encryption means that we do not have any additional space except sectors themselves and encryption must preserve sector access independence. It allows disk-encryption to be inserted in the middle of a sector processing chain without any requirements of the layer above or below.

Transparent encryption on the sector level is an old concept and was extensively studied [12, 13, 15, 20].

2.1   Existing Length-Preserving Solutions

We assume a security model where an attacker has access to an encrypted device only and can create snapshots or intentionally tamper with stored ciphertexts. The attacker can also perform full or partial replay attack (revert to a previous state of the device). Replay attack cannot be prevented without additional trusted storage.

The encryption itself is based on a symmetric block cipher operating in encryption mode over the whole sector (cipher block size is usually 16 bytes while the sector is 512 or 4096 bytes). A nice property is that sector size is always multiple of cipher block size, so we do not need to care about any padding. The reality is that only CBC [9] and XTS [11] modes are used in most commercial solutions.

A crucial part of an algorithm is an Initial Vector (IV) generator used for sector tweaking. All IVs used in FDE are at least partially derived from sector number. IV generator output based only on sector number is predictable, and output is visible to the attacker.

Tweaking by a sector number provides a countermeasure to possible intentional sector relocation and also ensures that the same content in different sectors generates different ciphertexts. As shown by Saarinen and others [21], CBC mode is not safe to watermarking attacks if IV is predictable. To provide resistance to watermarking, CBC mode usually uses keyed IV generator; one such an example is Encrypted-Salt-Sector-IV (ESSIV) [13].

The XTS mode [11] was specifically developed for storage encryption and its internal design (second key used for tweaking) allows using a predictable IV.

2.2   Integrity Protection

In the storage world, an integrity protection usually means detection of a random (and silent) data corruption [6]. FDE as the length-preserving encryption cannot provide sound integrity protection method. It can only provide *poor man's authentication* [12] that means that the user (application) can detect a corruption of data only by recognizing that decryption produced garbage.

FDE also produces the same ciphertext if the sector number and the input data are the same. If we model it under IND-CPA notion, we can see that FDE cannot be IND-CPA secure in this respect [15].

Additional metadata (length expansion) is needed to provide any integrity protection. There are proposals to implement metadata per-sector directly in hardware [14,19].

2.3 Another View of FDE Needed?

The *poor man's authentication* is apparently not secure and not seriously usable in reality. In combination with data encryption, we are expecting an active attacker and highly sophisticated tampering with data. Simple integrity protection (like CRC) is not enough; an authenticated encryption should be used.

The existing hardware solution [19] is inadequate because it doesn't provide enough space. Data Integrity Field (DIF) tag is only 8 bytes but split to several fields. Moreover, devices implementing DIF feature are very rare, expensive, require special disk controller and have never been used in laptops.

Solutions that suggest hardware or firmware modifications [8] (extending internal device protocols) are unsuitable for older drives. Even for new drives, it would require cooperation among hardware manufacturers.

There are also arguments to not provide integrity protection on this low level because an application can provide better integrity protection itself (for example filesystem knows which sectors are used). This is true; application data integrity should be implemented on a higher level. The problem is that not many applications do that (yet) and for older applications, it is even impossible to add it later. If a data integrity check is provided by a filesystem, it would be a nice trade-off. Unfortunately, even after many years, there are very few filesystems that implement cryptographically sound integrity protection. The FDE based solution then provides at least something to the rescue.

3 Our Proposal

We expect that we can provide and access additional metadata per-sector. To check that it is a viable concept, we have already implemented such a function on Linux. Our implementation is meant as a proof-of-concept for the idea of authenticated encryption and as a test-bed for various authenticated modes and extensions for FDE environment. The major goal is to use COTS devices so the existing systems can use our implementation just after a software update.

We split the implementation to module that provides metadata per-sector (storage part called *dm-integrity* module) and the second part that extends existing FDE of authenticated encryption (*dm-crypt* module).

3.1 Metadata Per-Sector

The additional metadata size per-sector is meant to be configurable (at initialization time). The provided metadata store can host integrity protection fields (authentication tag), random IV (or tweak) but also Forward Error Correcting Code (FEC) or any other extension in future.

The additional metadata are stored in special sectors that are interleaved with data sectors. To provide the atomic update of both data and metadata part, we use optional data journalling. Since tampering with journal metadata could cause additional data corruption (that would be detected later), journal metadata can be independently encrypted.

3.2   Authenticated Encryption

For cryptographic data integrity protection, we are proposing to use Authenticated Encryption with Additional Data (AEAD). The situation with AEAD algorithms is not settled yet, so our goal is to have a configurable system where we can easily switch modes, for example to another CAESAR [4] candidates.

Some modes are insecure if IV is fixed or repeated. Instead of inventing nonce generators we suggest to store random IV generated directly by a system RNG. As our test shows, it seems that RNG throughput is no longer issue on recent systems. We expect IV to be at least 128 bits (that is unfortunately not the case for GCM mode with 96-bit nonces).

For the AEAD algorithms, we already experimented with

- GCM [10] authentication mode (with AES),
- GCM-SIV [16] – GCM nonce-misuse resistant version (RFC proposal),
- existing mode combined with an additional authenticator (for example AES-XTS + HMAC),
- specific wrappers over ciphers like ChaCha20 with Poly1305 authenticator.

We define per-sector authenticated request that guarantees that sector number, IV and possible FEC extension are authenticated as well through Additional Authenticated Data (AAD). Our trivial per-sector format is illustrated in Table 1 and is compatible with the definition in IEEE 1619 [2,3] storage standard.

Table 1. AEAD sector authentication request.

AAD			DATA	AUTH
Authenticated			Authenticated + Encrypted	TAG
Sector #	IV	[FEC]	Data in/out	Tag

Forward Error Correction Code is here mainly for a demonstration that our concept is extensible. It could be useful for long-term storage with occasional bit-flip recoverable errors. The important question is if a combination of encryption and error correction is always secure.

3.3   Performance

The obvious argument against our solution is that it will have significant performance penalty and decreased storage size. The additional space occupied is fixed and depends on metadata size per sector. For example 128-bit metadata space per-sector decreases usable storage size of 3.03% with 512 bytes sector or 0.39% for 4096 bytes sector respectively. The performance measurement is out of the scope of this paper, but our trivial test shows that performance drop is still acceptable (but depends on many other factors). In reality, the same performance problems have been seen when FDE length-preserving encryption was introduced in software and the performance in following years increased significantly while the code was improved.

3.4   Security Effects

With random IV (even when applied only to non-authenticated mode) we achieve that the ciphertext differs even if the same plaintext is written to the same sector. This extension should achieve fully IND-CPA secure system.

The random IV also indirectly hides the problem of XTS mode leaks where every block inside a sector is encrypted independently, and the attacker can detect the change in the sector with the cipher block size granularity. With random IV the whole sector changes pseudo-randomly on every write while the internal parallel processing of blocks inside XTS mode remains. This has the same effect as a wide mode or an additional operation like Elephant diffuser in Bitlocker [12].

4   Conclusion

The length-preserving nature of FDE is perceived as a major hurdle to provide cryptographic integrity protection. Despite that, many high-level storage systems still use FDE as an underlying layer to provide encryption. The situation in open-source Linux filesystems is not any better, none of the widely deployed filesystems implement authenticated encryption (some implement length-preserving per-file encryption or non-cryptographically sound integrity protection).

Cryptographic integrity protection can be successfully used in the sector layer as demonstrated by widely used *Verified Boot* [1] for Android and Chromebooks. This solution provides only a read-only integrity-protected device without encryption (data sector hashes are stored in a separate area in a Merkle tree structure with root hash securely sealed in firmware).

We believe that we can provide authenticated encryption as a function of FDE layer. Current FDE installations are widely used, and with focus on existing COTS devices, our proposal can bring tamper-proof protection to many existing systems just by reinstallation (or with software update). Our approach does not replace need for an integrity protection on the application level, in fact, both concepts should be used together. With random IV per-sector we can achieve a pseudo-random change of the whole sector on write, this is the best possible output in the constrained FDE system (the need to access sectors independently is the limitation).

The question is if an integrity protection justifies FDE extension and if it is worth to implement it for real systems (lifetime of an encrypted storage is usually years or even decades). Based on our existing code we can already say that implementation (at least for the Linux kernel) does not require any wide system changes and mostly re-uses existing concepts.

Our per-sector metadata storage extension was already merged to the stable Linux kernel 4.12. We will continue experiments with authenticated encryption based on top of it.

Acknowledgements. I would like to thank Mikuláš Patočka for help with the implementation and Vashek Matyáš for helpful review and support of this work.

References

1. Verified Boot. https://source.android.com/security/verifiedboot/
2. IEEE 1619-2007 - Standard for Cryptographic Protection of Data on Block-Oriented Storage Devices (2008)
3. IEEE Standard for Authenticated Encryption With Length Expansion for Storage Devices. IEEE Std 1619.1-2007, pp. c1–45, May 2008
4. CAESAR: Competition for Authenticated Encryption: Security, Applicability, and Robustness (2016). https://competitions.cr.yp.to/caesar.html
5. LUKS: Linux Unified Key Setup (2016). https://gitlab.com/cryptsetup/cryptsetup
6. Bairavasundaram, L.N., Arpaci-Dusseau, A.C., Arpaci-Dusseau, R.H., Goodson, G.R., Schroeder, B.: An analysis of data corruption in the storage stack. Trans. Storage **4**(3), 8:1–8:28 (2008). http://doi.acm.org/10.1145/1416944.1416947
7. Brož, M., Matyáš, V.: The TrueCrypt on-disk format - an independent view. IEEE Secur. Priv. **12**(3), 74–77 (2014)
8. Chakraborty, D., Mancillas-Lopez, C., Sarkar, P.: Disk encryption: Do we need to preserve length? Cryptology ePrint Archive, Report 2015/594 (2015)
9. Dworkin, M.J.: SP 800-38A, 2001 Edition. Recommendation for Block Cipher Modes of Operation: Methods and Techniques. Technical report, Gaithersburg, MD, United States (2001)
10. Dworkin, M.J.: SP 800-38D. Recommendation for Block Cipher Modes of Operation: Galois/Counter Mode (GCM) and GMAC. Technical report, National Institute of Standards & Technology, Gaithersburg, MD, United States (2007)
11. Dworkin, M.J.: SP 800-38E. Recommendation for Block Cipher Modes of Operation: The XTS-AES Mode for Confidentiality on Storage Devices. Technical report, National Institute of Standards & Technology, Gaithersburg, MD, United States (2010)
12. Ferguson, N.: AES-CBC + Elephant diffuser: a disk encryption algorithm for Windows Vista. Technical report, Microsoft Corporation (2006). http://download.microsoft.com/download/0/2/3/0238acaf-d3bf-4a6d-b3d6-0a0be4bbb36e/BitLockerCipher200608.pdf
13. Fruhwirth, C.: New methods in hard disk encryption. Ph.D. thesis, Institute for Computer Languages Theory and Logic Group Vienna University of Technology (2005). http://clemens.endorphin.org/publications

14. Holt, K.: End-to-End Data Protection Justification (2003). T10 Technical Committee proposal letter. www.t10.org/ftp/t10/document.03/03-224r0.pdf
15. Khati, L., Mouha, N., Vergnaud, D.: Full disk encryption: bridging theory and practice. Cryptology ePrint Archive, Report 2016/1114 (2016). http://eprint.iacr.org/2016/1114
16. Lindell, Y., Langley, A., Gueron, S.: AES-GCM-SIV: Nonce Misuse-Resistant Authenticated Encryption. Internet-Draft draft-irtf-cfrg-gcmsiv-03, Internet Engineering Task Force, April 2016, work in Progress. https://tools.ietf.org/html/draft-irtf-cfrg-gcmsiv-03
17. Müller, T., Freiling, F.: A systematic assessment of the security of full disk encryption. Trans. Dependable Secure Comput. (TDSC) **12**(5), 491–503 (2014)
18. Müller, T., Latzo, T., Freiling, F.: Self-encrypting disks pose self-decrypting risks: how to break hardware-based full disk encryption. Technical report, Friedrich-Alexander-Universität Erlangen-Nürnberg (2012). https://www1.informatik.uni-erlangen.de/filepool/projects/sed/seds-at-risks.pdf
19. Petersen, M.K.: T10 Data Integrity Feature (Logical Block Guarding). Linux Storage & Filesystem Workshop (2007). https://www.usenix.org/event/lsf07/tech/petersen.pdf
20. Rogaway, P.: Evaluation of some blockcipher modes of operation. Technical report, University of California, Davis, February 2011. http://web.cs.ucdavis.edu/rogaway/papers/modes.pdf
21. Saarinen, M.-J.O.: Encrypted watermarks and linux laptop security. In: Lim, C.H., Yung, M. (eds.) WISA 2004. LNCS, vol. 3325, pp. 27–38. Springer, Heidelberg (2005). https://doi.org/10.1007/978-3-540-31815-6_3

Extending Full Disk Encryption for the Future
(Transcript of Discussion)

Milan Brož[1,2](✉)

[1] Faculty of Informatics, Masaryk University, Brno, Czech Republic
xbroz@fi.muni.cz
[2] Red Hat Czech, Brno, Czech Republic

I will be talking about disk encryption. I am working with disk encryption for several years. The full disk encryption is transforming the problem of maintaining a lot of data into a key management problem, but I will not be talking about the key management. I would like to talk about data storage and how to provide data integrity. I also have some proof-of-concept implementation to show.

What is full disk encryption? It is a very simple concept of a virtual layer placed between the disk and application or operating system. Disk operates over independent sectors. You can have a lot of processes reading different sectors in parallel, and if we use cryptography there, we have to use so-called length-preserving encryption and to preserve independent access. With ciphertext and plaintext of the same size, we do not have any metadata space for nonce or authentication tag.

We cannot store anything else. If I am encrypting the same data to a different sector, I do not want to have the same ciphertext. Every encrypted sector is tweaked by some value derived from the disk offset. That is the only external attribute entering the encryption, except the key. There can be some additional operations (like encryption) that make initialization vector (tweak) not predictable. In principle, it is still a value derived from the sector offset.

And here is another problem. Full disk encryption cannot provide indistinguishability under a chosen plaintext attack. When I model it under random oracle, the encryption is deterministic. The same plaintext in the same sector produces the same ciphertext. I can distinguish if the encryption is done with the same plaintext or not.

The size of the sector is larger than encryption block size, and we have to use some encryption mode. In most systems today only CBC and XTS modes are used. I would expect that a random change in plaintext will cause a random change in the whole ciphertext sector. We cannot expect more because of independent and parallel accesses. XTS mode is internally designed for parallel encryption, if you change only one bit, we can detect the change only in one block.

The problem I would like to talk about is that there is no data integrity protection. What can we do? First, we can just use a so-called Poor-Man authentication, which means that an application can try to recognize garbage from data produced by the decryption. That is of course not cryptographically viable.

F. Stajano et al. (Eds.): Security Protocols 2017, LNCS 10476, pp. 116–122, 2017.
https://doi.org/10.1007/978-3-319-71075-4_14

If I am encrypting random data, I cannot distinguish it from another random data; here it does not work in reality.

Partha Das Chowdhury: You mentioned earlier that a change in the same sector gives you the same change in the ciphertext. But for existing data in the ciphertext, even in the same sector you have this modification for each of the block that they hit, which means that the beginning of the sector will be different from the same thing at the end of the sector.

Reply: Are you talking about the situation where you are writing the same data to the same sector number? On input you have plaintext data, you have the encryption key that is the same, and you have sector number that is the same. So output must be the same. If you write the same data to another sector that is tweaked by another offset.

Bryan Ford: Presumably this is relevant only across time, right? If the same data gets written at different times in the same sector somebody, who is watching, will see snapshots. I think the essential is threat model, what is your threat model? The adversary, who just steals the hard disk, boom, it is gone. And he gets one snapshot and only one snapshot, in this case, it is not a problem.

Or is your threat model the NSA compromise or somebody compromised with firmware and is watching the transaction and leaking multiple snapshots? And in that threat model is it adequate also some traffic analysis protection, access pattern. What depth do you want to go in the threat model side if you go into the timing? If you give the adversary access to the time domain? I think that's a very essential.

Reply: Yes, that is a problem. If we have that simple common threat model, it is only if someone steals the disk. It can become a problem later, though. Yet still, there is no integrity protection. Someone still can access the device, do something with that and I have no way to help to detect that. If I had some external storage, like a cloud, and I am storing encrypted data, I probably have a problem. I would like to know that something happened there.

Bryan Ford: It seems like the integrity problem is not a problem in the threat model where an attacker steals the device and runs away with it. It is gone. It is only if the attacker modifies it and brings it back.

Reply: It depends on the model. If the device is stolen and game over, okay, that is true. Yet on the other hand, if someone just randomly writes something on my disk or just trying to crash my operating system, I have no way to detect that. But definitely yes, there should be threat models defined.

Mark Ryan: It is something like a gamer's console that someone is trying to cheat at the game. Do something like dump out the entire disk of the game console, put it back in it, dump out the disk again.

Reply: Just another idea here. When I was testing our proof-of-concept implementation, I found one problem that is close to an integrity check. Operating systems today usually expect that the disk can read any sector, but if I provide integrity checking and the integrity is not computed for that sector, nobody yet writes there, so it fails. Why operating system should manipulate with not yet written data? *"Don't read what you didn't write."* I would like to see a design of systems that we can detect *"This is the correct read. We are scanning for signatures that are not yet there."* Yet on the other hand, there can be applications wrongly written that try to read other data. And we can detect it with integrity protection.

The integrity protection is also intended to detect so-called silent data corruption. Something that flips bits when the device is dying. I would like to detect that on this lower level.

Ross Anderson: Disks, as rotating disks, are replaced by non-volatile memory. Then, of course, one has to revisit this because memory wears out, there are other potential raw hammer type attacks, emerging other technologies and so forth. Why not just expect the manufacturers will build integrity protection at the lower layer to which you can then access?

Reply: They are trying to do that on several layers. First, cheap devices, mobile phones typically, have a flash device. Yet every additional protection costs money. So they rely on software. Android is doing that for example. The dm-verity is exactly the system that tries to protect integrity on the block level. It is used in Android and Chromebooks devices, and it provides integrity protection but not encryption. And there are even extensions for forward error correction of data. Because the device does not use internally any checksums, if there is a bit flip, it is being propagated to the operating system. Google is exactly doing that on the software level.

And another example is an idea to add some metadata space for the sector. It was already there twenty years ago, maybe even more. And some devices provided that little external space. Yet it is not enough for a cryptographic integrity. It is just for CRC checks. And when I am talking to storage people, they still have problems to understand why we need cryptographic integrity.

It is designed for random changes, not for intentional integrity attacks. There is some hardware, but it will never be used in cheap laptops or cheap devices. We are simulating this data integrity field in software. You will receive sector plus metadata.

My intention is to try switch full disk encryption, which today provides only confidentiality, to something that could provide data integrity. And the design goal is to use devices without the requirement of any specific hardware.

I do not believe that we can rely on any hardware vendor to provide this in firmware. It would take years until we have some protocol for it. And it is still only for some devices. My goal was to use normal disk or SSD as it is today. It, of course, means that we cannot provide some prevention for replay attacks because you still can take the snapshot of the device and replace it back. Nobody can detect that without additional storage for external checksum. But I still think there is a good use case for that.

My second design goal was separate the storage and the cryptography part. The idea is that we can implement the storage part in software, but later we can switch to hardware, for example with persistent memory as a byte address-able storage. Storage part can change, but authenticated encryption algorithms remain the same.

Another design goal is to use authenticated encryption that provides both confidentiality and integrity. We need algorithm agnostic implementation so we can switch to newer authenticated encryption later. It should be generic software.

Operating systems, I mean mainly open source Linux, do not provide a real data integrity protection. Some file systems do integrity protection of metadata but without cryptographic algorithms. The integrity protection of data should be part of the operating system.

Tuomas Aura: How it is with sectors of the size of power of two? Can you steal space from them? Like the reason why they do all these games with the IVs is to avoid using space from the sectors. And the same with any integrity check that you have. And now I think with the SSDs, the solid state device storage, and again sectors have the very strict power of two sizes. And it is not even as easy to change as with magnetic storage. I do not know. I never understood this. Is it the service disk provides, do sectors sizes have to be the power of two?

Reply: That is based on the design of the device. Our solution still uses a fixed sector size. We are using the same sector size as the device and then just interleaving so-called metadata sectors where all the hashes or authentication tags are stored. It still uses the power of two sizes.

Tuomas Aura: That takes me to the next step. Now you are storing the data somewhere else. Not in the same sector with the data. That means you implement it in software on the computer, not in the device. Now you are writing multiple sectors in completely different parts of the disk. And the disk needs to promise to you this is an atomic product otherwise you will break the integrity quite often.

Reply: That is exactly what the storage part does. It does journalling and it provides atomic write of data sectors plus metadata sector.

Tuomas Aura: And if you are doing a hash tree integrity, but you are doing sector by sector, but if you do a hash tree, it becomes a hot storage area.

Reply: I am not doing anything like that. I am just storing metadata sector independently. Atomicity must be there, and it is there by design.

Tuomas Aura: And atomicity with a hash tree is a nightmare, because you have slow write pattern.

Reply: For example, dm-verity uses the Merkle tree, and they store the signed root hash inside the firmware. But it is a read-only device used only for system partition for verified boot. It does not work for a read-write device. That is not where I am heading. I have configurable metadata space per-sector. The lower layer provides the atomicity of the write. Then we can implement anything above that. It can be authenticated encryption, it can be just simple checksums, or there can be stored randomly generated initialization vector.

Partha Das Chowdhury: Can you explain why it is a problem to use AES-GCM if you have a space for authentication tags?

Reply: I can use GCM there, but GCM has several problems. There is the 96-bit initialization vector (nonce). I am generating initialization vector randomly, using a cryptographic random generator inside kernel in this case. But 96-bit for nonce can be a problem if we are writing a lot of data. We will have collision one day. And the nonce collision in GCM is the problem. Serious problem. That is why I would like to use something else, some collision resistant mode. The system should be easily configured for any authentication mode. If GCM works in that encryption model, then we can use it. And it can be accelerated in hardware.

Markus Voelp: Do you have an idea how much latency you would have to add for reads and writes in your approach?

Reply: I have a graph with some measurements, not latency, but throughput. We are already doing length-preserving encryption, so authenticated encryption should add only little latency there. Adding authentication encryption does not cause many problems. What causes the problem is the additional storage handling. As I said, you have to provide atomicity; we need to maintain a journal. And journal means to write data twice.

On the graph, you can see that there is a performance drop, but still, I think, it is usable. I can work with that proof-of-concept implementation on my laptop. For the "normal" work, you will not even notice that something like encryption is going there.

Yet performance is always the first question for the storage people. I do not want to have this as the first question. The first question should be if is it secure and if it protects data well. If it is, let's talk about optimization.

On the graph, we can see two measurements: solid state drive and rotational drive. We can probably focus more on solid state drive because all mobile devices and laptops in next years will probably use only solid state drives. Rotational drives will be more used for data centers archives. For the solid state drive writes, there is at least half performance drop, but we are still in usable numbers. If I used it for normal work, for example for a compilation of kernel, which uses both disk and CPU, we were under a 10% slow down.

Simon Foley: On the picture, for the rotational drive, the AES encryption is faster than the underlying device?

Reply: For a rotational drive, there is the influence of the I/O scheduler. For the measurement, I tried to run it in a system where nothing else is running. I think it runs ten times and the number is the arithmetic mean. It can happen, it is all software encryption. Yes, it is just what I measured, I do not want to present false data.

Markus Voelp: Have you also considered the energy issue because in particular for solid state drives, you are adding much more randomness just by encrypting everything and they are having one type of bits in the majority of the written data.

Reply: With SSD, that is problematic as nobody knows what it is doing inside firmware. Many SSDs today are doing encryption anyway inside, even if you do not use self-encrypting drives.

For other drives, there is also some deduplication inside. And there is possibly specific handling of zero blocks because you can just mark it is as zero blocks. Then such things like TRIM, some garbage collecting running. Maybe that is what happened even here for the encryption speed.

If you write a lot of data, the drive can decide that now is the time for the garbage collection and the throughput changes. After half an hour, it returns. Nobody knows what is going there. For me, I use abstraction; it is just operating on the sector level. The behavior depends on the drive vendor.

Markus Voelp: Maybe it is worth attempting to integrate your approach with SSDs because it already accesses data there.

Reply: You mean implementing it in firmware directly? That is another story, self-encrypting drives. Yes, the energy consumption is near perfect. My problem with self-encrypting drives is that how I get proof that the encryption key is from some trusted source? It is generated inside the drive. It is firmware, closed-source. For the performance improvement, yes, you are right. It will be faster.

Bryan Ford: It looks like in this design, each sector is authenticated independently of all other sectors, right? If an attacker can observe multiple versions of some sectors over time, then they could selectively roll back some of them.

Reply: Yes.

Bryan Ford: I am concerned in particular about operating system integrity attacks or PlayStation attacks or something where all I need to do is as an attacker, know or guess when an OS upgrade happened, find two particular sectors in the OS image where the new version of this part of the code and the old version with that part of the code will still work. For security circumvention, I bet you could find examples of that in the operating systems we have. I guess the question is how much do you think we need to care about that in the threat models you have in mind?

Reply: Yes, that is a question about the threat model. It is a trade-off. You can roll back sectors on your own if you have snapshots.

If I have a model that just cannot allow an attacker to have snapshots, no problem. If the attacker can do that, then it depends on what he can achieve here. My goal was to have something that I can implement in Linux in short-term.

I think I even have to mention another limitation, multi-user environment. I am expecting the laptop or external device where there is one user. If we have multi-user, multi-tenant environment, everyone who has the key can decrypt everything. It is not usable for that scenario.

I still hope there will be another level of integrity protection, like inside file system. If someone finally writes good file system that provides authenticated encryption for the enterprise, it would be perfect. But we still do not have that even after five, six years.

I know this is not a perfect solution. It is a trade-off, but maybe it motivates someone to write something better. I think that data integrity should be handled as the first class citizen, not just be ignored as it happens today.

Key Exchange with the Help of a Public Ledger

Thanh Bui[✉] and Tuomas Aura

Aalto University, Espoo, Finland
{thanh.bui,tuomas.aura}@aalto.fi

Abstract. Blockchains and other public ledger structures promise a new way to create globally consistent event logs and other records. We make use of this consistency property to detect and prevent man-in-the-middle attacks in a key exchange such as Diffie-Hellman or ECDH. Essentially, the MitM attack creates an inconsistency in the world views of the two honest parties, and they can detect it with the help of the ledger. Thus, there is no need for prior knowledge or trusted third parties apart from the distributed ledger. To prevent impersonation attacks, we require user interaction. It appears that, in some applications, the required user interaction is reduced in comparison to other user-assisted key-exchange protocols.

1 Introduction

Authentication is essential in any key exchange over insecure network. It helps each party be certain that the exchanged key is in fact shared with the desired second party, not an impostor. While authenticated key exchange has been widely studied, it is still a task with many complications. Most of the existing key-exchange protocols require some root of trust between the involved parties, such as prior knowledge on a cryptographic key or password [9,11,15,20,23,40], or trusted third-parties (TTP) [14,34]. In situations where these roots of trust are not available, such as device pairing, key exchanges usually rely on user interaction to achieve authentication [5,9,17,21,22,26,38]. The probability of a successful attack against these protocols mostly depends on the entropy of the user input. While more complex inputs bring higher security level, they might also cause usability issues.

To ease the requirements of a secure key exchange, we find the solution in blockchains and similar *public ledger* structures, which provide a new way to publish information and achieve consistency in a distributed system. They have been used as key directories that store bindings between identities and public keys [1,24,29,41]. In a public-key-based key exchange, a party can look up for the public key of the other in these directories. While these systems provide a reasonable user experience and do not depend on any single TTP, they restrict a party to use only the registered keys and thus, complicate key management. Furthermore, they require all interested parties to have a well-defined and unique identity, which does not always hold in reality. For example, two mobile devices of the same user may share the same identity, such as the user's email address,

© Springer International Publishing AG 2017
F. Stajano et al. (Eds.): Security Protocols 2017, LNCS 10476, pp. 123–136, 2017.
https://doi.org/10.1007/978-3-319-71075-4_15

or they may be identified simply by their presence in the user's hands. In any case, the key-identity binding requires the user or someone else to register the bindings.

In this paper, we present a new family of key exchange protocols that utilizes the global consistency property of the public ledgers. We refer to the protocols as the *public-ledger-based (PLB) protocols*. The idea is to bring transparency to a key exchange by publishing its parameters into the public ledgers. This enables the communication parties to check whether they are participating in the same key exchange, thereby detecting man-in-the-middle (MitM) attacks. Our protocols do not require any roots of trust between the parties or key-identifier bindings. In cases where the parties have public identifiers, such as phone numbers or emails, MitM attacks are prevented without any user interaction. When public identifiers are not available, our protocols still require the users to act as an out-of-band channel. However, the amount of information conveyed via the out-of-band channel is not a function of the desired security level. Thus, high security level can be achieved with little user interaction. Of course, instead of being MitM, the attacker could perform an impersonation attack against one of the parties. We will present application-specific solutions to the attack.

The rest of the paper is structured as follows. Section 2 covers the background about public ledgers. Section 3 gives an overview of our solution, and Sect. 4 describes the PLB protocols in detail. Section 5 presents a number of practical applications of the protocols. Section 6 discusses the denial-of-service attacks against the protocols and the privacy issues and presents some solutions. Section 7 concludes the paper.

2 Background

This section covers the literature about public ledgers and the threat model that we consider in this paper.

2.1 Public Ledger

The recent widely known compromises of popular service providers [2–4] and government surveillances [16,18,28] have motivated quite a few proposals for public ledgers that have no centralized management. These public ledgers are basically public logs of *events* with the following properties [12]: *immutability* and *global consistency* of the event history, *inclusiveness* in the sense that all valid data is included. The ledgers might also define a *linear order* or have some built-in concept of time on all data entries.

Two main architectures have emerged for the public ledgers [13]: (1) totally distributed with no central points of trust or (2) more centralized with one untrusted third party who manages the ledger's content and several trusted auditors who audits its behaviors.

Distributed ledgers. The most prominent representative of the distributed ledgers is Bitcoin [30]. In Bitcoin, an open peer-to-peer (P2P) network with no single party responsible for any critical operation maintains an append-only log of transactions, called *blockchain*. Transactions take place between public keys and are communicated as signed messages in the P2P network. They are mined into blocks approximately every ten minutes. Global consistency is achieved by compressing the global history of transactions into one cryptographic hash value, which can relatively easily be agreed on and communicated to everyone. Inclusiveness and immutability are guaranteed by a novel distributed consensus mechanism and a competitive mining process.

The Bitcoin's blockchain has become a reliable log for many other applications, such as CommitCoin [4], Factom[1], Proof of Existence[2], Virtual notary[3], and Tierion[4]. It has also inspired hundreds of alternative cryptocurrencies, such as Ethereum [39] and Namecoin [24]. A number of central banks and financial institutions have started investing in Bitcoin-based technologies [7,31,35].

Centralized ledgers. Although Bitcoin and its variants have achieved a large degree of success, the decentralized nature limits their ability to achieve widespread adoption. The reason is that, for the systems to be completely trustless, users must store the entire blockchain locally and track its progress. Thus, the amount of storage and communication traffic that they require increases linearly with the number of users.

To address the shortcomings of the blockchain, more centralized ledger architectures have been proposed in the literature, in which the ledger content is maintained by an untrusted third party instead of the P2P network. They rely on trusted *auditors* to achieve the desired properties.

Most of the proposals in this category are for monitoring security of the web PKI. Certificate Transparency (CT) [27] is a public log of all web certificates, which aims to bring transparency and accountability to the CA operations. The log is structured as an *append-only Merkle tree*, in which new records are added to the right of the tree. Accountable Key Infrastructure (AKI) [25] and its kin [8,37] are similar solutions, but they deploy an *ordered Merkle tree*, where the data in the leaf nodes is sorted by the domain name instead. Both append-only and ordered Merkle trees enable logarithmic-size proofs of existence and non-existence for certificates, though. In yet another variant of these ideas, PKI Safety Net [36] enables verification of both the issuing time order and the non-existence of records for a domain by maintaining two trees that are similar to those in CT and AKI, respectively. Independent *monitors* maintain a copy of the trees and audit their consistency.

Apart from web PKI, centralized ledger solutions have been suggested for other applications. CONIKS [29] constructs directories of user certificates. DECIM [41] keeps track of uses of a public key in a transparency log so that its owner can detect key misuse. Enhanced Certificate Transparency [33] extends CT to handle certificate revocation and shows how this extension can be used

---

[1] https://www.factom.com/.
[2] https://proofofexistence.com/.
[3] https://virtual-notary.org/.
[4] https://tierion.com/.

in end-to-end email or messaging systems. Bui et al. [12] apply public ledgers to group management in distributed systems where entities are represented by their public keys and authorization is in the form of signed certificates.

In this paper, we are not proposing any new ledger structure. Instead, *we assume that a public ledger with the properties mentioned above exists and we use it as an abstract to build our key exchange protocols.*

2.2   Threat Model

We consider a threat model where there are active attackers against key exchanges. The attackers can perform *man-in-the-middle (MitM)* attacks to intercept the communication traffic or *impersonation* attacks to pretend to be one of the involved parties. They can also perform *denial-of-service (DoS)* attacks to cause failures to key exchanges.

We assume that all the underlying cryptography is secure. Also, the communication channel between any party and the ledger, if exists, is secured under existing security protocols such as TLS/SSL.

3   Basic Idea

The key observation that motivated this work is that *in a key exchange that is free of MitM, the endpoints have a consistent view of the key exchange's parameters (i.e. the public keys of the endpoints or the shared key).* Suppose that when Alice wants to establish a shared key with Bob, Carol performs a MitM attack to intercept the communication. If Carol succeeds, there will be two different key exchanges — one between Alice and Carol and the other between Carol and Bob, as illustrated in Fig. 1. A secure connection, on the other hand, involves only a single key exchange. In other words, the MitM attack creates inconsistent views of the key exchange between Alice and Bob, while in the case of a secure key exchange, their views are consistent.

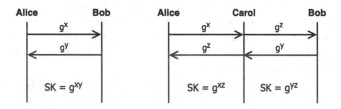

Fig. 1. A secure key exchange (on the left) vs a key exchange with MitM attacker (on the right)

Based on the above observation, *our proposal for detecting MitM attacks against any unauthenticated key exchange is to publish its parameters to a public ledger.* Let us assume such a ledger exists and (unrealistically) that there is only one legitimate key exchange taking place in the world ever. After the unauthenticated key exchange, one of the parties (e.g., the initiator) sends an event E containing the key exchange's data to the ledger, which can be, for example, a hash of the public keys or a hash of the shared key. When the ledger has made the event public, the parties separately query the ledger to check how many new events were entered into the ledger. If there is only one and it matches their view of the key exchange, the key exchange was secure. On the other hand, if two or more events were entered, there may be a MitM attacker around and both parties must discard the results of the key exchange.

Context. The scheme described above is impractical because it supports only one key exchange ever. To enable multiple key exchanges, our first attempt is to amend the key-exchange event E with a context C. The data submitted to the public ledger will be $\langle C, E \rangle$ and it is indexed by C. That is, one side submits this data to the ledger, both sides query it with the index C, and then they compare the received event E (if there is only one) with their view of the key exchange.

The context can be any information that the two parties agree on *naturally* or *out of band*. The following information is particularly suitable to be used in C:

- application identifier a,
- endpoint identifier i if one is already known to the other party,
- user input or user-compared code c.

The first and second elements are examples of natural contexts, while the last is an example of out-of-band contexts. A key exchange can use both natural context and out-of-band context. How much information the context should hold depends on how many parties are simultaneously writing to the ledger. The frequency of collisions for the index C should be sufficiently small to not frustrate the users.

Time window. We can see that by tagging each key exchange event with a context, once a context is used, it cannot be re-used for any other key exchange. To optimize the solution, we tag an event E not only with a context C but also with a time t. This way, we can do one key exchange per context per *time period* τ. Defining the time period is application-specific, and it must be agreed by the two parties in advance. An application, for example, can define that a context can be used once per minute or per hour.

We can consider time t as a part of the context C. However, it must be provided by the ledger because we cannot trust the communication parties to timestamp the key exchange events. Thus, the ledger must have a built-in concept of time. In Bitcoin, for example, a new block appears every ten minutes; thus, we can roughly determine the timestamp of a block by checking how many blocks are after it in the block chain.

Figure 2 illustrates an overview of the protocol with the addition of the context and the time period. The data submitted to the ledger will be $\langle C, E \rangle$ and it is timestamped by the ledger. When each party checks the ledger, they only query for events with context C that happened in the time period τ. The parties reject

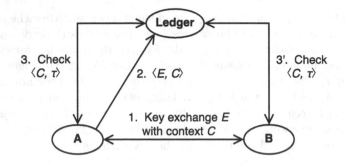

Fig. 2. An overview of the public-ledger-based key exchange protocol

the key exchange if there is more than one events that matches this query or if the retrieved event E does not match theirs.

4   Public-Ledger-Based Key Exchange

We now describe our PLB key exchange protocols in detail. We will start with a protocol where the communication parties agree on a context out of band and user interaction is required for the agreement. We will then build on it a protocol where the two communication parties must naturally agree on a context with each other and no user interaction is involved.

4.1   Public-Ledger-Based Key Exchange with Out-of-Band Context

Since the PLB key exchange protocol with out-of-band context requires user interaction, we require the communication parties to be equipped with the following: (1) a screen that can display a string, and (2) a "start" button where users can press to trigger an event.

The protocol involves four parties: the initiator A, the responder B, the ledger L, and the user U. It consists of six phases as follows.

1. **Unauthenticated key exchange:** In the first phase, the parties perform an unauthenticated key exchange to establish a shared secret key SK.
2. **Context acquirement:** The initator A requests the ledger for a context that is not in use. The ledger then returns a context C that matches the query. A then sends the context to B using the shared key. (An alternative way to acquire a context is for one party to generate it locally and try to use it. This way, depending on the entropy of the context, collision might happen, causing failure in the protocol.)
3. **Context comparison:** A and B display the context C on their screen so that user U can compare the context. If they display the same context, U presses "start" on both endpoints at the same time. After that, both parties immediately query the ledger to get the current ledger's time. Let S_A and S_B be the ledger's times that A and B receive, respectively.

4. **Commitment:** A commits the key exchange to the ledger. It submits an event E containing the key exchange's parameters along with the context C to the ledger. The ledger then stores E and indexes it by C. It also gives the event a timestamp t. If for some reason (e.g., network failures) the submission fails, A aborts the protocol and informs B about the abortion. Otherwise, A informs B that the commitment was successful via the encrypted channel established in the previous phase.

5. **Commitment verification:** When the ledger has published the event in the previous phase, both parties separately query the ledger for events with context C. A queries for events that happened only in period $[S_A - \triangle, Q_A]$, and B queries for events that happened only in period $[S_B - \triangle, Q_B]$, where Q_A and Q_B are the times when A and B make the query, respectively, and $\triangle$ is an application-specific constant that represents the possible difference in clocks between A and B. The ledger then returns a list of events that match the query and a proof that the list is complete. For each event in the list, the ledger also returns the respective timestamp. The parties verify the list. They abort if any of the following occurs: (1) the verification fails, (2) more than one event appear in the list, or (3) the only event in the list does not match their view. Otherwise, the protocol succeeds and the parties accept the shared key.

6. **Confirmation:** User U checks that the protocol succeeds on both sides. It it fails on either side, the user must abort the protocol.

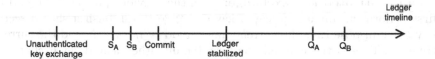

Fig. 3. Ledger's timeline of events for a PLB protocol using out-of-band context

Figure 3 illustrates all the events in the key exchange above in the ledger's timeline. We can see that if there is man in the middle, the party who queries last (B in the figure) will see that there are two key exchanges with the same context C and thus, abort the protocol. Impersonation attack is also not possible because the user will check that the protocol succeeds on both sides.

A notable property of the protocol is that its security level does not depend on the entropy of the context. In order for the protocol to succeed, each key exchange simply needs a unique context during its time period. How much information the context should hold depends only on how many parties are simultaneously writing to the ledger.

4.2 Public-Ledger-Based Key Exchange with Natural Context

In many cases, the user cannot be present at both sides to press the "start" button as in the previous protocol. However, the communication parties in these cases usually have a public identifier that is already known to each other. For example, in an encrypted phone call, the identifiers are the phone numbers or the email addresses. These identifiers can form a context on which the parties can naturally agree with each other. This section will present the PLB key exchange when a natural context is available. This protocol is more simple but requires more assumptions than the previous does because there is no user interaction.

The PLB key exchange with natural context involves three entities: the initiator A, the responder B, and the ledger L. Beside a context C, the initiator and the responder need to agree with each other on the following parameters in advance:

- A time period's length w, which indicates that a context can only be used once in a time period of length w. The first time period of a day starts at 00:00. We assume that the local clocks of the communication parties must be synchronized with reliable sources, and w must be larger than the difference between these clocks.
- A timeout α, which indicates the maximum duration of a key exchange.

These parameters can be pre-configured in the communication application. This way, by using the same application to communicate with each other, the two parties naturally agree on the parameters.

The protocol consists of three phases: *unauthenticated key exchange, commitment,* and *commitment verification*. The details of each phase are as follows.

1. **Unauthenticated key exchange:** As in the previous protocol, the parties first perform an unauthenticated key exchange to establish a shared secret key SK. Suppose that the current time period is $[t_0, t_0 + w]$ and the current time is t. The parties can only perform the unauthenticated key exchange if t is not within $[t_0, t_0 + \alpha]$ or $[t_0 + w - \alpha, t_0 + w]$. This is to ensure that the key exchange does not span over two time periods. Let S_A and S_B be the times when the key exchange starts on A and B, respectively. A will abort the protocol if it does not finish by time $S_A + \alpha$, and B will do so by time $S_B + \alpha$.

2. **Commitment:** The initiator A submits an event E containing the key exchange's parameters along with the context C to the ledger. The ledger then stores E and indexes it by C. It also gives the event a timestamp t. If for some reason (e.g., network failures) the submission fails, A aborts the protocol and informs B about the abortion. Otherwise, A informs B that the commitment was successful via the encrypted channel established in the previous phase.

3. **Commitment verification:** When the ledger has published the event in the previous phase, both parties separately query the ledger for all events with context C in the current period. The ledger then returns a list of events that match the query and a proof that the list is complete. For each event in the list, the ledger also returns the respective timestamp. The parties verify the list. They abort if any of the following occurs: (1) the verification fails,

(2) more than one event appear in the list, or (3) the only event in the list does not match their view. Otherwise, the protocol succeeds and the parties accept the shared key.

The protocol described above can prevent MitM attacks as follows. Assuming that there is a MitM attacker, the attacker must perform a separate key exchange with each party. However, the two key exchanges must share the same context C. With time synchronization and the timeout, we ensure that the communication parties perform the key exchange in the same time period. Thus, at least one of the parties will see two key exchanges with the same context published in the ledger and abort the protocol.

We can see that instead of being the MitM, the attacker could perform an impersonation attack against one of the honest parties (and denial-of-service against the other if necessary). Then, one party will be see the expected one key exchange in the ledger while the other will not even check. We will present application-specific solution to detect impersonation in the next section.

5   Applications

We now consider a number of practical applications of the PLB key exchange protocol.

5.1   Encrypted VoIP

We first present the most convincing application of the protocol — *encrypted voice over IP (VoIP)*, such as Cryptophone[5], SilentPhone[6], and Signal[7].

In these applications, each user is typically represented by a public-key pair, and the users use these key pairs to establish end-to-end encrypted phone calls. To verify that they are actually communicating with the parties they intend, the users can rely on trusted authorities who vouch for the users' public keys, such as the certificate authority in the X.509 Public Key Infrastructure. A major issue with trusted authorities is that they can vouch for fraudulent keys in an attack [2,3]. An alternative approach is that the users perform key verification out of band. A common approach for key verification is to compare key fingerprint, i.e. some representation of a cryptographic hash of the public keys. Key fingerprint comparison introduces severe usability because users have to manually perform key verification before communicating with a new partner. Shorter strings can be provided instead to simplify the verification [10,42]. A short authentication string (SAS) is a truncated cryptographic hash of the key exchange's parameters, which is usually represented by a human-friendly format. Participants compute the SAS based on the key exchange they observe and compare the resulting

---

[5] http://www.cryptophone.de/.

[6] https://www.silentcircle.com/.

[7] https://whispersystems.org/.

value by reading it aloud. The authentication is based on recognition of the other party's voice.

The PLB key exchange protocol can be applied readily to encrypted VoIP and improve the usability. Specifically, the parties perform the protocol with the context being the phone numbers (or user IDs). This context is inherent to both parties; thus, no out-of-band channel is needed for context verification. The use of the public ledger prevents MitM attacks, and the users will naturally start speaking secrets only if they recognize each other's voices. Therefore, the protocol achieves the same level of security as the SAS verification approach's but better usability because no user interaction is required.

Of course, users who have never heard each other's voice cannot rely on our protocol to establish a secure phone channel (same as with the SAS verification solution). Voice spoofing is also an issue of voice-based authentication [19,32]. Thus, we do not aim to completely replace the stronger methods of authentication, such as manual key fingerprint verification, but to complement them.

There have been attempts to publish bindings between user identities and public keys to public ledgers [1,24,29,41]. The main difference between these solutions to ours is that they restrict a party to use only the registered keys and thus, complicate key management. Our protocol, on the other hand, allows users to use arbitrary key pair for each communication, making the use of multiple devices with separate keys easier.

5.2   Device Pairing

Device pairing — the procedure of establishing a shared key for secure communication between two devices — is another application of the PLB protocol. In device pairing, there is usually no key management infrastructure or pre-shared secret between the devices. Thus, authentication solely depends on some form of user action, such as entering a passkey [9,17,21] or verifying numeric code [5,22,26,38]. The security level of these approaches depend on the entropy of the user input. In Bluetooth, for example, users have to compare six digits displayed on the devices and the probability of a successful attack is 10^{-6}. Using longer or more complex inputs would be more error-prone and reduce usability.

The PLB key exchange protocol might offer advantages other the existing solutions in this scenario. The devices can run the PLB key exchange protocol with out-of-band context, and the users compare the context displayed on the devices. If they are equal, the key exchange succeeds with impossibility of MitM attacks, regardless of the entropy of the context.

The protocol can be applied to group association where more than two devices want to establish secure communication with each other.

6   Discussion

In this section, we discuss denial-of-service attacks against the PLB protocols as well as their privacy issues.

6.1   Denial-of-Service

We have showed how the PLB key exchange protocols can defend against MitM and impersonation attacks. Another security vector to the protocols is the denial-of-service attacks where the attacker spams events to the ledger. This could prevent key exchanges to succeed because the endpoints could observe several key exchanges with the same context as theirs in the ledger and drop the key exchange as a result. In this section, we will analyze the causes of these attacks and how we can mitigate them.

The PLB key exchanges using natural contexts are attractive targets of DoS attacks. It is due to the fact that natural contexts are usually endpoint identifiers, which are known by everyone. To permanently prevent any pair of parties to communicate, an attacker can determine the context based on their identifiers and continuously send fake events with the context to the ledger. A solution for this type of targeted attacks is for the ledger to authenticate endpoint identifiers. Authentication could be easily adopted by centralized ledgers like Certificate Transparency. Also, the service provider can act as the ledger provider itself; thus, users can use the same credentials for the application and ledger.

The out-of-band contexts might also be guessed if their entropy is low. Thus, they must be random so that it is difficult to guess by the attackers but not too complex for users to compare. Using the ledger-provided contexts as in our protocol can limit the attack to some extent but cannot prevent massive spamming. Limitation on rate of submissions, posting fee (e.g. the transaction fee in Bitcoin), and proof-of-work of clients (e.g. client puzzels [6]), are some solutions to prevent massive spamming.

The ledger might be the source of context leak. Depending on the ledger's architecture, the attackers can read the contexts immediately when new events are entered the ledger and then post fake events with the same contexts. The blockchain with P2P network is an example of such designs, in which transactions are propagated through the network for a while before they are mined into blocks. Thus, to prevent context leak, the ledger could be designed so that it can only be queried for individual contexts and and the response for any individual query leaks no information about other events in the ledger. CONIKS's [29] is an example of such design. The ledger could also be round-based, meaning that events can be accepted in a round and only published in the next round.

6.2   Privacy

We now argue about the privacy issue of the PLB protocol that uses the communication parties' identifiers as the context. It is true that if a record is published in the ledger every time two parties communicate with each other, the protocol has serious privacy issue. However, that is not how applications work in practice. Two communication parties need to perform a key exchange only once and save the result locally for later uses. They do not have to perform another key exchange unless one of them changes its public key. Authentication also helps to prevent privacy issues. For example, a party can only query the ledger for the records that are associated with contexts containing its identifier. Further-more, unlike ledgers that store key bindings, the content of our ledger can be erased periodically without affecting any key exchanges. This not only reduces the footprint of the ledger but also might be of little help in preserving user privacy.

7   Conclusion

We have shown that it is possible to have authenticated key exchange proto-cols that take advantages of the global consistency property of blockchains and other public ledgers to detect and prevent man-in-the-middle attacks. While our protocol requires the users to act as an out-of-band channel, the amount of information conveyed out of band is not a function of the desired security level. Instead, it depends on the number of simultaneous key exchanges and thus, on the load of the public ledger; the out-of-band information simply ensures each key exchange gets its unique context string. Further work is required on the detailed requirements and design of the public ledger and on analysis of denial-of-service threats.

References

1. Blockstack, December 2016. https://blockstack.org
2. Comodo fraud incident, January 2017. https://www.comodo.com/Comodo-Fraud-Incident-2011-03-23.html
3. DigiNotar SSL certificate hack amounts to cyberwar, says expert, January 2017. https://www.theguardian.com/technology/2011/sep/05/diginotar-certificate-hack-cyberwar
4. Yahoo hack: 1bn accounts compromised by biggest data breach in history, January 2017. https://www.theguardian.com/technology/2016/dec/14/yahoo-hack-security-of-one-billion-accounts-breached
5. Alliance, Z., et al.: Zigbee Specification (2006)
6. Aura, T., Nikander, P., Leiwo, J.: DOS-resistant authentication with client puzzles. In: Christianson, B., Malcolm, J.A., Crispo, B., Roe, M. (eds.) Security Protocols 2000. LNCS, vol. 2133, pp. 170–177. Springer, Heidelberg (2001). https://doi.org/10.1007/3-540-44810-1_22
7. Barrdear, J., Kumhof, M.: The macroeconomics of central bank issued digital cur-rencies (2016)
8. Basin, D., Cremers, C., Kim, T.H.J., Perrig, A., Sasse, R., Szalachowski, P.: ARPKI: attack resilient public-key infrastructure. In: Proceedings of the 2014 ACM SIGSAC Conference on Computer and Communications Security, pp. 382–393. ACM (2014)
9. Bellovin, S.M., Merritt, M.: Encrypted key exchange: password-based protocols secure against dictionary attacks. In: Proceedings of the Computer Society Sym-posium on Research in Security and Privacy, pp. 72–84. IEEE (1992)
10. Blossom, E.: The VP1 protocol for voice privacy devices version 1.2 (1999)

11. Boyko, V., MacKenzie, P., Patel, S.: Provably secure password-authenticated key exchange using Diffie-Hellman. In: Preneel, B. (ed.) EUROCRYPT 2000. LNCS, vol. 1807, pp. 156–171. Springer, Heidelberg (2000). https://doi.org/10.1007/3-540-45539-6_12

12. Bui, T., Aura, T.: Application of public ledgers to revocation in distributed access control. https://arxiv.org/abs/1608.06592

13. Chase, M., Meiklejohn, S.: Transparency overlays and applications. In: Proceedings of the 2016 ACM SIGSAC Conference on Computer and Communications Security, pp. 168–179. ACM (2016)

14. Dierks, T.: The transport layer security (TLS) protocol version 1.2. RFC 5246 (2008)

15. Diffie, W., Van Oorschot, P.C., Wiener, M.J.: Authentication and authenticated key exchanges. Des. Codes Crypt. 2(2), 107–125 (1992)

16. Electronic Frontier Foundation: National security letters, July 2015. https://www.eff.org/issues/national-security-letters

17. Gehrmann, C., Mitchell, C.J., Nyberg, K.: Manual authentication for wireless devices. RSA Cryptobytes 7(1), 29–37 (2004)

18. Gellman, B.: The FBI's secret scrutiny, July 2015. http://www.washingtonpost.com/wp-dyn/content/article/2005/11/05/AR2005110501366.html

19. Gupta, P., Shmatikov, V.: Security analysis of voice-over-IP protocols. In: Proceedings of the Computer Security Foundations Symposium, pp. 49–63. IEEE (2007)

20. Hao, F., Ryan, P.: J-PAKE: authenticated key exchange without PKI. In: Gavrilova, M.L., Tan, C.J.K., Moreno, E.D. (eds.) Transactions on Computational Science XI. LNCS, vol. 6480, pp. 192–206. Springer, Heidelberg (2010). https://doi.org/10.1007/978-3-642-17697-5_10

21. IEEE Standards 802.11 WG, Part 11: Wireless LAN medium access control (MAC) and physical layer (PHY) specifications

22. IEEE Standards 802.15 1–2005, Part 15.1: Wireless medium access control (MAC) and physical layer (PHY) specifications for wireless personal area networks (WPANs) (2005)

23. Jablon, D.P.: Strong password-only authenticated key exchange. ACM SIGCOMM Comput. Commun. Rev. 26(5), 5–26 (1996)

24. Kalodner, H., Carlsten, M., Ellenbogen, P., Bonneau, J., Narayanan, A.: An empirical study of Namecoin and lessons for decentralized namespace design. In: Proceedings of the Workshop on the Economics of Information Security (WEIS) (2015)

25. Kim, T.H.J., Huang, L.S., Perring, A., Jackson, C., Gligor, V.: Accountable key infrastructure (AKI): a proposal for a public-key validation infrastructure. In: Proceedings of the 22nd International Conference on World Wide Web, pp. 679–690 (2013)

26. Laur, S., Nyberg, K.: Efficient mutual data authentication using manually authenticated strings. In: Pointcheval, D., Mu, Y., Chen, K. (eds.) CANS 2006. LNCS, vol. 4301, pp. 90–107. Springer, Heidelberg (2006). https://doi.org/10.1007/11935070_6

27. Laurie, B., Langley, A., Kasper, E.: Certificate transparency. RFC 6962, IETF (2013)

28. Lichtblau, E.: Judge tells Apple to help unlock iPhone used by San Bernardino Gunman, July 2015. http://www.nytimes.com/2016/02/17/us/judge-tells-apple-to-help-unlock-san-bernardino-gunmans-iphone.html

29. Melara, M.S., Blankstein, A., Bonneau, J., Felten, E.W., Freedman, M.J.: CONIKS: Bringing key transparency to end users. In: Proceedings of the USENIX Security Symposium, pp. 383–398 (2015)

30. Nakamoto, S.: Bitcoin: A peer-to-peer electronic cash system (2008)
31. O'leary, D., D'agostino, V., Re, S.R., Burney, J., Hoffman, A.: Method and system for processing internet payments using the electronic funds transfer network, US Patent Application number 13/789,826 (2013)
32. Petraschek, M., Hoeher, T., Jung, O., Hlavacs, H., Gansterer, W.N.: Security and usability aspects of man-in-the-middle attacks on ZRTP. J. Univ. Comput. Sci. **14**(5), 673–692 (2008)
33. Ryan, M.D.: Enhanced certificate transparency and end-to-end encrypted mail. In: Proceedings of the Network and Distributed System Security Symposium (2014)
34. Shamir, A.: Identity-based cryptosystems and signature schemes. In: Blakley, G.R., Chaum, D. (eds.) CRYPTO 1984. LNCS, vol. 196, pp. 47–53. Springer, Heidelberg (1985). https://doi.org/10.1007/3-540-39568-7_5
35. Shin, L.: Canada has been experimenting with a digital fiat currency called CAD-COIN (2016), March 2017
36. Szalachowski, P., Chuat, L., Perrig, A.: PKI Safety Net (PKISN): addressing the too-big-to-be-revoked problem of the TLS ecosystem. In: 1st IEEE European Symposium on Security and Privacy (2016)
37. Szalachowski, P., Matsumoto, S., Perrig, A.: PoliCert: secure and flexible TLS certificate management. In: Proceedings of the 2014 ACM SIGSAC Conference on Computer and Communications Security, pp. 406–417. ACM (2014)
38. Vaudenay, S.: Secure communications over insecure channels based on short authenticated strings. In: Shoup, V. (ed.) CRYPTO 2005. LNCS, vol. 3621, pp. 309–326. Springer, Heidelberg (2005). https://doi.org/10.1007/11535218_19
39. Wood, G.: Ethereum: A secure decentralised generalised transaction ledger. Ethereum Project Yellow Paper (2014)
40. Wu, T.D.: The secure remote password protocol. In: Proceedings of the Internet Society Symposium on Network and Distributed System Security, vol. 98, pp. 97–111 (1998)
41. Yu, J., Ryan, M., Cremers, C.: DECIM: detecting endpoint compromise in messaging. Technical report (2015)
42. Zimmermann, P., Johnston, A., Callas, J.: ZRTP: media path key agreement for unicast secure RTP. RFC 6189 (2011)

Key Exchange with the Help of a Public Ledger
(Transcript of Discussion)

Thanh Bui$^{(\boxtimes)}$

Aalto University, Espoo, Finland
thanh.bui@aalto.fi

In this talk, I am going to present an application of public ledgers, which is to support authenticated key exchanges. I will start by reviewing the current solutions for authenticated key exchanges and describe the observation that motivated this work.

We have been all familiar with man-in-the-middle (MitM) attacks where an attacker pretends to be Bob to Alice and pretends to be Alice to Bob so that it can then intercept all the messages between them. The traditional way to present this type of attacks requires some root of trust between the parties. For example, it can be some trusted third-party, such as a certificate authority in TLS, or it can be a shared master key or master password between the parties. In case of device pairing where there is usually not any root of trust between the devices, user interaction is required for key exchanges. Such user interaction can be, for example, key fingerprint comparison or short code comparison. Our observation is that these solutions help to guarantee a consistent view between the endpoints. We can see that when the conversation is in under a MitM attack, Alice and Bob will see different public keys and they also come up with a different shared secret.

Our proposal is that we can publish all the key exchange parameters to a globally consistent ledger. This way, when there is MitM attack, the endpoints will see that there are two key exchanges in the ledger, and they will stop the key exchange as a result. In the rest of the talk, I will explain in details the protocol and the applications that it might be useful for.

Now, I will talk about the public ledger that we require for this protocol to work. The main property that we need from the ledger is global consistency. It means that anyone that reads information from the ledger will not see conflict results. Another property that we require is fairness, meaning that the ledger has to accept all valid submissions. It might require some fee like the transaction in Bitcoin, though. Also, the ledger should not place too much trust on any single party.

At the moment, there are two common architectures for public ledgers. The first one is totally distributed. A notable example of this is Bitcoin. All of these properties that we need are guaranteed by an open peer-to-peer network and a competitive mining process. The second architecture is that of the certificate transparency. It is more centralized with an untrusted third party that manages all the ledger content and several independent auditors that audit its behavior.

© Springer International Publishing AG 2017
F. Stajano et al. (Eds.): Security Protocols 2017, LNCS 10476, pp. 137–143, 2017.
https://doi.org/10.1007/978-3-319-71075-4_16

We are not going to propose any new ledger design here, but we just assume that a ledger that satisfies all of our requirements exists and use it for our protocol.

Let's see how we can use the public ledger for key exchanges. I will start with the protocol for a simple but unrealistic scenario, where the ledger can only support only one key exchange ever in the whole world: First, the two entities perform an unauthenticated key exchange, such as Diffie-Hellman with each other. One entity then submits an event containing the key exchange's data to the ledger. The event can a hash of the public keys or a hash of the shared secret. Next, both entities check with the ledger that how many key exchanges have been done. If they see that there are more than one key exchange in the ledger, it means that there has been a MitM attack and they should drop the key exchange.

Hugo Jonker: How do you ensure that A and B have the same view of the ledger?

Reply: With a distributed ledger like Bitcoin, that can be ensured with the peer-to-peer network and the mining process. On the other hand, with a centralized ledger like certificate transparency, users can query the auditor to see whether they share the same view of the ledger.

Ross Anderson: I really like this idea but there are a couple of practical drawbacks, though. The first is if I set up a key for example with a calendar to communicate and we both post the hash of our view of the key exchange to the blockchain. It takes nowadays, what, twenty four hours? So this is an issue of latency and there is an issue of volume. If you've got a billion social networks and users, and we all make a friend a day. The transaction rate is way beyond the capacity with existing blockchains. Nonetheless, this is a good idea and perhaps may provide some incentive to think about authentication protocols and authentication that comes after the initial key exchange. Further it can be used to drive the construction of blockchains with very much more serious footprint.

Peter Y A Ryan: If I can ask a question not related to public ledger. A key establishing protocol is typically followed by a key confirmation step. Wouldn't that be here?

Reply: The key confirmation is just not shown there. You can do it afterward.

Bryan Ford: I really like this idea. I assume somewhere on the future slides you will be talking about how these parameters have to be only used once and you can use the block chain to check that and stuff, so maybe I should just encourage you to get to the next coming slide, because I'm waiting with bated breath.

So far we have seen a simple but unrealistic solution. How can we extend it to multiple key exchanges? The first solution is to tag each event in the ledger with a context C. This way, we can do one key exchange per context. The context here can be any information that the two endpoints can agree naturally or out of band. For example, the natural context could be the application name or the endpoint identifiers. In a phone call, it can be the phone number. Examples of the context that can be agreed out of band are user input or any authentication code that users can compare out of band. Anyway, this solution is still not good enough because once the context has been used, we lose it forever.

A better solution is to tag an event also with a time T. This way, we can do one key exchange per context within a period of time. We can actually consider time as a part of the context, but it must be provided by the ledger. The ledger may have already had built-in concept of time. For example, in Bitcoin, one block appears every ten minute. Thus, based on the number of blocks, we can approximately measure the time. In summary, the communication endpoints need to publish an event to the ledger with a context, and the ledger needs to timestamp it.

I have presented the protocol, and now I will show some use cases of it. As I have mentioned before, the context can be agreed naturally or out of band. Here I will list some applications that the two endpoints can agree on a context naturally.

Jiangshan Yu: How can the sender authenticate the recipient? Let's say if A talks to B and the attacker simply pretends itself as B to the ledger and B does not know he is receiving request from A. So do the users need to go through the entire blockchain for the entire history to detect this attack?

Reply: You're right. It's an impersonation attack, and I will come back to that later. Now I am just discussing about the MitM attack because it is the main idea of this protocol.

Let's get back to the applications of the protocol. The first one is IoT hub. When we want to associate IoT devices to a hub, those devices will connect to the first hub that they can discover. This hub can be in the local network, or it can be anywhere over the Internet. The context that can be used for the key exchange between the devices and the hub here would be the hub ID.

Partha Das Chowdhury: If I am a sensor and I connect to a hub, can the hub distinguish between a legitimate sensor and a malicious sensor?

Reply: If the hub accidentally exchanges key with the malicious sensor, then the real sensor's light doesn't turn on. The user will then notice that there is something wrong and reset the connection.

Another example of applications with natural context is in encrypted voice-over-IP. In this application, the context would simply be the phone numbers, and the endpoints naturally know this phone number when they make a phone call. Human voice recognition and liveness detection bind the call to a specific time window. Thus, we can prevent MitM attacks without any root of trust or user interaction. The endpoints do not have to speak aloud any key hash or key fingerprint. Of course, there is the problem of voice spoofing, but if we can assume that encrypted VoIP services like Cryptophone is secure, then we can achieve the same security level but with better usability. The next example is device pairing. Let's say a user wants to pair a computer to a printer. The user would simply select a printer from a list of printers that can be seen in the local network. It would then use the device identifier as the context for the key exchange.

Now I have talked about the MitM attack, and now I'm going to discuss about the impersonation attack. As we can see, the ledger can prevent MitM attacks, but it cannot do anything against impersonation. Specifically, the attacker can perform the impersonation attack against one endpoint and maybe denial-of-service against the other. This way, one endpoint would see one key exchange as expected, and the other wouldn't even know about this key exchange. Then, why do the protocol work for the applications that I just described? Well, the reason is that the user can check out of band that both endpoints have completed the key exchange. That is enough to ensure that there is no impersonation attack, because the ledger ensures that there can be only one key exchange and if both endpoints have completed the key exchange, then they must have done it with each other, not with any attacker.

Jiangshan Yu: If I am understanding correctly, what you are saying is that after the computation has been completed, you need another out-of-band channel to confirm that the conversation has indeed happened between the two parties, right?

Reply: We need an out-of-band channel to ensure that the key exchange has completed on both sides.

Jiangshan Yu: But do you mean both parties have to be online simultaneously? Can't there be communication starting from one party and the other party might not be presented?

Reply: It's a good point. One requirement for this key exchange to work is that both parties need to be online at the same time. So it's really an application-specific protocol.

Jiangshan Yu: Why can't we just use the out-of-band channel directly, saying that I just give you a call and this is the hash value of the key exchange?

Reply: The reason is that we want the out-of-band channel to be minimal. We don't really want any key fingerprint comparison, short string comparison, or anything like that. We just want to know that both endpoints has completed the key exchange, and it can naturally be done without any effort in many applications.

Mark Ryan: But with what data? If they just agree on a binary bit, that's not enough, because the attacker could still be doing a MitM attack.

Tuomas Aura: If you think of the example scenario where the user selects the printer that it wants to pair with, the implicit data it produces is what we call natural context. The user knows that it wants to pair with this printer.

Mark Ryan: So what is sent on this out-of-band channel?

Tuomas Aura: In this case, nothing is sent on the out-of-band channel. The only thing is if one device is paired in the end, and the other one is not. If one shows green light and the other one doesn't show green light, then something is wrong.

Mark Ryan: You're saying one bit is sent on the out-of-band channel. I don't think that would avoid man in the middle, because there could be simultaneous man in the middle and they both completed with the attacker.

Tuomas Aura: In that case, the log will have an entry saying that the device with a certain serial number has been attached to a hub. If the user interface of the hub shows that a device with that serial number is attached to me, then either it has done the key exchange directly with that device or there is a MitM attack, which means two key exchanges have been done with the same serial number for the device. Because both the device and the hub check the ledger, they would detect two entries in the ledger.

Mark Ryan: They just check that something is present in the ledger, but other things are present as well.

Tuomas Aura: No, they look for entries with that serial number of the device.

Mark Ryan: They have to search the entire ledger?

Tuomas Aura: How you search the ledger is outside this problem.

Khaled Baqer: What you want is a consistent view of how many updates the key would perform. This is what you need, right? In CONIKS[1], for example, it gives you updates about the key, the synchronization, and everything, so it's relevant to what you are doing. And asynchronous key exchange is probably what Signal does, and you can verify out of band with Signal numbers or something. Maybe you want to compare to that too. So maybe some relevant literature is usable here.

Reply: We are aware of CONIKS. The advantage of this protocol over CONIKS is that it doesn't require any long-term key. This way, users can use any key they want in a communication. Without long-term keys, it simplifies the use of multiple devices which have different keys. Also, not all entities have a public identifier so that they can use CONIKS. With our protocol, entities can agree on a context out-of-band, and that wouldn't require them to have public identifier.

Tuomas Aura: In some cases, the phone numbers or device ID are natural parts of the process, so the users would check, but you don't need to teach the users to do that. We can also add other context artificially like text codes, which the users actually has to explicitly check.

Bryan Ford: I'm trying to think around what the precise user interaction requirements are, minimal user action requirements for security are, and I like the fact that it looks like these devices don't necessarily need to have displays or display long strings or even short strings of numbers. Will this work securely if each device to be paired only has to have local area Wifi broadcast access to the ledger, a green light, a pairing button, and a confirmation button, something like that. Making the assumption that when two devices in the same general vicinity, in pairing mode and nobody's trying to attack them, and everything

---

[1] https://coniks.cs.princeton.edu/.

just happens. Only other devices around could cause DOS attacks in that case. Is this the right way to think about this? Or does that model fall over?

Tuomas Aura: At least one of the devices needs to have some kind of user interface where the user chooses or sees with whom it pairs.

Bryan Ford: Does that need to be a code? What's necessary and sufficient for that identification of the other device? Or is it sufficient to make the assumption that there will only be two devices that are trying to pair in this vicinity right now?

Tuomas Aura: That code needs to be long enough not to have collision accidentally because that would result in denial of service. For security, a minimum length code is sufficient. Let's say this protocol is used very rarely, you don't need anything to be put into the ledger. You're the only person who can pair two devices today. You do that and the devices became paired, then you check the ledger and see that today only two devices were paired, so everything is OK. That's the minimum interaction. But for public ledgers, you get collision of the public context, so that what you need to worry about.

Bruce Christianson: But you've got to be sure that the content in the ledger's the right one.

Tuomas Aura: Yes, it has to be the right one. If someone else is using the same context for another key exchange, that just results in failure of the key exchanges.

Partha Das Chowdhury: But your context is the device settings?

Tuomas Aura: It can be.

Partha Das Chowdhury: It can be, or it is in case of IoT sensors?

Tuomas Aura: I guess it would be then.

Hannan Xiao: Do you consider the man in the middle attacks between the endpoints and the ledger?

Reply: No, we assume that the connection between the endpoints and the ledger is secure.

Hugo Jonker: So, you're assuming an out-of-band. How realistic is it to have an out-of-band channel that the man in the middle can not interfere in? And if you can have that, why are you not using that channel for the key exchange?

Reply: Because we want to keep it minimum. As you can see in the example cases, the out-of-band channel that we require is the user sees that the key exchange has done.

Hugo Jonker: As you may or may not know, in Norway they had an election system that used an out-of-band channel. Then it turned out it was broken because the out-of-band channel they used was sending SMSs, and they had malware colluding on the computer and on the phone. And you have an assumption that there can be an out-of-band channel between a computer and a printer.

Tuomas Aura: The out-of-band channel is the user who sees the green light coming on the printer, meaning that it's paired, and sees the computer screen saying that "I'm here" with the printer. Then the user doesn't need to do anything. There's no communication this way, except one bit from each device to the user. If only one of them is paired, then it's up to the user to go, reset the printer and try again.

Reply: The key point here is that the ledger ensures that there can be only one key exchange per context. So if we see both endpoints have done the key exchange, then they must have been done together, not with some attacker.

Fabio Massacci: How does the printer know that it's not synchronizing with you but with me. The printer light is blinking and it might be synchronized with me. But you don't know it.

Reply: In this case, both the computer and the printer are connected to some device. However, the ledger ensures that there can be only one key exchange, so they must be connecting to each other.

Paulo Esteves Verissimo: So the model assumes that the printer can not be hacked. You have to guarantee that nothing else can lit that light, which is arguable. Otherwise, the attacker can lit the light and pair with the other device.

I will talk a little bit about denial-of-service. We don't really have a complete solution for denial-of-service for this protocol because the attacker can just spam events to the ledger. Here are some solutions that we have thought of. First, on the ledger side, we can prevent spamming by, for example, authentication the endpoint identifier. This way, the ledger becomes a trusted third party, who prevents denial-of-service attacks, but not for authentication. Another way is for the ledger to have posting fee. Of course, it can prevent massive spamming but not targeted attacks. We can also design the ledger so that it doesn't leak information about the context. For example, we can make it not completely public. An entity can only query about a context that it knows. The ledge can also be round-based, meaning that events can be written to the ledger in one round and become public in the next round. Although these solutions make it more difficult for the attacker to know when a key exchange happens, they don't prevent massive spamming. The context can be chosen so that it is difficult to guess. We can use long random device identifier as the context. However, that would require some out-of-band channel to compare the context, which is not really what we want.

Now, I will conclude this talk. I have presented an authenticated key exchange, where MitM attack are detected with global consistency of the public ledger. This protocol requires no root of trust and less out-of-band communication than previous solutions do. Furthermore, the security level does not depend on the entropy of the out-of-band message. However, we still need application-specific solutions to prevent denial-of-service and impersonation attacks.

Reconciling Multiple Objectives – Politics or Markets?

Ross Anderson[✉] and Khaled Baqer

Computer Laboratory, University of Cambridge, Cambridge, UK
{ross.anderson, khaled.baqer}@cl.cam.ac.uk

Abstract. In this paper we argue that the evolution of protocols is one of the most important yet least understood aspects of the governance of information systems. At the deepest level, security protocols determine the power structure of a system: who can do what with whom. The development, adoption, spread and evolution of protocols, and competition between them, are both political and economic activities. They may reconcile multiple objectives or be the battlefield in which one interest defeats another. They occur at all levels in the online ecosystem, from individual and small-firm action, up through organisations and networks to whole ecosystems – and may eventually play a role in shaping culture, values and norms. They play a key role in innovation: early movers may use protocols to establish a strategic advantage and lock competitors out. How can we understand such complex behaviour? In this paper we sketch a possible framework inspired by research in institutional economics.

1 Introduction

Security protocols often support not just a community of users but a business community, and evolve with it. It should be obvious that if a protocol is designed by Alice, we might expect it to suit her strategic purposes. But this can make Bob unhappy, and the protocol eventually needs to be redesigned. A mature discussion of security needs to take account of how protocols evolve. However, we rapidly get out of the space of two-player games.

Previous workshops on security protocols have discussed several examples of protocols acquiring new features until eventually they broke, as a result of feature interaction or implementation complexity. The system designed by IBM and others to encrypt PINs in a bank's ATMs was extended by Visa and others to support worldwide networks of banks, ATMs and point-of-sale devices. That led to API attacks which arose from unanticipated feature interactions [9]. It was extended further to deal with EMV smartcards, leading to further vulnerabilities and attacks [14]. The same holds for SSL/TLS, which is now more than 20 years old; it has accumulated options (such as export ciphersuites) and features (such as heartbeat) which have led to significant vulnerabilities. Because of the enormous number and diversity of users, fixes usually have to be applied at one end only; simultaneous upgrades to both clients and servers are hard [22].

© Springer International Publishing AG 2017
F. Stajano et al. (Eds.): Security Protocols 2017, LNCS 10476, pp. 144–156, 2017.
https://doi.org/10.1007/978-3-319-71075-4_17

This much is reasonably well known. At previous protocols workshops we have touched on economic models of protocols [5], asked whether in a democratic system there should be a 'loyal attacker', inspired by the 'loyal opposition' in parliament [7] and discussed crowdsourcing social trust [11]. In this paper we apply concepts from institutional economics to provide a framework for discussing the ways in which protocols evolve at different scales of organisation and time, and the effects on innovation.

The rest of the paper is organised as follows. Section 2 describes John Groenewegen's model of innovation in the electricity industry, and our proposed simplification of it for protocol analysis. Section 3 looks at protocol creep, bugfixes and tussles. Section 4 considers protocol complements and the scaling of innovation. Section 5 attempts to draw some conclusions – for the 'Internet of Things', for dispute resolution, and for the kinds of online conflict we have seen around recent elections on social media. Finally, we present our conclusions in Sect. 6.

2   The Groenewegen Model of Innovation

The institutional economist Groenewegen proposed a model of innovation in the electric power industry [16], which we copy in Fig. 1.

The point of such models is that technology evolves in ways that depend on scale, on networks, and on history. Once you've invented the battery, you can perhaps electroplate spoons with silver. In theory you could make and sell torches, but in practice the electric lamp was not invented until the dynamo came along, and electricity got much cheaper. Given these technologies, any town that already has gas lighting should replace it with electric lighting, which is cheaper. Once several towns have electric power companies, it's worthwhile for them to build a grid and perhaps even merge to get economies of scale. The utilities then become natural monopolies, which brings in regulation.

At a workshop at Schloss Dagstuhl in November 2016 we discussed this with Johannes Bauer, Thomas Maillart, Barbara Kordy, Gabriele Lenzini and Sebastian Pape and simplified it to four levels. For present purposes, we simplify it still further as in Fig. 2.

At the bottom, at level 4, are the actions of individuals or small firms; the person who invents a device, or writes a piece of software for their own use, and perhaps makes a few copies for friends. The time taken to do this can be very short, perhaps a matter of days to weeks.

At the next level up we start to industrialise, with the emergence of a substantial firm or network. This might be a physical network, such as the electric wiring installed to convert a town's gas light to electricity, or a virtual network, as where software runs on a particular type of machine. Both can support innovation. A power company that recovers its startup costs from a street lighting contract can then start selling electricity to homes, and once that's available it starts to make sense for people to invent appliances. An example of a virtual network is where firms started selling home computers in the 1980s, which led rapidly to the emergence of games companies that wrote software for them. The time constant for the emergence of a firm or network is typically 1–10 years.

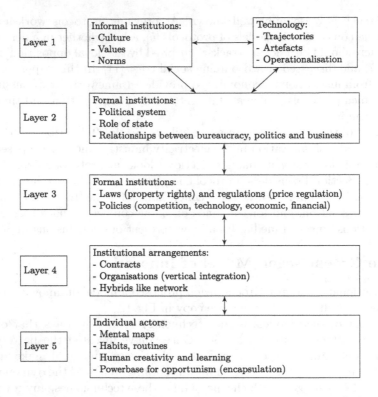

Fig. 1. Groenewegen's model of innovation, recreated from [16]

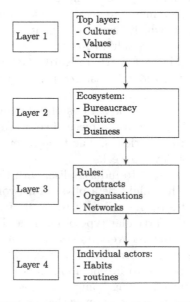

Fig. 2. Our innovation stack model

The level above that is an environment or ecosystem, of which our starting example is a power grid plus its associated regulation, standards and markets. A grid may cover a section of a large country (as in the USA) or several smaller countries or regions (as in the EU, or the grid covering Ireland and Northern Ireland). Similarly, the Internet can be seen as an environment, while large service firms like Microsoft, Google and Facebook try hard to maintain their own ecosystems: their products work better together than with their competitors' offerings. The time constant to build an ecosystem is measured in decades rather than years.

Finally, the top level is one of culture, norms, religions, or (as Groenewegen puts it) social embeddedness. Culture is slow to change, but it does indeed change in response to changes in a civilisation's underlying technology package. Putnam documented, for example, how the arrival of television noticeably cut participation in club membership and group social activities, and no doubt the spread of smartphones [21], while Pinker ascribes the Enlightenment to the spread of the novel [20]. The rapid adoption of smartphones, messaging and social media over the past decade will no doubt have an impact too. In general, the time constant of cultural change is measured in centuries; however it does occasionally happen that a noticeable change occurs in the course of a human lifetime. One might argue that the Enlightenment and the late 20th century rights revolution were such, and were at least in part facilitated by technological changes (printing and television respectively). Social conservatives may deplore one or even both of these developments; that such resistance can last for centuries merely underscores the slow pace of cultural change.

This 'innovation stack' seems an attractive way to describe and analyse innovation in fields other than electric power, as it reflects how technology entrepreneurs actually think. In the 1970s and 1980s, a small software company that had written a system to automate a sawmill (say) would then try to parametrise it and sell it to all sawmills; having done a project, you work to build it into a firm. From there, the next aspiration is to become a platform. The success of IBM, DEC and later Microsoft emphasised the value of being an ecosystem used by many industries rather than just one; during the dotcom boom, one startup after another would tell its investors it was going to be the Microsoft in some industry sector or another. Those who succeeded, such as Amazon, became household names, and this approach to business is discussed in detail by Shapiro and Varian's book "Information Rules" [23], which became the top business book in 1998. Now the largest firms such as Amazon, Apple, Google and Facebook attempt to embed themselves in culture, by not just building ecosystems around their core products but by shaping human behaviour around them and channeling it through them. At each step, ambitious firms try to move up to the next level in the stack; few succeed; but those who do reap tremendous rewards.

Can this framework give useful perspectives on how protocols evolve?

3   Protocol Evolution

We first consider three forms of protocol evolution: growth, bugfixes and tussles.

3.1   What Successful Evolution Looks Like

Our first example is the world card payment network, which can be seen as emerging from the local innovation of Diners' Club in New York in 1950; both credit and debit cards were first offered by single banks to local customers, then networked together first nationally and then internationally. The protocol history really starts with the first cash machines fielded by Barclays in 1967. Early ATMs used ad-hoc mechanisms for PIN security but rapidly converged on a methodology pioneered by IBM. A single bank could give each customer a PIN generated by encrypting their account number with a secret PIN Derivation Key, available in all the bank's ATMs and also to its central mainframe.

This was then adapted to provide dual control, so that no member of bank staff would ever see any PIN other than their own, with a view to both minimising insider fraud and defending the bank against claims from customers who had been defrauded (or pretended to be). The mechanism was to embed the cryptographic keys in tamper-resistant hardware, both in the ATM and in a Hardware Security Module (HSM) at the bank. The cards and PINs sent to customers could be sent from different data centres, or from the same centre on different days; and likewise the pairs of keys used to initialise ATMs [6].

The natural next step was to extend the communications to support interbank networking, a project driven by Visa and other card brands in the early 1980s. Further features were added, such as allowing customers to choose their own PINs. This allowed convenient worldwide ATM networking, and in due course a serpent appeared in the garden: things had become so complex that attacks started to emerge based on careless design [4] and feature interaction [14]. No sooner had the worst of these attacks been mitigated but the banks rolled out EMV, adding a further layer of complexity; and the inevitable attacks were found in due course [24].

The card payment system evolved from being a single-bank system (level 3) to being an ecosystem (level 2), and assurance failed because of a combination of bloat, feature interaction and institutional economics. As noted in [18], the implementation of EMV in Britain involves thousands of pages of specifications, as the cost of building the ecosystem was accepting backwards compatibility with a lot of legacy systems. The combination of features that led, for example, to the No-PIN attack is scattered around this huge corpus. The bank brands building the ecosystem had insufficient incentive to insist on formal verification or even adversarial review. The member banks also have conflicts of interest internally [17]: an acquiring bank that uses a less secure PIN entry device increases the risk of fraud across all local card issuers, yet it's unlikely to face more than a few percent or so of this fraud itself. Ultimately, the limits to security are about governance.

3.2   Dealing with Protocol Failure

At Indocrypt 2011, Rescorla asked why the Internet runs on pre-historic cryptography [22]. His point was that while the basic TLS protocol may be secure in theory (it was verified by Paulson in the 1990s [19]), it has been broken repeatedly in practice because of features that were not verified (such as error handling), emergent properties of implementations (such as timing), forced parameter choices (such as export ciphersuites) and add-ons (such as session resumption – to which we would nowadays add heartbeats). Yet it has proved almost impossible in practice to fix these flaws properly. A robust solution would in most cases involve changes at both ends at once, which is impractical. So long as a few percent of online shoppers still use IE version 6, almost no merchant will be prepared to move entirely to modern ciphersuites that would abandon these customers and their business.

The combination of scale and network effects means that it is cheap to tweak the code, but extremely expensive to change the architecture. TLS 1.0 dates to the 1990s; versions 1.1 and 1.2 were minor tweaks; the more significant upgrade to 1.3 is still a work in progress. Similarly, the move from magnetic-strip-based ATMs and POS transactions to the smart-based EMV involved pilots in the early 1990s, standardisation work in the late 1990s and finally a roll-out in 2002 – which is still not complete. This roll-out has involved substantial local customisation, and incremental changes are still being made to support new services and patch up vulnerabilities that get exploited. Even there, it can be slow; it took UK banks over 5 years to block the No-PIN attack [18]. In biological terms, we can see protocols as a case of punctuated equilibrium rather than gradualism. Cladogenesis – the creation of new species – is not however down to a near-extinction natural event, but to richer forms of competition and conflict.

3.3   Dealing with Conflict

Many of the interesting cases arise when an incumbent protocol is challenged. In 2012 we wrote of how the overlay payment service Sofortüberweisung (Sofort) challenged the incumbent giro payment system operated by banks in Germany and Austria [7]. Germany in particular has many small banks who did not operate very competitive payment services; Sofort built a system that would enable account holders to log into their bank accounts via its systems and make easy, rapid payments for online purchases. In effect, it was performing a Man-in-The-Middle (MiTM) attack on the German banking system, and providing a better, cheaper payment service that pleased both customers and merchants. The banks sued, accusing Sofort of inducing their customers to break the terms and conditions under which their accounts were operated. The competition authorities intervened, advising the court that the competition brought by Sofort was socially beneficial. The case was stayed and Sofort duly acquired a banking license.

In that case, the effect of a challenge to an established ecosystem was that the challenger established itself as a player and slightly improved or extended the ecosystem's services. The same pattern can be found in a number of other cases:

- During the dotcom boom, a number of new payment service firms sprung up to challenge the credit card industry, which is dominated by the Visa-Mastercard duopoly and thus somewhat slow-moving; the winner, PayPal, has in effect become a leading credit card acquirer, although it also has its own payment mechanism for personal account holders to use.
- The establishment by Android and Apple of phone payment mechanisms from 2011 was also intended as a challenge to the credit card duopoly[1] but did not really take off until after contactless credit cards became mainstream, leading retailers to upgrade their terminal fleets; it is now, like PayPal, a minor add-on to the credit card ecosystem.

There have also been cases where the absence of a viable incumbent enabled a protocol to establish a new ecosystem rather than just slightly extending an existing one:

- About 200 mobile-phone payment systems have been set up in various less developed countries, and about 20 of them have become mainstream[2]. In such protocols, the payer sends an encrypted SMS message or USSD command to a payment server ordering it pay a certain sum to a given phone number; the payee gets a message certifying receipt. The killer app was migrant remittances in an environment where most people had no access to conventional banking services but where mobile phones were spreading rapidly. The best-known is Kenya's M-Pesa whose operator Safaricom processes payments amounting to a substantial proportion of Kenya's GDP[3], becoming a larger payment service provider than any local bank, and has also become the monopoly Mobile Network Operator. In this case, regulation can be used after a monopoly establishes its presence to thwart attempts by newcomers to disturb the innovation stack and undermine the monopolist's control: the monopoly (Safaricom) uses regulation to accuse innovators of undermining its service, and thereby stalling the innovators' efforts in lengthy legal battles[4]. Moreover, attempts over the past ten years to set up similar phone payment systems in developed countries (such as Pingit and PayM in Britain) have

---

[1] Full disclosure: the first author assisted with the design of Android Pay while a scientific visitor at Google.

[2] See GSMA's 'Mobile for Development' website (using the *Mobile Money* filter): http://www.gsma.com/mobilefordevelopment/tracker.

[3] See mobile payment statistics at the Central Bank of Kenya: https://www.centralbank.go.ke.

[4] For example, see Safaricom's battle with Equity bank over the bank's use of overlay SIMs to circumvent the restrictions on phones (https://www.standardmedia.co.ke/business/article/2000135850/safaricom-loses-battle-to-block-equity-bank-s-thin-sim-card), and Safaricom's battle with BitPesa (https://www.bitpesa.co/blog/bitpesa-v-safaricom/).

generated little traction, as people in such countries already have plenty ways of paying both online and offline.
- The SSL/TLS protocol was different. It was the outcome of a challenge by Netscape in 1995 to a protocol suite, SET, that was getting too complex and difficult to implement. SET was a large collaboration between industry players (including Netscape and Microsoft) and the banking industry (Visa and Mastercard) to design a standard online credit card payment system. However, there were too many players, the specification got too complex, and implementing it would have required every bank to certify the public keys not just of its merchants but all its cardholders. It became clear that many banks would take years to even get online; large-scale certificate issuance was going to leave many potential customers stranded. SSL gave a quick and dirty way to get card transactions online, with only the merchants having to buy certificates – which they could do from third-party CAs.

In the case of SSL/TLS, the cost of not authenticating both ends of the transaction was phishing; but that only got going until 2005, ten years after SSL was first launched. SSL/TLS does however requires certification of the public keys of servers at least. This brings us to the topic of how the evolution of a protocol can be affected by externalities, such as required complementary services.

4 Protocol Complements and Scaling

Public-key cryptography started off as a monopoly protected by the Diffie-Hellman and RSA patents; the operating company, RSA Data Security, issued certificates as a service to customers. This was spun off in 1995 as Verisign, and as the patents reached their end of life, this company became the next big money-spinner [3]. During the dotcom boom, it established a dominant position by purchasing rivals such as Thawte. However various nation states and others pressured Microsoft to put their root keys into the browser, so as to facilitate interception, leading to several hundred organisations becoming 'trusted'.

Iran was excluded, and hacked DigiNotar so as to be able to run MiTM attacks on dissidents. This led to the industry, led by Google, excluding Diginotar and thus terminating its business. The resulting disruption, which included multiple Dutch government departments not being able to offer their usual online services until they had acquired new certificates from elsewhere, was a shock to the industry. The result was a 'flight to quality' with most extended-validation certificates now issued by Verisign (now owned by Symantec), with Comodo the next largest. These CAs are considered "too big to fail" despite the fact that Verisign also suffered a data breach in 2010 and the Iranians also got Comodo certificates at one point [10].

This is not the first time the fight has been over complements to an ecosystem; IBM used its patents on punched cards as a key tool in its fight against Remington Rand and others for dominance of the tabulating machine market in the 1930s [2]. Shapiro and Varian discuss other cases of complements being used for leverage in battles to dominate markets with network externalities [23].

A key question however is scope. For example, the 'Internet of Things' is shaping up to be not one ecosystem but many, in each of which the objects sold by a vendor communicate with its cloud services and through them to a user's phone. There is no real reason for the security protocols to be standard TLS, except perhaps in that the phone app may embed a lot of ad networks that need to rely on standards [8].

The lack of standards can cause real problems, such as in the failure to provide for the home area network (HAN) in the smart meter ecosystem promoted in the EU [1]. Different Member States adopted different standards for communication with appliances in the home, with none of them gaining enough traction to appeal to appliance vendors. As a result, it looks like the Google Nest standards may prevail. The EU regulators should have standardised local interconnectivity first if they wanted meters and appliances to communicate directly rather than via third-party service firms. In this case too, the scope of complements had a critical effect on scaling.

A further computer-science approach is to think in terms of centralisation versus distribution. In practical terms, the world of IT has spent 50 years centralising things and putting them online. But it does have limits, and these are often as much political as technical; data localisation laws, local telecoms regulation and bank supervision are three salient examples. Last year we talked about DigiTally[5], where an overlay network can be used to do an end-run round an incumbent payment system that's entrenched thanks to a mobile network monopoly; there too, however, there is a centralised issuer. In this particular case the multiple protocols (GSM for basic communications and then SMS or overlay for two competing or complementary payment systems) can compete in the normal commercial and political arenas. There we learned that one should always ask: where is the choke point? The incumbent's control of the agent network is one of the foundations of its monopoly, along with its control of the API and the dominant telco (that the government is a shareholder also doesn't harm them in this context). However, this is not always purely technological. For mobile payments in Kenya it is the 40,000 agents who turn banknotes into bits. The DigiTally case study reminds us that this is likely to come down to the sort of economics that competition policy people worry about, namely how institutions work in the real world, and the tussles between them.

5   New Directions

The established literature on information economics already notes the importance of innovation in the success of a platform [23]. Windows (and before it Unix and the IBM ecosystem) succeeded by providing a platform on which millions of programmers could innovate. When people bought the platform, they gained access to the products of other innovators in the same ecosystem. The

---

[5] See our previous SPW paper [12], CCS 2016 keynote (https://www.cl.cam.ac.uk/~kabhb2/DigiTally/docs/ccs-vienna-2016.pdf), and the DigiTally project: (https://www.cl.cam.ac.uk/~kabhb2/DigiTally/).

positive feedback thus created led to platform success. The smart meter HAN failed because people could not innovate; the default for an appliance maker is to enable their equipment to be controlled remotely by the customer's phone via their own server.

Innovation is not just a matter of software; people also innovate by setting up websites to support their hobbies and interests, or their social life. The effect of scale here is less studied. However, we might estimate that while millions of programmers benefited from the Windows platform as a space in which they could innovate, the world-wide web increased this by an order of magnitude. It enabled tens of millions of people to create websites by the mid-2000s; writing HTML is easier than writing programs.

Since then, social media has increased the scale by two further orders of magnitude. Facebook currently claims 1.9 billion active users, while networks in China and Russia have hundreds of millions more. All you need to do is upload a picture, click on a few friends and you're away. Part of Facebook's secret sauce was minimising the amount of expertise and effort required to join.

Once just about everyone's online, almost everything bubbles up, from cat pictures to hate speech. In fact, Grossman notes that much of the unpleasantness online is just a democratisation of the unpleasantness previously seen from tabloid newspapers and even state propaganda organisations: xenophobia, smears, doxxing and other personal attacks [15].

At this point, the protocol researcher might ask, 'What's missing?'

Our 'starter for ten' is recourse. Pinker describes how human conflict has dropped in stages from a high level in pre-state societies to the low levels found today in most societies, and that the largest single fall was associated with the emergence of the state.

The king provided justice, both as redress post facto, and as laws governing such matters as land and marriage to minimise the number of disputes arising in the first place. Gambetta's studies of organised crime show that where justice is not provided effectively by the state, there will be a temptation for private actors to do it – and we do indeed find various kinds of Mafia online, such as Dread Pirate Roberts and his Silk Road. Other options include industries able to provide recourse as a service, such as the credit card system.

But a purely technical solution cannot be enough. If the purpose of the state is to resolve disputes, it's not enough to have an army to monopolise military force in the jurisdiction and a college of judges to rule on individual cases. A state is more than that. States historically were tied up with culture and religion; they were as socially embedded as could be. From the elaborate negotiations used by pre-state tribes to end feuds through the gruesome public executions of early kings, justice evolved in society with splendid ritual: the English travelling judge in his wig and robes was the emissary of the King's Peace, and the jury men he swore to try cases embedded the verdicts in the local community (or at least in its elite). Law became democratic as society did; Blackstone describes its evolution as a 'long march from status to contract' [13]. This works at many levels; at the top level, of course, we elect our legislators, whose job it is to deal with gaps that emerge between laws and social norms. As a result, most of the people internalise the important rules most of the time.

The dispute resolution system must be one that people actually believe in. This belief ultimately has its roots in lived experience. The classic security engineering view that 'a trusted system is one that can break my security policy' [6] may be a good heuristic for reasoning about mechanism, but it is not enough to reason about how systems are embedded in society, especially when people feel anxious about globalisation, frustrated by call centres and infuriated when 'computer says no'. Perhaps it's not enough to assume we have an impartial "judge", who combines competence at cryptologic mathematics with effective competence in the real world. Perhaps we have to start asking "To whom am I really proving this?" Perhaps we have to start thinking about crowdsourced mediation or arbitration: in short, about juries.

6   Conclusions

Shapiro and Varian's classic "Information Rules" [23] is almost twenty years old but still has much to say about how security protocols succeed or fail. We have discussed a number of examples familiar to the protocols community, notably payment protocols and SSL/TLS. There are interesting issues around peer competition, and hacking everything from insulin pumps to tractors.

What we've tried to do here is organise the accumulated experience from 25 years of protocol workshops in an institutional economics framework.

Lessons learned include that if you want something to succeed you'd better think hard about how it will be open to innovation by others. Alternatively, as we've seen in mobile payment systems used in less developed countries, regulation can be used after a monopoly establishes its presence to thwart attempts by newcomers to disturb the innovation stack and undermine the monopolist's control.

Who are the innovators – programmers, micro-entrepreneurs from bloggers to small firms, or everybody? Who will resolve disputes, and how? The framework we've proposed suggests that it's not enough to have a resolution mechanism that can be verified using a logic of belief. It must be a mechanism in which people actually believe. This is a topic that protocol researchers have barely touched; the closest attempts so far may be on human auditability of digital elections. Yet even those require people to trust mathematicians and other experts. The events of 2016 suggest that expert opinion is not always enough. If protocols are the tools of power in a digital age, how can they win genuine acceptance? The crowdsourced reputation systems operated by firms such as Tripadvisor and eBay may indicate a possible direction of travel. If people feel they don't have a voice any more, to the point that using customer feedback properly can give a travel agency or auction house a real advantage, then in what circumstances might it be possible to extend this to dispute resolution?

Acknowledgements. We are grateful to Johannes Bauer, Thomas Maillart, Barbara Kordy, Gabriele Lenzini and Sebastian Pape for the discussions at Schloss Dagstuhl referred to in Sect. 2, and to workshop participants for the discussions there.

References

1. Directive 2009/28/EC of the European Parliament and of the Council of 23 April 2009 on the promotion of the use of energy from renewable sources and amending and subsequently repealing Directives 2001/77/EC and 2003/30/EC. European Parliament (2009)
2. The IBM punched card. IBM Inc (2017)
3. Verisign. Wikipedia (2017)
4. Anderson, R.: Why cryptosystems fail. In: Proceedings of the 1st ACM Conference on Computer and Communications Security, pp. 215–227. ACM (1993)
5. Anderson, R.: The initial costs and maintenance costs of protocols. In: Christianson, B., Crispo, B., Malcolm, J.A., Roe, M. (eds.) International Workshop on Security Protocols. LNCS, vol. 4631, pp. 336–343. Springer, Heidelberg (2005). https://doi.org/10.1007/978-3-540-77156-2_42
6. Anderson, R.: Security Engineering. Wiley, Hoboken (2008)
7. Anderson, R.: Protocol governance: the elite, or the mob? In: Christianson, B., Malcolm, J., Stajano, F., Anderson, J. (eds.) International Workshop on Security Protocols. LNCS, vol. 7622, p. 145. Springer, Heidelberg (2012). https://doi.org/10.1007/978-3-642-35694-0_16
8. Anderson, R.: Making security sustainable. Commun. ACM (forthcoming)
9. Anderson, R., Bond, M., Clulow, J., Skorobogatov, S.: Cryptographic processors-a survey. Proc. IEEE **94**(2), 357–369 (2006)
10. Arnbak, A., Asghari, H., Van Eeten, M., Van Eijk, N.: Security collapse in the HTTPs market. Commun. ACM **57**(10), 47–55 (2014)
11. Baqer, K., Anderson, R.: Do you believe in Tinker Bell? The social externalities of trust. In: Christianson, B., Švenda, P., Matyáš, V., Malcolm, J., Stajano, F., Anderson, J. (eds.) International Workshop on Security Protocols. LNCS, vol. 9379, pp. 224–236. Springer, Heidelberg (2015). https://doi.org/10.1007/978-3-319-26096-9_23
12. Baqer, K., Bezuidenhoudt, J., Anderson, R., Kuhn, M.: SMAPs: short message authentication protocols. In: Anderson, J., Matyáš, V., Christianson, B., Stajano, F. (eds.) Security Protocols 2016. LNCS, vol. 10368, pp. 119–132. Springer, Cham (2017). https://doi.org/10.1007/978-3-319-62033-6_15
13. Blackstone, W.: Commentaries on the Laws of England, vol. 2. Collins & Hannay, New York (1830)
14. Bond, M., Anderson, R.: API-level attacks on embedded systems. Computer **34**(10), 67–75 (2001)
15. Grossman, W.: Don't die interview, 21 October 2016. www.nodontdie.com
16. Künneke, R.W., Groenewegen, J., Auger, J.F.: The Governance of Network Industries: Institutions, Technology and Policy in Reregulated Infrastructures. Edward Elgar Publishing, Cheltenham (2009)
17. Murdoch, S.J., Bond, M., Anderson, R.: How certification systems fail: lessons from the ware report. IEEE Secur. Privacy **10**(6), 40–44 (2012)
18. Murdoch, S.J., Drimer, S., Anderson, R., Bond, M.: Chip and PIN is broken. In: 2010 IEEE Symposium on Security and Privacy (SP), pp. 433–446. IEEE (2010)

19. Paulson, L.C.: Inductive analysis of the internet protocol TLS. ACM Trans. Inf. Syst. Secur. (TISSEC) **2**(3), 332–351 (1999)
20. Pinker, S.: The Better Angels of Our Nature: The Decline of Violence in History and its Causes. Penguin, London (2011)
21. Putnam, R.D.: Bowling alone: America's declining social capital. J. Democracy **6**(1), 65–78 (1995)
22. Rescorla, E.: Stone knives and bear skins: why does the internet still run on pre-historic cryptography. INDOCRYPT (Invited talk) (2006)
23. Shapiro, C., Varian, H.R.: Information Rules: A Strategic Guide to the Network Economy. Harvard Business Press, Brighton (1998)
24. Youn, P., Adida, B., Bond, M., Clulow, J., Herzog, J., Lin, A., Rivest, R.L., Anderson, R.: Robbing the bank with a theorem prover. Technical report, University of Cambridge, Computer Laboratory (2005)

Reconciling Multiple Objectives – Politics or Markets?
(Transcript of Discussion)

Ross Anderson[(⊠)]

University of Cambridge, Cambridge, UK
ross.anderson@cl.cam.ac.uk

Ross Anderson: Well if we have to reconcile multiple objectives, game theory suggests that there are two ways of doing this: you can use politics or you can use markets. You can cooperate or you can fight. If you want to get something you can't produce yourself, you either produce something and trade it, or you go out with your friends with pointy sticks or with ballot boxes and take it some other way. Game theory gives us at least the beginnings of a framework for understanding how people make these choices.

For the past 25 years, this workshop has been about seeing protocols breaking as they evolve, and I think one thing we've learned over the period is that this is about power. It can be economic, or it can be political. In previous workshops, we've touched on this. In 2012 for example, we asked whether democracy calls for a loyal attacker, like a loyal opposition; I gave the example of Sofortüberweisung, the payment system in Germany that provides an overlay payment service to compete with Visa and Mastercard. Two years ago, Khaled and I talked about crowdsourcing social trust.

What we put our minds to this time is whether there's a more systematic way of modelling the politics of protocol change that's a bit north of basic game theory – fairly general, but gives us something that we can actually talk about. The inspiration comes from a chap called John Groenewegen who's a recently retired institutional economist at Delft, and who studies innovation in the electric power industry. He's come up with a model (which is too small to read here) and in any case is an inspiration rather than something we're going to use directly.

Last year at Dagstuhl, we brainstormed a bit about this with Richard Clayton and one or two other people, and we simplified it to a four-level innovation stack. This is taking away the industry-specific stuff from Groenewegen's model. At the top layer, you've got cultures, values, norms – civilization, call it what you will. This is the thing that persists for hundreds of years, and changes only very, very slowly.

The next layer down, you've got an ecosystem. You've got a confluence of economics, of politics, of business. This takes place over a period of decades. Examples of ecosystem change: collapse of the Warsaw Pact; Britain joining the EU in the 70s; Britain leaving the EU in a couple of years time. That's the scale of the ecosystem, of how things come together on a scale between culture and organisations.

© Springer International Publishing AG 2017
F. Stajano et al. (Eds.): Security Protocols 2017, LNCS 10476, pp. 157–170, 2017.
https://doi.org/10.1007/978-3-319-71075-4_18

And then you've got the everyday rules: the organisations, the contracts, the networks. This is where you get change on a period of perhaps a decade, that it might take you to build up a company, to establish a new protocol, to establish a new way of writing software or whatever.

At the bottom, of course, you've got individual actors. The things that we do every day, for and to each other – habits, routines, transactions – which may be mediated by markets or by manners.

The obvious thing here is that the time constants change between layers, and that crossing up to the next layer is hard. People try and build their businesses into ecosystems. A very small number succeed: IBM, Microsoft, Standard Oil, James Watt with his steam engines. He didn't get to control the ecosystem, but certainly the steam engine changed the global trading ecosystem because it made ship transport rapid and reliable.

If we use this as a framework, can we start to classify changes in protocols? I think that the usefulness of such a model is that it does give us a handle on the kind of protocol changes we've been discussing here over many years. ATM encryption is designed for single banks by IBM and some other companies; it extends to multiple banks by Visa; the company becomes an ecosystem; in the process, it acquires the complexity and we get the API attacks. EMV is an evolution of the same ecosystem and suffers from the same birth defects: too many legacy banks; too many legacy national networks; too many features; nothing like strict central governance. You get No-PIN attacks, pre-play attacks, and so on. Features plus institutional economics breaks the assurance, and this we can think of as a hallmark of when a company becomes an ecosystem. Or we could talk alternatively about how Windows APIs became horribly complex as Microsoft developed its ecosystem, and they were used in various lock-in and other plays. This is the same sort of thing going on.

Case two. Protocol bugfixes. We've seen a dozen attacks on TLS in the past 15 years or so. Kenny Patterson has some information collected on this. Whenever you find a new timing attack, or error attack or session resumption attack, then you have to fix it at one end, because there's still a few percent of shoppers using Internet Explorer version 6, and merchants are not prepared to say goodbye to their business. People like Eric Rescorla have written about this at great length. About how you end up being able to tweak open SSL code but not architecture, because that's the way things work once you get these two-sided market effects going. If you're going to talk about protocol evolution, this brings in mind the debate you have in biology between punctuated evolution and gradual evolution. Or as they say in zoology, 'the creeps versus the jerks'. This suggests that when we come to protocol evolution, these two-sided markets effects put us solidly in the category of punctuated evolution. At the level of business dynamics, you can see these as being minor skirmishes to defend an ecosystem – which, in the process, make it more rigid and in various interesting ways less adaptable.

Case three. Protocol tussles. See our paper on Sofort in 2012. Another example: Android Pay. Another example: SSL/TLS vs. SET, STT and SEPP, if you go back to 1996. This is standard incumbent versus challenger play, which you see written about at great length in Shapiro and Varian's classic book. What's happening here is that you've got all-out wars over ecosystem boundaries or mechanisms. Will it be IBM or will be Apple which controls the desktop – and all the things that come from that? This is something about which very large amounts have been written by people who write books on technology policy. Maybe we can just learn from these books and don't have anything to contribute ourselves.

Well, maybe not so fast, because in the protocol world, we've also got this interesting case of protocol complements. Jim Bidzos in the late 1990s realised the revenue from Public Key Partners was about to tail off because the RSA patent was due to expire in 2002. What do you do about that? Well, you set up Verisign, and you sell this wonderful idea of the certification authority, and you arrange that everyone needs to go and pay $10 every year to refresh their certificate. At the time, if you were around, you would remember that people got very, very bullish and bubbly about the prospects for Verisign and its former competitor Baltimore. Baltimore got into the FTSE 100 stock index by promising investors that within a few years, everyone would have to pay £10 every other year in order to refresh the public key certificate for their toaster. Well, the Internet of Things is about to happen, and perhaps you'll see that coming along.

Then, of course, you had this huge big fight whereby the spook agencies wanted to get their certs in too. There were big debates over whether, for example, the Turkish government's certs should be in software shipped in America and Britain, and Iran being excluded hacked Diginotar – and you've got the flight to quality and certificate pinning and all the rest of it. Now we perhaps have a good view of this fight, but it's an odd and interesting fight, because it's a fight over complements. If you've got an open ecosystem, which you might roughly call TLS, how do people make money? We fight about the secret sauce that you've got to have alongside it in order to make it all work.

How might the Internet of Things change things? Much could be said about this. Let me define an Internet of Things, and I'll use the capital T for Things. This consists of a microecosystem of a Thing, which is an object that has got a microprocessor and software and communications in it, which communicates to the cloud, which communicates to an app on your phone. So a Thing with a capital letter is a thing that you can control from your phone with the assistance of some third party who may or may not sell your information to the spammers.

So what can we predict with protocols here? The interesting thing about the Thing is that all of a sudden the dominance of the global ecosystem of TLS is shattered. There is no particular reason why your Things should talk to your phone through the Thing vendor's cloud using a standard protocol, except for the fact that there exists an API to call it – it's a few lines of code, you don't have to think, and so on and so forth. But the barrier to innovation is now very, very radically reduced. When you think about it, perhaps the only thing that says that a Thing still has to have an involvement with TLS is whatever ad network you're using in the mobile phone app.

Paulo Esteves Verissimo: I missed the point. Why would you not need standardised protocols? Things can be made by a lot of different kinds of firm. Standards are something you want.

Reply: This is the point that I'm coming to next, because the original idea that many promoters of the Internet of Things seemed to have had, is that things would talk to each other – and thus the vendor of the Thing would be deprived of the opportunity to monetize them. Why should anybody have the incentive to allow Things to do something as stupid as talk to each other is not entirely clear. My worked example is the HAN – the home area network. We were promised – gosh, at least 10 years ago, perhaps 15 years ago – that we would have home area networks where your fridge would talk to your toaster to your immersion heater to your boiler, and through your electricity meter to the network. And the network would be able to say, 'There's not an awful lot of wind at the moment, and the clouds are blocking out the sunlight to the PVs, so we would really like you to use less electricity, and I just put the price up to 30p' – whereupon your home would intelligently turn off the immersion heater, and start cycling the freezer a little bit less aggressively, provided it stayed below whatever threshold it was and so on. In other words, the idea was that you would have adaptive response for all sorts of worthwhile purposes in the home.

That failed to happen. Completely failed to happen – because when the European Union brought in the Electricity Directive in 2009 they put in a mandate for smart meters but they forgot to put in a standards mandate for home area networks. So when each member state transposed it, they adopted different standards, and so if you were Mr. Samsung, you don't want to make 27 varieties of smart fridge – especially when that would undermine your chance of monetizing any information from the fridge. So you will see to it that your Samsung fridge will talk to your Samsung server and to a Samsung app. Similarly, when Canon sells you a printer, that will talk to Mr. Canon's servers in Japan, which will talk to a Canon app, and so on and so forth.

The necessary preconditions for creating an ecosystem within the home were never even remotely close to being created. The incentives are all in favour of fragmenting these protocols rather than creating an ecosystem in which one particular protocol predominates.

Unless of course, you get a powerful player who decides otherwise. At present, of course, the player in that market is Google with Nest. Because Google, through the app store, has got some influence on what apps do, and if Google becomes a dominant player in managing home energy, then perhaps – at least this is what the guys at Google think – they can get the protocols around Nest adopted by vendors of devices, and they can get the platform economics going that way. From the point of view of protocols, this is an interesting worked example, or rather, non-working example. Yes?

Paulo Esteves Verissimo: Well we have one new mobile phone protocol, which is exactly is the combination of three existing protocols. Do you see something similar happening here? Do you just see two or three or maybe 10 protocols, which can then be merged into one conglomerate protocol and then to something where people start thinking about the next level?

Reply: Well, this brings us back to our perspective, which is the next slide. How does our perspective help? Recall the innovation stack. At the top, there's culture, values, norms. Controlling that is the aim of all good dictators. How do you get your worldview across to everybody? Then there's the ecosystem, which is what you're trying to do if you want to create an environment for home innovation and you're someone like Google.

How do you get to control an ecosystem? By controlling something at the next layer down. Contracts, organisations networks. You've got a killer app, for example, and if that killer app is controlling the home thermostat – the Google idea, maybe that's your way in. If it was controlling the buying and selling of energy, your gas meter, your electricity meter, and perhaps payments that you got from the sense of turning your immersion heater off, then that would have been another platform on which you could have made a bid for ecosystem dominance.

Now how does tech in general make a difference? In the old days, stuff used to bubble up at the human level. Ideology would be something that evolved out of zillions of conversations between individuals; or you could have an individual leader, a military leader, or a religious leader who would get a tribe together, and the tribe could become a nation, and then it could become a huge movement and then it could become a worldwide religion. It's an innovation system, but in a non-technical sense. Now what's happening is that technology enables this, and protocols – and in fact software in general – can be seen as an enabler of this kind of social innovation.

What one's doing with creating a protocol is trying to build out an idea into a firm or to build a firm out into an ecosystem. What are the conditions under which a protocol may enable you to do that? Remember the incentives facing individual actors. Actors want to maximise impact. They want to be rich, famous, or both. If they're pure Darwinian operators, they want to have large numbers of grandchildren but we've got other metrics too nowadays. And the strong and the smart succeed and then try and limit innovation by others. How can a protocol empower actors? How can a protocol enable you to turn your business into an ecosystem or turn your ecosystem into total world dominance?

Let's step back a sec, and look at recourse. If the theme of the workshop is where people have got conflicting objectives, then what sort of actors might adopt a protocol? Well, competition in the business sense is an obvious one. Sofort started off when merchants got fed up paying 2.5% to Visa and Master-Card, and somebody got the idea, 'We'll let them do bank payments directly, pay less money to Visa and MasterCard – and let us take a commission of the savings.' Another example is crowd innovation: insulin pumps, for example. You can buy insulin pumps if you're diabetic, which will automatically pump insulin in response to readings from a glucose meter, but these are rather crude devices, and some people like to reprogram them so that they can get finer grained control. In order to do this, they have to hack the pumps. This makes the pump vendors worry about liability, and raises all the issues about whether the protocol should allow a certain amount of latitude for innovation in the first place.

Or look at disputes. If things go wrong, people tend to go to the government, and the government can offer redress after the fact. You sell me a rubbish thing online, I go to the county court and get an order against some of your money. Or escrow before it: I decide to buy some drugs from you on Silk Road, and so I hand my money to Dread Pirate Roberts, and when I confirm that the drugs have been received and that they burn rather satisfactorily, Dread Pirate Roberts releases the money to you. This can be a governmental arrangement, a private arrangement, various kinds of arrangements – but there are ways in which you can put redress into a protocol.

The third sort of actor that you find where people adapt a protocol is for industry to specialise a protocol for their needs. You take something off the shelf and you adapt it to what is specifically required for cars, for healthcare or whatever.

From looking at a number of cases like this, one of the things that we begin to suspect is that a key factor for success in protocols is: does the protocol support innovation of some kind? Is it possible to take the vanilla protocol, and turn it to another use? We already understand this from software platforms. The reason Bill Gates has got an awful lot of money is that the Windows platform that he built, and the DOS platform before it, enabled anybody to use the existing deployed base of PCs to write new kinds of software. So you could write a new card game. You could just as easily write control software for a sawmill. In neither case did you have to crank up a factory to make all the computers from scratch. So a key thing here is that to get people to adopt protocols, you have to create the ability to adapt protocols.

The lesson that we then get from the failure of the home area network idea in Europe is that the regulators should have put a protocol there, and they should have done it first before they worried too much about the details of the mandates, about which country would have to see to it that how many of its population adopted meters for gas and/or electricity by such and such a date. If you had provided the platform in which people could have innovated, then there was some chance that you could have had app pull rather than legislative demand push.

And in fact if you look at the Daily Telegraph today, you'll see that there's an extensive article on page 23 and also on the website about how the whole smart meter episode is running out into the sand. The smart meters aren't working right; they're not interoperable; if you change suppliers the meter becomes unsmart; you then get an email telling you to go read the meter; and a smart meter is more difficult to read than a dumb meter because you've got to press half a dozen buttons in order to actually get out a reading in numbers that you can then copy on a piece of paper and carry indoors to type into an email to the power company. Yes?

Paulo Esteves Verissimo: Going back to the original thing. You talked about access conditions. Then you seem to talk about HANs as a thing from the past or something failed. You seem to point to the regulators that should have acted. I agree with what you say, your competition has made standards work, and most of the time that's how it works.

Reply: Mm-hmm (affirmative).

Paulo Esteves Verissimo: I don't think it's too late for HANs, because actually I think the whole thing is just starting. HANs, people talked about them for ten years, but it's actually, with the smart meter thing and with the concept of a network ... So there's a network that gets to the smart meter, which is the gateway. Then, that the market make the gold. I can see that working on both sides.

Reply: Well sure, a lot of people think it's a matter of religious preference, HANs should exist, but HANs don't exist. In different countries we don't even have agreement on what the underlying radio platform should be. Should it be a low-energy Bluetooth? Should it be a variant of Zigbee? And the thing that breaks that roadblock may very well be Mr. Google rather than bureaucrats in Brussels. But the point is that the people in Brussels were trying to pull the wrong levers when they said, 'Let's have a deployment mandate.' They should have engaged the tech community in the right way to begin with to see to it that there was a way for information to flow backwards and forwards.

Paulo Esteves Verissimo: These problems happen. See the car makers. Car makers are very powerful companies. A few of them think, 'Oh, no. I'm going to do it my way,' and so on and so forth, but they haven't really. There's a substantial level of standardisation of components, not just electronics, so that they can be interchangeable, because obviously that's the way to recheck the system.

Reply: Yep.

Paulo Esteves Verissimo: That's what I will believe will happen in houses, but it's probably not mature now.

Reply: Well, I could talk some length about safety and security in cars, but that's a different talk. We have peripherals in progress about that, and I'm happy to talk about it offline. For current purposes, here's the punchline. That platforms for innovation are really the key here, because if you want to turn your product into an ecosystem, let others innovate on it. Tuomas?

Tuomas Aura: I have been wondering about this, why we don't have any HANs. There's lots of proposals for home networks and home hubs and nothing really happened. There was the Xbox, and then there are the home routers, and I was googling about, and proposals for things that are smart. It seems that the problem is that they all got closed protocols.

Reply: Yes.

Tuomas Aura: And –

Reply: That's exactly the consensus in network economics.

Tuomas Aura: Is the problem you're suggesting is that someone like a big authority in Brussels, comes up with an open platform? Or –

Reply: No.

Tuomas Aura: Or do you think there's anyone who can make this open platform?

Reply: Okay, the purpose of this talk is to explain what's going on. The entrepreneurial action that follows from it is separate. If you believe that you can do a startup that will make home networking work, then these are the sort of things that you need to think about when you're planning that startup, right? And here are some examples of how stuff succeeded. You've got Windows, Linux, and Android have done well by creating two-sided markets that bring app developers in touch with users. You have HTML, right? which extended this to web developers – and Facebook, which extended it to everybody. And all of these are about innovation of one kind or another.

Now, the existing examples which allow greater or lesser amounts of innovation – such as ATM networks, contactless, and of course TLS – can also be seen in this light. ATM networks turned out to be adaptable enough to bring tens of thousands of banks on board and to extend from ATMs to point of sale, to subway ticket machines and all sorts of other things. This is, I say, a framework in which you can start assessing how a new protocol might be useful, And if it isn't, don't waste your money on a startup to produce it. Paul?

Paul Wernick: What I'm seeing here is a situation not unlike system dynamics, which shows who influences what in terms of arrows connecting things, because there are a fair number of actors around, and they all have different degrees of influence on each other. I think that would be as helpful as thinking about specific examples, because I think it's a generic problem that goes beyond computerised technology.

Reply: Well sure, it goes beyond computerised technology, but I prefer to see these things in terms of network economics. Partha, you had your hand up.

Partha Das Chowdhury: I can see this ability to create a backbone that can talk to various (alien) devices over a VN. What concerns me is how do you fix liabilities. Consider the case of the Mirai botnet, where the CCTV cameras were manufactured in a different country so the manufacturer is not liable to laws in that country where it was being used for an attack.

Reply: In the specific case of the Xiaomei cameras, the customs man at Rotterdam should have sent that container back to China, because if you put the CE mark on a product, you're saying it adheres to all applicable standards. And we do now have a couple of ISO standards on vulnerability lifecycle management. So if you ship a CCTV camera that's got an embedded factory root password that you can't change and there's no means to upgrade the software, then such a device should a priori never be sold on the soil of the European Union. It should not be allowed in at the harbour. We've got the laws, right? Nobody's enforcing them because nobody understands this yet. But believe me, that's going to change. Until you get a catastrophe, nobody pays attention. And perhaps people not being able to use Twitter for five hours was a sufficient catastrophe (laughter) that the customs officials will start doing their job. At least we'll certainly hope so. We hope it's not going to take any fatal accidents before they get off their behinds. Joan?

Joan Feigenbaum: I have an answer to your, 'Where might new protocols be useful?' Electrical outlets. Something to prove to, so we can innovate our way out of having to carry adapters around every time we take a flight overseas.

Reply: Yes. If everybody ends up using Mac adapters!

Joan Feigenbaum: Well, Mac adapters are not the most convenient things, so it would be wonderful if some great innovator could get me out of having to take all these adapters everywhere I go.

Sven Uebelacker: Actually, I wanted to make this argument for exactly the opposite, and say, are protocols irrelevant right now? Because we are so used to translating one protocol into the next one. And MAC adapters and even the new IP developments work this way. You just combine an antenna array with software, which makes your mobile work.

Reply: It depends how you define 'protocol', and I'm going to come on just now to show that we can think of that perhaps slightly more broadly for a virtual viewpoint.

Virgil Gligor: So I agree with you that protocols should be platforms for innovation. In terms of home area networks I think people didn't find the business case to start with –

Reply: Exactly.

Virgil Gligor: And if you look at the building automation, where there is a lot of innovation, it's all based on closed networks and it's all a handful of producers that don't interoperate with other, very fragmented and not much innovation ... public innovation. There is innovation for example within Honeywell, how to manage these large buildings, and ZMax and some others – but not in terms of open protocols. They eliminated a lot of manpower, a lot of salaries, everything else. So there was prior activity. However, we did not see that all that clearly in home area networks.

Reply: Well this is well known if you look at industrial control systems protocols. Where protocols like DNP3, for example, take about 40 years to change because there are too many powerful stakeholders. So we cannot put authentication into SCADA systems before about 2040 and there will still be plenty of the current legacy being used then. So we have to reperimeterize. And that's just an example of the accumulation of protocol tweaks causing fossilisation and the two sided-market effects as well.

On the home area networks side, bear in mind that despite Bill's huge power and wealth, Microsoft was never properly motivated to cause printers to work properly. Right? Because Microsoft didn't make money out of printers. Printers were a pain. Printers were things that you had to have hundreds of in a shed in Redmond, so that you could test out all your patches every patch Tuesday. They're a source of pain rather than a source of pleasure. Is it any surprise, therefore, that when you go and buy a printer nowadays, the printer doesn't talk to anything except a server in Japan? That basically you have to email a document to someone in Japan that you don't know, from your mobile phone, in order to have it come out of your printer in your kitchen?

Is it any surprise that people are abandoning physical printing altogether, now that it's largely possible to do so? Printing was something that the modern world never managed to engineer properly, and we may very well find that because of the impossibility so far of finding good HAN protocols that make business sense, that all sorts of other current activities will just die – because nobody can make enough money from them.

Virgil Gligor: In terms of home area networks and home automation, entertainment systems evolved quite a bit – Xboxes and the like. Very successful. Microsoft, not being a hardware company, invested in Xbox and did fantastically well. But that was the limit in terms of penetrating the homes. The question is, what's the next boundary? What's the next piece of innovation that would allow the Microsofts of the world to penetrate the home? Or the Googles or the Apples?

Reply: Well, let me go on to the next slide. Thinking about scale, things like Windows, Linux and Android enabled innovation by people who knew how to write software. Let's say to a first approximation that's a million people. It might be five million, ten million, I mean, who's a programmer? Lots of people write occasional bits of code. It's, in order-of-magnitude terms, probably in the low millions worldwide.

HTML comes along and suddenly the number of people who benefit and who are empowered as producers goes up by an order of magnitude. Because it's a lot easier to put together a website that sort of works than it is to write a program that does something sort of useful. Okay, so we get an order of magnitude scale-up.

And then something that perhaps people haven't particularly thought about is when social networks came along – Facebook – that gives you a further two orders of magnitude in scale-up, because for most people in the world, maintaining their own website is too much bother. HTML looks too weird and the tools that you can use to write it are either too difficult, like emacs, or too fiddly if it's a proprietary graphical editor. So isn't it what people actually want – to open an account, drop in a photo, recruit a few of your friends and you're fine. Takes you five minutes.

So this is a way of bringing innovation to the masses. What we've also –

Fabio Massacci: But it's not the same type of innovation –

Reply: Yes, I know.

Fabio Massacci: Uploading a photo's not the same as writing a usable program.

Reply: Yes, but then it enables different types of innovation, so that the existence of things like Twitter, for example, empowers all sorts of people. Including some people that we might prefer not to have been empowered such a certain New York property developer. Now, if that New York property developer had to sit down with a box of punch cards, and encode his entire campaign in FORTRAN, then perhaps –

Virgil Gligor: We'd have been better off.

Reply: Or he would at least have learned to be a little bit more careful and meticulous with the way he organises information.

And what we've also found is that the old idea that ideology was something that evolved out of gazillions of conversations is perhaps being supplanted by mechanisms whereby you get statistical machine learning from crowdsourced data. Which of course brings its own issues of autonomy and, if you like, who's actually taking control.

You then get other side effects such as the fact that political debate moves increasingly from public spaces to private ones. And all the various strange things that we had this morning on the radio about MPs saying, 'X should be done and Y should be done about' – what were they talking about? They were talking about ticket touting. And the people who are obviously lobbying for laws to prevent secondary sales of tickets, were people who could've solved the problem perfectly easily with their own websites where they sell concert tickets, by adopting even ten percent of the smarts used by Ryanair.

So what we're seeing is a dislocation as the world goes from innovation done by people – talking about stuff, doing stuff in old fashioned human ways – to technologically empowered innovation, whereby you go and you collect your supporters, your customers, whatever, by means of platforms, by means of protocols. And then use them to build your empire.

So, anyway, that's the kind of framework for thinking that we've been trying to develop. What we'd like to suggest is that people start thinking about slightly more socially difficult test cases.

Now, as a computer scientist, your first reaction is to look for problems that might be easily soluble using theoretical computer science concepts or small-scale engineering. For example, there's a huge debate about how we get new protocols to react to emerging scale issues – things like Bitcoin. If Bitcoin can't process enough transactions per second, and now there's a day's worth of transactions and the thing's breaking because it takes you a day to get your transaction though, do you increase the block size? Do you do something different? Do you set up a separate blockchain?

But when we look at many of the problems people wrestle with, they're about dealing with what lawyers call incomplete contracts, where people make agreements with each other without always knowing the exact details in advance. When you contract with a builder to build your house, they may very well find that there's a sewer or an electricity main in the wrong place, or that there's unstable soil or whatever, and you end up having to go back and renegotiate halfway through.

So if you're a private actor, you can fix this at small scale by specifying an adjudication in the contract. You can write a contract with your builder – and in fact your builder will usually do this if you buy a house in Britain – saying that if anything comes up because of any of the following things that can go wrong, there's a process for adjudication and a procedure to go and find someone to adjudicate on it.

If you're an entrepreneur, you can try to provide this scale. And one of the reasons that the Silk Road worked is that Ross Ulbricht, the Dread Pirate Roberts that set that scheme up, set up an escrow system so that people buying drugs would leave the money in escrow for a while, so that you can see whether the drugs arrived or not. That plus a reputation system enabled the thing to work while underground markets had not worked previously.

Social adjudication can also work. Examples perhaps are Grameen Bank. And these are examples where innovation has got the chance of breaking out of narrow computer science confines and perhaps coming up with something interesting and useful. Paul?

Paul Wernick: Paul: The example you gave of building a house is quite interesting because the Guardian has been pushing recent examples where people have had great pains getting builders to do what needed to be done. Like problems building houses are inevitable. So the power seems to be with the builders. The adjudicator is an organisation funded by, and returning its profits to, the builders. And the poor house buyers were obviously stuck.

Reply: Yes well if you sign a contract like that, then more fool you.

Paul Wernick: But to build a house, that's the contract you sign!

Reply: Well, build your own then. Or alternatively, run for parliament and change the rules. But you'll find that the house builders have got more money and more power.

But the main message here is basically this; we started off seeing protocol security as being something that was fundamentally logic and mathematics. The BAN logic was hot off the press when the first of these workshops was held 25 years ago...

Bruce Christianson: 24 years ago.

Reply: I stand corrected! And then we moved to engineering. We talked about things like robustness principles – can you do something a little bit more general to deal with protocols, where proofs might, for various reasons, be inadequate? From 2001 we've had economics, fixed versus variable costs of protocols. Then we've had things like psychology, social trust. Of course, that's also a bit about crowdsourcing.

And so what I've tried to suggest today is that approaches from institutional economics might give insights into the political economy of protocols. That this isn't just a straightforward matter of the welfare theorems or of network externalities. It also matters what sort of institutions you're trying to construct, what sort of scale they are and what the relative time constants are.

And societies, if you see them as machines, are machines with a whole lot of different wheels which turn at a whole lot of different speeds, and the game that smart players are usually trying to play is to power their innovation up from the rapidly moving wheels of individual action, through corporate action, through ecosystem control, and finally, perhaps for a very few lucky individuals, world dominance.

Now, in order to do that, I'm suggesting that you need to think about how you empower others to innovate. And perhaps the interesting question in the theme of the workshop today is, 'Can we support innovation in dispute resolution?'

That is a bigger and deeper problem than just trying to preset some trade-off between, for example, privacy and law enforcement. It's a bigger and more general problem, and if we see it in terms of enabling people to negotiate, where there is the real capacity to negotiate on both sides – right? So I'm less interested in cases where states can compel, or a house building oligopoly can compel. While these are of political importance, there's relatively little play in them from the point of view of a technologically mediated platform that enables stuff to go forward. Insofar as we can contribute by engineering innovation, it's likely to be in this mucky, sticky bit in the middle where you're trying to deal with dispute resolution in the real world, where things aren't perfect. And workable second-best solutions may actually bring real progress.

Tuomas Aura: Hello, I just wanted to comment on this. I think this kind of thinking about the real economics and politics around it is really important. So I think we don't generally mention that in the research papers, but hopefully take it into account to some extent. But then, when I give to my students a design problem for security architectures or protocols, many of them propose things like, 'Let's use the security cards for registering students,' or an IOT application that changes the field in IPSEC protocol. And these are things that we cannot do when we design a system. We are stuck, we can't deal with the phone operators or change the SIM card properties or we can't change the norms or standards just for our application.

But that's not always obvious in even these basic things, it's not always obvious to new people and students who come to that area. Even going further back to the basics of what's possible to do with productive elements and innovation, it would be useful to have that preconception.

Reply: That's basically why I wrote my book – so that students coming into this field could have enough concrete cases to perhaps get some feel for what generally works and what generally doesn't. Of course, that's only a start and there's much more to go. Mark?

Mark Ryan: Can you give a bit more detail about what kind of innovation you're mentioning? This space of law enforcement versus privacy? What can the individual do?

Reply: In the space of law enforcement versus privacy, perhaps there's no play in that situation at all anymore. Certainly in Britain, the government has declared itself to be omnipotent and omnicompetent, and has declared the debate to be over. Insofar as there is a debate, it's going to be about the situation in the rest of Europe where the European Court of Justice has ruled against data retention. It's going to be in the USA where, for the time being, for better or worse, most of the data to which UK police forces want access happens to be located. And so if you want to be a privacy activist in the UK, you have to work with European and American bodies. I do, I'm off to the EDRi General Assembly at the weekend and I'm also on the advisory council of EPIC. One has to see these things in the international context.

Now, there, I suspect it's mostly about political lobbying and action. But my point here is that there are potentially many other areas where engineering innovation can bring real benefits. We have seen many cases such as the eBay and Amazon reputation systems, where reputations can do good. And there have been other cases where perhaps it does harm by locking people in to exploitative monopolies. Understanding this is important if you're to find the opportunity to do a startup that does make a positive difference.

The Seconomics (Security-Economics) Vulnerabilities of Decentralized Autonomous Organizations

Fabio Massacci[1], Chan Nam Ngo[1(✉)], Jing Nie[1], Daniele Venturi[2],
and Julian Williams[3]

[1] Department of Information Engineering and Computer Science,
University of Trento, Trento, Italy
{fabio.massacci,channam.ngo,jing.nie}@unitn.it
[2] Computer Science Department, Sapienza University of Rome, Rome, Italy
venturi@di.uniroma1.it
[3] Durham University Business School, Durham, UK
julian.williams@durham.ac.uk

Abstract. Traditionally, security and economics functionalities in IT financial services and protocols (FinTech) have been perceived as separate objectives. We argue that keeping them separate is a bad idea for FinTech "Decentralized Autonomous Organizations" (DAOs). In fact, security and economics are one for DAOs: we show that the failure of a security property, e.g. anonymity, can destroy a DAOs because economic attacks can be tailgated to security attacks. This is illustrated by the examples of "TheDAO" (built on the Ethereum platform) and the DAOed version of a Futures Exchange. We claim that security and economics vulnerabilities, which we named *seconomics vulnerabilities*, are indeed new "beasts" to be reckoned with.

Keywords: Seconomics vulnerabilities · FinTech · Security protocols
Decentralized Autonomous Organizations

1 Introduction

Several researchers have traditionally assumed that security and economics functionalities are separate objectives. We argue that for "Decentralized Autonomous Organizations" (DAO) security and economics objectives should be considered as one. A failure of a security property is not simply an annoying part *outside the protocol* (e.g. law enforcement agencies knowing you are using Bitcoin to purchase porn or shady drugs). A *failure of a security property for DAOs may lead to the collapse of the entire economic functionality because such security attack could be combined with an economic attack*. We call such vulnerabilities *seconomics* vulnerabilities.

In the past security vulnerabilities would translate to safety issues only for safety critical systems (when potentially exploited by terrorists, criminals or

© Springer International Publishing AG 2017
F. Stajano et al. (Eds.): Security Protocols 2017, LNCS 10476, pp. 171–179, 2017.
https://doi.org/10.1007/978-3-319-71075-4_19

malicious governmental actors). Loosely speaking, for DAOs every vulnerability becomes a seconomics one. Different pieces of code are not just distributed but fully under the control of the *autonomous* entities. So at the same time we have the ability to subvert the system *and* the incentives to do so.

The organization of the remainders of the paper is as follows. We first give a general description of DAOs in Sect. 2. Next a popular DAO, TheDAO, and its hard fork as a result of an attack shortly after its launch are shown in Sect. 3. Then we present the DAOed version of the Futures Exchange (Sect. 4) followed by a possible security protocol (Sect. 5). A "Price Discrimination" attack mounted from anonymity failure is described in Sect. 6. Finally, we "conclude" the paper (Sect. 7).

2   Decentralized Autonomous Organization (DAO)

A DAO is a decentralized and allegedly "democratic" organization that is available on a distributed ledger through the combination of smart contracts and a rich scripting language, e.g. Ethereum [6]. Technically, a DAO is an implementation of a financial service by encoding the computations directly into smart contracts using the scripting language. The distributed ledger, e.g. blockchain, provides the secure environment to execute the computations and store the information across the whole network and hence eliminates the need of having a central trusted party.

Historically, Bitcoin [10] has been the first practical DAO that was launched as a payment transaction network in 2008. The applications of "Proof-of-Work" and "Blockchain" are the core components that allow Bitcoin to be decentralized [10]. Extensions of Bitcoin are later provided, e.g. ZeroCoin [9] as a coin washing service (later improved as ZeroCash [13] for private payments). Ethereum with a Turing-complete was the latest platform upon which DAOs could be built.

The first smart-contract-supported DAO, "TheDAO" was launched as a venture capital funding in May 2016. The crowd-funding was $150 million at peak value. TheDAO is supported by and stored entirely in Ethereum currency units (ETH). The objective of TheDAO was to create a venture capitalist fund designed to initiate other projects and demonstrate the creation of DAOs, see daohub.org.

Another DAO, Dash [5] also demonstrates great potential. The funding system witnesses quick growth in monthly revenue, from originally $14.000 per month in September 2015, to nearly $30.000 per month in March 2016.

3   The Seconomics-TOCTOU Attack on TheDAO

Perhaps when mentioning TheDAO, the most known event is the attack that happened shortly after its launch in June 2016. An unknown hacker was able to drain away 3.6 million ETH (which worthed $50 million at that time), approximately a third of the 11.5 million ETH that was committed into TheDAO.

That was a typical TOCTOU (Time of Check - Time of Use) vulnerability (see [15] for an introduction): an integrity violation by a race attack using a recursive call in TheDAO's implementation. This vulnerability could then be used to mount an economic attack on TheDAO. In economic term, TheDAO suffered from money pumps as TheDAO proceeded with account clearance prior to ledger update[1]:

> The bug is that when splitDAO() is called, it will then call the recipients code to transfer Ethereum coin, after which the recipients code will call splitDAO() again before finishing. This causes the process to repeat itself, transferring more Ethereum coin, then calling splitDAO() again, which calls the hacker's code, which calls splitDAO(), which calls the hacker's code, and so on. The process will continue endlessly, until it drains all of TheDAO's coin.

In this case, a security vulnerability (the user was authorized to draw money *only* in the *first* instance) has been combined with an economic attack (the recursive calls keep draining coin from TheDAO).

Several other attacks are possible on the Ethereum "smart contracts". The paper from [1] shows several of them. Yet the very paper fails to see that what is dangerous are not the vulnerabilities by themselves but the combination of the attack to the software with a tailgated economic attack.

Indeed most of the vulnerabilities classified in [1] as new types are classical vulnerabilities discussed, e.g. see [15] for concurrency and [2] for object oriented classes. For example the "call to the unknown" among the "Ethereum-specific" vulnerabilities is a classical problem of inheritance[2] dating back to faults about inheritance [4] where "long standing bugs have persisted because nobody thought to verify that deeply inherited methods [...] were overridden". By itself this would be a classical vulnerability. It becomes a seconomics one when a user can redefine a method that allows money to be sent or received.

Given the current level of enthusiasm over blockchains and the like in the FinTech sector we might as well assume that several other DAOs will emerge. The might be equally vulnerable (even if we assume integrity is not violated but just anonymity is) as we discuss in the next sections.

4 Another Potential DAO: Futures Exchange

Futures Market are among the largest markets hence it is likely that the Futures Exchange will be DAOed.

---

[1] More detail on this hack can be found at http://blog.erratasec.com/2016/06/etheriumdao-hack-similfied.html.

[2] When invoking a contract at another Ethereum address this may have redefined its methods or the fallback method. Therefore the new redefined method will be called instead of the original expected method.

Table 1. Key compositions and characteristics of futures market

Traders characteristics:	
Possible positions	Buy-side traders holding long positions
	Sell-side traders holding short positions
Possible actions	Submit (market/limit orders) and cancel (limit) Orders
Exchanges main functions:	
Price Discovery:	Disseminating the real-time market data to market participants; Providing a central limited order book: a consolidated tape with an electronic list of all the waiting buy and sell quotes organized by price levels and entry time
Matching and clearing	Matching engines use algorithms to match buy and sell quotes with a price and time priority principle. Clearing house is responsible for having a daily/ final settlement by the process of "mark-to-market"
Risk managements	Traders need to deposit an "initial margin" and maintain a minimum funding in the "margin account" above the "maintenance margin"; otherwise, they will receive a "margin call" to request for additional funding. Any traders fail to meet to minimum margin, will be forced to liquidate their open positions or even be "netted out" from the market

A futures contract is a standardised legal agreement between two parties to purchase or sell an underlying asset at specified price agreed upon today with the settlement occurring at a future date.

Fundamental participants in a futures market include traders and exchanges (see Table 1). The central player of a futures market is a futures exchange. Futures contracts are negotiated at futures exchanges, which act as a central marketplace between buyer and sellers. The basic functions of the exchanges are to provide efficient price discovery process in their trading platforms, to match and settle trading activities, and to manage the risks for trading activities [14].

According to different trading positions, traders can be classified as buyers or sellers. Buyers take long positions by purchasing a certain amount of futures contracts, whereas sellers take short positions by selling a certain amount of contracts. The basic rule of trading in the futures market is buyers prefer to purchase contracts at lower prices and sellers prefer to sell contracts at higher prices.

A Futures Exchange DAO must maintain some key security properties:

Confidentiality of Inventory. As the counterparty for each trader, exchanges are required to hold all the trading information and each traders identify, including the prices, volume, margin, order type etc. However, in order to maintain the economic viability, an exchange has to protect the trading information and traders credential without leaking to other opposite side traders.

Market Integrity. Futures exchanges need to frequently monitor the trading activities (market prices and matching orders), the settlement capability (margin account) of each transaction to ensure the integrity of the marketplace. Many other attempts such as enforcing a maximum limit for a trader's long/short position, etc. are applied to protect market integrity.

Order Anonymity. The exchange must prevent the linking of limit orders to uncover the trading strategy of a trader. This is done by the management of an anonymous central limit order book where only the bid and ask price in the order book is available for public. In this way, traders will not be able to identify the other traders and forecast others' trading strategies.

5 Security Protocol for Distributed Futures Exchange

A security protocol for a Futures Exchange DAO could be built on a number of existing cryptographic primitives as follows.

Anonymous communication network. e.g. Tor, recall that the futures exchange guarantees full anonymity of the traders. Since it is impossible to "create anonymity" from scratch, we assume an underlying anonymous network that hides the traders' identifying information (e.g., their IP address). This assumption was already used in several prior works, most notably [13].

Commitment Scheme and Secure Addition over commitments. We also assume **Zero Knowledge** ideal functionality for some standard NP relations for commitments as well as for exchange functionalities such as order fulfillment and mark to market.

Merkle Tree. [8] where the leafs are commitments to anonymously commit and retrieve trader inventory as in [12,13].

The overall protocol should implement 4 phases of the "traditional" Exchanges:

Initialization Phase. Every trader participating in the futures market has to commit a valid initial inventory (validity can be proven with the standard zero-knowledge proof for commitments).

Order Phase. Every trader can post a new order or cancel a previously posted order. S/he will have to prove (possibly in zero-knowledge) that one has enough funds. Whenever a match happens, all traders will compute the new inventories, possibly with a secure multiparty computation and prove (again possibly in zero-knowledge) that they can afford the new liquidity profile of the market.

Margin Settlement Phase. This phase is run immediately after the **Order** phase, in case one or more traders were unable to prove to hold a non-negative instant net position. The traders participating to this phase would see all their pending orders being canceled and their account billed for them.

Mark to Market Phase. (At the end of the trading day, e.g. between 13:59:00 and 14:00:00) The traders locally update their inventory then commit the new inventory.

Such protocol can be engineered [7]. What we are interested in discussing is that what happens if some security properties fail.

6   The Seconomics Attack on Distributed Futures Exchange

It is sort of obvious that a failure of integrity may be dramatic to the protocol. We show that anonymity may also be essential.

A fully anonymous network is a quite strong assumption in the context of futures markets. In fact, the anonymous network, e.g. Tor, is not so reliable. It has been shown that traffic correlation attacks could be launched if the adversary control the entry or exit node and the server to deanonymize users [3,11]. Besides, as incentives would be quite strong (downloading porn or posting politically sensitive material is not the same as betting billions) we could assume anonymity would be violated. Considering this matter, we illustrate an attack that anonymity is no longer a matter of convenience. In fact, if anonymity fails, severe damage could be done to the Futures Exchange DAO and drive away the traders.

If confidentiality and anonymity fail, some traders can act strategically and make so that other traders will be maliciously margin-called by artificially posting orders that they do not intend to honor.

Assume Alice, Bob, Carol and Eve are in a futures market. Alice acculates a large short position of 90 contracts selling at $10 each, the other traders buy 30 contracts from Alice each at this price. In other words, she has in her inventory 90 promises to sell.

To estimate a trader's exposure, the Exchange assumes that all contracts are bought and sold instantaneously at the current mid price of $10. So, to fulfill her promise to sell 90 contracts Alice would have to buy them first from the current mid price and reduce her cash availability to $1400 - 90 \cdot 10 = 500$. We are the situation in Table 2 (left).

If Alice could wait, she could instead post a buy order of $9.50. If somebody eventually matched her order later in the day she would obtain a modest profit (50c per contract).

If Carol and Eve know that Alice is a small investor and needs cash, they can generate an instant profit by changing the liquidity profile of the market. They can post buy orders at slightly higher prices, this changes the mid prices and pushes the liquidation price of the position higher.

Alice could try to sell to those buy orders, but this pushes the contracts more deeply negative in a rising market exacerbating her problem of being close to the margin call. Eventually, the liquidation price, e.g. $16, is high enough that Alice's net position is below the margin call threshold and Alice is cashed out,

Table 2. Forcing alice out of the market

Price = $10				Price = $16
Trader	Cash	Contracts	Position	Position
Alice	1400	−90	500	−40
Bob	1200	30	1500	1680
Carol	1200	30	1500	1680
Eve	1200	30	1500	1680

Alice accumulates 90 selling contracts currently at the price of 10 and have a cash margin of 1400. As the price fluctuates by δ_P her inventory liquidation price is $X_{\text{Alice}} = -90 \times (10 + \delta_P)$, and her net position is $N_{\text{Alice}} = 1400 + X_{\text{Alice}} = 500 - 90 \times \delta_P$. When $\delta_P = 0$, the evaluation of her account stays the same (at \$500). When $\delta_P = 6$, her net position drops to -\$40 and she has to be netted out from the market.

with a realized payout to the other traders, i.e. her \$500 is given to the other traders.

The other traders can then cancel their orders and the price could then decrease back to \$10 or even lower (when Alice's trades would have been profitable), but Alice cannot benefit from this price as she has already been cashed out. The other traders do not have to actually trade anything, they have forced Alice to a margin call just by adjusting their buy quotes upwards strategically.

Eve and Carol have price discriminated Alice: they performed a pricing strategy that could only work because they *knew exactly* how much was in Alice's pocket and therefore how much was needed to nudge her out. The opposite problem can be generated from a long position and the market then being artificially deflated.

7 Conclusion (?)

The same problem of TheDAO might happen to the Futures Exchange DAO subjects to seconomics attack combining anonymity failure and price discrimination. Some parties may ask for the reversal of some transactions perceived as "unfair". But they will have no way to reverse them without changing the very system and network of participants. If enough people refused to join this would "balkanize" the market.

This leads to a central question: *"When the entire system collapses how could parties fix it?"* As TheDAO is distributed there is no way to actually "fix" the protocol backward as this would violate the other still standing security properties.

In the attempt to reverse TheDAO financial crisis, Ethereum designers proposed a solution *outside the protocol* itself, i.e. the hard fork: encourage parties to upgrade to a protocol client version that makes it impossible for the "hacker" to monetize the solution.

The attempts to fix the TheDAO proved difficult as to rewrite the central nexus of contracts forming the organization requires the majority of members to agree and this level of cooperation proved elusive. Indeed, a large fraction of the members of the Ethereum Community refused to join the new redressed ledgers, issued a Declaration of Independence[3] and continued to maintain the "classic" ledger:

> Let it be known to the entire world that on July 20th, 2016, at block 1,920,000, we as a community of sovereign individuals stood united by a common vision to continue the original Ethereum blockchain that is truly free from censorship, fraud or third party interference.

We can therefore speculate that *seconomics vulnerabilities cannot be patched* as the economic damages they may cause are unlikely to be reversible by purely technical means.

Thus seconomics vulnerabilities are different "beasts" to be reckoned with.

References

1. Atzei, N., Bartoletti, M., Cimoli, T.: A survey of attacks on ethereum smart contracts. Technical report, Cryptology ePrint Archive: Report 2016/1007 (2016). https://eprint.iacr.org/2016/1007
2. Binder, R.V.: Testing object-oriented software: a survey. J. Softw. Test. Verif. Reliab. **6**(3), 125–252 (1996)
3. Chakravarty, S., Stavrou, A., Keromytis, A.D.: Traffic analysis against low-latency anonymity networks using available bandwidth estimation. In: Gritzalis, D., Preneel, B., Theoharidou, M. (eds.) ESORICS 2010. LNCS, vol. 6345, pp. 249–267. Springer, Heidelberg (2010). https://doi.org/10.1007/978-3-642-15497-3_16
4. Cox, B.J.: The need for specification and testing languages. J. Object-Oriented Program. **1**(2), 44–47 (1988)
5. Duffield, E., Diaz, D.: Dash: a privacy centric cryptocurrency (2014)
6. Ethereum: A next-generation smart contract and decentralized application platform (2015). https://github.com/ethereum/wiki/wiki/White-Paper. Accessed 30 Dec 2015
7. Massacci, F., Ngo, C.N., Nie, J., Venturi, D., Williams, J.: FuturesMEX: secure distributed futures market exchange. Submitted for publication (2017)
8. Merkle, R.C.: A digital signature based on a conventional encryption function. In: Pomerance, C. (ed.) CRYPTO 1987. LNCS, vol. 293, pp. 369–378. Springer, Heidelberg (1988). https://doi.org/10.1007/3-540-48184-2_32
9. Miers, I., Garman, C., Green, M., Rubin, A.D.: Zerocoin: anonymous distributed e-cash from bitcoin. In: 2013 IEEE Symposium on Security and Privacy (SP), pp. 397–411. IEEE (2013)
10. Nakamoto, S.: Bitcoin: a peer-to-peer electronic cash system. Technical report, Unknown (2008)

---

[3] Available at https://ethereumclassic.github.io/assets/ETC_Declaration_of_Independence.pdf.

11. O'Gorman, G., Blott, S.: Improving stream correlation attacks on anonymous networks. In: Proceedings of the 2009 ACM symposium on Applied Computing, pp. 2024–2028. ACM (2009)
12. Sander, T., Ta-Shma, A.: Auditable, anonymous electronic cash. In: Wiener, M. (ed.) CRYPTO 1999. LNCS, vol. 1666, pp. 555–572. Springer, Heidelberg (1999). https://doi.org/10.1007/3-540-48405-1_35
13. Sasson, E.B., Chiesa, A., Garman, C., Green, M., Miers, I., Tromer, E., Virza, M.: Zerocash: decentralized anonymous payments from bitcoin. In: 2014 IEEE Symposium on Security and Privacy, pp. 459–474. IEEE (2014)
14. Spulber, D.F.: Market microstructure and intermediation. J. Econ. Perspect. **10**(3), 135–152 (1996). http://www.jstor.org/stable/2138524
15. Yang, J., Cui, A., Stolfo, S., Sethumadhavan, S.: Concurrency attacks. In: Presented as part of the 4th USENIX Workshop on Hot Topics in Parallelism (2012)

The Seconomics (Security-Economics) Vulnerabilities of Decentralized Autonomous Organizations (Transcript of Discussion)

Chan Nam Ngo[(✉)]

University of Trento, Trento, Italy
channam.ngo@unitn.it

Our observation is that the money loss comes *indirectly* from a security vulnerability in a normal case. When your computer gets infected with a malware you don't immediately lose your money. Only when the hacker finds very complicated ways to monetize your assets then you suffer from the loss. In other words,

$$\text{security vulnerability} \neq \text{money loss}$$

However, it is different for Decentralised Autonomous Organisation (DAO) in which the organisation is basically a software running that has the information populated on the distributed ledger platform and the rules are all implemented with the smart contracts (e.g. TheDAO on the Ethereum network).

Our first claim, which follows the DAO definition, is that,

$$\text{code} = \text{company} \tag{1}$$

And typically organisations are vectors for money, hence,

$$\text{company} = \text{money} \tag{2}$$

Then, from (1) and (2), it follows immediately that,

$$\text{code} = \text{company} = \text{money}$$

As a result in this case money loss comes *directly* from a security vulnerability, i.e.

$$\text{security vulnerability} = \text{money loss}$$

Then we would certainly wonder "When we face a loss in a DAO, can we undo the damages?" Unfortunately, the answer is that there is no possible technical fix for the DAO, as the thing that happened is the balkanization of the Ethereum network.

In conclusion, for financial technology protocols, we always have to consider this kind of security economics vulnerabilities in which besides preserving the integrity or some other security properties we also need to consider the economics aspect of the application that we are trying to build because, for example, in

F. Stajano et al. (Eds.): Security Protocols 2017, LNCS 10476, pp. 180–185, 2017.
https://doi.org/10.1007/978-3-319-71075-4_20

TheDAO's case, any kind of ex-post fix is impossible (as we can see from the Ethereum network fork into the original Ethereum and the classic Etherum).

Paulo Esteves Verissimo: I think you have some very valid thoughts. But I think it's important to separate between the problems that arise from the specification and the problems that arise from implementation. In both, what you're saying is true but for different reasons.

Since there's some evolving, the specification may be getting obsolete. They may be well coded and the code is perfect, has no vulnerabilities, no defects, but still they will become insecure or undependable because the situation changed. That is one point, and then you may call for adaptivity and this kind of thing.

But there is, I think an even more important point, which is this hope that we will ever make perfect systems. Meaning that the specification is valid and your code is perfect, which I don't think we'll attain for a lot of reasons, even price. You say code is money because you can code well. It is worth a lot of money. But actually, isn't it the case that if you spend a lot of money to make the code perfect, then when you come in, you don't stand a chance of making a profit margin. If you spend too much money to try to make your code perfect, then when it goes to the market, the price of your product will be too expensive.

And this is of course, related to an unrelated area, that is dependability and security, which is to use fault tolerance techniques for security, assuming that not everything is perfect, so use some redundancy. If some pieces of code have certain vulnerabilities, you can get along without those pieces of code.

I just wanted to insert this comment, that there are two ways in which code might not be working.

Reply: Of course, we cannot make something perfect and push it to the market. But the important thing is that, in this case if we are trying to implement something that has thousand years of history, then we must learn from the past to avoid the mistake from it. From our computer science perspective you may think that this is secure, but actually from the economics point of view, it is not, as we just showed with the price discrimination attack: even though you preserve everything and your code is running fine, you still have a chance to suffer from such an attack.

Bryan Ford: I think it's good and important to continue thinking about working on how to make more secure organisations, whether that's real life human organisations or decentralised DAO type organisations on a blockchain or whatever.

But taking this comment further on the difference between the intent and implementation, the DAO disaster was mainly in the implementation body, and I think one of the real lessons here is that DAO and digital organisations just need to learn the lessons of conventional human organisations. Human organisations tend to have a CEO for example, and CEOs occasionally die unexpectedly, or they go crazy and start doing bad things. What do you do in that case? Well that's why organisations have a board of directors for. Elected by the shareholders, they can replace the CEO. Maybe DAO needs to have a board of directors with a *multisig* power to replace the code defining the contract, or something that doesn't have that bug in it.

My question: "Is it more complicated than that? Is the real fundamental issue kind of the security of the structure, or having a backup mechanism that makes sense, that some responsible body of people can fix things?"

Fabio Massacci: To make this software organisation very robust and very reliable, you have to invest a lot of money, and this is what you don't want to do. I take one of the citations from Jean Tirole[1], which is known for economics, is that: "firms are actually incomplete contracts because making them complete are making them too expensive." Therefore any software organisation is going to be incomplete by definition. The point that we want to make is exactly this. Because it's incomplete by definition, that now, the software is directly transformed to monetization then we have a direct path from vulnerability to monetization, while you cannot just make the CEO go crazy.

For this you have a number of organisations that the DAO I think can do it, but it's a lot more difficult to foresee possible evolutions. For the CEO, there are only a finite number of places where you can hire. But for software, there are a lot more options that you have around. You have a lot more dimensions in which you can go, while physical CEO can only go in three dimensional space.

Bruce Christianson: Can I ask you to say a few words about why you think balkanization is problematic? Why is balkanization a bad thing? You seem to imply that balkanization is something that we wanted to avoid, if possible. Why does it matter that there's Ethereum and Ethereum Classic, and it's actually more profitable to mine Ethereum Classic? Isn't it just that we don't know whether the Union or Confederacy won the war? It's really impressive, they just had their thermals that they fought hard for. So why is balkanization a bad thing?

Reply: Balkanization may not be a bad thing but it deviates from the original idea of creating this Ethereum. Because the idea of the public ledger is that you have a place where you can safely post information there and it stays there forever. Now if you split into two, the question is that which should you trust? You cannot tell. You have to pick for yourself and that is the problem.

Fabio Massacci: If you put the money in a place, you expect the place to still be able to return the money. If part of the bank split in two, and some people move away into London with the cash and some people move into Brussels with the cash. You want to know, where is your cash? Should you go to London to get it, or should you go to Brussels, with the split between them. That's why balkanization is a problem if it's linked to money. If it's linked to a ledger nobody reads, you don't care. If you have to throw your monthly rent into it, then you want to know where is your money.

Bruce Christianson: But you know your money is in both banks, so if you withdraw from each, it should add up to your monthly rent.

---

[1] The Theory of Industrial Organization, 1988, p. 16.

Paulo Esteves Verissimo: To confirm with Fabio, and actually this is a real story, I don't want to tell the names but I just want to tell you about the facts of code, where the money goes because of the fancy code. A colleague of mine did this study for chip manufacturing. It's a classical study for vulnerability detection, and in the end he came up with a list of bugs that were in the chips, over a certain set of chips. And they said, "Ah, well thank you very much. Yeah, these few, we knew about them. They were heisenbugs, you know, these bugs that come and go." And so the client said, "We're not going to take them, we're going to take the others, fantastic, thank you very much."

Markus Voelp: You mentioned a few key words in your talk which makes me think about whether we should spend tax-payers' money in order to support this entire line of research anyway. And some key words were: futures, and these kind of trading things. When I take a bunch of them, I take my students to a casino and ask them to cheat as a big Joe and so on. What's your opinion about this one? Should I do research in order to support gambling by banks and credit institutes and others.

Reply: [This is recorded. So I will skip answering your question.]

Paul Wernick: It was suggested earlier on that out of good specifications you can have a perfect implementation but it might be very, very expensive. I suggest it's worse now because, as the world evolves, software doesn't evolve unless you do something to it. Professor Lehman has pointed out in the past that every time you run a programme it's in the form of an experiment. You find out whether it succeeds or fails but the success or failure is down to the world, not programme changing. So however perfect your implementation and specification are, the world might have moved on your features a year along.

Reply: But again it is not the problem whether your implementation is perfect or not, because as you said, every run is an experiment. The problem is that we need to learn from the past that came before the experiment so that your first experiment can be meaningful to not find out the mistake that has already been discovered in the past. And in this case, for example the futures exchange implementation, if we don't care about the economic attack from the past that the economist has discovered and we just go on and push this out of market it can be a very expensive and useless experiment.

Fabio Massacci: Useful for somebody else.

Bryan Ford: This again kind of illustrates my point. Have any virtual organisation meets the real world basically? And things go wrong when the real world hits your perfect organisation, whatever it is. And then you learn and the organisation has to adapt and there has to be a mechanism to re-write the code of the organisation. Whether that's embodied in a bureaucracy under a CEO and re-writing the code means sacking the CEO or just telling them to do things differently. Or whether it's something else. There's got to be a graceful evolutionary path otherwise it gets naturally selected out of the market for obvious reasons which is what TheDAO did, right? You're going to lose a million dollars here and there on that big of "whoops", but the question is "Can you recover and evolve and what is the mechanism to recover and evolve?"

Partha Das Chowdhury: The system needs to be easy to change.

Bryan Ford: Well of course it needs to be. But maybe not too easy because if it's too easy to change, then some hacker is going to come in and figure out how to change it without the board of trustees.

Partha Das Chowdhury: But you identified the problems and then change the system, evolve the system.

Bryan Ford: Right. There has to be a mechanism to do that.

Fabio Massacci: I think you have the point right. But it's difficult, with respect to other organisations. I think it is something like Ross said, a "recourse". In pure software organisation, recourse is more difficult. And the organisation is an instance of this. So what do you have to do? You have to change the code. But then if the code is distributed, it's more difficult to have everybody agree that this is the right thing to do.

In a sense, if we want to connect to Ross's political economy of protocols. In the physical political economy, we have a number of infrastructures, like police and the state, that takes care for the adjudication. So you're unhappy about something, you go to the police or you use assassination as Paul was suggesting.

In a distributed organisation, unless you have the mechanism for adjudication, things may be more difficult to fix. So any security vulnerabilities may have consequences that are more difficult to fix.

Paul Wernick: It's more difficult in the software case perhaps because software is so complicated. It's less likely a CEO work himself to understand exactly the implications of making a software change. We'll see these sort of race conditions and that might cause vulnerability.

So, if it's something you can kick, it might be easier to see what the problem is and how to resolve it. But with software, I think it multiplies the problem, which is much more difficult, much more complex an artefact. It is more difficult to understand what the problems are and how to fix them. So the CEO's job itself becomes much more difficult.

Markus Voelp: If you don't take it down to the software already, would you be able to take a few lines in your protocol and say, "these lines have to be implemented in a good way otherwise it is going to be very risky, etc."

Paul Wernick: Maybe the CEO would like to do it.

Ross Anderson: There is precedence in these cases for some vulnerabilities being tolerated or at least there are being no attempts to fix them retroactively. The classic example of vulnerability is when we pull a tax law every so often that the current situation is that the tax laws stay behind, interact with feature of volume two, feature of volume seven of this book, and feature of volume thirteen. And bingo, our money comes out. There have been plenty of cases where legislation is rushed through parliament in one day but usually people will tolerate nuances over a finance bill. So if you're seeking to ultimate recovery from flaws caused by vulnerabilities, then again, perhaps you need to build a structure that's got multiple bills moving at different speeds.

Tuomas Aura: In online multiplayer games, there are vulnerabilities that are exploited and over time some of them are fixed and some of them become better established practises. So maybe you can think of multiplayer games as a smart contract that actually has this governing body that will fix flaws that may make money out of nowhere. Or actually just fix them multiple times over time to make it work better.

Bryan Ford: I think many tax codes including the US are indeed like online multiplayer games. A lot of people have figured out ways to cap and ways to keep companies from fixing those goals. Keep capping it year after year, this is the way it works.

Paulo Esteves Verissimo: Actually, the other day I was searching something. I can't remember what, and I came across the Oxford Comma in an article mentioning how Oxford Comma is the most beautiful malware-injecting law.

Hugo Jonker: Just to add to that, there was a ruling in the United States, basically, where lack of Oxford Comma cost the company 10 million dollars[2].

Paulo Esteves Verissimo: The article mentioned that, yeah.

---

[2] https://www.nytimes.com/2017/03/16/us/oxford-comma-lawsuit.html.

A Security Perspective on Publication Metrics

Hugo Jonker[1,2](✉) and Sjouke Mauw[3]

[1] School of Computer Science, Open University of the Netherlands,
Heerlen, Netherlands
hugo.jonker@ou.nl
[2] Digital Security Group, Sciences, Radboud University, Nijmegen, Netherlands
[3] CSC/SnT, University of Luxembourg, Luxembourg, Luxembourg
sjouke.mauw@uni.lu
http://www.open.ou.nl/hjo/
http://satoss.uni.lu/sjouke

1 Introduction

The importance of publication metrics, such as the h-index [9], has increased dramatically in recent years. Unfortunately, as Goodhart [7] already remarked: "when a measure becomes a target, it ceases to be a good measure". And indeed: hiring, grants and tenure decisions depend more and more on performing well in publication metrics. This leads to a perverse incentive for individual researchers and journals to "optimise" their perfomance. However, such behaviour undermines the utility of the measure itself, in the extreme case nullifying its value. The underlying cause is that besides the functional requirements on a measurement, there are also security requirements on them. As is often the case, these security objectives remain implicit. In this paper, we provide a much-needed security perspective on publication metrics.

There are different kinds of security issues that may arise. We distinguish between weaknesses in the design and weaknesses of a specific implementation. Moreover, problems can arise either without malicious behaviour, or due to a malicious actor. The case where a malicious actor abuses design weaknesses of a publication metric is overlooked in literature. We term such malicious actions "gaming". Gaming can be characterised as "those actions taken by a researcher that impact that researcher's publication metric, which he would not take in absence of that publication metric." For example, a journal editor is gaming when he insists that authors of submitted papers cite several previously published papers in the journal to game the journal's impact factor; or a citation ring of researchers is gaming when members of the ring systematically cite all other members, thereby artificially increasing their citation count.

There have been many discussions in literature on the use of and the methodology underpinning publication metrics. Concerning the h-index, for instance, an overview of discussions, weaknesses and alternatives can be found in [1]. This has led to an abundance of "improved" publication metrics and critiques, in turn, on these new metrics. The discussions mostly center around methodological shortcomings (e.g., skewing to young or old, to males or females, to researchers

© Springer International Publishing AG 2017
F. Stajano et al. (Eds.): Security Protocols 2017, LNCS 10476, pp. 186–200, 2017.
https://doi.org/10.1007/978-3-319-71075-4_21

in western countries, etc.). The fact that the methodology can be deliberately exploited by a malicious agent is hardly touched upon in literature.

Contributions. We develop a formal model of the publication process. This enables us to model various publication metrics, including the h-index and impact factor. Using this model, we can derive a given metric's "gaming surface". The gaming surface of a publication metric identifies every potential source of change in the model of the publication process that results in a change in the publication metric. Ergo, any changes in the publication metric must originate from this gaming surface. Having identified all potential sources of change, one can design mitigation strategies based on the standard security triad of prevention/detection/correction. We propose several detection heuristics. The foremost detective strategy in our view is semi-automated anomaly detection. Finally, we advocate an open publication process, including not only reviews, but also communications between editors, reviewers, and authors.

2 Categorising Weaknesses of Publication Metrics

Popular publication metrics have been avidly discussed and vivisected by researchers. For example, literature has strongly contested the h-index's suitability as an indication of a researcher's quality, see for instance [8,10,17] for specific critiques and [1] for an overview of discussions, weaknesses and alternatives. The perceived weaknesses of the h-index have led to a flood of alternative metrics, including the g-, e-, a-, and m-index (see e.g. [4] for an overview).

In order to make a clear distinction between the various types of weaknesses, we will order these along two independent axes. The first axis concerns the distinction between design and implementation, while the second axis concerns the distinction between weaknesses that can be observed already in a *friendly* environment and weaknesses that involve an *attacker*. These two axes imply the four types of weaknesses illustrated in Fig. 1.

Table 1. Four types of weaknesses related to publication metrics.

	Implementation	Design
Errors	Deficiencies	Methodological drawbacks
Attacks	Hacking	Gaming

I. **Errors**
  a. **Implementation deficiencies.** Software design involves making design decisions. Moreover, implementation is an error-prone process. Taken together, it is likely that implementations of publication metrics contain specifics that cause them to produce different output than other implementations of the same publication metric. Such errors are not restricted to simple encoding or algorithmic errors. They could also be introduced at the software design level.

Example: a researcher's h-index as computed by Google Scholar is (almost always) higher than his/her h-index as computed by Web of Science. This is because Web of Science uses a stricter definition of "publication" than Google Scholar.

b. **Methodological drawbacks.** A publication metric will have methodological limitations, due to the discrepancy between what the publication metric actually measures (e.g. citations) and its purpose to measure research quality or quantity. These limitations are already present in the system in regular usage, with honestly behaving agents.

Examples for the h-index: women score lower than men [10], citations in negative context contribute positively [18], retracted papers continue to contribute to the h-index [6], biased against developing countries [13], etc.

II. **Attacks**

a. **Hacking.** A publication metric's implementation can be affected by security vulnerabilities, such as buffer overflows, vulnerable cryptography, flawed protocols, insecure authentication, etc. Any such vulnerability may be exploited to change a publication metric.

b. **Gaming.** A publication metric is intended to reflect behaviour as done in absense of the metric. In essence, gaming weaknesses are possibilities to apply Goodhart's Law [7]. By crafting input specifically for the publication metric process, the process is unduly affected.

Examples: Publishing pacts [15], reviewing one's own papers[1], create bogus papers citing existing papers[2], create bogus papers all citing each other [11], asking authors of drafts to include a citation to your related paper [15], etc.

We pose that methodological arguments are to be discussed in the field of bibliometrics, while attacks are within the purview of the field of security.

Recall the notion of gaming, described as *"those actions taken by a researcher that impact a researcher's publication metric, which he would not take in absence of that publication metric"*. Thus, whether or not some activity is regarded as gaming clearly depends on an interpretation of the researcher's activities and underlying intent. The goal of this paper is not to determine intent, but to provide a method to determine the possibilities for gaming inherent in a publication metric, and to suggest countermeasures to prevent, detect or correct gaming if and when it should occur.

Various instances of gaming publication metrics are described in literature. For example, researchers have found evidence of gaming journal impact factors (see e.g. [2]); several researchers have set up sting operations to uncover sloppy review practices, e.g. [3,16]; and various researchers performed experiments to game the publication databases directly, bypassing the normal publication process completely (e.g. [11]).

---

[1] http://retractionwatch.com/2012/08/24/korean-plant-compound-researcher-faked -email-addresses-so-he-could-review-his-own-studies/.

[2] López-Cózar et. al. 2012 – deliberately not cited here as the researchers used their study to increase their own h-index.

All these works found a specific gaming attack on the publication process. However, a uniform approach to modeling and analyzing such gaming attacks is missing. To understand which gaming attacks can be executed, below we construct a model of the publication process, a so-called *publication structure*. This will help us to understand and possibly reduce the "gaming surface" of publication metrics.

3 Publication Structures

In this section we define the notion of a *publication structure* using simple set theory, which describes the relations between the basic notions of *author, paper, publication venue* and *citation*. These notions are considered at two levels of abstraction: the *data view*, which concerns raw publication data, and the *publication view*, which defines the abstract categories used to calculate the *h-index* and other publication metrics.

3.1 Structure of the Publication Process

Even if the definition of a publication metric seems clear, the devil is in the details. Take, for example, the h-index. Hirsch [9] describes the h-index as follows: *"A scientist has index h if h of his or her papers have at least h citations each, and the other papers have $\leq h$ citations each."* This informal definition seems clear, but it does not define clearly what a citation is nor, more pressingly, where these citations originate. Indeed, different *publication data processors*, like Google Scholar and Scopus, often calculate significantly different h-indexes for the same author, even though they use exactly the same definition of h-index. We observe that the calculation of an h-index (and, similarly, any other citation-based bibliographical metric) is relative to a particular interpretation of the notions of *author, paper, publication venue* and *citation*, and the relations between these. We call such an interpretation of reality a *publication structure*. From an abstract point of view, a publication structure for a given publication data processor describes the set of rules, algorithms and heuristics that the publication data processor uses when building, updating and interpreting its publications database.

An important observation is that publication data processors base their calculations on a particular selection and interpretation of *raw data*. For example, a publication data processor may consider only digitally available papers, and consider only the author names as they literally appear in a given pdf file. Indeed, an author's name can be represented in many different ways, e.g., by using initials, by leaving out accents, or by variations in its transcription to the latin alphabet. Consequently, we will make a distinction between the various representations of an author's name and the author itself. Similarly, we consider the abstract notion of a paper as opposed to its various representations, allowing us, for instance, to consider the pre-proceedings and the post-proceedings version of a paper as the same publication. Likewise, we make a distinction between publication venues and their representations.

Various practical and even standardized approaches have been developed that address the distinction between concrete representations in the publication process and their abstract entities. Examples are the ISBN number for books, the ISSN number for journals and the DOI for electronic documents. However, these notions do not necessarily line up with a publication data processor's notion of a publication. For instance, two editions of the same book may be considered as instances of the same publication for the purpose of citation counting, while they have different ISBN numbers. A promising initiative to define abstract author entities is the ORCID initiative[3], but it's still too early to observe its impact in practice. Consequently, publication data processors will continue to use their own proprietary abstract representations of authors, publications, and publication venues. We formalise this as a *data view*, expressing raw data, a *selection and interpretation function*, which represents a publication data processor's view on the raw data, and a *publication view*, which represents the publication data processor's selection and interpretation of the data view.

3.2   Formalisation

We assume the existence of *raw data* available to a publication data processor on the publication process – papers, venues, authors, citations. On this raw data we define a *data view*, which provides a selection σ of the raw data.

First we will introduce some standard mathematical notation used in the definitions below. Let $p: X \times Y$ and $q: Y \times Z$ be relations, then their *composition* is defined by $q \circ p = \{(x, z) \in X \times Z \mid \exists y \in Y: (x, y) \in p \wedge (y, z) \in q\}$. Let $\sim: X \times X$ be an equivalence relation on a set X, then the *quotient set* of X by $\sim$ is denoted by $X/\sim$.

The relation between the sets of author representations and paper representations is defined by $authored_\sigma$, where $authored_\sigma(a, p)$ means that author representation a (co-)authored paper representation p. The set of citations is denoted by C_σ, containing all expressions that, according to the publication data processor's standard, describe a reference to a paper. The citations occurring in a paper representation are expressed by the relation $contains_\sigma$, where $contains_\sigma(p, c)$ means that citation c occurs in paper representation p. Similarly, $refersto_\sigma(c, p)$ expresses that citation c refers to paper representation p. The relation $at_\sigma(p, v)$ states that publication representation p was published in venue representation v.

A publication data processor considers a specific subset of the raw data. Some papers may not be in its view – e.g., Google contains many more "publications" than Scopus. Moreover, the publication data processor will interpret its subset of raw data to unify double entries. We call this the *data view* of a publication data processor on the raw data.

---

[3] https://orcid.org/.

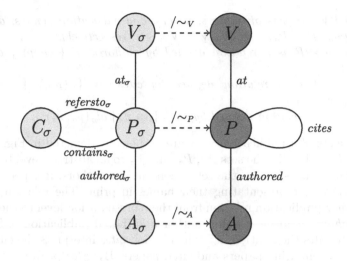

Fig. 1. Data view (left) and its induced publication view (right).

Definition 1 (Data view). *A data view dv is a selection σ of the raw data, i.e. $dv = (A_\sigma, P_\sigma, V_\sigma, C_\sigma, authored_\sigma, contains_\sigma, refersto_\sigma, at_\sigma)$, where*

- *A_σ, P_σ, V_σ, and C_σ are sets of author representations, paper representations, publication venue representations and citation representations, respectively,*
- *$authored_\sigma$: $A_\sigma \times P_\sigma$ is a relation defining which authors wrote which papers,*
- *$contains_\sigma$: $P_\sigma \times C_\sigma$ is a relation defining which citations occur in which papers,*
- *$refersto_\sigma$: $C_\sigma \times P_\sigma$ is a relation defining which papers are referred to in which citations.*
- *at_σ: $P_\sigma \times V_\sigma$ is a relation defining at which venue a publication appeared.*

The components of a data view are graphically depicted in Fig. 1 (left).

Remark that an author can be represented in a data view in different ways: with initials (A.N. Example), with first name (Alfred Example), full name (Alfred Nicholas Example), etc. Similarly, different objects may represent the same paper (PDF version, HTML version), and the same venue may also be represented in different ways (abbreviation, full name). Unifying these representations constitutes an *interpretation* of the data view.

Definition 2 (interpretation). *An interpretation ι is a tuple $(\sim_A, \sim_P, \sim_V)$, where the equivalence relations interpret which representations are referring to the same abstract object in the classes A_σ, P_σ, and V_σ, respectively.*

By interpreting a given data view, we arrive at a *publication view* – the abstraction of a data view.

Definition 3 (Publication view). *Consider a data view $dv = (A_\sigma, P_\sigma, V_\sigma, C_\sigma, authored_\sigma, contains_\sigma, refersto_\sigma, at_\sigma)$, and an interpretation $\iota = (\sim_A, \sim_P, \sim_V)$. The induced publication view $pv \in PV$ is a tuple $(A, P, V, authored, cites, at)$, where*

- *A, P, and V are sets of authors, papers, and publication venues, defined by $A = A_\sigma/{\sim_A}$, $P = P_\sigma/{\sim_P}$, and $V = V_\sigma/{\sim_V}$, respectively.*
- *authored: $A \times P$ is a relation defined by authored = { (a, p) | authored$_\sigma$ (a_σ, p_σ) }.*
- *cites: $P \times P$ is a relation defined by cites = { (p, q) | refersto$_\sigma$ ∘ contains$_\sigma(p_\sigma, q_\sigma)$ }.*
- *at: $P \times V$ is a relation defined by at = { (p, v) | at$_\sigma(p_\sigma, v_\sigma)$ }.*

The components of a publication view are graphically depicted in Fig. 1 (right). The sets A, P, and V lift the sets A_σ, P_σ, and V_σ to an abstract level by dividing out their equivalences. Thus, the set A contains all authors, irrespective of the possible variety in representating their names in print. The relation *authored* lifts the author-publication relation from the representation level to the abstract level, so *authored*(a, p) means that author a authored publication p. Similarly, the relation *at* lifts the relation at$_\sigma$. The relation *cites* interprets the citations as a relation between citing papers and cited papers. By *cites*(p, q), we mean that paper p cites paper q – abstracting away from the representation of p, q and from the representation of the citation. Note that in the case of paper r containing a citation c that links to two papers p, q, this results in both *cites*(r, p) and *cites*(r, q). Additionally, for the case where r contains two citations c, c' that both point to the same paper p, this results only in one citation *cites*(r, p).

Using the notion of a publication view, we can formally define a *publication metric*.

Definition 4 (Publication metric). *A publication metric pm is a function* pm: $PV \times Args \rightarrow \mathbb{R}$, *where Args is defined as*

$$Args ::= V \mid P \mid A \mid \mathbb{N} \mid Args \times Args.$$

The first argument is the *publication view* of the publication data processor. The remaining arguments allow us to define for which entity the metric is evaluated. For instance, the *h-index* has two arguments: a publication view and the author for which the *h-index* is calculated. When discussing publication metrics and their definition, we will often leave the publication view unspecified.

Some publication metrics make use of metadata that is not represented explicitly in our model. An example is the year of publication. Whenever necessary, we will assume that such metadata is implicitly represented in the model as an *attribute* of the concerned notion. For instance, we denote the publication year of a publication p as $p.year$.

In Fig. 2, we provide a schematic representation of the role of a publication structure in determining the value of a publication metric. It expresses that a publication data processor's *data view* is constructed by collecting and selecting raw data. The *publication view* is then derived by equating the various equivalent names of the sets of venues, publications and authors. Based on this publication view, the publication data processor calculates the publication metric.

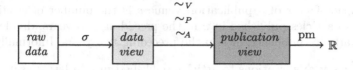

Fig. 2. From data to a publication metric.

3.3   Examples of Publication Metrics

In this section we show that a publication structure is not only rich enough to define the *h-index*, but also to express most publication metrics with a similar scope as the *h-index*. We start by defining two auxilliary functions. The first function expresses the number of times that a publication has been cited. For $p \in P$ this metric is defined by

$$numciting(p) = |\{\ q \in P \mid cites(q,p)\ \}|. \tag{1}$$

The second auxiliary function determines the set of all publications of author a. It is defined by

$$pubs(a) = \{p \in P \mid authored(a,p)\}. \tag{2}$$

Using these functions, we define the h-index of a as the largest subset of a's publications such that all its elements have at least as many citations as there are elements in the subset:

Definition 5 (*h-index*). *The h-index for a publication structure* $S \in \Sigma$ *is a function h-index*: $A \to \mathbb{N}$, *defined by*

$$h\text{-}index(a) = \max\{\ i \in \mathbb{N} \mid \exists_{T \subseteq pubs(a)} |T| = i \wedge \forall_{p \in T} numciting(p) \geq i\ \}.$$

In a similar way, we can define other publication metrics, like the g-index [5], or Google's i10-index. The i10-index is the number of articles (co-)authored by a with at least 10 citations. Formally:

$$i10\text{-}index(a) = |\{\ p \in P \mid authored(a,p) \wedge numciting(p) \geq 10\ \}|.$$

The g-index of an author a is the largest number i such that the i most cited papers of a together have collected at least i^2 citations. Formally:

$$g\text{-}index(a) = \max\{\ i \in \mathbb{N} \mid \exists_{T \subseteq pubs(a)} |T| = i \wedge \sum_{p \in T} numciting(p) \geq i^2\ \}.$$

Finally, we give an example of a metric for publication venues: the *impact factor*. For this publication metric we use the attribute $p.year$, which determines the year of a publication.

The impact factor of a publication venue v is the number of citations in a given year to articles published in v in the preceding two years, divided by the number of articles published in v in the preceding two years. Informally:

$$\frac{(\#\text{this year's citations to articles published in } v \text{ in last 2 years})}{(\#\text{articles published in } v \text{ in last 2 years})}.$$

We can make this more precise as follows. Consider a publication structure S.

The set of publications that appeared in venue $v \in V$ in any period $[y, y']$ is then given by

$$app(v, y, y') = \{q \in P \mid at(q, v) \wedge y \leq q.year \leq y'\}.$$

The impact factor IF of a specific venue $v \in V$ for year y is then given by

$$IF(v, y) = \frac{|\{\,(p,q) \in P \times P \mid q \in app(v, y-2, y-1) \wedge cites(p,q) \wedge p.year = y\,\}|}{|app(v, y-2, y-1)|}.$$

3.4   Extending the Model

Note that some publication metrics make use of information that is not represented in our definition of a publication structure. An example is the *acceptance rate* of a venue – the percentage of submitted papers that was accepted. It is a simple matter to extend the model to be able to also capture metrics that incorporate slightly more data than available in the basic definition. We illustrate this by showing how to extend the model to define the metric *acceptance rate*.

We extend the data view with a relation *submitted-to*$_\sigma$: $P_\sigma \times V_\sigma$, which defines the venue to which a paper has been submitted. After extending the corresponding publication view with generalized relation *submitted-to*, the acceptance rate AR of a venue $v \in V$ is defined as

$$AR(v) = \frac{|\{\,p \in P \mid at(p, v)\,\}|}{|\{\,p \in P \mid submitted\text{-}to(p, v)\,\}|}. \tag{3}$$

4   Gaming Surface

To determine where a change in a publication metric originates, we identify every potential source of change in publication structures – the *gaming surface* of publication structures. The gaming surface of a publication metric consists of exactly those sets and functions of the data view on which the outcome of the publication metric depends. Therefore, a specific change in a publication metric must originate from a change in the publication structure's gaming surface. More precisely, a change in a publication metric's output can only be the result of a change in the underlying publication view, and a change in a publication view must originate either from changes in the underlying data view, or from changes in the equivalence relations used to derive a publication vier.

This means for publication structures S and S':

- $\mathrm{pm}(pv_S) \neq \mathrm{pm}(pv_{S'}) \implies pv_S \neq pv_{S'}$,
- $pv_S \neq pv_{S'} \implies dv_S \neq dv_{S'} \vee (\sim_A, \sim_P, \sim_V) \neq (\sim_{A'}, \sim_{P'}, \sim_{V'})$.

Thus, someone attempting to game a publication metric should craft or manipulate raw data in such a way that it influences the sets V_σ, P_σ, A_σ, C_σ, their relations $contains_\sigma$, $refersto_\sigma$, $authored_\sigma$, at_σ, and/or the equivalences $\sim_{A'}$, $\sim_{P'}$, $\sim_{V'}$. These items form the generic *gaming surface*. Since a particular publication metric may not depend on all of these, their actual gaming surface may be reduced. We illustrate how to determine the gaming surface of a particular metric by considering two example metrics: the number of publications of an author and the *h-index*.

4.1   Gaming Surface for Number of Publications

Consider the metric "number of publications of an author", $a \in A_\sigma$, defined by

$$\mathrm{numpub}(a) = |\{p \in P \mid authored(a, p)\}|.$$

Thus, this metric is only affected by changes to the publication view's A, *authored*, and P. These, in turn, are affected by the following changes in the data view:

- A: A_σ, $\sim_A$.
- P: P_σ, $\sim_P$.
- *authored*: $authored_\sigma$.

Table 2 lists the gaming surface of this metric, including the effects of possible gaming actions. Some actions have the desired effect of improving an author's number of publications, while others have no effect or an adverse effect. Concrete examples of the actions with a positive effect are: produce and publish bogus papers under your name, an author with a common name can claim publications of other authors with a similar or identical name, slightly change the title of a paper between its publication in pre- and post-proceedings, the editor of a journal accepts a paper under the condition that he becomes co-author.

4.2   Gaming Surface of the h-Index

Recall the definition of the h-index (Definition 5):

$$h\text{-}index(a) = \max\{\, i \in \mathbb{N} \mid \exists_{T \subseteq pubs(a)} |T| = i \wedge \forall_{p \in T} num\,citing(p) \geq i \,\}.$$

This definition depends on three aspects: the given author $\bar{a} \in A$, the definition of the function $num\,citing$ (Eq. 1), and the definition of the function $pubs$ (Eq. 2). These two functions depend on the set P, and the relations *authored* and *cites*. This means that any change in an author's h-index must be triggered by changes to the underlying data view elements, i.e.:

Table 2. Gaming surface for "number of publications".

	Action	Poss. effect
A_σ:	Add an author	None
A_σ:	Remove an author	−
P_σ:	Add a paper	+
P_σ:	Remove a paper	−
$\sim_A$:	Unify two author representations	+
$\sim_A$:	Distinguish between two author representations	−
$\sim_P$:	Unify two paper representations	−
$\sim_P$:	Distinguish between two paper representations	+
$authored_\sigma$:	Add an author to a paper	+
$authored_\sigma$:	Remove an author from a paper	−

- From A: A_σ, $\sim_A$,
- From P: P_σ, $\sim_P$,
- From $authored$: $authored_\sigma$, $\sim_P$, $\sim_A$,
- From $cites$: $contains_\sigma$, $refersto_\sigma$.

In Table 3, we list all update actions that could affect one's h-index, keeping in mind the type of component. The table identifies what the potential immediate effect (if any) of the update is. As can be seen, not all updates have an immediate effect. For example, a newly introduced author is not linked to any paper, and therefore has no h-index. On the other hand, some effects require multiple updates. For example, to increase one's h-index with +1, a researcher needs to publish a new paper, and that paper needs to be cited. In the model, there is also a formal constraint: to extend $cites$ with p, p', there must be a pair p, c to $contains_\sigma$ and a pair p', c to $refersto_\sigma$. An update that adds only one of these pairs will not propagate to the publication view.

In the table, we find that some updates may lower a person's h-index. This implies that not only can an attacker aim to improve his own h-index, he can also work to lower his competitors' h-indices.

Moreover, we also find some actions which by themselves will not alter a h-index: adding an author to A_σ, adding a paper to P_σ and extending the relation $contains_\sigma$. Such alterations need to be followed by further alterations (linking the author to a paper, linking the paper to citations) to influence a subject's h-index.

Updates to $\sim_P$ deserve special mention, as the same type of update may have a positive, a negative effect, or no effect. Unifying two lowly-cited paper representations may give the resulting combination enough citations to let it contribute towards the h-index. Conversely, if two highly-cited paper representations are unified, this may lower the h-index as there is one less paper contributing to the h-index. Distinguishing two paper representations can have the opposite effect: breaking a paper that counts for the h-index into two that do not count for the

Table 3. The gaming/update surface of the h-$index$

	Action	Poss. effect
A_σ:	Add an author	None
A_σ:	Remove an author	$-$
P_σ:	Add a paper	None
P_σ:	Remove a paper	$-$
$\sim_A$:	Unify two author representations	$+$
$\sim_A$:	Distinguish between two author representations	$-$
$\sim_P$:	Unify two paper representations	$+, -$
$\sim_P$:	Distinguish between two paper representations	$+, -$
$authored_\sigma$:	Add an author to a paper	$+$
$authored_\sigma$:	Remove an author from a paper	$-$
$refersto_\sigma$:	Cite a paper	$+$
$refersto_\sigma$:	Remove a citation to a paper	$-$
$contains_\sigma$:	Inject a reference in a paper	None
$contains_\sigma$:	Remove a reference from a paper	$-$

h-index will lower the h-index, while breaking such a paper into two papers that both count will increase the h-index.

Finally, we point out that Table 3 identifies the effect on an individual's h-index. Group effects are not accounted for. For instance, getting into the top 5% of authors can easily be achieved by adding many (bogus) authors without publications.

5 Mitigation Strategies

We develop mitigation strategies based on an analysis of the involved parties and their incentives. We recognise the following parties:

- Targets of evaluation: researchers, journals, workshops, but also universities, departments, etc.
  Incentives: to score as well as possible on publication metrics.
- Stakeholders in the publication process: reviewers, editors, program committee members, publishers, etc.
  These may be evaluated by publication metrics as well. Their incentives therefore are the same as targets of evaluation.
- Publication data processors: Google Scholar, Thomson, etc.
  Incentives: provide reliable data.
- Evaluators: employers, evaluation committees, funding agencies, etc.
  Incentives: support the decision process based on an evaluation that correctly uses the right publication metrics.

Given the incentives and the gaming surface, it is clear where an actor can act to further his goals. This helps guide where mitigation can take place and where to place security controls.

Mitigation must be based on the data available. Curiously, in scientific publishing, details such as reviews, communication between authors and reviewers, communications between reviewers and editors, etc. are *not* publicly available. However, there are types of gaming that can only be detected in such data. One example is a reviewer who requires a paper under review to add a citation of his work.

Manipulations of the publication process often escape the attention of quality control. For example, quality control levels proposed by the *Transparency and Openness Promotion* group [14] extensively detail quality controls for the research process, but lack any considerations of the reporting process.

We therefore advocate that data concerning the *reporting process* must be publicly available.

We believe that the most relevant mitigation strategies are based on analysing the aggregated data to detect possible gaming. Borrowing from the field of intrusion detection, we discern two types of detective strategies:

- Signature-based detection.
  Signature-based detection identifies patterns in the data that are common to a particular gaming attack. An example of such a detector is the SciGen detector by Labbé et al. [12].
- Anomaly-based detection.
  Anomaly-based detection identifies deviations from the expected norm in the data. An example is the following check by Thomson for detecting a journal that is gaming: a very quick increase in impact factor of the journal, coupled with a high number of self-citations.

Currently, a few publishers are taking some initial measures in this direction. However, current efforts are far behind what is possible. We advocate the development and use of tools to automatically analyse data and identify anomalies. Remark that not all detected cases will be instances of gaming – some will be benign. For example, a detector that detects papers that are cited before their official publication can also trigger on a paper for which the publisher makes a webversion available prior to official publication. As such, the detection process can never be fully automated. Human evaluation will be required, but the effort necessary to identify gaming can be significantly reduced.

6   Conclusions

Publication metrics are playing an ever-increasing role in scientific careers and scientific standing of journals and other publication venues. This creates a perverse incentive for "gaming" a publication metric: taking actions that improve a metric, which would not have been taken in absence of the metric. Publication metrics suffer from various drawbacks, both in implementation and in design.

We showed that gaming is a category in itself, which has received scant attention in literature.

Gaming of publication metrics is a disservice to scientific advancement. We argue that steps are needed to prevent flagrant gaming. To this end, we introduced the notion of a *gaming surface* of publication metrics, and developed a formal framework to rigorously define the gaming surface of any specific publication metric.

Defences against gaming are then built upon understanding the given publication metric's gaming surface. We discussed potential security controls and classified these.

Such measures can help to not only safeguard publication metrics, but can also help to identify some forms of attempted fraud at an early stage. As such, we advocate ongoing research into designing security controls for publication metrics.

References

1. Alonso, S., Cabrerizo, F.J., Herrera-Viedma, E., Herrera, F.: h-index: a review focused in its variants, computation and standardization for different scientific fields. J. Informetr. **3**(4), 273–289 (2009). http://www.sciencedirect.com/science/article/pii/S1751157709000339
2. Arnold, D.N., Fowler, K.K.: Nefarious numbers. Not. AMS **58**(3), 434–437 (2011)
3. Bohannon, J.: Who's afraid of peer review? Science **342**(6154), 60–65 (2013). http://www.sciencemag.org/content/342/6154/60.short
4. Bornmann, L., Mutz, R., Daniel, H.D.: Are there better indices for evaluation purposes than the h index? A comparison of nine different variants of the h index using data from biomedicine. J. Am. Soc. Inf. Sci. Technol. **59**(5), 830–837 (2008). https://doi.org/10.1002/asi.20806
5. Egghe, L.: Theory and practise of the g-index. Scientometrics **69**(1), 131–152 (2006). https://doi.org/10.1007/s11192-006-0144-7
6. Glänzel, W.: What is the impact of fraudulent literature? Int. Soc. Scientometr. Inf. Newsl. **6**(2), 44–57 (2010)
7. Goodhart, C.: Problems of monetary management: the UK experience. In: Papers in Monetary Economics I. Reserve Bank of Australia (1975)
8. Guilak, F., Jacobs, C.R.: The h-index: use and overuse. J. Biomech. **44**, 209–209 (2011)
9. Hirsch, J.E.: An index to quantify an individual's scientific research output. Proc. Nat. Acad. Sci. U.S.A. **102**(46), 16569–16572 (2005)
10. Kelly, C.D., Jennions, M.D.: H-index: age and sex make it unreliable. Nature **449**(7161), 403–403 (2007)
11. Labbé, C.: Ike Antkare one of the great stars in the scientific firmament. Int. Soc. Scientometr. Informetr. Newsl. **6**(2), 48–52 (2010)
12. Labbé, C., Labbé, D.: Duplicate and fake publications in the scientific literature: how many scigen papers in computer science? Scientometrics **94**(1), 379–396 (2013). https://doi.org/10.1007/s11192-012-0781-y
13. Mishra, D.C.: Citations: rankings weigh against developing nations. Nature **451**, 244 (2008)

14. Nosek, B.A., Alter, G., Banks, G.C., Borsboom, D., Bowman, S.D., Breckler, S.J., Buck, S., Chambers, C.D., Chin, G., Christensen, G., Contestabile, M., Dafoe, A., Eich, E., Freese, J., Glennerster, R., Goroff, D., Green, D.P., Hesse, B., Humphreys, M., Ishiyama, J., Karlan, D., Kraut, A., Lupia, A., Mabry, P., Madon, T., Malhotra, N., Mayo-Wilson, E., McNutt, M., Miguel, E., Paluck, E.L., Simonsohn, U., Soderberg, C., Spellman, B.A., Turitto, J., VandenBos, G., Vazire, S., Wagenmakers, E.J., Wilson, R., Yarkoni, T.: Promoting an open research culture. Science **348**(6242), 1422–1425 (2015). http://www.sciencemag.org/content/348/6242/1422.short

15. Parnas, D.L.: Stop the numbers game. Commun. ACM **50**(11), 19–21 (2007). https://doi.org/10.1145/1297797.1297815

16. Sokal, A.D.: A physicist experiments with cultural studies. Lingua franca **6**(4), 62–64 (1996)

17. Waltman, L., van Eck, N.J.: The inconsistency of the h-index. J. Am. Soc. Inf. Sci. Technol. **63**(2), 406–415 (2012). https://doi.org/10.1002/asi.21678

18. Wendl, M.C.: H-index: however ranked, citations need context. Nature **449**(7161), 403–403 (2007)

A Security Perspective on Publication Metrics
(Transcript of Discussion)

Hugo Jonker[1,2](✉)

[1] Department of Computer Science, Open University of the Netherlands,
Heerlen, Netherlands
hugo.jonker@ou.nl
[2] Digital Security Group, Radboud University, Nijmegen, Netherlands

The presentation began with discussing the application of Goodhart's Law to metrics used in academia. Goodhart's Law says "when a measure becomes a target, it ceases to be a good measure." Due to the widespread use of various metrics to gauge academic performance, Goodhart's Law is slowly coming into effect. This warrants looking at the metrics from a security perspective: how can they be exploited, and what can we do against such shenanigans?

Hugo Jonker: So basically, what I'm doing here, off the record, is I'm hunting scientific fraudsters. The problem is: a good scientific fraudster will try to be indistinguishable from a good scientist.

Paulo Esteves Verissimo: Also indistinguishable from a good fraud salesman. (laughter)

Ross Anderson: What about string theory? Isn't that an entirely fake discipline?

Reply: That is possible. That is something I'm not quite sure about. But actually, I'll capitalise on this example by Ross. There's no way I can automatically tell actual fraudsters from brilliant scientists because the fraudsters are trying to emulate the brilliant scientists.

Ross Anderson: But how do you tell a good string theorist from a bad string theorist? You ask the other string theorist. No outsider has any understanding whatsoever, isn't that just absolutely perfect?

Markus Voelp: String theory is not a scientific theory because it doesn't allow you to run any experiment to confirm it. But of course you can also argue this about fusion which is kind of similar.

Hugo Jonker: Getting back on track: there's such a thing as citation stacking which is a citation ring by journals. These are editors which make sure that papers published in their journals cite other journals in the stack. And Thomson Reuters is looking for this behaviour, and has already punished journals by excluding them from their index databases. So fraud in the publication process has become so prevalent that Thomson Reuters is actively taking steps against it and catching fraudsters.

© Springer International Publishing AG 2017
F. Stajano et al. (Eds.): Security Protocols 2017, LNCS 10476, pp. 201–213, 2017.
https://doi.org/10.1007/978-3-319-71075-4_22

Tuomas Aura: Perhaps this is workshops like this with post-proceedings to ask people to cite each other's papers – when relevant.

Reply: Yes and this goes back to my previous remark. You're absolutely right. . .

Bruce Christianson: And not just from this year, by the way.

Reply: Indeed, do cite Bruce's brilliant paper from two years ago. So actually this was one of the fundamental things I probably mention a few slides on: to detect fraud, you need manual intervention. I believe that this cannot be avoided. But currently, we're already using human intervention to catch fraudulent behaviour. Maybe we can design tools to help automate parts of the process to help focus human intervention, because human intervention is expensive as we all know and computer time in contrast can be fairly cheap.

Frank Stajano: In cases like the one cited by Tuomas of this workshop, where there is a somewhat benign element, if you want to intervene, the problem is that it's not just isolated fraud, but it's more like "I'll scratch your back, you scratch mine because I will do a citation of your paper because of course the expectation is you will cite my paper as well."

Reply: Indeed. The thing is: it would be hard to distinguish between benign cases and fraudulent cases – I think that's your point. I agree. But there's low hanging fruit that we're also not catching such as Mr. Moon. Mr. Moon he setup fake Gmail accounts and when he submitted a paper to a journal he suggested reviewers, namely his other Gmail accounts.

And we'll see two "case files" in the slides. These concern people where what we observe seems not quite normal. Let's use these to fine tune heuristics. Let's look at these cases and see what do we think is different.

Markus Voelp: Yeah, love those pictures. Your premise is that we should kind of repair the broken system, isn't it? Like, the alternative would be to abandon using these indices altogether and find out something else?

Reply: Indeed, we should work to correct the system. I would say that our community does not have sufficient power to abandon these indices.

Markus Voelp: Why?

Reply: Because the requests for such indices come from higher up in the hierarchy – sometimes from university level, sometimes even higher.

Markus Voelp: Those with a professor title in front of their name are typically the persons sitting in committees appointing other people and as long as they abandon these indices. . .

Reply: That would be a nice idea. However, I think that overestimates our influence. . . Let me give you an example why. You're probably aware as most others here that as a computer scientist you need to travel to publish. Explaining this to a university hierarchy is a huge – and recurring – challenge. As a computer scientist, it is impossible to publish at the top of your field without travelling.

Yet I would imagine most professors in this room will have had debates within the university hierarchy about the size of or even necessity for a travel budget. So while I appreciate your suggestion, I don't think it's feasible for us researchers to cause research performance metrics to be abandoned.

So again, off the record, there's two ideas behind this talk. One is can we catch these guys? Can we do something to automate the process? And if you don't like that takeaway, the other idea is: can you become a better fraudster.

Frank Stajano: And now why should this be off the record?

Hugo Jonker: That's a good question, Frank. Because I would like my public record to be clean.

Back to the security view on publication metrics. We define the notion we call gaming as artificial manipulation to improve your scientific standing. The paper mostly focuses on author-level metrics like the h or Hirsch index. But the discussion applies equally to venue metrics such as acceptance rates or impact factors.

The h-index is the maximum number m, such that this author co-authored at least m papers, each of which was cited at least m times.

You can see that this increases quadratically in this picture. m papers, each m times cited, so the number of citations you need increases quadratically. So to improve your h-index optimally, that is, with as little effort as possible, you need quadratic effort to improve it. Most of you probably have papers that do not contribute currently to your h-index, which is below optimal.

Gaming is exploiting design weaknesses. It's different from hacking where you exploit implementation weaknesses.

Frank Stajano: What you do mean with quadratic effort?

Reply: The effort needed to increase your h-index is quadratic in the number of papers that contribute to the h-index.

Frank Stajano: My effort is on the writing paper. If I need another citation to increase my standings, for the sake of argument, it's not the case, then the fact that this needs 50 citations to instead of 49 or 48 is not extra effort for me because I don't do any active effort to get the citation.

Reply: And that's why your h-index is where it is.
   (laughter)

Ross Anderson: There are many other walks in life where gaming is not considered bad but good. In the practise of politics, for example, it's all about gaming. It's all about being nice to the prime minister and getting a promotion and assassinating the other MPs' reputations who might compete with you for ministerial jobs. It's all about sucking up to the press and doing down your opponents. This is just the business of gaming.

Reply: But in this area, academic ranking, it isn't. That's why we call the notion of gaming publication metrics "attacks". What we're going to do is we're going to formally define the publication process and then we can define publication metrics upon that. Then we will distinguish between two types of attacks.

One type is where, for example, you hack into Google's database and add your name to a bunch of papers. Alternatively, if you're in their database anyway, you could also just increase your h-index – it's probably stored in there somewhere.

Gaming, on the other hand, is really something different. Gaming is an attack where the attacker exploits the way that the attacked metric is computed. So hacking illegally changes the inputs for this metric, while gaming is about optimising legitimate inputs.

To give you one example, in Google Scholar you can unify two different papers. You can say these are the same paper. For example, that happened to me, one tech report was published at two institutions. If that happens, you can tell Google Scholar these are the same. Now suppose these two papers individually do not contribute to your h-index. Together, they might. So suddenly the joint representation of this work is above the threshold for inclusion in the h-index. So... if you unify two papers, each of which has almost enough citations to contribute to your h-index, and you will end up with one publication that contributes. So you can actually do this.

Paulo Esteves Verissimo: That's not so horrible, is it? If my team put down some biblio stuff I could have a paper in this journal that is cited and it's not gaming in the wrong sense. Why? Because that is flagged. So let me state my case. I'm an advocate of peer review. That's what should always exist. And then metrics should only serve to confirm the image that arises. This may be romantic, but that's the way some people work here including here in this country.

So anything that Google does, that it can verify, I think is fair game. I'm much more worried about these "citation clubs" where the cross citations happen. This case, on the other hand, is when two or more papers are merged. I think that is correct, because sometimes you have a conference and another version of the same work, and Google finds it, it puts an asterisk, so you get off.

Reply: Indeed, there are benign uses for this.

Basically while we're working on this, I have also an MSc. student looking into this, it seems like there is little automation in the current process of detecting. You'll see this reflected in the case files I think.

So we formalised the publication process. We begin from raw data, such as the internet. From this a selection is made: a data view, a database like Google Scholar. This a selection on the raw data that has somehow happened – how this is done is outside the scope of the formalisation. Next we have authors, publications, venues like journals or this conference, and citations. So all of your papers have at the end a list of citations and each citation refers to one or more papers. It could actually refer to more than one paper, it usually doesn't if you did it right, but this is one way where you can hack. You could just have one citation pointing to two different papers.

Frank Stajano: Can you expand on this?

Reply: You could, for example, add a title, a workshop, and a digital object identifier that don't coincide. So then I have a citation that points to two different papers, and while it looks like the paper has 15 references, if Google processes the paper, it might actually find that it refers to 16 papers. So conversely, if I happen to be a proceedings editor and I think wow, I'd like my h-index to be a bit higher, I make sure all citations have some digital object identifiers. Just hypothetically speaking.

A problem is that the same object can occur under multiple designations in the data view. To give a concrete example, sometimes SPW is written "SPW" in a citation list, sometimes it's written "Security Protocols Workshop". Sometimes the 25th edition is referred to as edition "XXV", sometimes as "25", sometimes as "2017". All of these designations refer to the same workshop, SPW 2017. So in the formal model, we "divide" to obtain equivalence classes. Similarly we use equivalence classes for authors. Sometimes I'm referred to by initials, sometimes by full name, etc. So the formal model makes a step from the data view to a view based on equivalence classes for authors, papers, and venues.

Using this formalisation, we can define publication metrics. To give you an example: on this slide is a definition of the h-index. This definition is based on the formal model. We can also formalise the i10-index: every publication that has more than 10 citations. Or the g-index, which is a slight twist on the h-index if you will. That is if you order your publications by citation number, descending, then g is the largest index such that the total number of citations squared is larger than the index in the list. And last but not least, with a slight extension, we can also define something like acceptance rate, which is really straightforward: the number of papers published by a venue divided by the number of papers submitted there.

And we can define a wide array of other metrics. We were working on that for a while, which was fun. But what I promised you was, though I haven't used this term yet, the gaming surface. We formally defined these metrics. We're using components from the formal model. So what we can do with this? We have a publication metric and we know exactly which components of the publication view it uses, namely: these. We know where the contents of those components originates from: from these components in the data view. The data view, that's where we can start playing. Now we can see, what happens if I start changing things in the data view or things in the equivalence relationships?

This slide shows the attack surface of the h-index. I'm not going to go into details, but if you want to improve your h-index, this is basically a short how-to. The attack surface lists what components an attacker may influence, and what the effect will be. For example: adding authors to papers, getting another paper, unifying two author at presentations, e.g. in DBLP. I think most of you know DBLP. You can mail DBLP and say, "Hey, this author and this other author, they are both me."

Markus Voelp: Why does having an extra author not help? Are you only looking at your own h-index?

Reply: Yes, I'm looking only at one author's h-index.

Paulo Esteves Verissimo: We agree that some of these things are just fair game. Because if you are represented in several ways, it's only natural for you to want to tell them "Hey, guys. I'm this one guy." Whereas others might be using a malicious or even rational way. So it wouldn't be better to separate them? Just as a suggestion.

Reply: In what sense do you mean?

Paulo Esteves Verissimo: Because consolidating several presentations of your name is not gaming, it's just regular behaviour.

Reply: Ah, that's a good remark. But suppose we're applying for the same jobs and I'm looking at your resume and think "Oh! Impressive." I want to make you look a bit worse. Maybe I can consolidate a few of your papers into one.

Paulo Esteves Verissimo: Actually, that's a very good question, but I think you can only do that if you log in.

Reply: For Google Scholar, you are right, but this formalism is agnostic of the underlying database. So *if* I can remove you as an author it will likely hurt your h-index, maybe that's an interesting approach for me to take.

Ross Anderson: Well, there are multiple layers of gaming here. . . Some people I suspect don't log onto Google Scholar because they get enough free extras from other people with the same name and don't want to disambiguate.

Reply: Yes. Correct. Like the prolific author, "et al."

Ross Anderson: Yes.

Fabio Massacci: So I think you're missing one important aspect of the attack surface: creating venues.

It's not in your attack surface, but it's one of the most important one because you can actually create venues. There is a researcher I know that managed to move from 18 to 70 in h-index, according to Google. Just by inventing the venue. Because Google does not authenticate the venue.

Reply: Indeed, Google does not verify the venue.

Fabio Massacci: It's very interesting in fact. If you're up for promotion, I can tell you tricks. It's very intriguing.

Reply: I can share one trick that I know. It was published, so this is already known. Google indexes the webpages of educational institutes. So if you put a PDF that looks like a paper on your institutional webpage, Google is likely to find it and count it as a publication. If you put an MSc. thesis that cites all of your publications, suddenly the citation count of all your publications will increase.

I've seen the lack of venue authentication happen with a tech report of mine, which was the full version of a paper. We put the tech report on our website, Google found it before the conference and counted it as a publication – counting the tech report as a citation to the published version.

Fabio Massacci: So this is an instance of venue creation?

Reply: Yes, it is.

So, you're right. The reason that I didn't include venue spoofing is because this is not in the attack surface of the h-index. So there's a meta level. That is in the selection of the raw data: how can you manipulate the selection that constructs the data view from the raw data?

On to mitigation strategies. What can we do about it? So far the discussion has been great, but let's actually try to do something to prevent this, not just talk about profiting from this.

There are two approaches to detecting malfeasance: signature-based detection and anomaly-based detection. Signature-based detection is what you can do, for example, to detect SCIgen papers. SCIgen is a paper generator that basically generates random papers to use a polite term. The words are completely random, Labbé et al. wrote how to detect such papers. There's an underlying pattern.

We wanted a more generic approach than that because we wanted to find people cheating in new and exciting ways. We want to look at DBLP, at the entire set of computer science authors in there. And we want to shake that up and see what comes out.

Remark that if we're doing that well, probably a few people in this room would come out. Because as I said in the beginning, we're looking for things that stand out and there are people in this room that stand out in the scientific community. And rightfully so.

This is the part where human intervention will come in again. How do we do this? Collect data and not just at one point in time. That's also important. You can gather the data once, but your Google Scholar page five years ago looks different from your Google Scholar page now because you published more papers. So you can't just look at it statically. One time gathering data gives you a data point. You will want to look at the dynamics, as well.

To achieve this, we need to understand typical characteristics of evolution, how researchers publish. And this was actually a bit challenging to come up with a cup of tea and a white board. So we turned to some interesting cases – if you know of any let me know offline. But I'll show you two case files. The idea is then that we would use these heuristics to identify outliers and then in stage two, we would actually zoom in on these outliers. So what this would give us, the first stage, that would give us, here are people who stand out of the crowd. I'm sure everyone in this room can name a few people. If you think about the security community you can probably think of a few people who should be standing out of the crowd. The people who are excellent scientists.

How do we zoom in on those? We're going to look at them and their peers. The idea is that we will compare their performance to the performance of their peers. And actually in the MSc. project I was talking about before, we're now looking to do that. Comparing, for example, papers published at one venue, at on workshop. Comparing how these papers gather citations and from where to all the other papers at that one workshop.

Real life cases. I've used a picture of a character from Donald Duck to keep the person anonymous. I don't know what the name of this character is in English, though.

Frank Stajano: Flintheart Glomgold.

Reply: Thanks!

At one point in Mr. Glomgold's life, this Mr. Glomgold had an h-index of 30 and then said "given quality and quantity of recent works, this figure will probably double in the next two years."

Now, you've asked me, "What do I mean with quadratic work?" I mean that this is suspicious. If you have an h-index of 30 and then two years later you have an h-index of 60, I'm thinking, "What's going on?".

So we started looking at this person. Frankly, I don't care if this case is benign or not. I'm just looking at this case to come up with heuristics. we found two publications which were almost the same – on the order of 10 different words a page. There was one paper from 2016 cited in 2015.

Bruce Christianson: Oh, but that's quite all right. But that happens all the time. A pre-print or something.

Tuomas Aura: It happens when some work stops where the publications appear two years later.

Vashek Matyas: I've just got an email from John Anderson who is responsible for SPW'16 proceedings and he's promising, soft promise, that in April he will deliver to Springer.

Hugo Jonker: Oh.

Vashek Matyas: April 1st.

Frank Stajano: Did he mention the year? (laughter)

Hugo Jonker: Okay, getting back on track. Being cited before publication is an actual phenomenon, especially nowadays with journals listing accepted papers online prior to publication. Colleagues of mine had an experience where an accepted paper was on the stack to be actually put into print for two years. Meanwhile, it was up on the journal's page and the journal was advocating, "Refer to it like this. Cite it like this." You know? So, this happens. This could be correct. It's becoming less weird. This particular paper that we were investigating was cited 50 times in 2015. I know there are people here in this room who do a lot better than I do H-index wise. But for me this will put it at the top of my publication list. And this is prior to publication.

Paulo Esteves Verissimo: Well, yeah... we should be careful about this. The point is, these could be, for example, two papers, a preliminary version and then a second version.

Reply: These two almost equivalent papers were published in two different journals.

Fabio Massacci: This is also common in economics because they publish a paper at a conference which is not formal proceedings. Then they put in SSRM [Social Sciences Research Methods - HJ] and then it is published into American Economic Reviews until I couldn't find this after that so it's possible in certain fields when the difference between conference and formal proceedings...

Reply: Exactly – so we cannot automatically determine the intention. The thing is: I just want to identify these cases. I want to apply my gut feeling to such cases. And then I want to put that feeling into a heuristic form that I can then program and apply to everyone in DBLP. Well, actually I want to explain those hunches to a student and let him do the work.

This next paper was cited 104 times by June. It got more than 80 citations from one journal. It got more than 10 from one other journal when we looked. So, 104, more than 90 of those citations, I think 95 of those citations, originated from two journals.

Paulo Esteves Verissimo: Do you have a subscription to those journals?

Reply: No. We did find an editor at the journal though... Mr. Glomgold. Now my spider sense starts tingling. This one person happens to be editor at a journal that within a very short time frame happens to cause about 90% of the citations. So, I don't know. Maybe this is still above board... That was what Fabio was getting at before. There are venues that are specialised and where the top performers are, of course, on the editorial board. And there are small specialised areas where there are like two journals in that field, or three. So yes, then this situation might possibly occur.

Tuomas Aura: Well, one typical paper-submitting trick is to check if there is any relevant paper by one of the people on the editorial board. Citing that is a good way of having your paper accepted. So this situation could be created like this, except that the numbers of suddenly appearing citations are too high, of course.

Reply: So you agree that the number seems quite out there. This is actually the whole point, because I'm not on the institutional review board of any journal. What I do want to do is: I want to be able to detect such things and tell these people, "This is maybe a case you want to investigate." I want to be able to do that.

Virgil Gligor: The author was of the biggest names. So who's the author?

Reply: Flintheart Glomgold. Here, I even have his picture.

Fabio Massacci: So is he in Computer Science?

Reply: This is in computer science. We're only looking at people who appear in DBLP. So these are people that, if they are cheating... I would not like their presence in the field. Because they're basically cheating where all of us are working hard for our careers.

The second case file is one of "De Zware Jongens," – Beagle Boys, I think, in English. This chap was doing self-citations. Occasionally, he was editor of a book and then he would also be editor of a chapter in the book... This is not necessarily impossible, but it's also not necessarily exactly what you would like. He also published almost identical papers in different journals.

So: how to detect things that warrant investigation. That's basically what we're now trying to do. We check, "Is there an above average increase in publications and/or citations?" Then we would go and find peers of this person and then compare the characteristics of publications of the outlier with the characteristics of the publications of his peers. Initially we wanted to simply compare the peers and the outliers directly, but then we figured that if someone is publishing mostly in databases or in computer graphics and he makes one effort into computer security, maybe there's a different citation culture there. So maybe what would be very weird in one area is a lot more normal in another area. So initially, you should look at the papers.

Markus Voelp: How would you deal with areas like real-time systems? Which actually have two sub-areas. One is for theory papers where you can get a paper every month and the other is for experimental papers where you need months in order to set up your experiments to run.

Reply: So how would I deal with that? I would work in the first area, not in the second. More seriously: what we do is we check a publication. And then for the publication we check, where is it published? This is what the student is working on now. And then retrieve all the other publications from that issue of the journal, or from that workshop, or conference and then see how is this one cited, how are the other ones cited. So these should be, in that sense, comparable. And, of course, we're now running into the problem where we're pushing too many requests to Google.

Ross Anderson: The remark I was about to make is that I have a research student who is from Korea and who observed that many people from East Asian countries do research in their relevant fields because of the language gap. They do stuff that was cool here 10 years ago. And because they can't read papers as fast as we can, because of language, so what my student set out to do was to write an algorithm which would tell him what was hot and what wasn't in any field. So, quite simply, you look for a few people in the field of interest. You then pass the publication tree and you find the people who are the outstanding people in the field, the leaders, and you see what they're interested in and what their peers are interested in. With a few tweaks to these algorithms, you can determine more or less automatically that, for example, security protocols are hot and petri nets are not without having to read a million words of text, which is for a non-native speaker, a handicap. Perhaps a bigger barrel of techniques like this is a way forward.

Reply: It's actually interesting, it sounds very related to what we're doing here. Yes?

Bryan Ford: I would be concerned the moment that mechanism becomes a metric, I would be very concerned that... what was it, Campbell's law?

Reply: Yes, or the Cobra Principle.

Bryan Ford: It started with coming back, inviting us again, being used as a game-able mechanism to make me see it as an influencer. My topic is hot, and that other one isn't, right?

Frank Stajano: In response to Ross, well maybe not a response, actually. I can see why someone with a language problem would not be able to read as many papers as you, but why would he have to read the papers that are 10 years old at this case? Why can't he read just fewer of the modern papers?

Ross Anderson: Well, if you suffer from such a handicap, what sensible tools are available for bridging the gap and looking at master data is an obvious thing to look at.

Frank Stajano: This is all fine. I believe the tool would be improved if we look at all the papers.

Hugo Jonker: I agree, but I think the tool that Ross was describing, a tool that can do that would address the problem.

Markus Voelp: I want to ask Bryan. Can you tell me the difference between this student's system, grid computing, cyber-physical systems and what was the next buzzword... and what if we find a new topic, which is going to be hot by definition?

Bryan Ford: That's a real good question. To me, blockchain is just the new buzzword term for distributed system, peer-to-peer systems. These themes, buzz words, come in waves. I don't know how that works, I'm just saying I would be suspicious of a mechanism that kind of tries to turn buzzwords into concrete metrics because I bet Hugo would come along and figure out how to game that too, right?

Reply: That I would certainly try.

Virgil Gligor: In answer to your question, Frank, about Ross's comment is that some of the people in Asia, for example, have found this to be typical of Korea. They read the background papers. They go to the reference list and they go to the reference list of the reference list and so on and they find that a paper early on in the topic, and they discover a flaw. Then they publish the paper on discovering the flaw and correcting it without realising that this particular topic is no longer of interest and they have a hard time publishing it.

I've noticed this time and again as an editor and chief of IEEE Transaction on Dependable and Secure Computing, with people from Asia and from Korea in particular. Good work, but kind of obsolete.

Paulo Esteves Verissimo: This is first a very interesting topic. Some of the things that you were talking about could and should obviously be filtered out by a competent panel of peer reviewers. It's also important to think about that. One of those is, for example, the amount of self-citations. Actually, there's a couple tools that discern self-citations that can be used if you're looking at... And, so that you know, there are guys who did research about the typical self-citation profile of areas. Ours is 20-something percent. You know, particle physics is at hundreds because the papers have two hundred or one thousand authors.

These are the kind of things that you can go and try to see. The other thing is that we were talking about serious peer review, you can filter the guys who surf the big waves, which is this guy has a lot of citations and very poor h-index and then you'll see he has four papers with 1000 citations because he's just jumping from one area to the other. Then you have to think, what can I expect of this guy if you're trying to evaluate the guy.

We should give metrics no more importance than they deserve. One of the worries is that people are getting wrongly focused on H-indices, that's very damaging.

Reply: Yes, I think that is worrying.

Bruce Christianson: I think what you were arguing when we came in, that it's important not to turn the metrics into targets. It's important to use them for the purpose of motivating. . .

Reply: Yes, precisely. Use metrics not as a target but for a purpose.

Frank Stajano: When you say peers, how do you define peers? Is it people who have a similar H-index at the time? Is it people who work in a similar field, because some of the things I expected would be definition of peer authors, which is what you're actually looking for down there.

Reply: Good point. What are peers? This is a thing we can tweak in our approach. In the MSc. project, we're looking at the first iteration of ideas. The first idea we had is to actually take the peers we can readily identify, knowing that it'll not be perfect.

Our initial approach is to look at coauthors. Of course, supervisors publish with their PhD students, so we know these are only peers in a limited sense. Another thing that we're looking at is editors for a journal. So, if you're an editor, the others on the editorial board are your peers. We assume they were elected because in some certain sense, they stand out from the crowd like you. That should be the general idea.

Then, these people should also have roughly similar publication characteristics. The core concept is not that we can fine tune, "Oh, you have a 0.1 difference," but if hypothetically speaking, we would find that Virgil is publishing twice as much and each of his publications is cited eight times as much as any of his co-editors, then either Virgil really needs to move on from that journal, or there's something weird. It's these huge things that we're looking for.

Ross Anderson: Let me give you one outline. Chuck Thacker won a Turing award, his H-index is five.

Paulo Esteves Verissimo: This gives hope.
  (silence)

Hugo Jonker: In conclusion, editors and journals: use a plagiarism checker. These things already exist to check homework. How can it be that folks publish almost literally the same paper twice? As we said before: I don't know to what extent this is self-plagiarism or not, but I also don't have confidence that publishers are using adequate plagiarism checkers at this moment.

I have a bunch of other conclusions. Basically, systematic detection of certain classes of gaming can be partially automated. This will help focus the human intervention. You cannot do this without human intervention because computers can only look at the numbers and say, "Hmm, this number's big. It's bigger than expected." Okay, maybe it's bigger because this guy's the next Einstein, maybe it's bigger because he's the next big scientific fraudster.

So: we can partially automate finding such cases, and also diving into such cases to substantiate why this person showed up, which helps distinguishing between the fraudsters and the Einsteins.

That's all we have time for, thank you for your feedback.

Controlling Your Neighbour's Bandwidth for Fun and for Profit

Jonathan Weekes$^{(\boxtimes)}$ and Shishir Nagaraja

Lancaster University, Lancaster, UK
{j.weekes,s.nagaraja}@lancaster.ac.uk

Abstract. We carry out a systematic study of the attack-resilience of flow-rule replacement strategies for switch caches in Software-Defined Networks. Flow Rules are inserted into the switch at the request of the network hosts to direct traffic- replacing older rules when the switch flow table is full. Malicious hosts can leverage the flow rule replacement strategy to launch cache flushing attacks. This results in substantially reducing the network throughput of their neighbours forcing their traffic to slow down dramatically. We describe and evaluate the attack on the First-In-First-Out strategy- the defacto SDN flow-rule replacement strategy.

1 Introduction

Programmable switches are a foundational component of Software-Defined Networks (SDN). One of the key strengths of SDN switches is its fast line rate. These switches contain rules in TCAM which provide instructions as to where to forward the traffic they receive. TCAM memory provides fast lookup of rules (tens of nanoseconds) [1]. However, to reduce manufacturing costs, the size of TCAM memory on a switch is limited. Thus a switch can only hold a small number of rules (between a few thousand to a few hundred thousand) within its flow table. Being a scarce resource, a well configured flow table is essential for switch performance as it will otherwise result in 'cache-miss' for arriving packets, increasing their transmission time. An attacker who can exert influence on the state of the flow table has the potential to lower network throughput and increase latency.

SDN uses cache-misses to trigger controller activity to configure the flow-table. A Cache-miss however forces the packet to register a significant delay in arriving to its target due to the fact that it takes additional time for the controller to reconfigure the flow table to accommodate it. Under normal circumstances, it is only the first packet of the flow that registers this delay (of the order of ms) [5] with the remaining packets of the same flow being processed at line rate.

SDN's intrinsic nature of allowing users to influence the state of the switch's flow table allows malicious users in the network to launch various attacks aimed at reducing or controlling the performance/throughput of the network. A malicious user of the network may launch a cache flushing attack by requesting

© Springer International Publishing AG 2017
F. Stajano et al. (Eds.): Security Protocols 2017, LNCS 10476, pp. 214–223, 2017.
https://doi.org/10.1007/978-3-319-71075-4_23

enough rules to fill the entire flow table with his/her own flows causing all other flow rules to be evicted from the switch. The rules inserted by the attacker are purely for the purpose of ensuring the legitimate rules are removed from the switch. By doing this, the attacker ensures that the next packet of a legitimate flow experiences the delay of a "first packet" while the switch awaits instructions from the controller. By repeatedly causing legitimate rules to be evicted, the attacker can ensure that a high percentage (if not all) of the packets of the legitimate flows experience this delay which results in the aggregate speed or throughput of the flows in the network being reduced.

The default replacement policy in SDN is the First-In-First-Out policy. However it does not perform optimally even under benign circumstances due to the fact that network traffic follows a power-law distribution [2]. Since FIFO does not consider the usefulness or popularity of a flow-rule before evicting it, it does not service network traffic particularly well. In the context of an attacker, FIFO faces an extreme vulnerability as the attacker can maliciously force a switch to dump heavy-hitter rules from the cache resulting in service-denial attacks.

So what rule-replacement strategies can designers of SDN switches and controllers adopt, when building a network, to provide performance and attack-resilience? There is significant literature on cache-design in distributed systems which suggest a number of strategies. Is it possible to achieve attack-resilience by retaining heavy-hitter rules in the flow table, as current traffic distributions suggest (LFU)? Or, is the key to attack-resilience to minimise the attacker's control of which rule is evicted by evicting randomly selected flow-rules (Random Replacement). Or, is evicting the least-recently-used rule the best way to rid the switch of spurious rules induced by attacker traffic?

2   Motivation and Threat Model

2.1   Motivation

The ability to control a target host's throughput in a network can to be a powerful weapon. An attacker may be motivated to throttle a target host's throughput in order to launch a number of insider attacks. The attacks proposed in this work provide an attacker with the ability to introduce arbitrary delays to the target host's incoming and outgoing traffic. Here we look at two scenarios demonstrating how this ability can be useful to a malicious entity while detrimental to the rest of the network as well as the abilities required of an attacker attempting to perform these attacks.

Trading Markets: Environments such as currency trading, stock markets and energy trading, require traders to be able to buy and sell commodity units in real-time. A trader with the ability to delay another trader's transactions, can gain a significant upperhand. For example, a trader company - Malequities Ltd, deploys malware within another - WeakTraders Ltd's recently upgraded network infrastructure composed of SDN. Launching cache-flushing attacks on the SDN switches at crucial times from within WeakTrader's network, gives Malequities

Ltd an edge in purchasing cheaper stock before its victim does so, and selling it just after WeakTraders Ltd makes a purchase. Thus WeakTraders Ltd ends up paying for Malequities Ltd's profit margin by inducing latency at the right times. The attack completely undermines the fairness property of the stock exchange and allows the attacker to obtain a first-mover advantage.

Video and Audio: Video and audio streaming have quality-of-service requirements in terms of the maximum latency the application codecs will tolerate. For instance, both video and audio codecs will drop packets that don't arrive at the destination within a certain amount of time, or reduce bit-rate in response to deteriorating network (bandwidth) conditions. Cache-flushing attacks proposed here can reduce the network bandwidth in such a way as to render video and audio streaming inoperable while under attack. Organisations are increasingly dependent on the availability of VoIP to conduct business and any disruptions have the potential to cause significant financial and reputational damage.

Denial-of-Service Attacks on Critical Infrastructure: SDN lowers capital cost and offers centralised management of network infrastructure. For these reasons, SDN is a good candidate for network infrastructure in cyber-physical systems (CPS). Latency plays an important role in ensuring systems integrity. A delay in flows or packets from sensors to actuators can lead to a rapid build-up of risks from simply unsafe to outright dangerous. For instance, delays in reporting the moisture levels of a tank of sulphuric acid can result in a blast with potentially fatal consequences. Thus an attacker who is able to induce flow latency can cause damage in a wide range of situations: A hospital under such an attack can result in alerts notifying staff about critical changes in their patient's conditions being delayed causing lives to be lost; An airport which has its network throughput reduced may be unable to co-ordinate the departures and landings of planes properly resulting in collisions and traumatic near misses; A sewage system unable to receive timely instructions can cause tanks to overflow causing urban pollution.

2.2 Threat Model

From the above scenarios, we can see that there is sufficient motivation to warrant this attack. In evaluation of these attacks, we make the following assumptions and place the following restrictions on the attacker.

- We assume the attacker(s) is a regular user of the network who does not have admin access to the network equipment or any hosts on the network except the ones he/she has compromised.
- The attacker may have compromised or otherwise has root access to a small subset of the hosts in the SDN network excluding the hosts whose traffic he/she is attempting to control.
- The attacker is not able to directly access or control the physical switches or controllers but is able to influence the state of the network using traffic from the hosts he/she controls.

These assumptions show that our attacker is a relatively standard user of the network with no special abilities and a secure SDN network should have the robustness and intelligence to handle a user (or small subset) who suddenly turns malicious. To reduce the potency of such a situation leading to these attacks, the network should be able to distinguish between legitimate and malicious flow requests- classing malicious flow requests as ones which are simply issued for the purpose of disrupting regular use of the network. Ideally it should be able to distinguish between malicious and legitimate requests from a single host such that in the event of the host becoming infected with malware, the network is still able to provide appropriate service to the host while defending itself against the effects of the malware. In addition to this, the issue of fairness as a security requirement arises. As a QoS assurance the network should ensure that use of the network's resources are appropriately apportioned among its users and no single user has the ability to abuse more than their fair share of the resources.

3   Background

The key to inducing a delay in network traffic is flow rule eviction. SDN switches hold flow rules in the TCAM which direct traffic through the switch. TCAMs typically hold 4000–8000 rules (some hold more). Due to the size of the network and the large number of flows per switch, SDN networks often employ active flow eviction strategies in which the controller explicitly removes flow rules from the switch to make room for new flows.

The ability of a user to request a rule which leads to the eviction of another rule in the switch provides a vector for malicious users to launch attacks. In the absence of a rule to direct a packet arriving at the switch, the switch is forced to send the packet to the controller for direction. This is called a cache miss and adds additional latency to the packet. Subsequent packets of the flow usually do not register this delay because the controller places a flow rule in response to the cache miss, however by causing the regular eviction of this flow rule, a malicious user causes a large majority of the packets in the flow to register cache misses giving the aggregate flow a higher latency, inducing a delay.

Various strategies can be used in deciding which flow rule to remove from the switch TCAM. The most common one is First in First Out- meaning the rule which has been in the TCAM the longest is removed. Least Frequently used- the rule which has the lowest number of packet hits per second, Least Recently Used- the rule which has not been used for the largest amount of time and Random Replacement- selecting a rule at random to be removed are also potential rule replacement strategies. Without active flow removal, once the switch flow table is filled, no new flows can be routed resulting in denial of service to some hosts.

4   Attacks

4.1   Determining the Switch Table Size

The aim of the attacks is to fill the switch's flow table with flows such that the legitimate flows in the network are continuously removed. As such, the attacker must, in each instance, determine the size of the flow table in question. Here we describe a "reconnaissance" attack an attacker can use to determine this value. Depending on the flow replacement strategy, this will involve probing the network in various ways. Because this part of the attack is not the focus of this work, we only demonstrate a probe under the FIFO strategy which gives the attacker an idea of the flow table size.

Abiding by the attacker model defined above, the attacker controls two physical hosts on the network. Determining the size of the flow table is simply a matter of requesting rules until one of them expires. Within one of these hosts (Host2), the attacker creates a large number of virtual interfaces, assigning each a valid network IP address. From Host1 the attacker can then regularly ping one IP address (IP1) on Host2. Once this is in action, the attacker sends a single ping to each of other the IP addresses on the interfaces created on Host 2. The number of other IPs which can be contacted in this manner before Host1-IP1 pings register a delay (which indicates a cache-miss) will give an idea of the number of rules in the flow table.

The main factor affecting the accuracy of this probe is the amount of surrounding network traffic as the attacker conducts his/her experiments. It is crucial that the attacker picks a time when there is expected to be as little traffic as possible on the network (e.g. late at night). Repeating the experiment several times will also help reduce the noise-induced errors (due to possible other traffic on the network). Even with this, there is not a 100% guarantee of accuracy, however it will give the attacker a general idea of how large the flow table size is.

4.2 First In First Out

The First In First Out (FIFO) flow rule replacement strategy is the default for OpenFlow Switches. When the switch's flow rule capacity is filled, it evicts the oldest flow rule in favour of new ones requesting space.

To induce a delay in a network user's traffic, the attacker must ensure that as many of the victim's packets as possible register a cache-miss forcing the switch to go to the controller for direction. To remove the user's rule (to achieve the cache-miss), the attacker must send enough traffic to fill the switch's flow table. The FIFO policy means that the number of packets the attacker sends in a particular flow after the first is irrelevant, as long as they are sent after the victim's rule has been put in place, the attack rules will be favoured over the victim's rule. With this in mind, the attacker sends a single packet to a range of destinations large enough to cause rules which fill the flow table and have the legitimate user's rule removed. Enough destinations cause the table to be filled with the attacker's rules which is the goal of the attack. Because the initial packet of a flow experiences some delay while the controller maps out the path and puts the rules in place, the constant removal of a legitimate flow's rule will have the effect of slowing down the entire flow effectively reducing the bandwidth of network.

Deterministic rule replacement strategies give the attacker a 100% chance of success if he/she is able to meet the criteria. In this instance, the criterion is simply to cause enough rules to get the victim's rule evicted as often as possible. The use of virtual interfaces and PINGs mean that the attack does not require a large amount of computing power and is only limited by the attacking host's bandwidth. The bandwidth will dictate the rate at which he/she can request new flows. The rate at which the victim sends packets through this flow also affects the attack. If the victim sends 1000 packets at line rate, the attack will be much less effective than sending 1000 packets at a rate of 10 per minute, in which case the attacker will likely have enough time to remove the flow rule between each packet. The number of compromised hosts the attacker controls also factors into the effectiveness of the attack. The more hosts the attacker controls, the more attack rules that can be requested per second. Very little physical effort is required of the attacker as well since the entire process can be automated with a short script and a list of the ip addresses.

5 Evaluation

5.1 Network Setup

To evaluate the various attacks described above, we utilise the network shown in Fig. 1 below. Up to this point we have only evaluated the success of the attack on the FIFO strategy. The results from this indicate a promising line of research. The key evaluation criteria is how much we can slow the bandwidth of the benign users when an attack is launched.

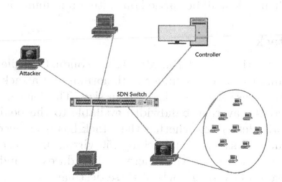

Fig. 1. Network setup

The network contains a Pica8 3297 SDN Switch, a ryu controller which installs the flow rules for communication in the network and four (4) Linux hosts. Two (2) of the hosts are used as "compromised hosts" and the other 2 as benign hosts on the network. Because of the small size of the experimental network, we constrict the size of the switch table to hold 90 flows. In a regular network where the switch flow table size is unrestricted, a switch can hold several thousand flows. The attacker would simply have to scale up the attack to be effective i.e. compromise enough hosts to support enough flows to facilitate the attack. This is not an unlikely scenario.

5.2 Determining the Switch Table Size

We evaluate this attack by testing the ability to accurately determine the number of flow spaces available in the switch. We launch 100 virtual interfaces in one compromised host and carry out 5 rounds of the attack described above. The results are given below.

Table 1. Determination of flow table size

Round	Num of Pings
1	45
2	44
3	46
4	45
5	44

From the results we determine we are able to ping between 44 and 46 interfaces before the first rule was replaced. Thus, we conclude that the switch has enough flow spaces for communication with no more than 46 machines. This is relatively accurate since the switch was set to hold 90 rules (each ping requires two (2) rules- source to destination and destination to source for the reply). With this in mind, each attack shall be carried out with a minimum of 50 destinations.

5.3 FIFO Attack

To evaluate the effectiveness of the attack, we conduct 10 file transfers from one benign machine to the other under both normal and attack conditions and compare the differences. Each file is 1 GB in size. The length of time the file transfer takes and the average bandwidth available to the benign hosts under both conditions will determine whether the attack has been successful or not.

We carried out the attack by launching 250 virtual interfaces on one "compromised" host, assigned them valid network IP addresses and had the other compromised host rapidly ping each of these destinations in quick succession. From the recon attack, 250 targets would be more than enough destinations to fill the switch flow table. The attack was repeated every 0.5 s thereby constantly renewing the rules in the table. It should be noted that this attack can be scaled up or down by increasing or decreasing the time between attack repetitions and/or using more compromised hosts, allowing the attacker to increase or decrease the victim's bandwidth at will. The results are documented below in Table 2 and Fig. 2.

6 Discussion

This work examines the impacts of cache-flushing attacks within an SDN network. The results in Table 1 show that the cache-flushing attacks slow down file

Table 2. Time taken and average bandwidth for file transfers under bening and attack conditions

Round	Benign conditions		Attack conditions	
	Time - secs	Avg BW - Mb/s	Time - secs	Avg BW - MB/s
1	8.741	106.5	20.234	50.4
2	8.733	119.8	21.667	47.9
3	8.732	119.8	21.580	45.6
4	8.730	106.5	28.557	34.2
5	8.732	119.8	26.605	36.9
6	8.734	119.8	22.985	43.6
7	8.732	106.5	30.115	32.0
8	8.733	106.5	21.428	45.6
9	8.735	119.8	21.803	45.6
10	8.733	119.8	23.534	43.6

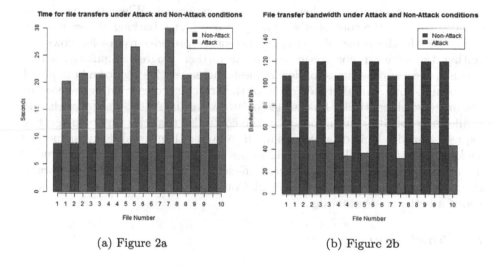

(a) Figure 2a   (b) Figure 2b

Fig. 2. Experimentation results

transfer significantly. Figure 2a and b show the file-transfer duration and the average bandwidth recorded. Under normal conditions, the recorded bandwidth was 106.5–119.8 MB/s while under attack conditions the recorded bandwidth was 32.0–50.4 MB/s. Under attack conditions, the transfer duration was increased by 400–600% compared to normal conditions, making this a successful attack.

In the evaluating the attack, we flush the flow table twice every second to achieve the increase in file-transfer duration. Several factors must be considered in the attack including the rate of flushing, size of the table and rate of flow rule installation. Increasing or decreasing the rate of flushing is likely to drive the available bandwidth down or up respectively. For example, flushing the table twenty times per second will cause more first-packet delays than twice per second providing the attacker with a tool to adjust the victim's throughput as desired. The size of the flow table dictates the number of destinations the attacker must send to in order to flush the table. As the flow table size grows, it is likely to become more difficult to flush the flow table unless he scales up the number of attack sources. This is achievable through the use of botnets and should not present a difficult challenge. Finally, the rate at which the controller can install rules will determine how quickly the table can be flushed and by extension the maximum number of flushes which can be executed per second.

Our analysis of cache-flushing attack is in its preliminary stages and we make several assumptions. First, we assume that the controller is sufficiently provisioned and does not suffer overloading as discussed by Kloti et al. [3] and Shin and Gu [4] during the attack. Second, we assume that controller-switch link [6] also does not suffer congestion as a result of the attack.

Both controller-capacity and the availability of the link between the controller and the switch are important considerations for attack performance. Due to the attack, a large number of flow requests are generated. When the number of requests exceeds the controller's capacity, it develops a backlog of flow requests or crashes. In the event of a crash, it no longer provides routes for flows and neither the attacker nor victim can make further progress. Similarly, with a backlog, the response times for flow requests increases, slowing down both attack and benign flows. Another side effect of the attack is congestion in the control-channel (switch controller link) which occurs when the switch-controller channel is filled to capacity causing delays in the controller response times when a flow request is made. This delay brings about a larger than usual delay in the first packet of the flow while the switch awaits the flow rule. We have not studied the impact of these variables on attack efficiency. Future work will move towards isolating the effect of rule replacement from the other issues in order to bring about a better understanding.

7 Conclusion

In this work we propose attacks against rule replacement strategies in Software Defined Networks and evaluate the attack resiliency of the FIFO flow-rule replacement strategy with the intention of carrying out similar evaluations of other prominent strategies. We demonstrate that the FIFO flow-rule replacement strategy is easily susceptible to attack which can then be used to throttle the bandwidth of neighbouring hosts in the network.

References

1. Kannan, K., Banerjee, S.: Compact TCAM: flow entry compaction in TCAM for power aware SDN. In: Frey, D., Raynal, M., Sarkar, S., Shyamasundar, R.K., Sinha, P. (eds.) ICDCN 2013, vol. 7730, pp. 439–444. Springer, Heidelberg (2013). https://doi.org/10.1007/978-3-642-35668-1_32

2. Katta, N., Alipourfard, O., Rexford, J., Walker, D.: Rule-caching algorithms for software-defined networks. Technical report. Citeseer (2014)
3. Kloti, R., Kotronis, V., Smith, P.: Openflow: a security analysis. In: 2013 21st IEEE International Conference on Network Protocols (ICNP), pp. 1–6, October 2013
4. Shin, S., Gu, G.: Attacking software-defined networks: a first feasibility study. In: Proceedings of the Second ACM SIGCOMM Workshop on Hot Topics in Software Defined Networking, HotSDN 2013, pp. 165–166. ACM, New York (2013)
5. Tavakoli, A., Casado, M., Koponen, T., Shenker, S.: Applying nox to the datacenter. In: HotNets (2009)
6. Wang, A., Guo, Y., Hao, F., Lakshman, T., Chen, S.: Scotch: elastically scaling up SDN control-plane using vSwitch based overlay. In: Proceedings of the 10th ACM International on Conference on Emerging Networking Experiments and Technologies, CoNEXT 2014, pp. 403–414. ACM, New York (2014)

Controlling Your Neighbour's Bandwidth for Fun and for Profit
(Transcript of Discussion)

Jonathan Weekes[✉]

Lancaster University, Lancaster, UK
j.weekes@lancaster.ac.uk

Software Defined Networks (SDN) are a type of network characterised by its separation of control and data planes. Control of the network's flow paths is given over to a centralised entity (the controller) which has a global view of the network. The controller installs "flow rules" which are stored in "flow tables" in the switches to provide instructions on where to forward packets of a flow. The OpenFlow protocol (the defacto protocol of SDN) dictates that any packets the switch receives for which it has no rules should be forwarded to the controller for instruction. The controller then installs the necessary rules and the packets are forwarded.

Within this protocol, the first packet of every flow experiences a delay as the switch forwards it to the controller then waits on the rule installation. Under normal circumstances, the other packets in this flow do not experience the same delay as the rule is already in place. The TCAM memory which SDN switches use to store their flow tables is very fast but also very expensive. As a result, the tables are usually restricted in size to a few thousand flows. To avoid the situation in which the table is filled and no new flows can be routed, SDN switches can be configured to employ active eviction in which it removes the oldest flows in the switch to make room for the incoming ones.

A major vulnerability in this system is that the value of the flow to the network is not considered when making space for new ones. As a result, several small flows may displace a heavy hitting flow rule causing the next packet of the heavy hitter to be forwarded to the controller since its rule has been removed. We exploit this using a "spray attack" which creates a large number of small flows resulting in a large number of rules with very few packets going through them. Creating enough rules within a short space of time allows us to completely flush the flow table of any rules that were previously there ensuring that any further packets for flows which were previously running through the switch experience the first packet delay. By repeatedly flushing the flow table in this manner, we ensure that a large percentage of the packets in the flow experience this first packet delay which increases the aggregate time of the entire flow. Thus from the end user's point of view, when under attack, it appears that his/her bandwidth has suddenly decreased. We demonstrate this attack under the threat model of an attacker who has compromised a small subset of the nodes on the network but does not have direct access to either the switches or the controllers.

© Springer International Publishing AG 2017
F. Stajano et al. (Eds.): Security Protocols 2017, LNCS 10476, pp. 224–231, 2017.
https://doi.org/10.1007/978-3-319-71075-4_24

Fabio Massacci: In this way it's also the attacker itself because it's in the same network that experience first packet delay, or am I wrong?

Reply: That is correct. The attacker would also experience a first packet delay. But I would argue that this doesn't matter, because he doesn't care about the speed of his flows particularly in this scenario. All he wants to do is make sure that the speeds of the other flows in the network are affected.

Fabio Massacci: What would be threat model for this. So you're sitting on the same network at the end of the day.

Reply: Yes.

Fabio Massacci: So what would be the goal of the bad guy in this case? Why would you like to essentially delay everybody else including itself?

Reply: Okay. Well I was going to discuss the impacts at the end, I should have brought it to the beginning. The impacts of this would range from simple, fun impacts to more serious ones. Simple fun impacts meaning your neighbor's trying to download a file from the Internet and it's suddenly remarkably slowed down. More serious implications would be stock trading business for example where transactions are time sensitive and if you see a stock at a particular price you want to send your transactions as fast as possible. If I'm able to slow down your transactions I could potentially drive you out of business.

Fabio Massacci: This is the wrong business model. For the financial transaction, because we have a project on this, and actually the people who do these fast things they buy their own dark fibre directly to the exchange because they want to make sure that they beat the other milliseconds. So they don't sit on the same network. They actually sit on separate dark fibre. You can even see on the Internet from Chicago American-style exchange to the NASDAQ in New York. That is these fibre that's owned by Goldman Sachs and all the others, so you need to find a better example than this one. People sitting on the same network.

Paulo Esteves Verissimo: Or, on the other hand, that might help the big guys to make sure little guys don't butt in at all. They might unify to make sure that smaller traders can't get in, whilst they're doing their transactions on a big fund.

Reply: Just let me answer the question. I think that it is important in any scenario in which you need a good bandwidth, even if you're having something like Skype conference calls or something like that. Someone who can suddenly lower the quality of your Skype call, as he sees fit, causes a lot of dropped packets. It may be a little more potent in such a scenario.

Tuomas Aura: I'm not sure if you're attacking bandwidth or latency, but at least you relay back latency. You will also affect latency. And the place where in our services aspect that causes latency yo take place is online gaming. So let's say a network in a gaming tournament, maybe all in one building, built on SDN. It would be quite tempting to do this to your opponents.

Reply: Agreed.

Bruce Christianson: How can you do it to your opponents without doing it to yourself?

Reply: Yes. So, in this particular attack, it's assuming that the attacker does not also have a vested interest at that exact time, when he is conducting the attack. So he may conduct the attack, suddenly stop the attack, carry out his transaction, and then continue the attack, to give himself the fine tuned window of a good network speed. Yes?

Markus Voelp: You may want to look into these edge cloud control live scenarios, where you try to offload some of the control bus to your base station or even closer into the cloud. In this case you have this real time traffic which must arrive in time or otherwise your car will crash or you will hit someone. And in parallel, you can still have traffic which is in your data center, which would not be affected by the latency delays.

Reply: Yeah.

Markus Voelp: But still it's latency and not bandwidth.

Reply: It is technically latency, yes. What would happen with the, for example, TCP transactions, because it's sending packets back and forth due to dropped packets, what you would see was the overall length of the transaction would increase, whereas the size of the file that is being transferred stays the same. In which case, if you're calculating throughput or bandwidth, it would seem like your bandwidth has been lowered. I'll illustrate that in a little while with some examples, but technically yes, it is latency that is being affected in some of the packets. With the attack, the next packet coming in after the flow table has been flushed receives this delay, and repetitively doing that ensures that a high number of packets in the flow experience a delay. In our preliminary evaluation, we carried it out in a physical network rather than using the mininet implementations of virtualised networks just to see how it performed on real hardware. So we used a Pica8 switch, controller machine using RYU which is, if you're familiar with SDN, a controller application that installs flows, and four rack servers, assuming two of them were malicious and two of them were trying to do legitimate transactions. They all had a standard 10 Gbps network interface card, just like the host machine in any office or home, for example. And this was the effect: under normal circumstances you see the first ping taking much longer time than the rest of them. So the first ping takes 10 s there, and the rest of it takes about 0.6–0.7 s.

Audience: Milliseconds?

Reply: Milliseconds, sorry. Forgive me. Milliseconds. Yes, 10 s for a ping would be an attack in itself. This may be a little bit difficult to see, so I'll just say what is highlighted there. So this is being run under an attack. The first ping takes 9 ms to complete. The second one takes 0.8 and then 0.6, and then we switch on the attack. Pings from the time we switch on the attack take 5 ms, 4 ms. We step up the attack. It goes up to 113 ms for a ping. So 113 ms versus 0.6 ms.

And as we turn down the attack and then turn it off, it drops to 7 ms, and then goes back to its regular 0.6 ms. Question?

Partha Das Chowdhury: A potential application can be railway tendering systems. In my country what happens is we have cartels in various parts of the country. So they don't allow other competitors to come in and participate and submit their bids within the time of the tendering process. And now they have all moved to Internet so the tendering is all done electronically. So that can be a potential application where somebody can harm others without compromising his own interests because he's not in that process at that point in time.

Reply: Yes, I agree. So moving on ...

Fabio Massacci: Maybe a different threat model would be the misconfigured machine on network cloud or something like this, and I have a misconfiguration in a part of the attack, it may generate all these connections by mistake. So this may be another threat model that you may want to consider rather than the malicious. Just because of the misconfiguration, the virtual machine that you have on one side all of a sudden start generating all these connections. So this may be an alternative-it may generate this behaviour.

Reply: Okay, thank you. We also carried out some tests in file transfers. This is just the preliminary testing. The blue bars that you see there are the file transfers under regular conditions, so no attack is happening. And you can see it happened generally about the same amount of time, in about 8 s, and the red ones are for the file transfers under attack conditions, so we're running the attack. It's a lot more erratic, but most importantly it takes some of them almost five times the amount of time as under no attack conditions. So this was the point I was making about the bandwidth seeming to have seemingly dropped. An unsuspecting user of the network at this point would be contacting his IT administrator saying, "Hi, for some reason I'm downloading my files extremely slowly. I need to get my work done." And the IT admin then tests the bandwidth. He finds it's slow. The attacker turns off the attack. He gets a normal bandwidth and he can't figure out why this is happening. Currently, there are no logging systems for rules that are moving in and out of the network as it is because it just assumes that this is normal behaviour. But, an attacker would be able to stealthy launch this attack, stop it at his will, move it up and down as necessary, as in throttle the bandwidth up and down as he wanted to. So this is what the bandwidth looks like under the attack and under no attack. With the attack it's very low, about 40 or 50 megabytes per second. Whereas, under no attack, it's closer to 120 megabytes per second. As we were discussing before, the potential impacts of this: video streaming quality, gaming, file downloads, Skype call quality, the financial transactions that we just mentioned, critical infrastructures, this one can carry some serious implications as well, hospitals that have time-sensitive treatments that need to reach their patients on time.

Ross Anderson: Another example is critical infrastructure, such as DNS. There is a DYN DNS attack in October from the Mirai botnet that managed to bring down twitter for several hours in the US Eastern seaboard, only because the guys at DYN DNS took that long to figure out what was happening to it. It's not just about spray attacks, it's about DDOS attacks, generally. The fact that people, even people who should know better, like people running the DNS services, often don't know the tools or the clues and the requisite combination to see what's happening.

Reply: Agreed. Some of the critical infrastructures-airports that are trying to tell planes when to land, sewage systems that have reaction mechanisms that should catch it before it overflows, it could flood a city, these types of critical infrastructure would be affected by drastically reduced bandwidth.

Hugo Jonker: How would a reduction to 40 megabytes per seconds address VoIP call quality?

Reply: Sorry?

Hugo Jonker: You claim that your attack in the previous slide reduced bandwidth to about 40 megabytes.

Reply: Mm-hmm (affirmative).

Hugo Jonker: Correct? And now you say that it will affect VoIP call quality?

Reply: Right. Now, what is important is that is not a set limit. So, in testing I've also been able to jam the file transfer that we were doing entirely. So, completely shut down the bandwidth because of the rate that we were cycling, the rate at which we were flushing the switch. So, we titled the paper "Controlling the Bandwidth" because you can literally turn the bandwidth from zero to maximum as you step up or step down the attack. So, to answer the question, the voice, the Skype call packets would be dropped, the sound would stop coming through, these would be sort of errors. And, Skype being the UDP protocol that it is, it would not be resending packets. So, your call freezes and you don't know why. Yes.

Hannan Xiao: Have you considered Quality of Service provisioning in the network?

Reply: Yes.

Hannan Xiao: Because FIFO is used normally for best effort service where they don't care about delay or bandwidth- it's that the application, we can adapt to that. But, traditionally a route may use FIFO in forwarding packets, but now you use SDN when you try to get the route from the controller so that's another schedule there. So, if you are going to be delay sensitive or bandwidth-sensitive applications, when a packet comes in it would be wrong to use FIFO to try to get the route from the controller.

Reply: Yes, so this is just the preliminary findings, but at the end of it I would like to show how quality of service will be affected throughout. Things like adaptive bit-rate videos that go through, if we can show that we can drastically reduce the quality that it brings in, it would look like you can't guarantee quality of service as long as you're moving these rules in and out. So, yes, thank you. Future work, we would like to explore other flow replacement policies and taking from CPU cache replacement policies that look at how data needs to be moved in and out of the cache. We'll be looking at least frequently used, so the flows that have the most packet hits, the highest value flows will stay in the network, which should be the most obvious solution. If a flow is receiving a high volume of traffic, it's important to the network, let's keep it in the network. We'll be looking at least recently used, the flows that have the most recent hits, packet hits will be kept into network. Random replacement, so it doesn't matter how long a flow has been there, how many packets it used. We pick a flow at random, chuck it out, and put in the new flows. With regards to these, however, there is no guarantee that they will work because if I, as an attacker, can generate a steady stream of data through the switch, my flows will seem more frequently used than the flows that are, for example coming from the internet, which might have a lower bandwidth than a flow that is generated on the network itself. Question?

Markus Voelp: Since most of your scenarios are quality of service or even real time oriented, you may also want to look into SDN scheduling related issues and papers.

Reply: SDN Scheduling?

Markus Voelp: Yeah, like, try to schedule real-time traffic in Software Defined Networks.

Reply: Okay.

Markus Voelp: There are a few papers out there.

Reply: Okay, thank you. Mm-hmm (affirmative). So, yes, an attacker generating enough high volume flows to take up the entire flow table would be a possible attack on both least frequently used and least recently used because it would ... transferring these streams across the network would have a higher bandwidth than someone trying to download a file, for example. Random replacement, we could potentially just use the same spray attack and hope for the best, hope that the flow that is removed is the legitimate flow that I'm trying to get out of the switch. Potentially we could use hybrids, but that would be future work and any potential, other flow replacement algorithms that you can think of. Yes.

Paulo Esteves Verissimo: What I'm going to ask doesn't take anything away from your work. It's about future, about something we're doing. If stronger authentication is used between controllers and devices, would any of your attacks succeed?

Reply: Between controllers ...

Paulo Esteves Verissimo: And devices.

Reply: Devices as in the hosts and the network or the switches?

Paulo Esteves Verissimo: No, the switches.

Reply: The switches? I don't think it would because the attacker model that we have in this scenario doesn't touch the switches. You see, it doesn't have any administrative rights on the switches. All he can do is request flows to be put into the switch.

Paulo Esteves Verissimo: They're put into the switch?

Reply: Yeah, by the controller. So, the switch is not malicious and the controller is not malicious.

Paulo Esteves Verissimo: The controller is fooled?

Partha Das Chowdhury: So the devices are internally connected, I guess.

Reply: Yes, they are internal.

Paulo Esteves Verissimo: So, the bad flows are installed in the devices, but the controller ... there is something that I'm missing, how or why does the controller send incorrect those into the devices?

Reply: Right, because at this point in SDN, there are no mechanisms to classify a flow as bad or good. A flow that has one packet going through it ...

Paulo Esteves Verissimo: No, but if I have authentication, you don't have bad guys trying to fool the controllers. That's good.

Reply: Right, I understand. So, the point I'm making is that there is no fooling the controller because he doesn't consider anything bad. So, everything is good to him, and, therefore, as charitable as he is, he can't be fooled. He's happy.

Paulo Esteves Verissimo: Okay, okay, okay, okay. So, if the interaction with the control were authenticated, so that the good people would be able to talk to the controller, but not the bad people. Again, this would be foiled.

Reply: Yes.

Partha Das Chowdhury: How do you know who the bad people are?

Paulo Esteves Verissimo: No, no, no ...
   Unknown: They are packets.

Reply: Yeah.

Paulo Esteves Verissimo: Different question.

Reply: So, presumably, at this point, the users have been already authenticated to the network and are subsequently compromised. So, possible solutions for this attack detection. The difficult thing about this is that as Paulo was highlighting, the controller accepts anything that is given to it. So, there is no such thing as a bad flow. Any flow that is given is installed to the switch, so how do we then detect which flows are bad or not? If we use IP blacklisting, potentially that could start spoofing addresses. Any address on the network that is valid is sending a flow request, and then we're back to square one. At this point, the research is its early stages, so we're still working out whether all the attacks work. I haven't gotten to the attack detection yet, but I'm very much open to solutions for this particular attack. If it's confounded people, well then that'll be great and I could potentially be cited a lot due to the fact that no one knows how to break it.

Permanent Reencryption: How to Survive Generations of Cryptanalysts to Come

Marcus Völp[✉], Francisco Rocha, Jeremie Decouchant, Jiangshan Yu,
and Paulo Esteves-Verissimo

CritiX, SnT—Interdisciplinary Center for Security, Reliability and Trust,
University of Luxembourg, Luxembourg City, Luxembourg
{marcus.volp,francisco.rocha,jeremie.decouchant,jiangshan.yu,
paulo.esteves-verissimo}@uni.lu

Abstract. The protection of long-lived sensitive information puts enormous stress on traditional ciphers, to survive generations of cryptanalysts. In addition, there is a continued risk of adversaries penetrating and attacking the systems in which these ciphers are implemented. In this paper, we present our work-in-progress on an approach to survive both cryptanalysis and intrusion attacks for extended periods of time. A prime objective of any similar work is to prevent the leakage of plaintexts. However, given the long lifespan of sensitive information, during which cryptanalysts could focus on breaking the cipher, it is equally important to prevent leakage of unduly high amounts of ciphertext. Our approach consists in an enclave-based architectural set-up bringing in primary resilience against attacks, seconded by permanently reencrypting portions of the confidential or privacy-sensitive data with fresh keys and combining ciphers in a threshold-based encryption scheme.

1 Introduction

Many application areas today produce enormous amounts of privacy or otherwise sensitive data and metadata while often underestimating its longevity. Human genotypes, sequenced for research and medicine, are a prominent example of such data as it combines long-time valuable information with a general desire to keep this data online accessible for medical research and other applications[1]. Current next generation machines sequence genotypes at an enormous pace of around 10^{11} raw base pairs per day. As a result, the costs of sequencing a human's DNA dropped below 1000 USD, and more and more genotypes are being sequenced,

---

This work is partially supported by the Fonds National de la Recherche Luxembourg (FNR) through PEARL grant FNR/P14/8149128.

[1] In fact we have selected genomic information for precisely this combination, but for the remainder of this paper and in hindsight of the workshop, please consider it as only one example of information with such properties and possibly not the best one. The interested reader is here directed to the transcript of the talk and the controversial discussion it triggered.

© Springer International Publishing AG 2017
F. Stajano et al. (Eds.): Security Protocols 2017, LNCS 10476, pp. 232–237, 2017.
https://doi.org/10.1007/978-3-319-71075-4_25

with protective measures barely keeping pace. Besides indicators allowing unique identification of individuals in a group, DNA may carry also stigmatizing information such as an individual's susceptibility to illnesses and its sensitivity to drugs.

DNA inheritance is a perfect example of an often overlooked aspect of sensitive data: its longevity. Such long lived data, originally collected in a legal way (e.g., to diagnose a patient), may be used for less ethical reasons in the future. For example, one could imagine the political impact in a presidential election if indicators for a serious disease in the genotype of a candidate's ancestor are made public. These threats are neither science fiction nor do they go unnoticed. For example, Gymrek and colleagues [6] were able to re-identify 13.1% of the donors contributing to the 1000-genome project, even though their data was anonymized, and Backes et al. [1] warned about the potential erosion of genomic privacy.

Naturally, a wealth of solutions exist at the protocol level, including synchronous [3,5,11] and asynchronous [2,13] proactive secret sharing approaches [7] to limit the time of share exposure in (t, n)-threshold ciphers [9]. The (t, n)-threshold thereby ensures that attackers, who are able to compromise up to $t-1$ out of n locations while reencrypting shares every epoch of size T prevents adversaries from recombining secrets learned at different epochs. Similarly, an efficient proactive encryption scheme [12] is also introduced to periodically update the secret keys for decryption. In particular, there is a unique public key in the system for data encryption, and this public key and all ciphertexts in the system do not need to be updated. All secret keys are updated periodically, in the way that a sufficient number of the secret keys in any single epoch can decrypt the data encrypted using the non-changed public key. So, all users in the system only need to remember a single public key, and use this single public key for encryption in the life time of the system, even though the corresponding secret keys (possessed by the corresponding decryption servers) are updated. However, with data whose life-spans exceed 50 years, we must also take into account two further threats:

T1. long-term cryptanalysis using leaked ciphertexts and
T2. revealed vulnerabilities of ciphers, both at the protocol level and below.

The contributions we are working on are therefore:

1. a system architecture to safely consolidate shares in a single location while limiting the probability of revealing plaintext but, equally important, of the rate at which ciphertext can be revealed; and
2. a heterogeneous (multi-cipher) proactive sharing scheme to mask vulnerabilities in individual ciphers, in their implementation or in the execution environment they execute in.

It is paramount to consider system-level attacks while constructing novel ciphers because the protection of many systems is flimsy at best. For an account of the protection state of sensitive systems, consider the recent testimony given in front of the Committee on Oversight and Government Reform [8] where US Department of Homeland Security revealed that it still relies on known to be insecure Windows 2003 server installations with a transition planned only for the fiscal year 2018. Combined with the increasing availability and sophistication of tools to penetrate and attack systems, this positions data loss as one of the most paramount risks long-lived information is facing, even if data is revealed partially or fully encrypted.

2   Threat Model

In this work, we consider threats mounted by external attackers on computer systems used to process data whose value remains high for several generations. Attackers may eventually escalate privileges and become "insiders", but must attain their goals through remote exfiltration of information. Thus, we exclude attackers with local and/or physical access, or any other kind of attacks whose attainable ciphertext extraction bandwidth exceeds the practical bounds of any reencryption system our system may use. Indeed, such insiders might simply steal or copy the disks. In particular, we therefore assume appropriate access restrictions and supervision of maintenance works. We assume a locally synchronous setting with reliable timing information available to all components and shielded from attacks. Network-only access and hypervisor-only adjustable timers justify this assumption.

We generally assume advanced and persistent threats and highly skilled adversaries capable of penetrating any exposed system. More precisely,

1. adversaries penetrate systems from the outside through any possible connection and proceed from there to penetrate further components;
2. adversaries can only exfiltrate information by remote means (including covert channels), with a bounded and known extraction bandwidth;
3. adversaries have unlimited external storage for storing plain- and ciphertexts; and
4. they will eventually learn about prospective vulnerabilities in the ciphers or their implementation.

However, we assume the impenetrability of trusted-trustworthy components and a sufficiently strong isolation of enclaves to limit data exchange between compromised entities to a bandwidth bounded by b_{max}.

Our working hypothesis, which remains to be validated as part of our future work, is that given an assumption about the minimal amount C of ciphertext needed for a successful cryptanalysis attack — even taking into consideration vulnerabilities, which may shrink the search space and diminish that amount — by restricting the amount of ciphertext material an adversary may extract to be less than C, we maintain confidentiality.

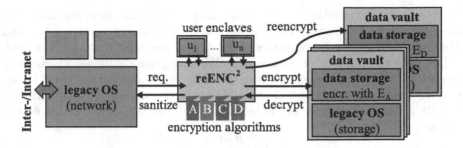

Fig. 1. Permanent reencryption architecture

3 Permanently Reencrypting Enclaves

To address on the one side potential future compromises of ciphers (both at the protocol and implementation levels) and, on the other side, breakthroughs in cryptanalysis and improvements of adversarial computing power, we take a more-shots-on-goal approach and use diversity, through a collection of replaceable encryption algorithms to protect the confidentiality (and likewise integrity and privacy) of stored data and metadata.

More precisely, on the architectural side, which we depict in Fig. 1, we decouple the data vaults from the networked legacy operating system (OS) by channeling all accesses through our $reENC^2$ component. Our goal is to limit the rate at which the ciphertexts of sensitive data are revealed to adversaries. We do not preclude covert channels and similar means to communicate between the data vaults and the networked legacy OS as long as the bandwidth between the two is lower than an upper bound b_{max}. In particular, we do not preclude the possibility of vulnerabilities in the legacy OSs (network and storage) and hence the possibility of compromise. $reENC^2$ is the trusted-trustworthy permanent reencryption enclave in our hybrid system design [10], whose role is to mediate user access to the data vault for operations (ideally directly on the ciphertext [4], but if necessary also by decrypting the data, and by reencrypting it after these operations complete). The actual operations are thereby located in user-provided enclaves u_j, which receive the decrypted data after successfully passing an access control check. Moreover, u_j communication is sanitized by $reENC^2$ to prevent unintended exposure of plaintext. We assume existence of sufficiently strong data sanitizers for all user operations and leave it as future work to construct such trusted-trustworthy sanitizers (possibly by requesting a proof of how u_j processes the data, which can then be matched against the data-release policy).

Ciphers plug into $reENC^2$ and are provided the keys and data to process. The coupling has to be such that faults do not spread to other enclaves or to the legacy OS. Dedicated access to FPGA-based implementations or software implementations with dedicated message buffers are examples of such a decoupling.

Besides granting access and redirecting data into user enclaves, the second primary role of $reENC^2$ is to permanently read data from the vault and reencrypt it with a fresh key and periodically also with a fresh cipher. To prevent a compromised data vault from keeping old data and, by this, from extending the time of ciphertext exposure, we redirect the output of reencryption to a fresh data vault and recycle the resources of old vaults once their data is transferred.

Let v be the number of data vaults. We anticipate vaults are executed in parallel. Hence, illegitimate channels between the vaults and the untrusted legacy OS have a maximal bandwidth of vb_{max}. Let c_i be the amount of ciphertext kept in vault i. Then adversaries are able to exfiltrate the tolerated fraction θ of c_i within

$$T_{leak} = \frac{\theta \ min_i(c_i)}{b_{max}}. \tag{1}$$

To prevent leakage of a large enough fraction of ciphertext, vaults have to be rejuvenated faster than T_{leak}. From this we can derive minimal bandwidth requirements between $reENC^2$ and the old and new data vault of

$$b_{min}^{par} = \frac{2 \sum_i c_i}{T_{leak}} \tag{2}$$

in case of parallel re-encryption and of

$$b_{min}^{seq} = v \ b_{min}^{lpar} \tag{3}$$

for sequential re-encryption of one enclave at a time.

3.1   Long-Term Data Encryption

The remaining questions are now: "How can we encrypt data such that we drastically reduce the dependence on the correctness of a cipher?" and "How, by reencrypting the data, can we maintain this situation for the life-span of the data?". The properties which must be enforced are that:

1. all data that is encrypted with a given key needs to be reencrypted with a fresh key before the adversary gets hold of enough ciphertext material to succeed in the cryptanalysis of this data; and
2. all data that is encrypted with a given algorithm must be reencrypted with an alternative algorithm, before an adversary learns how to break the algorithm (e.g., once a vulnerability is discovered).

Of course, adversaries may learn about zero-day exploits before an algorithm is replaced. To keep our long-living data protected, we therefore propose a proactive two-stage encryption scheme, using techniques drawing from fault and intrusion tolerance, where we combine f_1-threshold crypto with f_2-cipher diversity, where f_1+1 and f_2+1, respectively the number of shares to be captured and the number of diverse ciphers to be broken, for a successful attack, define the parametric protection of the data. By putting the evaluation of these parameters in context with the above-mentioned C parameter, in a real system, we claim that we will be able to reduce the probability of a successful attack below a tolerable residual risk, over a long life span. We plan to evaluate our approach through a security analysis and field experiments.

References

1. Backes, M., Berrang, P., Humbert, M., Shen, X., Wolf, V.: Simulating the large-scale erosion of genomic privacy over time. In: 3rd International Workshop on Genome Privacy and Security (GenoPri) (2016)
2. Cachin, C., Kursawe, K., Lysyanskaya, A., Strobl, R.: Asynchronous verifiable secret sharing and proactive cryptosystems. In: Proceedings of the 9th ACM Conference on Computer and Communications Security, CCS 2002, pp. 88–97. ACM, New York (2002). http://doi.acm.org/10.1145/586110.586124
3. Desmedt, Y., Jajodia, S.: Redistributing secret shares to new access structures and its applications. Technical report ISSE-TR-97-01, Department of Information and Software Engineering, George Mason University (1997)
4. Gentry, C.: A fully homomorphic encryption scheme. Ph.D. thesis, Stanford, September 2009
5. Gupta, V.H., Gopinath, K.: G_{its}^2VSR: an information theoretical secure verifiable secret redistribution protocol for long-term archival storage. In: International IEEE Security in Storage Workshop, pp. 22–33 (2007)
6. Gymrek, M., Golan, D., Rosset, S., Erlich, Y.: lobSTR: a short tandem repeat profiler for personal genomes. Genome Res. **22**(6), 1154–1162 (2012)
7. Herzberg, A., Jarecki, S., Krawczyk, H., Yung, M.: Proactive secret sharing or: how to cope with perpetual leakage. In: Coppersmith, D. (ed.) CRYPTO 1995. LNCS, vol. 963, pp. 339–352. Springer, Heidelberg (1995). https://doi.org/10.1007/3-540-44750-4_27
8. Power, D.A.: Federal agencies need to address aging legacy systems. Testimony Before the Committee on Oversight and Government Reform, House of Representatives, May 2016. http://www.gao.gov/assets/680/677454.pdf
9. Shamir, A.: How to share a secret. Commun. ACM **22**(11), 612–613 (1979)
10. Sousa, P., Neves, N.F., Verissimo, P.: Proactive resilience through architectural hybridization. In: ACM Symposium on Applied Computing, SAC 2006, Dijon, France, April 2006
11. Wong, T., Wang, C., Wing, J.: Verifiable secret redistribution for archive systems. In: International IEEE Security in Storage Workshop (2002)
12. Yu, J., Ryan, M., Chen, L.: Authenticating compromisable storage systems. In: IEEE TrustCom 2017 (2017)
13. Zhou, L., Schneider, F.B., Van Renesse, R.: APSS: proactive secret sharing in asynchronous systems. ACM Trans. Inf. Syst. Secur. **8**(3), 259–286 (2005). https://doi.org/10.1145/1085126.1085127

Permanent Reencryption: How to Survive Generations of Cryptanalysts to Come (Transcript of Discussion)

Marcus Völp[✉]

SnT - University of Luxembourg, Luxembourg, Luxembourg
marcus.voelp@uni.lu

Today I'm presenting permanent re-encryption. How to survive generations of crypt analysis to come. [...] And, I was told by Frank that I should use the first five minutes in order to convey the important message. So, thanks a lot. Thanks for your continuing excellent work in exploring, novel ciphers, cryptanalysis, in really building new crypto algorithms, and, in particular, into breaking them. Thanks for your recent advances in this field. And, a very special thanks to the team in Amsterdam and Google for breaking Sha1 just a week ago, because this gives me a perfect introduction into my talk.

What will it be about? I would like to start talking a bit about, genomic information, your DNA, and why it is worth to protect the privacy and the confidentiality of this information for at least the next 50 years? And, taking this as an example, I would like to make two points: First, since all of you are doing such an excellent work, we may have vulnerabilities, or we may find in the future vulnerabilities in the ciphers that we are using them. Like, in Sha1 where we now have the first collision. And hackers make exploit implementation vulnerabilities and also break you ciphers.

The big question is now, can we still protect sensitive data, which we want to use for a lifetime of 50 years by coming up with a combination of a clever architecture and protocols, such that we really achieve long-term data encryption? That we are sure to protect data for generations of cryptanalysist to come. So, this is my five minutes, and now you are free to interrupt any time you like. *[The presentation continues with an introduction of genomics as the motivating example]*

Ross Anderson: Marcus, I don't believe that genomics gives you the even remotely plausible application for long over-time encryption. I hear this all the time from people trying to sell quantum cryptography. And it strikes me as a lack of application knowledge. The slide you have there sums it up entirely. Genomics is becomes pervasive. It's very, very cheap to do. Right? You leave DNA everywhere. And what's more, you can get all that matters about a population by sequences a subset of living people in the past. Now, the threat to genomic privacy is not about people deciphering encrypted genomes in the far future. The threat is statistical inference control. The threat is inference attacks. It's an entirely different lecture series, not the lecture series of long term cryptography.

© Springer International Publishing AG 2017
F. Stajano et al. (Eds.): Security Protocols 2017, LNCS 10476, pp. 238–246, 2017.
https://doi.org/10.1007/978-3-319-71075-4_26

So I do accept that there are cases where you do need to protect stuff long term, but I don't believe that this is a good example to go through it.

Peter Y A Ryan: A good example then might be voting. Encrypted votes.

Marcus Voelp: Yes, maybe. So for both voting, and also in a certain way for DNA, and not answering to your question right now, Ross. You still have the problems that you have to reveal part of the data, which we partially addressed with our architecture, but, which is becoming a little bit difficult.

Answering Ross's question, currently we are doing it the wrong way, because companies gain control of our DNA, and we don't have any kind of control over it. In parallel, we have to process this huge amount of data in unsecure environments, in the cloud and so on. So I still believe that we need a protections scheme, which works for quite a long time, although there are alternative ways to gather DNA.

Ross Anderson: But the protection mechanisms that work here, are around the law of ethics. Right? The kind of problem we have in Britain is the hundred thousand genomes project now to be the fifty million genomes project. It could be a government scheme to sequences everybody, and keep everything online in the health service through a test account database lookups around DNA. That's wrong. That has to be fought at a political level. Because, if you go around saying, "We've got a wonderful encryption scheme which will make the fifty million genomes project safe" then politicians will use that as an argument to do it anyway, and they'll forget to do the encryption because it's too expensive. That's the problem that I was raising in the context of Joan's talk on Monday.

Paulo Esteves Verissimo: We have separate issues. Actually, now it's not all about law. I think it's about law and technologies. You were saying that there is no point protecting data, because anyway people will get to it?

Ross Anderson: No that's not what I said. I was one of the officers of the National Biometrics Council to report on exactly this, of what happens in medical ethics in the world of code-based medical records for basic genomics. There are many deep and interesting issues, but this isn't among them. Now, I think this is mistaken, because there are good and useful and interesting things to say about long-cover time cryptography. For example, how do you go about re-authenticating old contracts. Right? What about contracts for the sale of a real estate for example? If you're just using some kind of hashing function in a time-stamping service. So there are really good applications for this, but genomics is a bad example to choose as a motivating example.

Paulo Esteves Verissimo: It's forbidden to break into houses. And this is not the excuse for people who use lock. People use very secure locks. Why? Because there's a law enforcing that you get arrested when you break into a house. Still people do it. And if they do that, it creates damage, and, it maybe irrecoverable, but there are still valuable paintings and all that. So, even if I'm agreeing with you, this is more generic. I don't completely agree about the case for genomics. Why? Because we need, and I know we agree, laws that protect the genomic information. Until we have those laws and enforcement of the laws, we better use technology to protect what we can.

Ross Anderson: But we do have laws. The section is in the European Convention on Human Rights, chartered on fundamental rights, it's all there.

Paulo Esteves Verissimo: I'm not talking about that. I'm talking about laws that don't discriminate, that prevent discrimination of insurance companies and so on. But, anyway, let's agree that this is just one example, that there are other examples.

Joan Feigenbaum: I'd like to hear the rest of the talk, regardless of whether Ross thinks the motivating example is a bad one. And, I'd also like to address the point that whatever should be fought at the political level. I think that's true. In this case and in the same argument that Ross was making in my talk two days ago, but I do think that even while you fight things at the political level, you have to think about cryptography, to protect things and using cryptography correctly to protect things, which includes re-encryption. And even the people you're fighting with at the political level would ask you about cryptography protection.

Tuomas Aura: I guess many of us have documents that we don't want to be revealed, at least not in our lifetime and some of us might live more than 50 years, so that's one need. Then there are laws that require the documents to be kept secret for tens of years.

Marcus Voelp: Yes, one reason I picked this kind of example is that it both shows the need to protect information for a very long time, but it also shows that at the same time, we need to make it available, to have this information networked. For your case, also solutions to print it or store it somewhere, put it in the cupboard and leave it there and don't touch it anymore would work, for most of the documents. Here you really have the need to access it, and the solution which I now would like to come to ...

Tuomas Aura: Oh, I'm storing my documents in the cloud.

Marcus Voelp: I wouldn't trust my cloud currently to keep it safe for 50 years. *[Presentation continues with mentioning of Herzberg's secret sharing scheme]*

Here *[in Herzberg's proactive secret sharing]* the question is: should we in addition to coming up with these protocols where we essentially protect the key information, we protect the points that are used for these polynomes, should we also protect the ciphertext from leakage so that before enough information about the ciphertext is leaked, we are entering a new epoch so that the old ciphertext won't be usable anymore?

Fabio Massacci: Just a question, this because all these schemes normally work for the data being very small? When you actually protect the data you typically protect the key, the symmetric key with which the data is actually encrypted because, I don't think you can use this polynomal for a DNA that's one gigabyte if you have such an application. So in reality you have a symmetric encryption and then you just break the symmetric encryption at the end. You would just let this secret sharing stay and just break the last step.

Marcus Voelp: Yes, you are completely right. This is simply showing that we already have a few algorithms which think in the right direction. And I'm presenting you another version of it, which hopefully is really able to protect data for a very long time. *[The presentation continues with the assumptions, one of them being that the adversary has no physical access]*

Partha Das Chowdhury: So you're not considering applications like smart locks that have to remain secured for 20 years of their life. There you have physical access.

Marcus Voelp: The solution I will present here doesn't protect against physical attacks to the system. Let me phrase it in this way, so if you have additional solutions like hardening, hardware shielding and all this kind of things, then you may use this kind of architectures *[in environments where adversaries have physical access]*. Here I'm simply excluding these types of attack by assuming that I have some cloud environment and physical access is limited so you can't spend days in your cloud server room in order to run these attacks. Simply because I don't know exactly how good the hardware protection mechanisms are currently in order to survive for the next 50 years, probably another interesting question. *[The presentation continues with a description of the architecture and protocol]*

Now if you have such a piece, we encrypt this piece and this gives us ciphertext based on the different algorithms which we are using here, so now we have algorithmic diversity plus cipher diversity in our system. And then, if we find that the key of one of these algorithms is likely to be revealed after some time, then before this happens we just re-encrypt with the same algorithm and with the same *[must be a different]* key. Our assumption is that key material are leaked much quicker than adversaries find vulnerabilities in the ciphers. Before such a vulnerability could be found for enough of this data, we could also re-encrypt by changing the algorithm.

Marios Omar Choudary: Instead of doing this re-encryption of different algorithms for different chunks, why don't you do the re-encryption of all chunks but several times, and re-encrypt with different algorithms every time?

Marcus Voelp: We do it proactively with different algorithms and on the individual chunks.

Marios Omar Choudary: And what is the advantage compared with the two approaches?

Marcus Voelp: So for the Herzberg secret sharing algorithms there is the single algorithm, if you break it then you have broken the entire system. Here, you need to both combine enough of these shares — so you need access to these ciphertexts in order to make sense of the whole secret — and in order to gain access to these shares you must be able to gain access to all these ciphertexts.

And before the ciphertext is leaked we are changing the encryption, either by the more lightweight version, by changing the key which we are using for this encryption, or if we find vulnerabilities by replacing the algorithm.

Marios Omar Choudary: What do you mean by "before the ciphertext is leaked"? How do you know when this is the case?

Marcus Voelp: We assume a certain maximum by known bandwidth that the adversary has in order to exfiltrate ciphertext from the enclave. We don't assume that the protection is perfect, but it's limited in a way that you can exfiltrate only so much data in any given period of time. So now before a significant part, a threshold of the ciphertext is leaked that would be enough — and I don't know where this threshold is — to later on run a ciphertext-based attack and reconstruct your initial secrets once you have found all these vulnerabilities here, before this happens we are re-encrypting the data in order to store it in a new enclave which hadn't seen any of these encrypted data yet.

Tuomas Aura: I'm wondering if you actually have the physical architecture for implementing something like with this limited bandwidth to the enclave. Because the communication bandwidth that you need to the re-encryption engine that has to be high enough to do the re-encryption in one re-encryption round. That shows that your vault actually has enough bandwidth to spit out all the ciphertext in one re-encryption round before you have done it. I don't see how you can limit the bandwidth, except for some very slow serial bus whatever that this worm communicates over to reduce it to a few bits per second, but basically to reencrypt you need to have a maximum bandwidth.

Marcus Voelp: What is not shown here in this picture [*Figure 1 in the paper*] is the enclave provider we envisage. If you would put everything into a many-core and you trust your enclave provider, which in this kind of architecture you have to do, then you have legitimate channels which work at much higher bandwidth than would be accessible for exfiltrating the state. Just think of an application running on your legacy OS within your same manycore architecture. An application which needs to talk to of the data enclaves. If it doesn't have the permission granted by the enclave provider, it would have to use side channels in order to exfiltrate this information, which is a much lower bandwidth than an allowed communication between enclaves. For now SGX doesn't provide enclave-to-enclave communication.

Tuomas Aura: But you are not going to convince me that Intel hardware security will last 50 years.

Marcus Voelp: No. I'm not even trying to convince you that Intel SGX is the right architecture for that.

Tuomas Aura: I might buy it if you say, "Well, each one of these vaults and re-encryption engine, each part of this, the hardware protection maybe will last for a year." Then we can replace every single part there. But now you are saying that there's some underlying layer that stays there for 50 years.

Marcus Voelp: No, what I'm saying is, in order to implement this architecture, you need to distinguish between allowed and unallowed communication. The bandwidth for the allowed communication must be much higher than the bandwidth that an adversary would get when exfiltrating information by other means. So all the cover channels which exist in your architecture, no matter how you construct it, you could use different machines to run the data vaults and a network connection and then have the network layer programmed in such a way that you have a direct connection in here *[between the vault and the re-enc component]*. And you may be still able to leak some information by modulating the timing when these requests are done and all these kinds of things.

So this gives you the cover channel bandwidth from the data vault into your adversarial code. And now you have this bandwidth gap here, and yes, the bandwidth here *[at the legitimate channel]* must be large enough in order to actually do real work, and to do the re-encryption and in particular the bandwidth ... The cover channel bandwidth here much be low enough so that we have enough time to do such a re-encryption step before enough of the cypher text is leaked.

Fabio Massacci: I like the idea that you were chopping physically as I understood it now, right? Not only digitally, but periodically, especially if you're thinking of 50 years, you need to reconstruct the whole thing again. Just you need to think the format of data because maybe the Acrobat PDF don't exist anymore, it reads the data that is 15 years old, or 20 years old. So you need to have something periodically to make the whole thing whole and then chop it again. You think that this keep working?

Marcus Voelp: I hope so because for constructing it and for redistributing it, so the easy case. This is done inside one of these re-encrypting enclaves for really re-encrypting to a different format. You still have these user enclaves where you can say, "Okay, now I need to really change my format. So I have one of these user enclaves which takes the old format, comes up with a new format and then writes it back into the next data vault."

Fabio Massacci: No, but I understood in your scenario that it's just a single bit that did change. What I liked the first you collect all the things together and then redo the split again, because you cannot just change the individual bits.

Marcus Voelp: No, the re-encrypting part gets access to the complete chunk. And for most applications you need to have this access unless you do homomorphic encryption stuff and so on. But only this component here *[the re-enc enclave]* has access to it and this is the one which we assume to be trustworthy.

Paulo Esteves Verissimo: We wanted to test fundamentally two things because this is a work in progress. One is, Thomas, great question. It's how reasonable and feasible is our hypothesis of having a differentiated bandwidth. And actually we can reply to your question, this re-enc2 imagine that it could have a much narrower bandwidth to the left *[to the legacy OS]* than to the right *[the data vaults]*. But this is what we want to test if you feel that this is feasible.

The other is this assumption that there's a certain amount of ciphertext which can become a percentage that we say, "If we don't leak more than this, we're safe." We'll also want to test if that makes sense, because this all is based on the fact that the adversary just gets a piece of the ciphertext which is parametric.

Tuomas Aura: So, Thomas, let's say you don't ... It's not trusting the hardware, and you say, "Ah, this Intel processor, probably five years' time, someone's going to break it." And I want to move my data vault to new hardware. Now there has to be a channel now that process this air gap between the old vault and the new vault. Within that five years. You have to transfer the data there using some encryption algorithm or combination of millions of algorithms. But you had to do that anyway with the current algorithm technology. So I record the step when this communication happens.

Paulo Esteves Verissimo: You take the Internet out.

Tuomas Aura: And now we've had to take all those algorithms, I think it seems that you can never move it to new hardware outside your current Intel processor.

Marcus Voelp: Yes and no. Yes, I can't do it because exactly if I would use an encryption algorithm to move data from one side to the other side, then I'm running into the same problems again. But what I can do, because that's just such a rare event that I'm really starting to distrust all the cores in my system. I can survive all the cores of a certain type by having enough cores in my manycore architecture and switching simply from Intel to ARM or whatever unless ARM is broken. But as long as this data transfer is rare enough, I have still the option to really shut down the entire system physically move the data from A to B and then use it there.

Bruce Christianson: When the heckling began, several people gave examples where the primary security service required was integrity rather than secrecy. And, on the principle of threat/service duality, there's a related question. I claim that I broke one of your secret texts. But can I prove that it's actually a break of the cryptotext that was originally there, and that it isn't a break of a retrofit that I've somehow substituted for the original? Which is clearly the same problem. Does your infrastructure give you integrity for free, or is that a completely separate problem?

Marcus Voelp: I don't know.

Peter Y A Ryan: If you don't know and go looking for proof, the answer is that that's part of the problem.

Ross Anderson: Could I perhaps come in at this point? I can see lots of applications for this. 20 years ago I was working on an AES candidate: Serpent. The U.S. government in its wisdom chose a faster but weaker algorithm for the certification of weaknesses, in my opinion, of no account. But this gives people an excuse to push other algorithms. The Chinese, for example, have SM4. The Russians have GOST. This leads to trade friction.

If you have a framework within which people can do triple encryption with replaceable algorithms, then that provides a technical way forward. To do that requires some real protocol engineering to-do, because to make ciphers commute you want to use them in streamcipher mode, and if you want to make the integrity work too, you need to think carefully about how you can deal with multiple authenticator attacks. If you could put a framework like that together and work out a system of engineering of appropriate roles of operation to do things like full disc encryption, that would be a real benefit and it will also give you a real potential benefit in that if you are doing three different encryptions with three different cores, for example, or three different encryptions with the same core. Then there are interesting pluses and minuses from the point of view of timing attacks and power attacks, which are a real concern.

During the last AES conference, people asked whether people might potentially use more than one AES finalist. So probably should be a reserve finalist kept in case the finalist was broken. And the concluding view was that yes, if AES were to fall into misuse it would be because of some completely different type of attack. Of course, the attacks that have been developed since then are thing like timing attacks and power attacks. So with all this context, yes, multiple replaceable encryption does potentially have some uses if you can get the protocol engineering right to do both the encryption and the authentication in a way that makes sense.

Marcus Voelp: I completely agree and in particular that's kind of in part what I put here at the remains-to-be-done list. We have to work on the protocol level how these algorithms work together.

Ross Anderson: I think that's actually a motivating example. Can you kill timing attacks and power attacks? And can you encrypt the DES and SM4 and Serpent for example, or whatever the combination is.

Tuomas Aura: Your attack model is such that you have this long-term sequence that don't change. I think you might be more plausible to do this re-encryption if you're actually worried about chosen-plaintext attacks which all require dynamic encryption. If it's instead of permanent general data, it's a database where the users continuously issue reads and writes. Then the real attacks would be something where the attack chooses the plaintext for the ciphertext. For that, you could kind of ignore the fact that the attacker may get hold of the old, static data. But you can prevent, by updating algorithms, that the attacker can in the future use these old algorithms for the chosen-plaintext attacks.

Ross Anderson: I agree, but this is a really big thesis, this piece of work.

Paulo Esteves Verissimo: Doesn't this enter into the amount, because then with chosen-plaintext attack, he gathers this amount of ciphertext that he needs, right? That goes probably into how much ciphertext we allow to be leaked, right? What you're suggesting is that it's probably less than ... If it's just any ciphertext, we can release more. If it derives from chosen-plaintext attacks, maybe he gets leverage and we should be more careful about the assumption. Because this can go out, if I understand it well, we're protecting this thing whilst it's here. We need it to be used outside, and that's where you enter your information.

Tuomas Aura: That wasn't really the point I was trying to make. Let's say you suspect now some cipher has become weak, and it's vulnerable to chosen-plaintext or chosen-ciphertext attacks. Now, you can update your old data to the new cipher, and the attacker will never be able to choose plaintext or ciphertext for the whole data because that is discarded, even though that may be published in the Cloud, or something. But your working set, the changing data, is now with the new set.

Virgil Gligor: Well, so you have to re-code it, because the data itself, as far as the cipher goes its genome. So it won't work, because the tactic cannot change. You can re-code it but if you leak it once, it's gone.

Marcus Voelp: That was one of the basic assumptions which we are making here, or the question which we are asking. "Do we, in addition to protecting the plaintext also have to protect the ciphertext?" Because once the ciphertext is leaked and then later on someone finds a chosen-plaintext attack, will he be able to take the leaked ciphertext and decrypt it based on the knowledge that he now has gathered on the broken algorithm?

Security from Disjoint Paths: Is It Possible?

Sergiu Costea, Marios O. Choudary$^{(\boxtimes)}$, and Costin Raiciu

University Politehnica of Bucharest, Bucharest, Romania
{sergiu.costea,marios.choudary,costin.raiciu}@cs.pub.ro

Abstract. We propose a work-in-progress protocol to detect man-in-the-middle attacks during the communication between two parties, by leveraging the existence of disjoint paths between the communicating parties. Our protocol allows us to detect attackers either at the protocol level (through delay measurements) or at the user level (if the attackers tamper with the data).

1 Introduction

Authentication in computer networks is a great challenge today. Since the proposal of the Diffie-Hellman key exchange protocol [1], many security protocols have tried to provide some sort of guarantee that a host is communicating with the intended party. This has been implemented mostly by means of trusted third parties (e.g. certificate authorities, ticket-granting services) or using long-term secrets (passwords and secret keys). One of the most widely used security protocols today for secure communications, Transport Layer Security (TLS), relies on a certificate authority (CA) to authenticate a secret key for use in secure communication, very much in the manner that was proposed by Needham and Schroeder back in 1978 [2]. Since then, most of the scientific effort has been focused on securing the practical implementation of the protocol and making the implementation fast, in particular for very short-lived communications (see e.g. the recent effort on TLS v1.3 [4]).

However, the required trust on the CA (i.e. on a trusted third party) represents a fundamental weakness of the current TLS approach. If attackers manage to compromise a certificate authority, they can issue fake certificates to decrypt the communication. This has happened in the recent past, with the cases of the Comodo and Diginotar certificate authorities. In the case of Diginotar [11], the attackers were able to issue over 500 fake certificates that were used to connect to major websites, including the CIA, Google and Microsoft. In this case, the Diginotar certificates were revoked from all Internet browsers, effectively closing its business. However, this does not solve the underlying problem. Furthermore, the hack on Diginotar was only found and revealed several months after the system was compromised, so there is no assurance that a CA is not compromised.

Another weakness of TLS is that powerful state adversaries can issue deliberately fake certificates or use their influence to control CAs. That is, we have no guarantee that a nation-wide adversary, such as China or US, will not influence a CA in order to get access to some communications.

F. Stajano et al. (Eds.): Security Protocols 2017, LNCS 10476, pp. 247–253, 2017.
https://doi.org/10.1007/978-3-319-71075-4_27

Finally, enterprises might want to analyse all the data traffic inside their network. This is done by inserting fake certificates into organisation computers. While this can be motivated by the need of defending against viruses, it also infringes on the privacy of employees whenever they communicate personal information.

We propose to explore a different approach: to establish a secure communication between two parties by using at least two paths through public networks like the Internet. This is interesting now, since the use of multiple communication paths is becoming popular, particularly since multipath TCP [5] has been implemented in iOS in 2013 and network operators in Korea started to use it to increase their bandwidth [6].

There has been some previous research on using multiple channels for security, such as multichannel security protocols [7] and two-factor authentication, but these approaches assume the existence of a secured channel, such as a visual channel or a carrier-secured message/voice channel. Instead, we want to focus only on public channels, without relying on third party servers or prior security between communicating parties.

In particular, in this paper we want to discuss the possibility of obtaining secure communications from disjoint paths, i.e. paths that never intersect, except at the sender and receiver sides, without relying on certificates or pre-established long-term secrets between the communicating parties. Additionally, we want to look at the strongest possible attackers: those that are simultaneously present on all disjoint paths and are willing to modify traffic. Is this possible? This is what we will discuss and partially answer in this paper, leaving the door open for better solutions and more practical implementations.

2   Obtaining Disjoint Paths

A first question is whether we can actually obtain disjoint paths in practice and if we can guarantee that they remain disjoint from end to end over a public network, such as the Internet.

A first idea is to use mobile devices equipped with multiple interfaces such as WiFi and cellular. When both WiFi and cellular connectivity is available, mobile phones can use these interfaces to setup two channels to any destination, as in the example shown in Fig. 1. Unfortunately, in this example, the two paths start out on different networks but converge a few hops away from the server.

Another option, that may allow us to obtain path diversity uses long-lived tunnels that cross jurisdictional and geographical boundaries. To set up such tunnels, regular users could rely on cloud computing and rent virtual machines in other countries. For example, in Fig. 2 a user based in Europe sets up a long-lived tunnel between his machine and its VM in the US. This user will have IP address A1 in Europe, and address A2 inside the USA cloud. The tunnel is secured using a secret decided when the user first registers with the cloud, and

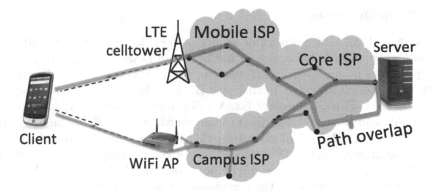

Fig. 1. Path diversity available to mobile users.

will be used to create path diversity for *all connections* this user makes with other parties.[1]

The service provider B must also setup a similar tunnel, but in many cases such tunnels already exist. All major providers, (including Microsoft, Google, Facebook, Amazon, etc.) have multiple datacenters spread around the globe which are already connected via encrypted long-term tunnels. Smaller providers rely on content distribution networks to achieve similar geographical footprint.

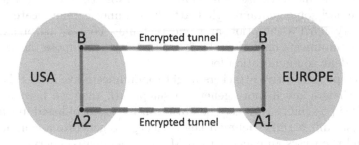

Fig. 2. Using long-term tunnels to ensure path and jurisdiction diversity.

On the server side, B must be able to use the connection ID to "recognize" channels belonging to the same client-server connection arriving at different datacenters it owns and direct them to a single backend server. This problem is called multipath load-balancing, but a scalable solution has recently been proposed that we can leverage [8].

---

[1] This is the only time the user will have to use one of the undesirable solutions such as password-based authenticated key exchange, but this only needs to be done once per user.

2.1   Open Questions

Although we have shown a possible approach, how do we get the IP address of the server endpoints? One option would be to use DNS. A will perform a DNS lookup for B's name using its A1 address; provider B will use A1 location to select the closest datacenter, in this case B1, and the client can now setup the A1-B1 channel. Then, to discover B2, A will perform another DNS lookup from address A2, and B's load balancing mechanism will return B2. A can now setup channel between A2-B2. Unfortunately, this leaves us open to possible man in the middle attacks on the DNS replies, so we cannot fully trust the response from DNS. A possible approach might be to rely on block chains, as has been done recently to decentralise the certificate authorities while still providing a trusted name service [9].

Other issues also surface. How do we deal with services that do not operate on multiple continents? What if the users do not have a VPN connection to another continent?

3   Security from Disjoint Paths

Say we have practical methods for obtaining disjoint paths, e.g. using the VPN solution presented earlier. How do we use this for obtaining secure communications?

One option would be to use secret sharing [3] to split the secret data across the paths, if we had some guarantee that attackers cannot communicate. However, this is a very hard assumption and one that may be easy to break, even if attackers communicate only after the fact (it is easy to compose the secret from the independent communication logs).

If we accept that active attackers might communicate live across the disjoint paths (which is a much more general assumption), then we need a different solution. One possibility is to use the data transfer protocol listed in Fig. 3. The protocol first runs a Diffie-Hellman key exchange to generate a communication key K_C and then uses an encrypt-then-MAC authenticated encryption method as follows. User A generates a fresh key K_T, which is used to create a Message Authentication Code (MAC) $t = \mathsf{MAC}_{K_T}(C)$ over the ciphertext C. The key K_T and the MAC t are sent on a long-delay path. The client waits time equal to the round-trip between $A1$ and $A2$, and then sends the N-blocks long ciphertext $C = \mathsf{Enc}_{K_C}(M)$ on a short-delay path. While the keys K_C and K_T may be compromised by active attackers, the goal of this protocol is to make a successful attack difficult[2].

Say the client originates its data from $A1$ and the server receives (i.e. combines) all data at $B1$ (see Fig. 4). In our protocol the client only sends the temporary key K_T (new for each sent message) and the authentication tag over the long-delay ($2T$) channel ($A1$-$A2$-$B2$-$B1$), while the bulk of the encrypted

---

[2] By successful we mean that attackers can remain part of the conversation, while honest users exchange messages, without being detected.

Procedure ClientSend(M)

$K_T \xleftarrow{\$} \mathcal{K}$

$C \leftarrow \mathsf{Enc}_{K_C}(M)$

$t \leftarrow \mathsf{MAC}_{K_T}(C)$

$\mathsf{Send}_2(K_T, t)$

$\mathsf{Wait}(2T)$

$\mathsf{Send}_1(C)$

Fig. 3. Secure multipath data transfer

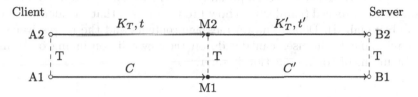

Fig. 4. Secure multipath data transfer protocol when attacked by two communicating active adversaries.

data (C) over the short-delay (for simplicity, we assume this delay is 0) channel ($A1$-$B1$). The roundtrip for $A1$-$B1$ without an active MITM attack is $4T$ and the total communication cost used across the long-delay channel is the size of K_T and t.

An active attacker that wishes to intercept the communication (i.e. decrypt and re-encrypt) first needs to tamper with the communication key K_C in order to use different keys K_C^A and K_C^B with A and B. Then, the attacker must to perform one of the following: (a) wait for the ciphertext C, decrypt, re-encrypt as C' and send a new tag t' (and possibly new K_T') from $M1$ to $M2$ – and this forces a delay of $4T$ between $A1$-$B1$ (so a RTT of $8T$); (b) forge/fake the re-encrypted data C' to avoid the previous costs.

This protocol makes the job of such adversary much more difficult than opportunistic encryption methods such as TCPCrypt [10]. This is because in order to avoid detection, the adversary must introduce false data into the communication. Therefore, users might eventually detect that they are not getting the expected content.

However, The data transfer protocol presented here has several security issues. Whenever the client sends an encrypted message the attackers can choose to stop forwarding messages to the server. This breaks the communication between the client and server. However, the attackers have already gained access to the first ciphertext and can decrypt it. Thus, they compromise the confidentiality of the first message without incurring high network communication costs. The client notices that something is wrong with the session, but can do nothing about the leaked contents in the first message.

Also, since the server provides no identity information, it is impossible for the client to distinguish between the legitimate server and the attackers. In this case, we rely on the user somehow noticing that the content in the server's reply is forged. Whether the user can be used to verify some types of Internet communications is an interesting question for future work.

Another issue is how to continue after an attack is detected, either in a true positive scenario (when an attacker caused the delay) or a false positive one (where network congestions or route changes delayed communication). Note that from a single run of the protocol, it is difficult to discern between the two. One tempting solution is to run the protocol again. However, since the first message is leaked an attacker can reliably replay the message the second time without causing any delay. In such cases, a possibly better solution would be to query the user on how to proceed (similarly to how browsers signal that the identity checks for a website failed). Depending on message contents and the repressiveness of their environment, the user can decide on their own if continuing or trying a different means of communication is safer.

4   Certifying Identity

A last important problem that we discuss in this paper is that of identity. Besides protecting from possible man-in-the-middle attackers between the client and the expected destination, the certificates used in TLS also prove that the entity you are connecting to is really that entity (e.g. your bank). Unfortunately, as mentioned in the introduction, the possibility of rogue certificates means that in practice we don't really have this guarantee, so we are left just with an ideal trust that all the certificate authorities are doing their job well.

Since we are in the context of disjoint paths, it would be very useful to leverage them also to certify the identity of the other party. One possible research direction is to rely on block chains, such as Bitcoin, to link the identity of a service provider with its pair of IPs.

Acknowledgement. We thank Virgil Gligor and Ross Anderson for very interesting discussions during the Security Protocols Workshops and for great ideas on how to improve our work.

This work was sponsored in part by the European Commission, through the SSI-CLOPS H2020 project.

References

1. Diffie, W., Hellman, M.E.: New directions in cryptography. IEEE Trans. Inf. Theory **22**(6), 644–654 (1976)
2. Needham, R.M., Schroeder, M.D.: Using encryption for authentication in large networks of computers. Commun. ACM **21**(12), 993–999 (1978)
3. Shamir, A.: How to share a secret. Commun. ACM **22**(11), 612–613 (1979)
4. Krawczyk, H., Wee, H.: The OPTLS protocol and TLS 1.3. In: 2016 IEEE European Symposium on Security and Privacy, pp. 81–96 (2016)
5. Ford, A., Raiciu, C., Handley, M., Bonaventure, O.: TCP Extensions for Multipath Operation with Multiple Addresses, IETF RFC 6824, January 2013

6. GigaLTE, news of Multipath TCP in Korea.http://blog.multipath-tcp.org/blog/html/2015/07/24/korea.html
7. Wong, F.L., Stajano, F.: Multichannel security protocols. IEEE Pervasive Comput. **6**(4), 31–39 (2007)
8. Olteanu, V., Raiciu, C.: Datacenter-scale load balancing for multipath transport. In: Proceedings of the 2016 Workshop on Hot Topics in Middleboxes and Network Function Virtualization, HotMiddlebox 16 (2016)
9. Namecoin. https://namecoin.org/
10. Bittau, A., Hamburg, M., Handley, M., Mazieres, D., Boneh, D.: The case for ubiquitous transport-level encryption. In: USENIX Security Symposium, pp. 403–418 (2010)
11. The Guardian: Diginotar SSL certificate hack amounts to cyberwar. https://www.theguardian.com/technology/2011/sep/05/diginotar-certificate-hack-cyberwar

Security from Disjoint Paths: Is It Possible? (Transcript of Discussion)

Marios O. Choudary[⊠]

University Politehnica of Bucharest, Bucharest, Romania
marios.choudary@cs.pub.ro

During my SPW talk, I presented the work that we did in the SSICLOPS European project on how to provide secure communications in a very difficult context: when we may not trust third party servers (e.g., Certificate Authorities) and we may not have long term secrets either.

In the following, I summarise the part of my talk until I was interrupted the first time (this was around minute 17' in my talk). Then, I present all the discussions we had during my presentation.

The most common protocol to exchange a secret key with another party with whom we have no prior secrets is the Diffie-Hellman key exchange protocol. However, in order to protect against Man-in-the-Middle (MITM) attacks, we need to authenticate somehow the public key obtained from the other party. The most common solution for this is to rely on certificates in order to validate for example the identity of a server. However, we cannot always rely on third parties, as we saw in the case of the DigiNotar Certificate Authority, which was hacked in order to issue fake certificates.

In our solution, we leverage several *public* channels to derive some amount of security, without relying on third parties or prior knowledge between participants. But even in this scenario, if we allow adversaries to communicate across these multiple channels (which is the more general scenario), we cannot guarantee a secure key exchange, simply because adversaries can always perform an active MITM attack. However, for some applications (e.g., voice chat or other applications) that involve bi-directional data transfer for some amount of time, we can increase the cost of a MITM attack to such extent that it even becomes detectable. This is the main idea behind our solution.

At this point, I presented our protocol, which you can also find in our paper. In short, we rely on a secure channel between a user's computer and some remote server across continents (e.g., a VM at Amazon) to provide secure communications with anyone in the world. We only need to establish this secure prior connection once to communicate with anyone. On the other side, we expect to communicate with services such as Google and Microsoft which also have connection points across continents. In this setup, I presented our protocol which manages to detect an active MITM that wishes to intercept a long bi-directional communication by decrypting and re-encrypting data. The detection happens because such active MITM will be forced to introduce a double amount of delay compared to the scenario without MITM.

© Springer International Publishing AG 2017
F. Stajano et al. (Eds.): Security Protocols 2017, LNCS 10476, pp. 254–259, 2017.
https://doi.org/10.1007/978-3-319-71075-4_28

Note, however, that our protocol cannot protect against attackers that only wish to intercept the first message of a communication (e.g., a GET HTTP REQUEST), because the attacker will see the request (and response) before we get a chance to detect the induced delay.

Markus Voelp: What are your assumptions about the Alice-to-Alice and Bob-to-Bob links? What happens if the adversary introduces artificial delay on these links?

Reply: Our assumption is that once you established the secure channel with the virtual machine across the continent, then you also measure the time, so you measure the base time before the start of any communication.

Ross Anderson: I really like this idea. And I'm not too bothered about the fact that there is a delay attack that frustrates it. Because in many applications the critical thing to know is whether anybody is attacking it. And if by having proxies in three different continents and running key exchange there, you can force an attacker to come out of the shadows and make himself known, then that in itself is of value, I would say, in some applications. But it's a neat idea that it hadn't before occurred to me that you could run protocols simultaneously in several continents across multiple channels thanks to Amazon.

Fabio Massacci: The idea of running the protocol across different continents is neat, but how do you know that you are in the right continent? Do you need a distance bounding protocol?

Reply: Indeed, it is difficult to calculate the lower bound for the timing. At the moment, we rely on the initial measurements.

Virgil Gligor: There is also a requirement that links A1 to A2 and B1 to B2, over time, use the same communication technology. Because if you use different communication technology over time, then the time T may vary. So even if you have bounds for one technology, but the providers change the communication technology, then you get a different result.

Reply: What we can do is basically rely on physical bounds. So basically we can rely on speed of light and just say: "assuming speed of light..."

Virgil Gligor: That's what we are talking about, so distance bounding.

Reply: Exactly that, so we can just rely on that as the minimum because the short-delay link we expect to be negligible compared to the long-delay link even at speed of light. So, we can rely for speed of light and say is the minimum distance we expect. For example, rely on the delay at speed of light between Bucharest and New York and that's it.

Virgil Gligor: So even that's problematic with the current Internet, and I'll tell you why. Your communication between say, Bucharest and Sophia may be routed through Minsk or through Beijing. So, consequently that link that you assume is low latency is going to be quite high or variable latency. So, I think that this may work with some communication technologies but not with others.

Reply: Well, we actually did some measurements across many machines we had available in Europe; and it turns out that for many links in Europe, there's no delay that comes even close to what you get over the long-delay channel across continents, even at the minimum, when you think just in terms of the speed of light.

Virgil Gligor: Most of the time I agree that it works.

Reply: So you have at least a range where it's easy to compute the average time to actually detect the difference between the short and long delay. So, even if you get rerouted, the short-delay link is going to have a much lower delay than when you go from Bucharest to New York. So, I think is fairly plausible to say that in most situations you are going to get enough distance between the two: between the minimum delay across the long-delay channel and the average delay across the short-delay channel.

Virgil Gligor: I was more referring to false positives, so to the problem of detecting a problem when in fact it's not.

Reply: Yes, it could be.

Joan Feigenbaum: So I also really like this idea. I'm wondering, if it is realistic: is there a potential problem that the same governments that want to do mass surveillance will discover the existence of these proxies and destroy them? Are there going to be great problems to keep these proxies up and running and not disappear?

Reply: Yes, I think it's a problem. I guess if everyone starts to use Amazon cloud for this, then probably what the U.S. can do is just go to Amazon and say: "give us access to these clouds because we need to intercept the communications". Then it's game over. So from that perspective, I think it's very difficult. I guess what you can do then is just to run your service. Maybe rely on things like TOR, on something that is no maybe as exploitable as common services that really do there businesses by staying in that country. Because in the U.S., if the government comes to a company like Amazon, well maybe you need to give them the keys because otherwise then you're out of business.

Joan Feigenbaum: I'm not sure TOR is the right way to start.

Reply: I'm not sure either.

Joan Feigenbaum: So I think it's a great idea. I'm just worried that these proxies won't survive very long, that would be my argument.

Reply: I was thinking at some point of the TOR hidden services, which Kaleed mentioned at some point, and this might be an idea towards that. But, we haven't explored that direction much yet.

Ross Anderson: Danah Boyd, who does ethnographic research of privacy behaviour of teenagers, shows that, in order to get privacy from parents, teachers etc., the teenagers organise flash crowds, where half a dozen friends will throw in like 20 comments on some particular random link from Amazon to set up their weekends activities. There is another example of random, pop up proxies that could be used, at least in the integrity surface.

Khaled Baqer: Are you assuming that the location of the proxies is hidden, or is that known?

Reply: At this point they are known.

Khaled Baqer: Okay, maybe I'm missing something, but maybe it doesn't matter that a person is anywhere in the network and you have to be close to the entrance. So if you run this on TOR, whatever route you take, even if I don't use the location, it matters that at the end point I'm listening to whatever has been coming to you.

Reply: So it doesn't matter if you are close to the server or the cloud, it doesn't matter. As long as you have an attack on one channel and one on the other channel.

Khaled Baqer: So what I'm saying is that what is of concern here is that I listen to the incoming connexions to you. Because I know your location, I'm just listening to everything that's communicated. It doesn't matter if it's multi-disjointed communications, what I'm listening to is everything that is incoming to the points of interest.

Reply: Yes, but the problem is that you have a long delay between the two adversaries. That's my point. When you are listening you're also able to tamper with it but, at some point this is going to communicate with this one within a time bound, and you're not going to be able to do stuff with this one without going through these long delay channels.

Khaled Baqer: No matter how this is delayed, it's not going to help you if I'm listening to all the incoming stuff. I can wait as long as it takes.

Reply: The point here is that you can indeed monitor all the traffic and at the end you could try to put everything together and do whatever you want with it. But you're not going to be able to do this in real time when I'm sending data with someone without being detected, and that's what we're trying to do here. So when you're trying to communicate real time over several exchanges, you're not going to be able to do this within the time bounds that I'm expecting, without giving me a high chance of detecting you. So that's the point of this protocol.

Khaled Baqer: So it's detectability then, that's what we're looking for?

Reply: Yes, that's what we're looking for. For detectability, yes.

Markus Voelp: I really like this protocol, but what happens if the time delay between B1 and B2 is significantly shorter than between A1 and A2? Just assume I'm sitting in Frankfurt and whatever the correspondence is in the U.S.

Reply: Well, the problem is that you can put the attacker anywhere you want. So, if the link B1–B2 is significantly shorter than A1–A2, that means that also the time for the attacker is significantly shorter. It would be great if you could have a scheme where the delay between A1–A2 and B1–B2 is much shorter than the delay between the adversaries, but it's not really possible to do anything like this in practice because, wherever you have the shortest distance, you just put the attackers next to it and basically that's the time you have also between the attackers.

Markus Voelp: Yes, but it would be natural for Amazon to really go and relocate to places where they have a high connexion, even across the ocean. I mean, you have a direct link between the two Amazon sites. But they are much better connected than I am with my mobile phone.

Reply: Ah, I see your point. So, you are saying that we expect the link B1–B2 to be smaller than A1–A2. That's likely, but as long as these delays (even B1–B2) is significantly longer than the short-delay links (A1–B1, A2–B2), then this should still work.

Markus Voelp: OK.

Virgil Gligor: What benefit would you prove from running multiple runs of this protocol? Would that help in any way?

Reply: Well I'm not sure. What do you have in mind?

Virgil Gligor: So I'm thinking again of false positives, because if you have false positives, you can't rely on this one.

Reply: Right, so I guess the idea is that either you have a very long communication, so you have a voice chat for several minutes where you can kind of get a good estimate of the average. Or as was mentioned, think of mass surveillance scenarios and basically you have this persistent threat that is trying to spy on all the communications. Basically because, let's say you have a large number of people using this protocol. Then, these different runs of the protocol are not necessarily between me and you, who are trying to have a conversation, but is different people running the protocol, so the adversary will increase its chance of being detected on at least one of these runs.

Virgil Gligor: Right, so the larger point was that if you have a single round of this, and you detect an attack falsely, we are stuck. You know that you assume that there is an adversary. What do you do then? So you have to have some alternative. And perhaps the alternative, perhaps, might be having multiple runs, or a different protocol. But, it's not enough to be able to just say, well I detected the adversary. Now what? What's the recourse? That's what I'm saying, that there is something more you have to do besides detecting the adversary, if you really want to communicate securely as always.

Ross Anderson: I'm not so sure, merely knowing that the bad guys are after you is worth an awful lot. And perhaps that's one of the ways in which the spooks are led into the open.

Virgil Gligor: Yes, for some people that's true. I would certainly agree that knowing that spooks are after you is important.

Ross Anderson: In repressive countries it may be all important, because it may enable you to motivate you behaviour in such a way that you don't end up being killed because of a result of non-computer information leaks.

Virgil Gligor: That's true, but again. There are cases where you want to actually communicate. In which case you've got to have an alternative.

Ross Anderson: If the spooks are after you, you may have to communicate differently.

Virgil Gligor: That's exactly what I'm saying. You have to have some alternative. You've detected the spook, now we have to do something.

Reply: Indeed, there are scenarios in which you can actually go a step forward. There are approaches, but this idea mentioned in this talk is just about detecting the problem. Then, there are several possible things to do after detecting.

End to End Security is Not Enough

Dylan Clarke[1](✉) and Syed Taha Ali[2]

[1] Newcastle University, Newcastle upon Tyne, UK
dylan.clarke@newcastle.ac.uk
[2] National University of Sciences and Technology, Islamabad, Pakistan
taha.ali@seecs.nust.edu.pk

Abstract. End-to-end (E2E) security is commonly marketed as a panacea to all of a user's security requirements. We contend that this optimism is misplaced, and that E2E security, as offered by services such as WhatsApp, Telegram, Mega, and Skype, is not sufficient in itself to protect users. In this paper, we discuss various means by which these systems may be compromised in spite of their security guarantees. These include exploitation of flaws in the implementation or even deliberate backdoors in the system. In some cases it may be easier for attackers to bypass the E2E secure channel in the system and attack the communication endpoints instead. Furthermore, the lay user generally has no convenient and convincing mechanism to verify that the system is indeed fulfilling its E2E security properties. We illustrate each scenario with prominent examples of actual real-world security failures and we discuss potential mitigation strategies that users may employ.

1 Introduction

The notion of end-to-end (E2E) security has become mainstream in the wake of the Snowden revelations and E2E terminology has started to enter the popular lexicon. A variety of applications and services have emerged which claim to offer E2E security, ranging from messaging services like Whatsapp, Signal, and Telegram [1], to email platforms like ProtonMail [2], and cloud storage services such as Mega [3].

The E2E security paradigm ensures that a system guarantees a specific security property from one endpoint to another. Secure messaging applications typically offer **E2E encryption**, i.e. messages are encrypted or decrypted only by users at the endpoints of a conversation and cannot be read by eavesdroppers in the path or even the messaging service and users' Internet service providers. Certain next-generation elections systems offer **E2E verifiability**, i.e. voters can audit the voting platform at every key step in the election. Voters can confirm that the system has correctly recorded their vote in favour of their chosen candidate and that the election tally has been correctly computed.

A fundamental goal of such systems is *implementation independence*, i.e. knowledge of whether the system has fulfilled its E2E security properties should

© Springer International Publishing AG 2017
F. Stajano et al. (Eds.): Security Protocols 2017, LNCS 10476, pp. 260–267, 2017.
https://doi.org/10.1007/978-3-319-71075-4_29

not depend on the underlying hardware or software and should be apparent from the output of the protocol [4].

In practice though, this may not be possible for various reasons. Protocols may theoretically be secure but the implementation may introduce vulnerabilities. The system's individual building blocks may have vulnerabilities which attackers can exploit. Malicious actors may even build deliberate backdoors into systems, compromising them without users' knowledge.

Using systems with E2E security properties may also motivate attackers to shift their focus to the system endpoints themselves which may be relatively easier to compromise. And, most importantly, systems today usually do not provide an convenient mechanism for a user to confirm that she is indeed getting E2E security. In some cases, a security failure may be apparent to the user, but there may be no way for a user to prove it to a third party.

In this paper, we contend that E2E security by itself is not sufficient. We present four fundamental arguments to demonstrate how E2E security guarantees, as commonly understood and advertised today in several popular applications, may be subverted. These concerns are straightforward and implicit within the definitions of the E2E security paradigm, but are rarely recognised as such outside of the security community.

Our second contribution is a discussion of various mitigating strategies that users may employ to address these concerns. These may be treated as basic guidelines and may serve as a first step towards formulating best practices for deploying E2E security applications.

The rest of this paper is organised as follows: in Sects. 2, 3, 4 and 5, we present our arguments, supported with various examples from real-world applications. We recommend potential strategies and solutions in Sect. 6. We conclude in Sect. 7.

2 Implementation Vulnerabilities

It is an unfortunate and all too common trend that protocols and solutions that appear secure on paper are easily hacked or broken once implemented. This may be due to any of several reasons: first and foremost, translating a design on paper into a real-world implementation can itself introduce security vulnerabilities into the system. Practical realities do not easily match with idealised theoretical assumptions.

A relevant example is the case of cloud storage service Mega which makes the following claim on the company website: "Unlike the industry norm where the cloud storage provider holds the decryption key, with MEGA, you control the encryption, you hold the keys, and you decide who you grant or deny access to your files, without requiring any risky software installs. It's all happening in your web browser!" However, security researchers have pointed out that this model is insecure [5]. To undertake data encryption, the encryption code is downloaded from Mega servers into the user's web browser where it is executed. It is trivially easy for Mega, or anyone else with access to Mega servers, to modify the code without the user's knowledge. Such a party could easily turn off the encryption and even steal the user's private key. Users therefore still have to fundamentally trust Mega to secure their data.

Second, attackers may exploit vulnerabilities in the underlying platform or individual building blocks to compromise the overall system. For instance, last year it emerged that hackers could defeat the E2E encryption offered by WhatsApp and Telegram by exploiting a vulnerability in the underlying Signalling System 7 (SS7) technology. This particular vulnerability allows an attacker to trick the telecom network into routing all messages intended for the victim's phone to the attacker's own phone. The attacker can create a new WhatsApp or Telegram account and fool other users by pretending to be the victim [6].

Another prominent issue is poor engineering practices. Security professionals often complain - and as security audits of commercial systems have demonstrated time and again - system security is generally not accorded high priority by developers. In many cases, security is usually grafted on to a system near the end of the product development cycle instead of right from the start.

There are several examples of security failures due to poor implementation. The landmark vulnerability analysis of Diebold voting machines conducted by Avi Rubin's team in 2004 discovered numerous such instances [7], including the fact that all votes on the machines were being encrypted using a single DES key hardcoded in all systems over a period of several years. In another instance, hackers demonstrated that the Sony Playstation 3 gaming platform always used a static 'random' number to create its ECDSA private keys [8], thereby enabling any party to generate signatures which the platform recognises to be as valid as Sony's own official signatures.

More recently, implementation faults in Snapchat allowed malicious users to harvest user data and mass-register thousands of accounts [9]. These faults did not affect the supposed E2E security of communications on the Snapchat platform, but they did demonstrate that such faults can still impact user privacy in unexpected ways. This case is also interesting because it exemplifies the attitude some companies take towards security. In this case, the hackers claimed to have brought these vulnerabilities to Snapchat's attention in the past. It was only when the company repeatedly proved "reluctant" to resolve the issues that the group mounted the attack to publicly pressure Snapchat into fixing the bugs.

3   Backdoors

Another way E2E security may be defeated is if developers were to build deliberate backdoors into their systems. This fear is not unwarranted in the current political climate in the West where governments actively conduct mass surveillance on citizens and seek to subvert E2E encryption [10]. There are several prominent examples of such backdoors.

Researchers have identified a security vulnerability in the WhatsApp messaging service, a custom implementation of the well-known Signal protocol, that allows WhatsApp and other parties to eavesdrop on users' communications [11].

A backdoor was also discovered in Skype, allowing the software to access web links sent in a supposedly E2E secure conversation. This particular feature checks the links for malware but could theoretically enable eavesdropping as well [12].

Individual system components have also been undermined with deliberate vulnerabilities with a view to exploiting them to compromise entire systems. In 2013, as part of the Snowden leaks, it emerged that the NSA had signed a secret $10 million contract with security industry leader, RSA, to promote and distribute the Dual Elliptic Curve random number generator as part of its BSafe security kit. This generator had flaws known prior to the NSA, thereby giving the agency a backdoor into several widely-used encryption products [13].

4   Security at the Endpoints

A truly E2E secure system may still fail to provide the required security, in a sense, if the communication endpoints are compromised. In this case an attacker does not have to break the system's encryption protocols; in most cases he simply has to hack the user's personal computer or smartphone. Indeed, as E2E security becomes more mainstream, it is only to be expected that attackers will shift their focus from the communication channels to the endpoints themselves.

We have witnessed similar attacks in the past targeting SSL/TLS. In 2011, researchers reported that the Torpig botnet was able to fake HTTPS connections [14]. Users accessing services such as online banking on infected machines were presented with modified web pages which mimicked those of the original banking websites, complete with the SSL padlock icon. When users entered their banking credentials on the page, the malware forwarded them on to the botmaster.

The Snowden leaks also revealed that the NSA was covertly tapping the internal networks of companies like Yahoo and Google [15]. Whereas users communicated securely with Yahoo and Google's Internet-facing servers using a direct SSL link, user traffic routed on the internal networks was unencrypted at the time. The agency could easily eavesdrop on user communications without having to subvert the SSL link.

5   E2E Security Properties and Verifiability

A rarely recognised concern in this domain is that there is usually no convenient and convincing mechanism for users to verify that a system indeed provides the E2E security properties that it claims. We consider the case of WhatsApp as an example: WhatsApp provides a code to each user enabling them to check that their shared connection is secure by comparing the codes through an alternate channel. As per WhatsApp, if the codes match, there is no eavesdropper and the channel is secure from one end to the other. However, it is not immediately clear to the lay user what these matching codes really signify and if they actually prove the channel is indeed protected. There is always the possibility that a malicious party in the middle provides both users with matching codes to give the impression of a secure channel.

Extending this line of thought, it is theoretically possible for attackers to fool users by creating fake versions of genuine E2E secure applications. These fake versions may change the protocol, leak information, or introduce other malicious software to compromise user security. Given the deluge of fake smartphone apps nowadays and the immense effort involved in regulating them [16], we may reasonably expect such a threat to materialise in the future.

6 Recommendations and Guiding Principles

Here we briefly propose strategies and general guidelines from the security literature that users and vendors may employ to address these concerns.

6.1 Implementation Issues and Backdoors

To avoid security issues due to poor implementation or deliberate backdoors, users would be well advised to use systems which have been rigorously vetted. Some companies make a point of subjecting their products to public scrutiny by making the codebase publicly available for security testing and by commissioning regular security audits.

Users should steer clear of products which opt for secrecy and the principle of security through obscurity. One example is secure messaging service Telegram which encrypts user communications using a new custom protocol [17]. This homegrown protocol, MTProto, has not been extensively audited yet and its security remains an open question.

Vendors can further cultivate trust in their solutions by instituting processes to effectively report and respond to newly discovered security vulnerabilities. Technology giants such as Google, Facebook, and Microsoft have had considerable success with bug bounty programs which financially reward hackers for reporting vulnerabilities in their systems.

Regarding the role of governments and agencies in compromising system security, the straightforward recourse for users is to work towards securing legislative protection and oversight. Users should also consider using services that are based in territories with more favourable data privacy laws. In this context, some companies deliberately advertise their location and jurisdiction as a selling-point. ProtonMail, for instance, specifically highlights the fact that all user data is protected as per stringent Swiss privacy laws [2].

6.2 Insecure Endpoints

The security literature has various strategies to address security issues at the endpoints. Threats such as malware, which mimic SSL connections to trusted websites, may be detected by deploying two and three-factor authentication and verification mechanisms.

Revisiting our earlier example of NSA eavesdropping on the internal networks of Google and Yahoo, users could employ overlay solutions like Confidante [18] or the Mailvelope browser extension [19]. These solutions install PGP functionality on top of webmail services like Gmail and Yahoo! Mail, thereby facilitating E2E security across insecure network segments. Even though Google now claims to encrypt all traffic on its internal network, using a secure overlay is an extra precaution, preventing the user from having to rely entirely on Google.

However it may not be possible to ensure security for every scenario. In these cases it may be a good strategy to undertake a risk assessment and formulate strategies for worst case scenarios. Considering the case of E2E encryption, the user may take precautionary measures to protect herself, perhaps by limiting the amount of personal information she reveals in communications, or by using pseudonyms or other mechanisms which give her plausible deniability in case her communications are hacked.

6.3   Verifiability of Security Properties

Devising usable mechanisms to verify system security is an open area of research. The fundamental challenge here is typically the lay user who does not possess a background in security and may find typical verification strategies cumbersome and non-intuitive.

One common strategy is to borrow techniques from the domains of reliability and fault tolerance to augment system security. In the case of online banking, inserting redundancy into the protocol, in the form of two-factor authentication and transaction verification using a mobile phone, can help convince the user that she is indeed communicating directly with her bank. In a similar vein, the StarVote end-to-end verifiable voting system advocates adding a voter verifiable paper trail to the system. After the electronic results are tallied and announced, the paper trail can be used to conduct post-election audits to inspire greater confidence in the system [20].

However, there is considerable work to be done in this domain. Currently, even configuring security settings on their systems can be a challenging experience for typical users.

6.4   General Suggestions

As a general overarching principle we must attempt to ensure that mechanisms we deploy to enhance E2E security do not end up introducing new security vulnerabilities of their own. A good example is the case of provenance. Indeed, it is considered good security practice to maintain system logs which, in the event of system failure, allow for detailed forensics investigation. However as Braun et al. convincingly argue provenance itself may pose a security risk in certain cases and securing it may prove a challenge [21]. Event logs, data provenance information, and associated meta-data may leak confidential information or open up new avenues of attack. Traditional security protocols are typically formulated to protect individual data items or processes, and are not well-suited to secure provenance, which maps the relationships of items and is approximated by a directed acyclic graph structure. Provenance therefore may require its own security model, perhaps distinct from that of the actual data.

7   Conclusion

In this paper, we have argued that E2E security, contrary to how it is commonly marketed today, does not provide universal protection against all possible security threats. E2E secure systems may fail - and indeed do fail - for various reasons. The system implementation may introduce security vulnerabilities into a design that is theoretically secure. The system may rely on building blocks with vulnerabilities which attackers can exploit to compromise the system itself. Government agencies have been known to pressure companies to insert secret backdoors into their systems. Attackers may bypass E2E secure channels and attack the endpoints of the system instead. Furthermore, it is often challenging and impractical for the lay user to verify that a system is actually providing the E2E security guarantees it claims.

Unfortunately, there is no straightforward solution. We discuss broad high-level recommendations which mitigate some of these concerns. We hope our effort encourages the security community to think along these lines and devise security mechanisms that complement and extend the E2E security paradigm.

References

1. Barrett, B.: Don't let Wikileaks scare you off signal and other encrypted chat apps. Wired, 7 March 2017. https://www.wired.com/2017/03/wikileaks-cia-hack-signal-encrypted-chat-apps/
2. ProtonMail: Secure email based in Switzerland. https://www.protonmail.com
3. Mega. https://www.mega.nz
4. Ali, S.T., Murray, J.: An overview of end-to-end verifiable voting systems. In: Real-World Electronic Voting: Design, Analysis and Deployment, pp. 171–218. CRC Press (2016)
5. Greenberg, A.: Researchers warn: Mega's new encrypted cloud doesn't keep its megasecurity promises. Forbes, 21 January 2013. https://www.forbes.com/sites/andygreenberg/2013/01/21/researchers-warn-megas-new-encrypted-cloud-cant-keep-its-megasecurity-promises/#6e4b540150f1
6. Fox-Brewster, T.: Watch as Hackers Hijack WhatsApp Accounts Via Critical Telecoms Flaws. Forbes, 1 June 2016. https://www.forbes.com/sites/thomasbrewster/2016/06/01/whatsapp-telegram-ss7-hacks/#39455d21178b
7. Kohno, T., Stubblefield, A., Rubin, A.D., Wallach, D.S.: Analysis of an electronic voting system. In: Proceedings of the 2004 IEEE Symposium on Security and Privacy 2004, pp. 27–40. IEEE (2004)
8. Bendel, M.: Hackers describe PS3 security as epic fail, gain unrestricted access. Exophase, 29 December 2010. https://www.exophase.com/20540/hackers-describe-ps3-security-as-epic-fail-gain-unrestricted-access/

9. Shu, C.: Confirmed: Snapchat Hack Not a Hoax, 4.6M Usernames and Numbers Published. TechCrunch, 21 December 2013. https://techcrunch.com/2013/12/31/hackers-claim-to-publish-list-of-4-6m-snapchat-usernames-and-numbers/

10. Lomas, N.: We want to limit use of e2e encryption, confirms UK minister. TechCrunch, 5 June 2017. https://techcrunch.com/2017/06/05/we-want-to-limit-use-of-e2e-encryption-confirms-uk-minister/

11. Ganguly, M.: WhatsApp vulnerability allows snooping on encrypted messages. The Guardian, 13 January 2017. https://www.theguardian.com/technology/2017/jan/13/whatsapp-backdoor-allows-snooping-on-encrypted-messages

12. Goodin, D.: Think your Skype Messages Get End to End Encryption? Think Again. Ars Technica, 20 May 2013. http://arstechnica.com/security/2013/05/think-your-skype-messages-get-end-to-end-encryption-think-again

13. Menn, J.: NSA infiltrated RSA security more deeply than thought. Reuters, 31 June 2014. http://www.reuters.com/article/us-usa-security-nsa-rsa-idUSBREA2U0TY20140331

14. Stone-Gross, B., Cova, M., Gilbert, B., Kemmerer, R., Kruegel, C., Vigna, G.: Analysis of a botnet takeover. IEEE Secur. Priv. 9(1), 64–72 (2011)

15. Welch, C.: Google encrypts Gmail between data centers to keep the NSA out of your inbox. The Verge, 20 March 2014. https://www.theverge.com/2014/3/20/5530072/google-encrypts-gmail-between-data-centers-to-keep-out-nsa

16. BI Intelligence: Apple is still struggling to keep fake apps out of the App Store. Business Insider, 11 November 2016. http://www.businessinsider.com/apple-still-struggling-to-keep-fake-apps-out-of-the-app-store-2016-11

17. Turton, W.: Why you Should Stop using Telegram Right now. Gizmodo, 24 June 2016. http://gizmodo.com/why-you-should-stop-using-telegram-right-now-1782557415

18. Lerner, A.A., Zeng, E., Roesner, F.: Confidante: usable encrypted email. In: IEEE Euro S&P (2016)

19. Mailvelope. https://www.mailvelope.com/en/

20. Bell, S., Benaloh, J., Byrne, M.D., DeBeauvoir, D., Eakin, B., Fisher, G., Kortum, P., McBurnett, N., Montoya, J., Parker, M., et al.: Star-vote: a secure, transparent, auditable and reliable voting system. In: Real-World Electronic Voting: Design, Analysis and Deployment, pp. 375–404. CRC Press (2016)

21. Braun, U., Shinnar, A., Seltzer, M.I.: Securing provenance. In: HotSec (2008)

End to End Security is Not Enough
(Transcript of Discussion)

Dylan Clarke$^{(\boxtimes)}$

Newcastle University, Newcastle upon Tyne, UK
dylan.clarke@ncl.ac.uk

The idea behind this presentation originated when I was looking at e-voting. I was looking specifically at end-to-end systems, implementing them and considering what can go wrong. Now, there's a bit of factionalization within e-voting research. A lot of people believe end-to-end verifiability is all you need for integrity. Then there's a smaller faction who believe, "No, it's more about reliability. It's audit logs. It's things like that". I was giving some talks on this and one thing that came up a lot was the Estonian e-voting system. The Estonian system tends to get a lot of criticism in the literature because initially it wasn't end-to-end verifiable, and there's still debate about whether it is now, but on the other hand the Estonian system has some very nice things to do with logs and auditability in it, which I think maybe some other systems could learn from.

As I was giving these talks, I got speaking to Taha Ali, who pointed out that what I was noticing could be generalised to all types of end-to-end security. That's really what I'm looking at here.

End-to-end is pretty much everywhere now. We've got end-to-end secure email, end-to-end e-commerce solutions, end-to-end messaging apps, and end-to-end verifiable e-voting. So we can ask, "Well, what actually is end-to-end when we see the phrase so much?" The idea, essentially, is that security is at the endpoints and there's implementation independence. What we mean by that is when you run, say, a system with a particular protocol, you don't worry about how the back-end server that you're interacting with works, or how the communication channel's been implemented. You have a protocol, and your protocol can tell you whether what you're doing is secure or not. Ultimately, you can just look at it and say, "I've got a secure connection or I've not got a secure connection." It's often used in the area of confidentiality, but it's also used for other properties like the integrity of e-voting, as I mentioned earlier.

The key point I want to look at here is this; it's common to market things as end-to-end secure now, but end-to-end security isn't enough on its own. There are plenty of things that can be done to enhance the security of E2E systems, a lot of which we already know about, but which aren't necessarily being used in E2E systems.

I divided up the issues into four key sections. The first one is: How secure is the implementation? Your E2E secure system might be secure on paper but not be in practice. There can be things like your threat model may not include some things that actually happen. You may have modelled the protocol but not things like how people use the system or how people acquire the system. The

© Springer International Publishing AG 2017
F. Stajano et al. (Eds.): Security Protocols 2017, LNCS 10476, pp. 268–277, 2017.
https://doi.org/10.1007/978-3-319-71075-4_30

building blocks might be insecure; things like your random number generation, your time stamping, and so on. The implementation might just have issues, even if the system on paper is perfect.

One good example here is the Norwegian e-voting system. It seemed to be a pretty good system on paper, and they looked to have a pretty good implementation, but in practice there was a problem with their random number generation. The first time you generated a random number in any usage, you got a random number. The second time, you got a fixed number. The third time, you got a fixed number again, generated from that last fixed number. So, it ended up being totally insecure just because of this bug.

Another good example is Snapchat. There's the Snapchat protocol, which is supposedly quite secure. Then there are third-party Snapchat apps, which will use the Snapchat protocol, and if we assume that was secure, that would be fine, but the apps are also leaking your information to their own servers. Then there's Skype, which is promising end-to-end security, but it's also promising that if you use the text chat on it, and you put in a link, it will check whether that link is to a malicious website or not for you. So, you've got a situation where supposedly Skype itself has no access to your link, but at the same time, it's telling you things about your link. That's in the terms and conditions.

Now, here are some strategies that we could use to address these issues. First of all, publicly available code, which is something we've probably all talked about a lot before. Regular audits, depending obviously on the type of system. Something like e-voting should certainly be being audited on behalf of the election authorities and the major players candidates in the election. Commercial software should be being audited by the developers, and extra audit encouraged by bounty programmes. Legislation and economic incentives are also important, as are a lot of the ideas from security economics. I've also said in the past that we possibly need careful consideration of security assumptions, but that's something I may be a little less sure on, because we're then asking, "Well, who is carefully considering the assumptions?" One person may look at a system as it's designed and say, "Well, this is absolutely fine," whereas another might actually spot the problems with it.

The second area we looked at was that the implementation might have deliberate vulnerabilities. There might be trapdoors in the cryptography, for example, you have Dual Elliptic Curve, where you knew that there could be values there to allow a trapdoor. There might be data exfiltration interfaces, as has happened in cases where a company's been persuaded to put things in to allow the intelligence services to get data out, or where the company itself wants to access users' data. Then there are fake applications. We actually tried, during some of our banking security research, to see if it was possible to put a fake application in the Google app store. This app didn't actually steal your bank details, but it did something untoward with a mock-up banking page that we put together. We had no problem uploading the app, then we deleted it before anybody downloaded it.

The strategies here are; firstly, legislation again. Auditing current implementations to check if they have back doors. Authentication techniques. Things like fingerprinting applications. We're also suggesting maybe using the blockchain to store authentication data, because obviously there's a possible attack if you've fingerprinted apps, that somebody could attack the fingerprint data. That was talked about in Alex Halderman and colleagues' paper on attacking the Estonian e-voting system. That it was perfectly possible that the digital fingerprints could be changed, or man-in-the-middle attacks could be used to provide fake ones to users.

The third thing we looked at was: How secure are the endpoints? It's all very well having end-to-end security, but if end-to-end means from your app to the person you're communicating with's app, then you've also got the issue that your data has to go through your computer, so malware on your machine could compromise security in a variety of ways. The data could just be stolen before it's encrypted, say if your machine was root-kitted, or maybe if a more limited piece of malware was able to access your copy buffer.

Financial transactions could be changed before they're sent. We looked a bit at that in a paper that's still undergoing review. The idea is that for certain banks you could trick people into using two-factor authentication to authenticate a different transaction from the one that they wanted to. Then there's altering protocols: your machine could have malware that actually changes the steps that you do, so you're not actually performing the protocol that you thought you were.

Now, here are some possible strategies for preventing these issues. We could look at multiple endpoints, two-factor authentication being an obvious version of that. When we're looking at the more limited types of malware then things like overlays could be used. For example, if you have an overlay which encrypts your data before it goes into your email, that wouldn't stop a root kit from getting the data, but it would stop something that was just seeing your copy buffer or was just seeing what went into the email client. Then there are TPMs or physical mechanisms. For example, part of your protocol could be being done on secure hardware that nobody has access to. Then, in some cases the only viable strategy might be accepting that end-to-end security might not always be possible and planning accordingly.

One good example I was given of this came from a discussion in the area of military intelligence, about what can be done if confidentiality is breached. The example given was a leak of submarine plans, and they came to the conclusion that the only thing that could be done was compensatory action, where they also leaked a number of fake plans as well. So there is always the option, if you know your security might not be one hundred percent, to take actions like that; to make sure that if the data is leaked then it can't necessarily be used.

The fourth issue we looked at is: How can someone verify that they have end to end security? The verifiability mechanisms have to be usable. Also, a lot of users might not have the skill that they need to verify the security properties. Even if they do, they also need to be able to act on the information that they receive.

One example is WhatsApp, which provides end to end secure communication channels, using some sort of key exchange scheme. In the documentation they tell you that you can check that your communication channel's secure; because a number derived from the key will be shown in your version of WhatsApp, and a number derived from the key will be shown in the version of WhatsApp that the person you're communicating with has. If you're near to each other, you could just look and see those numbers were the same. Alternatively, you could use another channel to share those numbers.

Their claim is this proves to you that your communication's secure. Well it does if you know that you're using a genuine implementation of WhatsApp. On the other hand, if you're not, it will be perfectly possible for whoever is intercepting your communication and has control of the apps to just show each of you a number. All they need to be able to do is generate a number and make sure the same one appears on both apps.

Khaled Baqer: When you have a group of people communicating using Signal or WhatsApp for example, if one the people in the group provided their own source of the Signal app, then failure in that protocol would affect security for everyone.

Reply: Yes.

Khaled Baqer: I understand that this is a problem if you download it from the app store for example, even though you can provide your own stuff and then you can't detect it: I can show you a random number here and a random number here, this doesn't mean that anything is encrypted. But in the case when someone can compile their own stuff, it's like, now you can show me that something's wrong.

Reply: Yes, that's a very good point. I think you could maybe generalize that even a little bit further and say: if multiple groups have implemented their own apps, and you've got several of them running, then you're fine as long as there isn't collusion between all of those groups. So that improves things.

Paul Wernick: But that means that everybody has to be able to read all of the source code of that app and understand it, and know which little bits they have to check, and trust the compiler they've used, and the infrastructure they've used when they compiled it. I think it just moves the security round a bit rather than actually giving you perfection. And it implies that everybody's good at programming and can read the code.

Reply: Yes. Although you could also say threat models come in to that as well. It depends on who you're trying to defend against. If you're having to trust your compiler and your hardware then you are vulnerable, yes. But if that is all you're having to trust, you're probably vulnerable only to a higher class of attacker than if you are having to trust the app that you downloaded from the internet.

Paul Wernick: It reduces rather than eliminates them.

Reply: Yes.

Khaled Baqer: We have to make some assumptions. If you don't trust any component, then nothing will be ever safe. We've all been over this in security protocols I think. So what I am trying to say is you can detect it if you compile it on a different platform. In this case, is I think protection is kind of the theme of the session, this is the one we're looking for.

Reply: Yes, you can certainly detect it if you have got your own implementation, and your own compilation of it. I think coming from what Paul was saying as well, once you're doing that, you're now protected from a lot more people than you were before. Not trusting your compiler may be reasonable if you are being targeted heavily by security services. It's not reasonable if you are worried about somebody trying to steal your photos on the internet.

Partha Das Chowdhury: In the voting case, you might not need verifiability. It might not be a very good feature to have because, in countries like I come from, most of the voting happens on bullets and ballots. So, the system will try to introduce verifiability, for anybody who voted to get a printout, so they can verify it. But it might not be a good thing to have verifiability. Because we are a large democracy and we are mostly using electronic voting. If I come out of the voting booth with a paper in my hands say that I voted for X, my wife might not be happy and I can get shot.

Reply: Yes. The verifiability that we use in e-voting is a bit more complicated than that. You've got to be receipt-free, so it doesn't prove who you voted for. It's more to prove that the protocol ran correctly.

Partha Das Chowdhury: But we have the receipt to say I voted for X, in India they came out with the receipt.

Peter Y A Ryan: You do have to be careful to ensure that verifiability doesn't conflict with receipt-freeness. The better designed systems do that.

I'd like to follow up on some of the other comments about voting. First of all I was a little bit puzzled because most of the people I speak to intuit verifiability as primarily about integrity, not so much about confidentiality, I don't think any of the people I talk to claim that end-to-end verifiability is enough, and they have a very precise sense of it which means that you can basically audit things. And that may get you into a canary thing, because in order to audit things you need to have an independent implementation of the algorithms to do the audit.

But you seem to be mixing issues of confidentiality and integrity. In the voting context, end-to-end verifiability is primarily about integrity, it's not about confidentiality. You need extra mechanisms, you need accountability, you need confidentiality, you need comparability, and you need lots of other things. So, I don't know who you've been talking to who claim that end-to-end verifiability is enough.

Reply: I'm going to touch a bit more on e-voting in a while and that is going to be about the integrity part of it. The confidentiality part is when we look at other end-to-end systems.

Tuomas Aura: These kinds of thing where you have receipt-free verifiability they can be dangerous if it's some kind of politically or ideologically hot thing that you're doing, like voting, because then you can always claim that the verification failed. In an election there could be a large number of people who claim their vote wasn't counted correctly, even though it was. And they always do this I'm afraid, and that problem could apply to other security systems. So in that sense this verifiability might cause more problems unless you actually get the receipt and have the public proof.

Reply: Yes.

Peter Y A Ryan: Having the receipt is also a problem.

Tuomas Aura: In voting it is, but for something else it might not be.

Peter Y A Ryan: You also need accountability sometimes for dispute resolution. If someone claims that something's wrong, you need to be able to look up whether it was really the system that went wrong or whether it's just them. If they claim that I took this candidate into the encryption device, and I audited the encryption and it comes out as a different candidate, that's one of the situations where it's difficult to figure out: is the guy lying, or is it really the encryption device that screwed up the encryption? So you need dispute resolution as well. That's another sense in which end-to-end verifiability is not enough.

Ross Anderson: Does this not then require comprehensibility, in the sense that a wooden ballot box with a metal hasp and brass padlock is comprehensible to people with ordinary science degrees. Whereas electronic voting systems ... who trusts experts anymore?

Peter Y A Ryan: Yes comprehensibility is another design issue. It's not so easy with crypto-systems.

Reply: Now, I've just got an example to go on to, which is e-voting, and that's the SEEV voting system, otherwise know as DREi, which I have been involved with the implementation of. We have the following issue. To explain it briefly: You tell the machine who you want to vote for. It gives you a cryptogram, which is part of some scheme which can prove the right vote was cast and maintains your confidentiality and so on. Because the machine could cheat and give you the cryptogram for "don't vote for this person" rather than the cryptogram for "vote for this person, we use a cut and choose protocol.

Essentially, the machine gives you a cryptogram and a proof that it is a cryptogram and then says to you, "Do you want to submit this one or do you want to audit it and check who it was for?" If you say submit, it goes in. If you say audit, the other cryptogram is revealed and you can say, "Yes, these do have the right relationship," but then it can't be used. Obviously, because the machine's committed to the first one, if it cheats there's a good chance it will be caught, because you might audit it.

So what do we do to make sure it genuinely commits it and you can prove that to other people? The machine digitally signs your first cryptogram. Generally that's fine. An issue arises though, if the machine gives you an invalid cryptogram with an invalid digital signature. Then you can go to somebody and say, "This machine, it's failed. It hasn't done it right. I've got an invalid digital signature." All that proves is that machine didn't sign it. Yet we found that usually, when it's discussed, people are quite happy when you get to the point where you say, "Well, there's a digital signature there. They must be secure. There's a digital signature."

Something we've had to think about is what you do if the digital signature fails. One answer in practice is, when you're using voting machines, you get your receipt which includes your digital signature printed on a piece of paper which is watermarked in some way. Then we're not really relying on the digital signature. We're relying on the watermarked paper. Then we start wondering, does the digital signature actually give us anything?

Another thing that's been suggested when it's done electronically, is that you can check the digital signature before using the cryptogram. But the average voter can't check a digital signature on their own. Well, you could just build it into the client. Assuming that the client works properly, you're fine. So there are ways around this.

The other thing I'll mention relates to Classroom Voting, which is our current implementation of SEEV. We've been using it in our department for the best paper award, which is an award with a cash prize. Last time we used it, the verification failed. It's an end-to-end protocol so that's fine. Election invalid. Just cancel it. Everything's okay. Except we're not allowed to cancel the election. We're only allowed to do it once. So the verification is not allowed to fail, right? So I had to audit the system.

Fortunately, we've got decent logs. I discovered somebody's voting client had failed half way through, which we have fault tolerance for. When that happens it cancels the vote. The fault tolerance code had failed. So I went in, fixed it and ran it again. Everything came out. It was fine. Everyone was happy with it, because we're all computer scientists so I could explain what had happened and show them the code changes I'd made. Not really ideal in a general election.

Peter Y A Ryan: So you fixed the election is what you're saying.

Reply: Yes. Fortunately, I didn't vote in it and my paper didn't win, so people were reasonably happy with that. Then we basically told people, "Don't worry. It was just a false positive. It's fixed."

About a week later our system got hacked. At the moment it's temporarily unavailable. Essentially what happened was that some hacking group saw it on the web. They discovered some way to escalate privileges, get into a folder with a document that had been set to have the wrong read access on it, and were able to get a password that gave them read access to our database, printed out a picture of the database schema, emailed it to us and said, "We've hacked you. We've done no damage. If you pay us $500 we'll tell you exactly how we did it and help you fix it." We had to figure out how they'd done it ourselves, and told the university who promptly closed our server down because they wanted to check that we haven't got any identifying information on it. That's where we're at now. So we had both the false positive and the failure in a quite close space of time, and that failure, which could have equally been a bad verification failure, did close our system down for a bit.

Now let's look at possible strategies to handle these issues. First of all, you need explicit mechanisms for reporting security failures. It's definitely not enough to say, "There's a digital signature. Keys need to match up. People could check." You need to figure out ahead of time, especially for something like voting, how are we going to handle disputes? What evidence is going to allow you to do that?

As was mentioned in some of the questions, what happens when somebody wants to destroy your system by coming along and claiming verification failed when it didn't? What happens when somebody doesn't understand your verification system, and they think it's failed when it hasn't because of something they've seen? We do an online cyber security course. I've seen students on that course, who are members of the public learning for the first time about cybersecurity, suggest that when they've gone to a supposedly secure website and a page hasn't loaded, that means it must be insecure. Similarly, that could happen with a secure e-voting system. People could genuinely believe that if there's a reliability fault, then there must be a security fault.

You also need legislation and regulations for handling claims as well, so that they can't just be brushed under the carpet, or so that they don't become a bigger problem because people feel they aren't handled properly. We need audit logs, so that people can actually look and find out what happened when verification failed, not just treat it as an end to end black box and say, "Well, the election's failed. What can we do?" Or, "The communication channel appears to have failed. Now what?"

The audit logs mustn't be a security issue themselves. They mustn't leak things. If there's sensitive information in them, we then need to control who can access that. How do you get the public to trust that the people who can access it are looking at it properly? There's also a need for usability analysis. I would suggest that comes after all the other things, because it's very easy to make a system usable and then add on a verification mechanism, and not concern yourself with whether the verification mechanism is usable.

In conclusion, I would say that end to end security is not sufficient in itself. It's a very, very good technique in a lot of areas, but certainly, when it comes to marketing, it is being pushed as the only thing in some places. I would say, from what we've looked at, security analyses need to model the circumstances in which the software is acquired and used, not just the protocol itself. That includes dispute resolution mechanisms, and also attacks on dispute resolution mechanisms: who's going to be using it and what understanding they'll have. Also, any strategies we use mustn't compromise security themselves.

Mark Ryan: Just a quickie on your classroom voting. You said that attackers attacked it remotely. I just wondered, in what sense is it available remotely?

Reply: The current idea is that it can be used by people at different universities. Anybody can get an account from us to create their own elections, which they would then use in their classroom.

Mark Ryan: I see, on your server.

Reply: We're looking at building a commercial prototype at the moment. The one that got hacked is only intended for local use. You need a local account. What we think happened is the hacking started off with one of the hackers knowing somebody who had a student account at our university, and then went on from there.

Fabio Massacci: The interesting thing is that in fixing the system, you fixed the election. So, should this mechanism for recounts, let's call it this, be included when you have a security protocol? So the recount is an implicit part of the protocol itself.

Reply: Yes. I think you definitely need that. In one of the trials of e-voting in the UK, essentially there were trials and they were shut down, and the electoral commission decided we weren't going to use any of the systems. One of the problems was a tallying operation failed, so somebody from the company providing it typed in a few lines of code, ran it again, and it worked, but there was no documentation of what those couple of lines of code were. In that case, they said "right, we're not going to consider e-voting in the UK anymore." Obviously, if it's a real election, you do need to be able to say "Here's a handbook. This person will type in these two lines of code while these other five people watch them to make sure that they're typing exactly these two lines of code. Then there will be an explanation of why they were needed."

Paul Wernick: The way the elections are run in this country, representatives of each candidate are allowed to attend the count. So presumably, representatives of each candidate who are computer scientists have to be able to watch the person typing in the change of code.

Reply: That would be a good idea, yes. There was a presentation I gave here a number of years ago about e-voting in the UK[1]. When they did these trials, one of the problems was that there was no procedure for what people were or weren't allowed to observe. This wasn't actually a full election they were doing it on. For example, one of the companies said, "For security purposes, don't let anybody see the screens of the computers." So you had all these computer literate observers stood around with somebody else shielding the screens from them in case it leaked privacy in some way.

Paul Wernick: At the cost of losing vote viability for the candidate.

Reply: Yes.

Fabio Massacci: In the medical field you don't know whether what they are giving to you is actually a dietary supplement or antibiotics. You trust a doctor, who is a certified medical professional, that he's giving you the right thing. Do you think that we should have something similar, the same way a doctor has, so when somebody claims this is a secure protocol, there should be a certified

---

[1] LNCS 7622, pp. 126–144.

computer professional that says, "Okay, I'm a security expert," and there's a bar or an order or a charter that says only these people can certify this software is secure?

Reply: I'm undecided on that. One of my worries with something like that would be who decides who gets to be certified.

Fabio Massacci: It is the same for doctors, I mean. Who decides that doctors are certified?

Peter Y A Ryan: Did you hear about California's top to bottom report on electronic e-voting. These were systems which supposedly had been certified by various companies, but when they went in, the security engineering was absolutely dreadful. The certification was a complete joke. It was basically done by companies that were paid by the manufacturers.

Fabio Massacci: Lobotomy was given a Nobel Prize. Lobotomy. The guy that invented lobotomy got a Nobel Prize. So doctors are also a problem. It's the same thing. Professionals can cheat, or can give wrong things or give wrong suggestions and the wrong brand to fix them, but still we have a process which we trust in the long run. When you go to the hospital, you're not going to be lobotomized just because some guy eighty years ago thought it was a good idea.

Peter Y A Ryan: A good process would be good.

Reply: There might be an argument of scale on that as well, that there's a lot more people being treated by doctors in the time scale than there are elections being run. Over the years it would take a lot longer to weed out all the bad election providers through failed elections than it would to weed out the bad doctors.

Auditable PAKEs: Approaching Fair Exchange Without a TTP

A. W. Roscoe[1] and Peter Y. A. Ryan[2(✉)]

[1] Department of Computer Science, University of Oxford, Wolfson Building,
Parks Road, Oxford OX1 3QD, UK
Bill.Roscoe@cs.ox.ac.uk
[2] University of Luxembourg, 2, avenue de l'Université,
4365, Esch-sur-Alzette, Luxembourg
peter.ryan@uni.lu

Abstract. Roscoe recently showed how HISPs, a class of protocol to allow humans to contribute to the creation of secure authentic channels between them, can be made auditable in the sense that a failed attack on them cannot be disguised as communication failure. In this paper we study the same issue for PAKEs: password authenticated key exchange protocols. We find that because this second style of protocol relies on long term state, it is harder to make them auditable, and that to do so we have to develop new ideas on how to approximate fair exchange without a TTP.

1 Introduction

In [11], the first author showed how HISPs (Human-Interactive Security Protocols [9]) could be transformed to allow a pair of users to detect when an attacker had deliberately tried to break into their run. This was achieved by using the construct $delay(x, T)$ which allows a user to put the data x beyond anyone's reach for time T, but which the users themselves can eventually open. Some options for implementing $delay$ are discussed in [11]. These are based on trusted third parties or alternatively sequential computation. We say that a protocol is *auditable* if the legitimate players can distinguish online guessing attacks from network failures.

The purpose of this paper is to describe how PAKEs (Password Authenticated Key Exchange protocols) may be rendered auditable in a manner analogous to HISPs. Like HISPs, conventional PAKEs are vulnerable to guess and abort style attacks: an attacker attempts a protocol run with a legitimate party and aborts as soon as he knows that his guess at the password is false. By suitable choice of role and timing the attacker can ensure that the legitimate party does not hold enough information to determine whether she has been interacting with an attacker or has simply been the victim of a network failure.

PAKEs are structurally quite different to HISPs. As a consequence the technique used to render HISPs auditable is not enough to achieve complete auditability in PAKEs. In essence this is because PAKEs, unlike HISPs, have

© Springer International Publishing AG 2017
F. Stajano et al. (Eds.): Security Protocols 2017, LNCS 10476, pp. 278–297, 2017.
https://doi.org/10.1007/978-3-319-71075-4_31

persistent state, meaning we need to protect this state (the password) between runs. To do this we need a more elaborate scheme to achieve auditability, and in fact only achieve a stochastic result: if an attacker makes a guessing attempt then in order to have a chance of gaining information, he has to yield an approximately equal chance of being caught. To achieve this we develop some new stochastic approximations to *fair exchange*, which we hope will find other applications. Nevertheless, the *delay* construct used to make HISPs auditable is once again invaluable.

The rest of this paper is structured as follows. In the next section we outline PAKEs and their structure, and in Appendix A we give a number of examples. In Sect. 3 we examine the important differences between HISPs and PAKEs, and show that copying the auditability transformation used in [11] for IIISPs does not, in fact, work because PAKEs have an extra attack vector that is not present in HISPs. To solve this problem we require an exchange of information to be as fair as possible, We describe a new approach to achieving exchange using *delay* that, while not completely fair, can be made as close to *stochastic fairness* as we choose. We then introduce the transformation to the confirmation stage of PAKEs that gives them an auditability property.

We believe the stochastic fair exchange mechanism we introduce here will find uses beyond making PAKEs auditable, and discuss this in Sect. 6. Appendices give an overview of PAKEs and of key derivation and confirmation mechanisms.

2   HISPs and the Roscoe Transform

Human Interactive Security Protocols rely on the existence of an unspoofable, low-bandwidth out-of-band channel to authenticate the key establishment. Thus the key establishment takes place over high bandwidth unauthenticated and non-private channels. Authentication of the end points of the key establishment is then performed using another non-secret but authenticated channel to communicate short digests of the session key to confirm agreement. A couple of examples will serve to illustrate:

Line of sight: suppose Anne wants to send a confidential document from her portable device to a nearby printer. Suppose further that the printer can display short codes. The devices run a key establishment and then display an agreed digest of the session key. Alice can check by eye that the codes agree and thus be confident that the resulting channel is indeed between her device and the printer.

Voice: The Silent Circle BlackPhone uses voice as the OoB channel. Suppose that Anne and Bob want to establish a secure channel between their phones. After running a key establishment, both phones display a number of *trust words* that are derived from the session key. They speak these words to each other and assuming that they recognise each other's voice this serves to confirm and authenticate the channel.

The fact that the digests are short means that an attacker, e.g. Man In The Middle, has a non-negligible chance of injecting a DH terms that will yield the same digest as displayed to the legitimate parties. Hence care must be taken to detect and limit such attempts. A possible attacker strategy is to mask guessing attempts as network failures: arrange to be first to learn the other's digest, and abort if it does not agree. The Roscoe transform is a way to transform conventional HISPs to a form which counters such a strategy.

To transform a HISP to render it auditable we simply wrap appropriate information in a delay that will keep the contents concealed for a period exceeding the timeout of the protocol. In particular, in a two-party protocol, we wrap the information that allows the first digest to be computed in a delay. Now, when an attacker receives this he cannot tell immediately if his guess is good, so he must either respond with his digest, and so reveal his attempted attack if wrong, or he aborts. In the latter case he will discover whether or not his guess was correct when the delay opens, but by then the other party will have aborted. Crucially, knowing that his guess was good in one run does not help him in future runs, as all runs are independent.

3   Reviewing PAKEs

Password Authenticated Key Establishment protocols (PAKEs) provide a way to establish secure channels in the absence of a PKI (or web of trust or similar), and without requiring empirical channels as is the case for HISPs. Instead, they rely on the parties having a previously shared, low-entropy secret: such as a password. We assume that the parties have been able to previously agree this secret via some authenticated, private channel, e.g. meeting in person over a cocktail. This password will be used repeatedly in authenticating future session key establishment protocol runs.

The goal of a PAKE is for the parties to establish a secret, mutually authenticated, high-entropy session key that can subsequently be used for secure communication. What PAKEs and HISPs have in common is that authentication typically involves human participation, in one case agreeing, remembering and typing in passwords, and in the other communicating a short seemingly random string between devices. In both cases this means that there is a distinct trade-off between humans' appetite and willingness for cognitive effort, and the amount of security obtained. In both cases the compromise in security is a small but non-negligible probability that an attacker can break authentication. In the case of PAKEs this is that the password may not be strong enough and so might be guessed. A crucial difference is that HISPs are stateless while PAKEs are stateful, in the form of the password.

PAKEs work by authenticating a key establishment protocol using common knowledge of a password between the parties involved, all over insecure (Dolev-Yao) channels. They work by each of the parties P_i computing a value V_i that is a function of the fresh entropy exchanged and the password. Subsequent key confirmation involves exchanges of values based on the V_i allow the various parties to determine whether the other parties with whom they have been running the protocol indeed computed the same values, and by implication share the same password.

Note that, in contrast to AKEs where a PKI is available, it is not possible to explicitly authenticate the messages of the PAKE. If we were to try to it would have to be on the basis of the password and so would provide an attacker with the possibility to launch offline dictionary attacks. Consequently the authentication in a PAKE has to be implicit as a result of the key confirmation steps.

Our proposal is to add features to PAKE protocols, including delay terms and time-outs, so that by the time any man-in-the middle has discovered whether or not the password guess he has made is correct, he has, with high probability, had to deliver confirmation messages (perhaps delayed) to the attacked party, or parties, which will ultimately reveal his presence in the case of an incorrect guess.

For concreteness in what follows we will describe the modifications required in the case of two-player protocols, but the techniques can be readily adapted to multi-party protocols.

The PAKEs known to us all follow the same high-level pattern: some key establishment steps, typically Diffie-Hellman based, with the password s folded into the calculation of the session key in some way. Thus, each party contributes fresh, high-entropy values and the session key is computed as a function of this fresh entropy and the low-entropy, long-term password. If the messages are not corrupted and both parties used the same password they will compute the same session key.

The key establishment phase is followed by a key confirmation phase that allows the parties to confirm that they have computed the same key, thus providing implicit authentication. Note that the key establishment and key confirmation phases may overlap: the first party to reach a state where it can compute the session can issue key confirmation data along with key establishment data in the next emitted message.

Care must be taken in the design of the entire protocol, key establishment and confirmation phases, to ensure that an attacker, passive or active, cannot launch an offline dictionary attack based on terms derived from runs of the protocol. Thus, the attacker, with polynomially bound computational power, should never derive enough information to confirm or eliminate password guesses with better than negligible probability.

The attacker can of course always launch online guessing attacks: simply interacting with a legitimate party with a guess at the password and observing if this succeeds. This cannot be avoided. The goal therefore is to ensure that this is the optimal attack strategy. Thus, the goal of the design is to ensure that an attacker can test at most one password per attempted run with a legitimate party. The situation is thus analogous to that for HISPs, which seek to ensure that no meaningful combinatorial attack can improve the attacker's chances to more than what they would be with a single completely random attempt at a man-in-the-middle attack.

We identify a difficulty with existing PAKEs analogous to the one discussed for HISPs in [11]: an attacker can disguise attempted guessing attacks as network communication failures. Specifically, he can arrange the attack so that he learns whether his guess is good before the legitimate participants learn of a confirmation failure. When the attacker learns that his attack has failed, i.e. his guess was wrong, he can block subsequent messages. When the attacked party time-out, there is no difference in what it will have seen to a communications failure at the same point in the protocol. Consider the following example based on the SPEKE protocol [6] with key confirmation:

$$1. \quad A \to B : X := hash(s_A)^{2x}$$
$$2. \quad B \to A : Y := hash(s_B)^{2y}$$

A computes $K_A = K = Y^x = hash(s_B)^{2yx}$ and B computes $K_B = K = X^y = hash(s_A)^{2xy}$.

$$3. \quad A \to B : hash_1(K_A, A, B)$$
$$4. \quad B \to A : hash_2(K_B, A, B)$$

Here the first two messages allow A and B each to compute a putative session key based on their respective values s_A and s_B of the shared secret. The key feature of SPEKE is that the DH generator is not publicly known but rather is computed by the parties as a function of the password, hence K is a function of the password. The final two messages allow them to confirm that they have computed the same K and hence, with high probability, $s_A = s_B$, implying that they have each been running the protocol with the intended party. $hash$, $hash_1$ and $hash_2$ are different cryptographic hash functions which each offer no information about each other in the sense that knowing the result of applying each to any x conveys no information that allows us to compute the others.

Note that the agent playing the role of Bob receives Message 3, the one which confirms (if true) that the party she is running the protocol shares knowledge of the password $K_A (= K_B)$, before Alice gets the reverse confirmation, provided by Message 4. Thus if "Bob" is actually fraudulent and has made a guess at the password, he will discover if this guess is correct before he has to send the message that will give Alice the same information. If this guess was correct, he will carry on, and Alice will be (incorrectly) convinced of the authentication. If not, he can abandon the run at this point and Alice will have no direct evidence of the attacker's presence: all she sees can be explained by a communications failure. This analysis replicates that for HISPs done in [11], except that here life is easier for the attacker because there is no need for the real Alice and Bob *both* to be present. The danger is that the attacker may be able to perform repeated attacks without the participants being sure that they are subject to attack. In the case of PAKEs he can potentially attack both of the owners of a password separately, doubling his chance of obtaining it.

Even if a legitimate party in a PAKE reached the point at which she sees that the computed keys do not match, there may be an innocent explanation: that one of the parties mistyped their password. It would therefore be greatly to our advantage if we could eliminate such mistakes for PAKE users: we hope to introduce such a method in a subsequent paper. In the rest of our present discussion we will assume that a password mismatch in any run is indicative of an attack.

With the strategy of making failed guesses look like communications failures, the attacker can expect to increase his chances of success, by allowing him to make more attempts before the legitimate parties start to suspect an attack and take evasive action. Such a strategy would be particularly effective where the attacker attacks many nodes in parallel.

In [11], one of us showed how to transform HISPs to prevent this by systematic transformation of the protocols, i.e. how all HISPs could be transformed in essentially the same way to eliminate these attacks.

The fact that known PAKEs essentially all follow the same structure, of a key sharing phase followed by a confirmation phase, suggests firstly that a similar approach might work for PAKEs and that the place to concentrate on is the confirmation phase.

Our objective is thus to find a similar transformation for PAKEs that ensures that the legitimate parties can distinguish with high probability any online guessing attack from a communications failure of the network. The legitimate parties will therefore be able to take remedial action and warn others.

While there are similarities between HISPs and PAKEs, there are also some significant differences.

- The absence of an out-of-band channel and the need to keep passwords secret make it much harder for Alice and Bob to discriminate between a mistake they may have made and an attack. If Alice simply types in the wrong password, Bob may think he is being attacked.
- A second, and more significant, difference is that PAKEs employ long term shared secret state (the password between a pair of parties) whereas all runs of HISPs are completely independent. It follows that even though an attack on a PAKE may have little chance of succeeding in the sense of getting a faked connection for the attacker on the same session, it may reveal useful things to him about the long term state. This difference means that we cannot simply apply the transformation that Roscoe developed for HISPs to PAKEs in order to render them auditable. While this can prevent an attacker successfully carrying out a one-off attack that simultaneously carries no chance of revealing the attacker and yet gives him a chance of completing a connection, it does not prevent one that can possibly reveal the password to be used in a second session.

Roscoe's HISP transformation sends data to allow comparison under a *delay* that opens too late to complete the present session: this prevents the attacker getting any *useful* information about whether this attack will succeed or fail. Nor does it assist in future attacks, since no state is shared between HISP runs. However, the PAKE attacker can afford to wait for this delay to open when he aborts immediately after receiving it: if his password guess was right or wrong in *this* session it will also be right or wrong in the *next*. And even if it is wrong the attacker can eliminate it from his search.

For example, Roscoe's transformation on SPEKE would replace the final two key confirmation messages by the following sequence:

$$3. \quad A \rightarrow B : delay(hash_1(K_A, A, B), T)$$
$$4. \quad B \rightarrow A : hash_2(K_B, A, B)$$
$$A : intime(hash_1(K_A, A, B))$$
$$5. \quad A \rightarrow B : hash_1(K_A, A, B)$$

in which the first message is sent delayed so that B must send his confirmation before he can know whether the delayed confirmation from A was correct or not.[1]

If B is an attacker, he has no chance of using a correct guess at the password to obtain connection in *this* run without giving away his presence (if is guess was wrong) by sending Message 4. The same holds if A is an attacker, because she has had to give away the delayed version of the confirmation for Bob to continue to Message 4, If she sent it honestly, Bob will be able to open the delay eventually and discover if her password guess was correct, and if she sends a wrongly formatted Message 3 this will also give her away.

On the other hand, Bob as attacker can now simply accept Message 3 and then abandon the run. This particular run will fail to complete, but he can wait for $delay(H(K_A, A), T)$ to open and thus find out if his guess s_B was correct. If correct he can either use the password in a future run, or, if incorrect, reduce his search space for future attempts. No similar strategy is useful for HISPs.

- A third difference is that the security level can easily be varied dynamically in HISPs: the length of a digest can be increased when there is evidence or suspicion of attack attempts. In PAKEs the password pre-agreed by Alice and Bob cannot be changed so easily: essentially the only way of reducing the likelihood of an attack in the presence of a known attacker is to restrict or ban use of the protocol.

It is clear that in performing this type of fishing-for-information attack, it is necessary to play the role of the first of the two parties to get the confirmation message in the original PAKE (the responder B in the case of our SPEKE/key confirmation example above).

In all standard PAKEs, the issue of who sends this type of information first is determined by which role a participant in playing: Alice or Bob. We need to improve on this. Note that the difficulty with the transformed SPEKE above is that the attacker knows exactly at what point he has the relevant information and so he can abort as soon as he reaches this point, even if the information

---

[1] There is no need for B to check that the correct value was delayed in Message 3 if he gets the correct Message 5 here. This would have not have been the case if the third and fourth messages of the original protocol were $H(H(K_A))$ and $H(K_B)$, namely nested hashing, because the former can be computed from the latter in the case where $K_A = K_B$ without knowledge of K_B. Since opening delays is potentially expensive, this explains why we used the form of confirmation messages we did.

is temporarily inaccessible to him due to a delay wrapper. In the next section we exploit this observation by introducing a stochastic element to the points at which the key information is transmitted.

A slight improvement on the above is to have the parties in effect toss a coin to decide who goes first. (There are cryptographic solutions to doing this fairly, including have each of the two send a delayed random bit[2] with each requiring the other before its own delay opens, and xor-ing them. This is a case where Roscoe's transformation does work, because no state is carried from one toss to the next.) Using this would mean that the attacker would not know at the outset whether he will be able to get Alice to reveal her confirmation value to him first, but he will know that he will have a 50% chance of achieving this and can abort the run if the coin goes against him. Thus the odds of detection are only slightly improved and we need to improve on this.

4   Two-Party Stochastic Exchange

Ideally we would like to achieve *fair exchange* of the confirmation values V_A and V_B: we would like B to get V_A if and only if A gets V_B. We assume that these can be revealed publicly at appropriate junctures without giving away the the key: they may for example be hashed versions of the two sides' keys.

It is known [10] that complete fair exchange, where one party gets what they want if and only if the other party or parties do also, is not possible without a Trusted Third Party (TTP) or a majority of honest parties. In this context we have only two parties, and the use of a TTP seems inappropriate: it necessitates additional trust assumptions and introduces a bottleneck and single point of failure[3]. In particular this means that in the two party setting we cannot achieve complete fairness. We can however get close to achieving what we term *stochastic fairness*: ensuring that the probability of each party getting what it wants from an aborted exchange is always equal.

What we actually achieve is to bound the difference between these probabilities to be below any positive tolerance. This is done by ensuring that A and B are ignorant of which of a number of messages they send or receive actually communicates V_A or V_B. This involves a combination of randomisation, blinding and delay: each sends the other a series of messages, knowing that one of the messages in each direction actually communicates V_A or V_B but such that neither of them know which until this process is complete because either these messages or something that enables them is delayed. Here, by "communicates", we mean that if A, say, receives all messages from B up to and including this one, then it will *eventually* (i.e. perhaps after waiting for one or more delays to open) be able to calculate the value V_B without any further input from B (or anyone else).

---

[2] In the case where the delay construction is deterministic, it will be necessary to salt these bits with a random nonce.

[3] *Optimistic* fair exchange protocols, e.g. [1] where TTPs are only used in the case of disagreement, counter some of these.

The key intuition is to arrange things in such a way that the two parties each holds a list of terms, one of which contains their confirmation value while the others are worthless fakes. This is done in such a way that neither knows which term in the list holds their real value. Thus, when they start to swap terms according to some schedule, neither knows at what point they release their real term, or when they receive the other's real term.

At a very high level, the way this is achieved is as follows:

- Each creates fake terms, blinds their real term and inserts this at a random point in the list.
- Each sends their list to the other.
- Each applies their own blinding to the received list and applies a secret permutation and sends this back.
- On receipt of this list, each strips off their original blinding from these terms.

They are now ready to start exchanging the terms according to some pre-agreed schedule.

Note that when unblinding a list, the same factor must be used, given that they do not know which is the real term. This means that the blinding function must satisfy the following properties:

(i) receiving multiple messages blinded under the same factor does not significantly diminish security (as it would with Vernam, for example) and
(ii) $\mathcal{B}(b1, \mathcal{B}(b2, M)) = \mathcal{B}(b2, \mathcal{B}(b1, M))$ for all M, $b1$ and $b2$.
(iii) For each b there is a key b^{-1} such that $\mathcal{B}(b^{-1}(\mathcal{B}(b, x)) = x$ for all x. Thus unblinding fits into the commutative framework implied by (ii).

The natural candidate for such a blinding is exponentiation in a suitable Diffie-Hellman type group, i.e. one in which taking discrete logs is deemed intractable. Thus, for example if we work in Z_p^* for a suitable, large prime p:

$$\mathcal{B}(b, m) := m^b \ (mod \ p)$$

We still need to ensure that during the exchange phase neither party knows at which point they release or receive the critical values, and so we still need to wrap the exchanged terms in delays, to prevent them being accessible before the exchange phase has completed.

The obvious way of introducing the delay is to apply it to all the relevant terms that are sent in the exchange. However, where a party is sending a list of terms to be delayed, an equivalent and probably more efficient one is for each of A and B to send a single delayed message containing an encryption key and wrap the terms in an encryption under this key. Thus they might exchange $delay(k_A)$ and $delay(k_B)$, with the MA_i and MB_i being encryptions of k different things, only one of which is V_A or V_B respectively. The improved efficiency of this approach would be apparent when auditing a failed run since only a single delay term would need to be opened.

This technique set out here is not a fair exchange in the classical sense defined above, because either side can abort the exchange when either might unknowingly have made the reveal to the other. However it approximates what we termed stochastic fairness, meaning that in this case the probabilities of the reveal having been made either way is itself fair. Because of the particular approach we have taken to swapping messages in the reveal phase, the agents will alternately have a $\frac{1}{k}$ advantage in this probability.

We call this technique and the variants introduced below *stochastic exchange*.

There are two important things we have not addressed in the above: efficiency and preventing fraud by one of the parties in what messages he sends. The former, as in the auditable protocols in [11], can be helped by ensuring that $delay(x, T)$ terms only need to be opened during the auditing process as opposed to normal complete protocol runs. The amount of cryptography (particularly with expensive functions) and number of messages sent and received plainly have a major effect on efficiency. It follows that there will be a trade-off, determined by the choice of k, between how much work the parties do and how close they come to stochastic fairness.

The latter is achieved by commitment to subsequent sends in advance, on the assumption that the attacker does not want to be caught cheating.

4.1   Putting the Pieces Together

We have described the various pieces of plumbing we require and we now put these together in the full protocol. For ease of presentation we opt for the $(1, 2, 2 \cdots, 2)$ pattern of exchanges where both parties generate $k - 1$ fake values. We suppose that A and B have just run a PAKE and so have computed K_A and K_B respectively, and they now wish to establish in a probabilistically fair fashion if $K_A = K_B$. We suppose further that they have assigned a session Id to the run: SID. In fact, they will not of course reveal these K values in the clear but rather values derived in a one way fashion from these, e.g.:

$$V_A := Hash(K_A, A, B, SID)$$
$$V_B := Hash(K_B, B, A, SID)$$

4.1.1   Phase 1-Setup
A generates a random seed value s_A from which the the fake key values $M_{A,i}$ will be generated, an index c_A for the real V_A, fresh keys k_A and sk_A, and blinding factors b_A and b'_A:

$$s_A \in_R \mathcal{K},$$
$$k_A \in_R \mathcal{K}$$
$$sk_A \in_R \mathcal{K}$$
$$c_A \in_R \{1, \cdots, k\}$$
$$b_A \in_R \mathcal{B}$$
$$b'_A \in_R \mathcal{B}$$
$$\pi_A \in_R \Pi_k$$

Here $\in_R \mathcal{X}$ indicates drawn at random from the set $\mathcal{X}$ and Π_k denotes the set of permutations of k objects. $\mathcal{K}$ is the space of keys, which we will assume is the same as the blocksize of the cipher $\mathcal{C}$, e.g. 256 bits. $\mathcal{B}$ is the space from which the blinding factors are drawn. The unprimed blinding factors b_X will be used by the parties to blind their own M terms, while the primed factors b'_X will re-blind the M terms received from the other party. We need a suitable, injective mapping g from 2^{256} to $\mathcal{G}$, the group in which we perform the blinding.

A now computes:

$$M_{A,i} := Hash(i, s_A), i \in \{1, \cdots, k\}/c_a$$
$$M_{A,c_A} := \{V_A\}_{k_A}$$

A now maps these terms into $\mathcal{G}$ and blinds the M_{A,c_A} term using her first blinding factor b_A.:

$$M^*_{A,i} := g(Hash(i, s_A)), i \in \{1, \cdots, k\}/c_a$$
$$M^*_{A,c_A} := \mathcal{B}(b_A, g(\{V_A\}_{k_A}))$$

In the simple, illustrative case that we are presenting now we don't actually need a full permutation on k objects, simple cyclic shifts will suffice. However, for more general constructions, where we share the critical information over several terms for example, we would need full permutations, so we retain them here.

B performs the corresponding calculations with $A \leftrightarrow B$.

4.1.2   Phase 2-Commitment

They now exchange a Delay term containing the key sk_X and an encryption under this key of the following terms: the index c_X (to the term containing their real V_X), the permutation, π_X the seed value s_X and the second blinding terms b'_X, but b_X crucially. At the same time they append the blinded M^*_X terms:

$$A \rightarrow B : Delay(sk_A), \{c_A, \pi_A, s_A, b'_A\}_{sk_A} \langle M^*_{Ai} \mid i \leftarrow \langle 1, \ldots, k \rangle \rangle$$
$$B \rightarrow A : Delay(sk_B), \{c_B, \pi_B, s_B, b'_B\}_{sk_B} \langle M^*_{Bi} \mid i \leftarrow \langle 1, \ldots, k \rangle \rangle$$

Thus, when the delay opens the ephemeral key is revealed and the terms under encryption are also revealed. Note that the Delay terms serve a dual purpose: to conceal the contents for some lower bounded time period and to commit the sender to the contents.

4.1.3   Phase 3-Reblind and Shuffle

Now A re-blinds the M_B terms that they have just received from B under their own second blinding key b'_A, and she permutes the resulting terms under her chosen permutation π_A. B performs the analogous operation on the terms he received from A, using his own second blinding term b'_B and permutation. Each sends the resulting list back to the other:

$$A \rightarrow B : \langle \mathcal{B}(b'_A, \mathcal{B}(b_B, M_{B, \pi_A(i)})) \mid i \leftarrow \langle 1 \ldots k \rangle \rangle$$
$$B \rightarrow A : \langle \mathcal{B}(b'_B, \mathcal{B}(b_A, M_{A, \pi_B(i)})) \mid i \leftarrow \langle 1 \ldots k \rangle \rangle$$

On receipt of these terms, each can strip off their own b_X blinding factor to yield a list of their own M_X terms but blinded and shuffled by the other. For the dummy terms the unblinding with b_X^{-1} won't cancel, but this does not matter as these are just random terms anyway. Consequently, neither knows which term in either list contains the critical V term. Thus A now holds the list: $\langle \mathcal{B}(b_B', M_{A,\pi_B(i)}^*) \mid i \leftarrow \langle 1 \ldots k \rangle \rangle$, which has $\mathcal{B}(b_X', \{V_A\}_{k_A})$ at some unknown place in the list, and similarly for B.

4.1.4   Phase 4-Fair Exchange

Now they are ready to start exchanging these terms progressively according the prescribed alternating schedule, for example the $(1, 2, 2 \cdots, 2)$ schedule:

$$A \rightarrow B : \mathcal{B}(b_B', M_{A,\pi_B(1)}^*)$$
$$B \rightarrow A : \mathcal{B}(b_A', M_{B,\pi_A(1)}^*), \mathcal{B}(b_A', M_{B,\pi_A(2)}^*)$$
$$A \rightarrow B : \mathcal{B}(b_B', M_{A,\pi_B(2)}^*), \mathcal{B}(b_B', M_{A,\pi_A(3)}^*)$$

$$\cdot$$
$$\cdot$$

$$B \rightarrow A : \mathcal{B}(b_A', M_{B,\pi_A(k-1)}^*), \mathcal{B}(b_A', M_{B,\pi_A(k)}^*)$$

Each can strip off their own blinding factor to reveal the other's M_X^* terms, one of which should be the encryption of V_X and the others dummies.

4.1.5   Phase 5-Reveal

Assuming that phase 4 runs to completion they can now exchange their encryption keys sk_X and k_X, permutations π_X and seed values s_X:

$$A \rightarrow B : k_A, sk_A, \pi_A, s_A$$
$$B \rightarrow A : k_B, sk_B, \pi_B, s_B$$

Now that they know the other's permutation, with the knowledge of their own index, they can identify which term should contain the real V_X and they can decrypt this with the newly revealed k_X.

4.2   When Things Go Wrong

If either party fails to receive the expected response in a timely fashion it sends no further message and abandons the protocol. If the protocol is aborted before Phase 4, neither node has received enough to determine if $K_A = K_B$ in the exchange.

If it is aborted in Phase 4, and once the delays have opened, an honest node can audit the messages received so far to determine whether all the messages it has received are coherent, and whether it should hold sufficient information to determine the other's V_X. That is, it extracts the other party's permutation from the Delay and from this along with knowledge of the index it used can determine if the real V_X term should be in the set received to that point. It also knows if its own V_X has been revealed.

If it is aborted after Phase 4, an honest node can audit as above but now certainly has the information to determine V_X, or establish that the other party cheated in the construction of the terms.

The delays only have to be opened in an aborted run because in a completed run the values V_A and V_B will have been exchanged and can be checked against the values committed earlier.

4.3   Auditing

Here we detail the auditing steps that a party X should take. In the event of the protocol aborting, these may have to tale place after the delay wrappers have been opened:

- Check that the other party Y has provided a valid key $k_Y \in \mathcal{K}$, a valid index c_Y in the range $(1, \ldots, k)$, valid blinding terms b'_X, b^*_X, a valid permutation π_Y over k objects and finally a valid seed value $s_Y \in \mathcal{K}$.
- Check, using knowledge of π_X, b^*_X and b'_X, whether Y performed the committed permutation of the re-blinding.
- If the protocol aborts at some point in Phase 4, say after X has received l terms from Y, then X computes $\pi_X(c_Y)$ and if this is less that l then the $\{V_Y\}_{k_Y}$ terms should be in the set X has received. X should decrypt this term and can now establish if $K_X = K_Y$. If $\pi_X(c_Y) > l$ then he has not received the critical term and cannot conclude whether $K_A = K_B$ or not.
- For all the terms received in Phase 4, X should check that they are correctly formed, i.e. of the form $M_{i,Y} = Hash(\pi_X^{-1}(i), s_Y)$, for all $i \leq l$ and $i \neq c_Y$. This check should be performed even if Phase 4 competes, i.e. if $l = k$.

By this means, each will be able to tell if the other has followed the protocol correctly. If not, it is highly likely that an attacker is present. If the terms are correctly constructed he can tell if $K_A \neq K_B$ then Y has made an incorrect guess so is assumed to be an attacker.

5   Playing with Probability

Imagine the following scenario. In a given network there are $2N$ parties who will pair off and try to connect to one another in N protocols runs. The probability of an individual password guess by an intruder being correct is ϵ. Each pair are prepared to make T tries at pairing if they think that communications failings are getting in their way. Therefore, if the pairs use some PAKE to establish their links without using our modified protocols, the intruder can expect to have approximately $NT\epsilon$ successes in breaking into the pairs without any chance of being discovered. (The approximation is because the intruder only needs to break each pair once, and so will stop attacking a given pair before the Tth if it succeeds before then. It is however a good approximation provided the probability of it succeeding in T tries is significantly less than 1, something we would expect in practice.)

If the protocol were now changed to one of our auditable PAKEs, this expectation would decrease to $\frac{N(T-1)\epsilon}{2k}$: the -1 is explained because in order to break in with no chance of being detected a run must be abandoned, so cannot be the last of T. (The discovered password is then used on a subsequent run within the T.) If on each run the intruder is willing to give away a $(1-\epsilon)/k$ chance of being caught (i.e. give away one of his MB_i) this will multiply the expected successes by 3 (rather than only getting only one share in half the runs he will now get one in half the runs and two in the other half), but will have an expectation of being discovered approximately $\frac{N(T-1)(1-\epsilon)}{2k}$ times. This means near certain discovery in many cases. In effect the intruder playing this game would give him 3ϵ successes for each time he is discovered.

With the pattern of exchange we nominated earlier, the ratio of successes gets worse for the attacker as the number of MB_i that he is willing to send increases. For example if he is willing to send 2 or 3 it reduces to $(5/3)\epsilon$ or $(7/5)\epsilon$. (In essence if prepared to give up r, the intruder has a 0.5 probability of giving up $r-1$ for r of Alice's and a 0.5 probability of giving up r for $r+1$, depending on who starts the exchange.

By picking a different sending strategy to the $1, 2, 2, 2, \cdots$ one we could keep all the ratios below 3ϵ and substantially reducing the number of messages sent. For example sending $1, 2, 3, 4, \cdots$ would still result in rations converging to 1 as the attacker yields more shares, with first term 3ϵ, but use only about $\sqrt{k}$ exchanges. However picking k large enough to keep $\frac{N(T-1)\epsilon}{2k}$ sufficiently small may require nodes to create and blind more MX_i than is ideal.

One can reduce the amount of work the nodes have to do by replacing what we might term the *linear* division strategy (i.e. the probability of being able to deduce V_X grows linearly with the number of MX_i one has seen) by a *quadratic* one. In this there are two specific MX_i that are required to deduce V_X, meaning that the probability of having them both grows quadratically with the number one has, in the initial phase of the exchange. For example X might initially send $\{\{V_X\}_{kx1}\}_{kx2}$ under a delay, making the MX_i a number of keys that include $kx1$ and $kx2$. Of course one could extend this to higher degrees. In the quadratic case with k messages in all, one must have $r > 1$ of them to have any chance of having both the two crucial ones, with the probability then being $\frac{r(r-1)}{k(k-1)}$.

If, for example, we picked $k = 10$ and the MX_i exchanged using the $1, 2, 2, 2, \cdots$ pattern we assumed previously, the attacker could give away one key without fear of giving himself away, and could (if willing to go no further) expect a $\frac{1}{90}$ chance of having his guess checked, and therefore a $\frac{\epsilon}{90}$ chance of obtaining the key. This improves from the $\frac{\epsilon}{20}$ chance using $k = 10$ with the linear approach. The amount of blinding (which is likely to be comparatively the most expensive part of our approach, computationally) is exactly the same in these quadratic and linear examples.

Therefore this quadratic approach reduces the chance our attacker has of breaking any of the N runs without giving away a much bigger chance of being caught.

The designer of any implementation is of course free to choose an approach to devising and exchanging tokens that is believed to be optimal in terms of the perceived threat, communication costs and computation costs. What we have shown in this section is that there are many options other than the linear $1, 2, 2, 2, \cdots$ one adopted earlier.

6   Game Playing: Other Uses of Stochastically Fair Exchange

What we have demonstrated is how to build PAKE protocols in which we can make the rate at which an attacker can gain information about keys without yielding evidence of his existence as small as desired, while the number of guesses at passwords he can check by other means will give away his existence to the trustworthy parties approximately the same number of times (stochastically).

The main part of this class of protocols is something we did not need at all for HISPs, a way of ensuring a nearly fair game between two players who are each supposed to give each other something, in the absence of a TTP.

Clearly the probabilistic fair exchange mechanisms proposed here could find application in other contexts, for example contract signing. In place of the V_X values we might have signatures and use the probabilistic fair exchange to provide *abuse-freeness*. The idea here is to avoid situations in which one party is able to gain some advantage by being able to prove to a third party that they have the ability to determine whether the protocol will complete successfully or abort.

Note that there are some interesting issues of incentives here: in our application to PAKEs the attacker wants to provide the correct confirmation value if possible. There is thus no incentive for him to provide an "invalid" V value. On the other hand, it is in his interests to try to identify the point at which he received the critical value from the honest party, or at what point he emits his critical value, which he potentially could do by constructing the fake terms in such a way that they are related by known exponents. This explains the hash construction of the fake terms and the need for each to audit that the other follows this aspect of the protocol.

In contrast, in say contract signing, each party may be incentivised to submit invalid signatures. The standard way to handle this is to introduce optimistic protocols: that will invoke a judge or TTP in the event of problems. In this context it is not clear that our stochastic fair exchange construction provides any advantage over such optimistic protocols. However, our construction would help to achieve abuse-freeness by ensuring that neither party can determine, and prove to the third party, at any point that they can control whether the protocol completes or aborts.

7   Analysis

Our goal in this paper has been to devise a protocol to prevent an attacker being able to test guesses at the password in a way that will not be detected by the honest participants, or more precisely, in way that they cannot distinguish from network failures. Ideally we would like to ensure that if the attacker can determine that his guess is wrong then the honest party will also know that the keys do not match. We cannot achieve perfect fairness in this sense, at least in the two-party setting without TTP, but we argue that the protocol described here allows us to get arbitrarily close to this. More precisely, we achieve the following property:

Definition 1. δ *Stochastic Fairness:*

Let p_X be the probability that X possesses the necessary information to establish whether $V_A = V_B$, possibly after delay terms have been revealed.

A protocol Π satisfies δ stochastic fairness if, at any point in the execution of the protocol we have:

$$|p_A - p_B| \leq \delta$$

Our basic protocol above satisfies $1/k$ probabilistic fairness.

7.1   Sketch Proof of Stochastic Fairness

Up to the end of Phase 3, neither party has any access to the V terms. They do have access to a term that contain the other party's V term but these are wrapped first by an encryption under a key that is under a Delay but more importantly the encryption is shrouded by an unconditionally hiding blinding b_X. These blinding terms are not revealed when the delays are opened.

Thus, if the protocol aborts before the end of Phase 3 neither party learns the other's confirmation term, and in particular, the attacker learns nothing about the validity or otherwise of his guess at the password.

If the protocol runs to the end of Phase 4, the fair exchange, then it is clear that both parties will have enough information to establish if $V_A = V_B$, or that the other party provided inconsistent terms. The interesting part is if the protocol aborts at some point during Phase 4.

First we will analyse phase 4 under the assumption that the two parties follow the protocol, later we will discuss how it deals with possible departures from the protocol if one of the parties is adversarial.

By the end of Phase 3, each party will have received back a list of M terms blinded and shuffled by the other party. We need to show that they cannot determine which term contains their real V. The blinding/shuffle construction is essentially the *exponentiation mix* construction of [12]. As long as the terms that are input to the mix are independent in the sense that there is no pair M_{Xi}, M_{Xj} for which the attacker knows y such that $(M_{Xi})^y = M_{Xj}$, then it can be shown that breaking the secrecy of the shuffle is reducible to the DDH assumption. On the other hand, if the attacker can arrange for a pair of inputs such that he knows the discrete log then it is easy for him to trace these through the mix. It is to avoid this that we use the hash function construction for the fake M_X values: the party has to commit to the seed value that is fed into the hash along with the index values to generate the M terms. Assuming that the hash is such that computing pre-images is intractable then he will not be able to produce dependent M_X values consistent with the committed seed s.

This establishes the key property: each party will not know which of the shuffled terms contains their real V and consequently they will not know at what point in Phase 4 they pass this term to the other. Equally, they will not know at which point that have received the term containing the other's real V term because, although they know what shuffle they applied they do not know which index the other used. Thus, after the first send B will have a $1/k$ chance that he has V_A (still concealed under a Delay). After the next send of two terms from B, A will have a $2/k$ chance of having V_B, etc. We see that, for this schedule of exchanges, the difference in their advantages is always bounded by $1/k$. As explained earlier, we can improve on this bound by suitable threshold constructions and scheduling, but the arguments will be essentially the same.

Of course, either party may chose to depart from the protocol by for example sending random terms rather than the actual terms, but this will only result in either the other finding that the keys do not match or the deviation will be evident on audit in the event of an abort.

8   Conclusions

In this paper we show that PAKEs, like HIPSs, are vulnerable to an attacker disguising guessing attacks as network failures, We have shown that PAKEs present significantly more challenges than HISPs to making them auditable, and outlined the approach we will take to solve this. The new construction, stochastic fairness, is likely to find application beyond PAKEs, e.g. in fair exchange schemes.

Appendix A: a brief survey of PAKEs

Here we briefly describe a number of representative PAKE protocols. This is purely for illustrative purposes; the techniques we describe below should work for all PAKEs. For simplicity we omit various checks that need to be performed. A comprehensive survey of PAKEs can be found in Chap. 40 of the Computer And Information Security Handbook 2nd Edition, Ed J Vacca, Elsevier 2013.

Such protocols come in two phases: key establishment and key confirmation. The first establishes a key based on the shared password, and the second allows each party to confirm that the other knows the password, implying that the key establishment phase was run with the intended party. These phases can generally be chosen independently of each other.

PAKE key establishment

EKE (Encrypted Key Exchange)

The original EKE, [2], is essentially Diffie-Hellman with the DH terms encrypted with a symmetric key s^* derived from the shared password s using a public, deterministic function f, $s^* = f(s)$:

$$A \rightarrow B : \{g^x\}_{s^*}$$
$$B \rightarrow A : \{g^y\}_{s^*}$$

The session key is formed as $K = g^{xy}$.

The original EKE has undergone several fixes to counter flaws, notably the fact that an attacker can eliminate a large number of putative passwords by decrypting the exchanged terms with a guessed password and observing if the resulting plaintext lies in the subgroup.

SPEKE (Simple Password Exponential Key Establishment)

SPEKE, [6], is essentially a D-H protocol but with the difference that the generator is not fixed and public but rather is computed as an agreed function of the shared secret s, for example:

$$h(s) := (H(s))^2 \pmod p$$

The squaring guarantees that g lies in the appropriate subgroup assuming that we are assuming a safe prime p where $p = 2q - 1$ with q also prime. The protocol is thus essentially a D-H protocol using the shared secret generator.

$$A \rightarrow B : h(s)^x$$
$$B \rightarrow A : h(s)^y$$
$$K = g(s)^{ab}$$

PKK

A rather elegant protocol, PKK due to Boyko et al. [3], is in simplified form for illustration:

$$A \rightarrow B : X := h(s_A) \cdot g^x,$$
$$B \rightarrow A : Y := h(s_B) \cdot g^y$$

Here h denotes a suitable mapping from the password space to the DH group.
A computes: $K_A := (Y/h(s_A))^x$
B computes: $K_B := (X/h(s_B))^y$

J-PAKE

J-PAKE, [5], uses a quite different approach: the so-called juggling of D-H terms. The original J-PAKE involved both parties generating and transmitting two D-H terms. For simplicity of presentation we describe here a lightweight version, [8], that requires just one D-H term from each party but involves a so-called Common Reference String (CRS) construction.

J-PAKE-CRS

Here we assume that there is an agreed element h of the group G with unknown log w.r.t. g (in effect a so-called Common Reference String CRS).

$$A \to B : g^x, ZKP(x,g)$$
$$B \to A : g^y, ZKP(y,g)$$

Round two:

$$A \to B : X := (h \cdot g^y)^{(x.s)}, ZKP(x.s, h \cdot g^y)$$
$$B \to A : Y := (h \cdot g^x)^{y.s}, ZKP(y.s, h \cdot g^x)$$

A computes: $K_A := (Y/g^{y.x.s})^x$
B computes: $K_B := (X/g^{x.y.s})^y$
Thus, if $s_A = s_B(= s)$ then $K_A = K_B = h^{x.y.s}$
$ZKP(x,y)$ denotes Zero-Knowledge Proofs of knowledge of a discrete log of x w.r.t. the base y.

Appendix B: Key Derivation and Confirmation

Having established a DH shared secret we typically need to derive a suitable session key for a symmetric algorithm. Various approaches have been proposed and we will not go into the details here but we refer the interested reader to, for example the NIST recommendations, [4], and Krawczyk [7]. A typical approach is to derive the key from the DH value is to use a suitable hash function that yields a close to flat distribution over the key space and include parameters associated with the session:

$$SK := Hash_1(K, A, B)$$

Where K is the DH value. Now the parties have to compare their keys, which they might do by, for example, exchanging hashes of the form:

$$A \to B : Hash_2(1, K_A, A, B)$$
$$B \to A : Hash_2(2, K_B, A, B)$$

An alternative approach is to segment the derived key into three parts:

$$SK = sk||k_A||k_B$$

Where $||$ denotes concatenation. A and B now exchange the appropriate segments as follows:

$$A \rightarrow B : k_A$$
$$B \rightarrow A : k_B$$

A and B now check that the received values agree with those they computed internally. Assuming that they do indeed find agreement they can proceed to use sk as the session key. This may require the calculation of a much larger key than normal, possibly requiring key expansion, see [7].

References

1. Asokan, N., Shoup, V., Waidner, M.: Optimistic fair exchange of digital signatures. IEEE J. Sel. Areas Commun. **18**(4), 593–610 (2000). https://doi.org/10.1109/49. 839935
2. Bellovin, S.M., Merritt, M.: Encrypted key exchange: password-based protocols secure against dictionary attacks. In: IEEE Symposium on Research in Security and Privacy, pp. 72–84 (1992)
3. Boyko, V., MacKenzie, P., Patel, S.: Provably secure password-authenticated key exchange using Diffie-Hellman. In: Preneel, B. (ed.) EUROCRYPT 2000. LNCS, vol. 1807, pp. 156–171. Springer, Heidelberg (2000). https://doi.org/10. 1007/3 540 45539-0_12. http://dl.acm.org/citation.cfm?id=1756169.1756186
4. Chen, L.: Nist special publication 800–56C recommendation for key derivation through extraction-then-expansion (2011)
5. Hao, F., Ryan, P.Y.A.: Password authenticated key exchange by juggling. In: Christianson, B., Malcolm, J.A., Matyas, V., Roe, M. (eds.) Security Protocols 2008. LNCS, vol. 6615, pp. 159–171. Springer, Heidelberg (2011). https://doi. org/10.1007/978-3-642-22137-8_23. http://dl.acm.org/citation.cfm?id=2022815. 2022838
6. Jablon, D.P.: Strong password-only authenticated key exchange. SIGCOMM Comput. Commun. Rev. **26**(5), 5–26 (1996). https://doi.org/10.1145/242896.242897
7. Krawczyk, H.: Cryptographic extraction and key derivation: the HKDF scheme. In: Rabin, T. (ed.) CRYPTO 2010. LNCS, vol. 6223, pp. 631–648. Springer, Heidelberg (2010). https://doi.org/10.1007/978-3-642-14623-7_34. http://dl.acm.org/citation.cfm?id=1881412.1881456
8. Lancrenon, J., Skrobot, M., Tang, Q.: Two more efficient variants of the J-PAKE protocol. Cryptology ePrint Archive, Report 2016/379 (2016). http://eprint.iacr. org/2016/379
9. Nguyen, L., Roscoe, A.: Authentication protocols based on low-bandwidth unspoofable channels: a comparative survey. J. Comput. Secur. **19**, 139–201 (2011)
10. Pagnia, H., Gärtner, F.C.: On the impossibility of fair exchange without a trusted third party. Technical report, Citeseer (1999)
11. Roscoe, A.: Detecting failed attacks on human-interactive security protocols (2016)
12. Wikström, D.: A sender verifiable mix-net and a new proof of a shuffle. In: Roy, B. (ed.) ASIACRYPT 2005. LNCS, vol. 3788, pp. 273–292. Springer, Heidelberg (2005). https://doi.org/10.1007/11593447_15

Auditable PAKEs: Approaching Fair Exchange Without a TTP
(Transcript of Discussion)

Peter Y. A. Ryan[✉]

University of Luxembourg, Luxembourg, Luxembourg
peter.ryan@uni.lu

This is some work I did last year with Bill Roscoe. I was on sabbatical so it's a kind of "What I did on my sabbatical" talk. I guess it fits with what seems to be an emerging theme in these sessions of the detection of attacks. I should perhaps explain that the use of term emphauditable was I think coined by Bill, to indicate the design of a protocols in such a way that legitimate parties can detect when they're under attack. That I hope will become clear in a moment.

So let me just give you the outline. The ideas came from some earlier work that Bill had done on what the Oxford people tend to refer to as HISPs: Human Interactive Security Protocols, but I think that this is synonymous with out-of-band channels, the kind of things we've been talking about. If they're not synonymous I'm happy to have someone correct me. So I'll just very quickly hint at those. I'll talk about "under the radar" guessing attacks, where an attacker tries to make guessing attacks undetectable, to look like a network failure or similar. An abort of the protocol rather than an explicit attack. Then I'll mention quickly Bill's general transform for making HISPs auditable in this sense, and then I'll briefly talk about PAKEs; Password Authenticated Key Establishment Protocols, and the distinctions between HIPSs and PAKEs.

The natural question which came up while I was in Oxford, was: "can we apply these techniques to make PAKEs auditable?" At first glance it seemed as though it should be trivial, in fact it turns out it isn't, which I'll try to illustrate. We had to develop some new techniques, which we think may have independent interest of their own: the stochastic fair exchange. So that's the outline, let's see if we can do it in the half an hour.

I think that you're probably all fairly familiar with HISPs, or out-of-band channel protocols. The idea is that there is some low bandwidth unspoofable channel that the participants can use to confirm that they've established a shared, secret key, via, for example, a Diffie-Hellman based protocol. So they don't use PKI and we don't assume a shared password or anything like that, the authentication comes purely from this unspoofable out-of-band channel.

The point here, and I think this was Bill's observation, I'm not sure anybody had hit on this before, is that an attacker can try a man-in-the-middle attack, or a masquerade attack at one end, just trying to guess. So for example he tries a guess at the randomness he injects in his Diffie-Hellman term, and hopes that it'll lead to an agreement of the short digests that they compare at the end. Of

F. Stajano et al. (Eds.): Security Protocols 2017, LNCS 10476, pp. 298–305, 2017.
https://doi.org/10.1007/978-3-319-71075-4_32

course if it doesn't then the parties don't continue. But the problem is that the attacker potentially can arrange, if he plays the appropriate role in the protocol, to learn the other person's digest before he reveals his digest, and if they don't agree, he can simply abort. And that is potentially interpreted by the legitimate party as a network failure or the other party having crashed.

So by this means the attacker can multiply the number of guessing attacks he can make before the legitimate parties start to be aware that they're under attack, and take evasive action, block further guesses, extend the length of the codes, seek other channels, and so forth. If you're just attacking a single node that perhaps doesn't buy you very much, but if you multiply it up by attacking a network of nodes, then you start to get some traction out of this. Okay, so that's the under the radar type attacks, so the goal is to try to counter that kind of strategy.

What Bill suggested was a very simple transform to these protocols, which relies on a *delay* construct, which I think in the past is sometimes called time-locked crypto. There are various ways you can implement this concept, you can do it with a third party, that is broadcasting decryption keys at various intervals. Or you can use time puzzle style problems. The idea is you try to guarantee that the information buried under a delay wrapper will be concealed for some suitable period of time, but will be revealed in due course. In this case that means comfortably beyond the timeout period for the protocol in question. This may depend on assumptions about the computational power of the attacher of course.

So here this works very easily. The first player to release their digest does so under a delay term, so now the attacker's strategy no longer works, because he doesn't yet know if his guess is good. If he tries to abort at that time, just allows the thing to timeout, then clearly the session doesn't continue, and basically he doesn't learn anything. If he tries to continue, he has to put in his guess at the code, perhaps also under the delay, and then his attack is revealed, potentially after the delay period has elapsed.

Khaled Baqer: Can you elaborate on how these protocols work?

Reply: I think it's very similar to the kind of scenarios we talked about before. Two parties perform, let's say, a Diffie-Hellman exchange, over WiFi or whatever, and then they want to establish that it was really between them, so they exchange, say over the phone, with voice authentication, short digests.....

Khaled Baqer: So they exchange short codes derived from the session key?

Reply: Yes, right. A short hashed code, a digest.

So, the real point of this talk then, is to see whether we can do the same kind of thing with PAKEs, make them auditable. At first glance it seems like the same trick should work straight off, but in fact after a little thought we realised that actually it doesn't, and there are some significant differences between HISPs and PAKEs, which means that it's not so easy.

First of all let me just say a few words about PAKEs. Here the idea is that we're not relying on a PKI, or out-of-band channels, rather we're assuming that the two parties have, as Bruce likes to say, met on a blasted heath and exchanged a password, or low entropy secret beforehand, and that is the basis of the authentication. So typically what happens is, and there's a whole bunch of these protocols, at its core it's a Diffie-Hellman key exchange, but somehow the low entropy secret is stirred into the computation of the keys. You have to do this very carefully to avoid offline dictionary attacks of course, but the final computed keys at either end are a function of the fresh entropy, plus the supposed shared secret. So they follow this up with some kind of key confirmation, exchanges of hashes of the key say, to confirm that they've both computed the same underlying session key. Thereby implicitly authenticating the other. I guess everyone's familiar with that.

A very simple example is the PPK protocol, so here we have some hash function which takes you from a dictionary password space into the group. So they both compute this ... Ideally of course they have the same password so they compute the same H-value here. This is multiplied into the Diffie-Hellman terms, and at the end when they compute the key, they factor out their own H-values, and as long as they were using the same password the H-terms will cancel, and so they get an agreed Diffie-Hellman term. If they don't share the same password then they will likely derive different H-values, so they don't cancel and in the computed session key you get a random value raised to the x or y. So that's a simple example. They then perform a key confirmation.

Okay, so our first guess was that we could just do the same transformation, just add delay terms to the hash key confirmation terms that are exchanged at the end. We realised actually that's not true, because there are several differences between HISPs and PAKEs, but the crucial one is that HISPs are stateless: there's no state going from one session to another, whereas clearly PAKEs are stateful. The password information is carried from one session to another. So that means that this delay transform doesn't work. All the attacker has to do, when he gets the delayed confirmation term, is just abort, sit it out, and wait for the delay to open. He then discovers whether his guess at the password was correct or not, and, of course, he can use that information into future sessions. So, either he's got the right password word in which case he can now set up a spoof communication, or he's at least eliminated a potential password. Yes Paolo?

Paulo Esteves Verissimo: Within your threat model could the timing out be hacked?

Reply: The timeout or the delay?

Paulo Esteves Verissimo: The delay. Conceptually does your threat model include tampering with the delay?

Reply: Right. I think the answer is for the purpose of this talk we're assuming that the delay works. Does what it's supposed to do: always keep values concealed until beyond the timeout has elapsed. In some of Bill's work on HISPs he actually did consider the possibility that the delay mechanism would fail and so built in sort of secondary safe guards -

Paulo Esteves Verissimo: Right, so my second question is: if the assumption fails would that hurt the protocol?

Reply: I think with the protocol I'm going to present now, if the assumption fails we're in trouble. We need to think more if we can make this protocol somewhat robust against such failures.

Okay. So Bill's transform doesn't work if you just apply it naively to PAKEs, basically because of the shared state. So what we then realised is that we need some form of fair exchange. Some guarantee that if A gets to see B's confirmation hash value then B will also get to see A's value, and vice versa. And this led to a construction for fair exchange that, as far as I know, is novel. Again, if someone's seen something like this before please let me know. We call it Stochastic Fair Exchange so the idea is basically to set things up in such a way that at any point in the unfolding of the protocol the probability of one party seeing the crucial value is approximately equal to the probability for the other party.

More precisely, suppose that we have the probability P_x that the party x has the appropriate information to be able to compute the confirmation term, possibly after the opening of delays. Then we can say protocol satisfies δ Stochastic Fair Exchange if the difference between those two probabilities is bounded by δ at all points of the protocol execution.

So the kind of set up we have in mind is we've run a PAKE and they compute some kind of hash values to exchange, which, probably to avoid reflection attacks, will be computed distinctly, but you can see how after exchanging these they can establish if they have computed the same underlying key. And so the key idea is to set things up in such a way that neither party knows the point at which they've transmitted the term containing their crucial value, or received the value from the other. And so that's basically it, at a very high level. I'll go into more detail in the next few slides.

Each party produces $k-1$ dummy terms. The real confirmation term, encrypted under a freshly generated key and blinded by a b term, is then inserted in this list at a random point. This blinding has to be commutative and one-way for reasons, which I think will become clear shortly. Each party sends this list across to the other party and then on receipt, the other party re-blinds these terms with a blinding factor of their own, this b', does a secret shuffle of the terms and sends them back. So each party gets back their list but re-blinded and shuffled by the other party. At that point, of course, each can now strip off their own blinding from these terms.

Basically, after this has happened, what they end up is a list of their terms, blinded and subjected to a secret shuffle by the other party. So they don't know where in this list their crucial term lies. All right? That's the key trick. And then, of course, they can start exchanging these backwards and forwards according to some schedule.

So in slightly more detail. I think we do have a bit of time. Each party has to generate a secret index i chosen from one to k, a seed value, which we'll explain in a second, a secret permutation, two blinding factors, and an encryption key. They compute the i-th M term as the encryption of the critical confirmation value under the secret key and blinded by their first blinding factor. And the others, the other $k-1$ terms will be computed in an appropriate way, e.g. counter mode, as a hash function of the seed. And that's significant. We'll come to that in a second.

So that's the set-up phase. Both parties compute these values and now they commit to them. They send to each other a list of these values, the index, the seed, the key, the permutation and the second blinding term, under delay and then the list of these M terms blinded by their first blinding factor. Okay. So they exchange these. Now they do what I hinted at earlier: they do a re-blinding of all the M terms, shuffle them, and send them back.

So now we get to the fair exchange phase. They unblind the M terms using their first blinding factor and they exchange them according in some alternating fashion. So, for example, A might send the first M term to B, then B sends two terms back, then A sends two terms and so on. And once all that's happened then, of course, they can strip off their second blinding term and reveal the raw end terms. And if all that completes fine then they just finish up with a reveal phase: they just send each other their index and their secret key, which allows each to identify and decrypt to reveal the other's confirmation value. Note that they should emit their M terms in the order that they received them back from the other party, i.e. preserving the permutation applied by the other.

I don't know how much this helps, but I tried to fit it all into one slide. So you can see it's quite an elaborate clockwork. Does the flow of the protocol make sense? I hope that the key high level idea is clear enough. Okay. So if something goes wrong, or actually even if it doesn't go wrong, the parties should perform various audit checks. These may have to wait until those delay terms open up, but they basically check that the terms that were sent out in the first commit were all appropriately formed in the sense that I explained in the setup phase.

Okay. So we probably don't need to go into all the details of the audits at this point. So a quick few words of the analysis. We've only done an informal analysis at the moment. We would like to do a more formal analysis in due course. It should be fairly clear from the way things have been set up that until we start the fair exchange phase, neither party has enough information to compute the critical values. Basically the M terms at that point are all shrouded in the blinding factor of the other party. Of course we have to be a bit careful about what kind of blinding we use because they have to use the same blinding factor to all the k terms because, of course, they come back shuffled. So to un-blind we can only do that if it's a single blinding factor. So we have to make sure that this isn't a security concern. We need something like taking exponents in an appropriate group. We could for example work with a prime modulus rather than an RSA modulus. So, in that sense, until the fair exchange starts, neither party should have enough information to work out the other's b value. If an abort occurs during the fair exchange phase they can then wait until the delays open. They can then extract the index term, at that point, with the knowledge of their own shuffle, they will know whether they should have received the appropriate critical term and they can open it up with a key. Then they confirm whether it's the correct value or not.

For the analysis, what's rather nice about this construction I described is that it's analogous to the exponentiation type mixes which sometimes we use in voting systems for example, which I think go back originally to Doug Wikström. The idea of taking terms to a common exponent, shuffling them and then posting them on the next column on the public ledger if you like. So that's a known, proven construct although this is a novel application of it. We know we can borrow some of the properties of that. So that's been proven to hide the shuffles, as long as you're talking about a passive attacker.

If you have an active attacker who can inject terms into the mix, you then have to be very careful because he can use that capability to inject a pair of terms related by an exponent that he knows, then of course this algebraic relationship is preserved through the mix so allowing him to trace things. So you have to prevent that possibility and that's basically where the hash function construct came from. Assuming that he can't compute pre-images of the hash or discrete logs he shouldn't be able to launch this kind of attack. If he tries such an attack it will be detected in the audit.

So the argument here is that when they receive back these blinded, shuffled terms from the other party they won't be able to identify which is their critical term in the list. So when they're going through an exchange process they don't know at what point they're releasing their critical term or at what point they receive a critical term from the other party. So that means the attacker no longer has the strategy of knowing when he can safely abort and learn whether his guess was right without revealing the attack to the other party.

Okay, so that's the basic construct. You can of course play various games with the fair exchange sequence, the schedule. You can extend further: you don't necessarily have to have the critical information buried in one term. You can have a secret share over several terms which gives interesting possibilities. Hopefully you got the idea how this new construct, this stochastic fair exchange construct allows us to transform PAKEs to make them audible in Bill's sense. But note: we still need the delays.

The construct is in itself quite interesting and as far as we know it's a novel way of doing fair exchange. Of course an obvious question is can we apply it elsewhere? Potentially, presumably in any situation where fair exchange is called for, this could perhaps be a useful construct. In particular it is obviously useful if you're concerned about abuse freeness. Abuse-freeness is where you want to avoid a party being able to prove to a third party that they control whether the protocol will complete or not. This kind of construct would seem to counter that kind of problem.

So we're currently thinking about other applications of this construct.

Bryan Ford: I really like the idea.

Reply: But?

Bryan Ford: No, no but. So fair exchange is something that a lot of people are talking about using block chain protocols to do. So one question is: have you thought about whether you can do this kind of thing in block chain but then the complementary question: Is this is an interesting, potentially new way to do fair exchange, can you build a more, do interesting consensus and have block chain fairness protocols out of this construct? There's a lot of anti-censorship or censorship and fairness risks the issue that their at the heart of a lot of block chain protocols. I wonder if this a potential tool in that.

Reply: I will talk to the first part of your question, perhaps I should have stressed: we're very deliberately trying to avoid trusted third parties. We're trying to make it very much a peer to peer kind of protocol.

Bryan Ford: Right. Well of course block chain protocols are trying to be a trust distributed not a centralised trusted third party. Whether you want to call that a trusted third party I'm not sure.

Reply: But I tend to think of it still as some sort of public ledger. It's still a third party. If you've got a two party protocol running they're still having to communicate with this ledger in some way right?

Bryan Ford: Sure. Sure.

Reply: So I think we were very much trying to avoid that. The delay construct in certain approaches might involve a trusted third party as I mentioned. Broadly speaking we're trying to avoid that and make it purely peer to peer.

Bryan Ford: Okay.

Reply: So this is the two party case. Of course you could extend this to multiparty but that goes beyond this talk. So I think that would be my answer to your first question. The second question, well I think that the answer is that we haven't thought about that. It sounds like an interesting line of thought. I'm not sure I fully understand what the sort of fairness issues with blockchain are. I'd certainly be happy to talk more about it either now or later.

Bryan Ford: Yeah, we should follow up later. In many of the consensus protocols that people exploring in this space, issues of if you have leader-based protocols. There's the question of how much can the leader decide, how much of an advantage does the leader get in deciding what transactions go in and what transactions go out. If there are better ways to commitment and delay the decision or delay the knowledge, prevent the leader knowing what transactions he's trying to bias against or something like that. That could be useful to this space.

Reply: It seems like this could well work. Yes.

Bryan Ford: It could be useful for that.

Reply: Yes, I'd be happy to talk more about that.
I see that I didn't make it controversial enough!

Bruce Christianson: Is there an assumption that delay is at all symmetric between the two parties? Because this is similar to the zero-knowledge stuff where you have a number of rounds, and each round they talk to each other and each gets a little bit more of the information they need in order to unlock the value of the exchanged secret. The idea here is that if the protocol aborts sufficiently late that one party can force through the protocol discovery process single-handedly, then so too can the other party. But if the attacker has vastly (many orders of magnitude) greater computational power, then they have an advantage. Can such an attacker unlock the delay significantly more quickly in your case?

Reply: Well I think this goes back to the earlier question. At the moment we're assuming that the delay does guarantee that things will remain concealed beyond the timeout period of the protocol. How feasible that is, is something that's not entirely clear to me. If you have a trusted third party then it's probably reasonably easy to do that kind of stuff. But we're basically assuming, well there could be an asymmetry. Yeah, the attacker might have more computational power but we're still assuming that it's not sufficient to break the delay construct within the timeout period.

Bryan Ford: So trying to respond along those lines. So I don't know if, I'm not deeply familiar with these kind of delay function when they're available or fill those rules. But are you familiar with, I know Arjen Lenstra developed this slow hash primitive where it was specifically trying to address this question. Trying to be a very non-parallelizable thing. So delay in a way that even if the attacker had massive parallel power, it wouldn't help much in terms of reducing the delay. Of course that was a slow hash, not a slow decryption kind of thing which slowly produced a random output as opposed to slowly producing something put in by hand but I don't know if something along those lines is usually adapted to that.

Reply: That's the kind of thing I think that Bill has in mind. I haven't looked at them too closely myself. But yes, you have to guarantee that you can't parallelize the computation. That's clearly crucial and there are some fairly standard ways of doing that.

Author Index